Language, Gender, and Professional Writing: Theoretical Approaches and Guidelines for Nonsexist Usage

Francine Wattman Frank and Paula A. Treichler

with contributions by
H. Lee Gershuny, Sally McConnell-Ginet, and Susan J. Wolfe

Commission on the Status of Women in the Profession
The Modern Language Association of America
New York

Copyright © 1989 by The Modern Language Association of America

Library of Congress Cataloging-in-Publication Data

Frank, Francine Harriet Wattman, 1931–
     Language, gender, and professional writing : theoretical
approaches and guidelines for nonsexist usage / Francine Wattman
Frank and Paula A. Treichler : with contributions by H. Lee
Gershuny, Sally McConnell-Ginet, and Susan J. Wolfe.
     p.   cm.
     Bibliography: p.
     Includes index.
     ISBN 0-87352-178-1 — ISBN 0-87352-179-X (pbk.)
     1. English language—Usage.   2. Nonsexist language.
3. Authorship.   4. English language—Gender.   I. Treichler, Paula
A.   II. Modern Language Association of America. Commission on the
Status of Women in the Profession.   III. Title.
PE1460.F64   1989
428'.008804—dc19   88-38161
                                                                          CIP

Published by The Modern Language Association of America
10 Astor Place, New York, New York 10003-6981

For our parents,

Irma Wattman and William Wattman
Jessie Cambron Treichler and Paul F. Treichler

Contents

Acknowledgments

The project that eventuated in this book was conceived and supported by members of the Commission on the Status of Women in the Profession of the Modern Language Association. We wish to thank those responsible for initiating discussions of the sexist language question, including Phyllis Franklin, Julia Penelope, and Guadalupe Valdés, as well as the various members of the commission during our own tenure, when the book in its current form was proposed and developed. Special thanks for support are due the commission chairs, including Evelyn Torton Beck, Madelyn Gutwirth, Mary Jacobus, Deborah McDowell, Helene Moglen, and Annette Niemtzow. We are grateful too for the suggestions we received from commission members Tey Diana Rebolledo, Eve Kosofsky Sedgwick, and Hortense Spillers and liaison representatives Joanne Glasgow of the Women's Caucus for the Modern Languages, Nan Maglin of the Division of Women's Language and Literature, and Paula Bennett and Tucker Farley of the Gay and Lesbian Caucus.

We are greatly indebted to a number of people at the MLA, surely one of the most professional of professional associations today. Walter Achtert, Director of Book Publications, generously gave astute advice and intelligent direction throughout the book's evolution. Ann Hull, who worked most closely with the commission, assisted us in many ways, for example in helping us reconstruct the history of the sexist language debate within the MLA. The three executive directors during whose terms the book has taken shape—Joel Conarroe, English Showalter, and, of course, Phyllis Franklin—deserve thanks for their support not only of this feminist project but of others as well. Adrienne Marie Ward conscientiously took charge of preparing the index. Finally, we thank the MLA's anonymous consultant readers for their useful and knowledgeable suggestions on the manuscript.

Our greatest source of technical help came from the incomparable editorial staff of the MLA. Under Judy Goulding's direction, they contributed a detailed and uncompromising analysis of the first draft, identifying additional problems that scholars and editors commonly encounter and furnishing us with a number of useful examples. Claire Cook's extensive editing of the final manuscript contributed profoundly toward making this a better book.

At the University of Illinois College of Medicine, Urbana-Champaign, our thanks go to Denice Wells for her expert preparation of the final manuscript, as well as its earlier incarnations, and to Anne Balsamo and Jefferson Hendricks for their bibliographic research assistance. We are also grateful to Daniel K. Bloomfield, dean of the College of Medicine, and Harold M. Swartz, chair of the Medical Humanities and Social Sciences Program, for providing additional support.

We are indebted to many others who have assisted us throughout this project. Cary Nelson carefully reviewed the entire manuscript, and Dennis Baron read selected portions from a technical point of view. Our colleagues and friends Carol Thomas Neely, Constance Penley, Joan Schulz, and others discussed the project with us or sent us material and suggestions. We also thank our contributors—Lee Gershuny, Sally McConnell-Ginet, and Susan Wolfe—for their patience and counsel.

Since the early 1970s, many people have worked to illuminate the consequences of sexism in language and to establish the vitality of language and gender as a field of study. Our bibliographic citations cannot fully acknowledge our debt to these teachers, scholars, and activists; they include Dennis Baron, Ruth Borker, Isabel Crouch, Betty Lou Dubois, Suzette Haden Elgin, Sue Fisher, Nelly Furman, H. Lee Gershuny, Marlis Hellinger, Nancy Henley, Cheris Kramarae, Robin Lakoff, Wendy Martyna, Sally McConnell-Ginet, Casey Miller, Claudia Mitchell-Kernan, Patricia Nichols, Alleen Pace Nilsen, Julia Penelope, Geneva Smitherman, Marsha Houston Stanback, Kate Swift, Deborah Tannen, Barrie Thorne, Alexandra Dundas Todd, Senta Trömel-Plötz, Varda One, Sharon Veach, Mary Vetterling-Braggin, and Susan J. Wolfe.

Francine Wattman Frank and
Paula A. Treichler

Introduction: Scholarship, Feminism, and Language Change

This book addresses the issue of linguistic sexism in scholarly and professional writing, presenting relevant ideas and research and a set of guidelines for nondiscriminatory usage. Since it is designed for scholars, teachers, students, professionals, and general readers concerned with language—an audience already sensitive to questions of wording—it would be inappropriate to dictate linguistic conduct. Rather, we seek to demonstrate the importance and value of avoiding biased language and to stimulate readers to think seriously about the matters we discuss.

Acknowledging that language change is a complicated business, we begin with a series of essays that place the sexist language question in a theoretical and historical context. The guidelines that follow do not attempt to replace one set of prescriptive rules with another, but they recognize that language is a rich resource with many alternatives to discriminatory usage. This book is thus not written primarily for people who want quick advice about how to fix objectionable wording. Although we include such advice and make it easy to locate through a detailed index, sexist language cannot always be hastily "fixed," particularly the special, often highly complex types that occur in scholarly and professional writing. What is called for is a broader understanding of sexist language, coupled with an ongoing editorial effort to eliminate such usage. To promote that understanding is the goal of this book.

We believe that a book on nondiscriminatory scholarly and professional writing is timely for several reasons. First, two decades of empirical research support claims by feminists that sexist language can have negative real-world consequences, especially for women and girls. Second, recent theoretical writing has clarified what sexist language is and how it functions. Third, while the many existing guidelines in this area provide alternatives for authors, few address the complexities and unique problems encountered in attempting to rid scholarly writing of sexist language. Fourth, the connections between this question and other crucial issues—language policies and language planning, the relation of language to material reality, and the relation of language to power (and thus to the ways some varieties of language come to be privileged)— have special importance for scholarly writing, where mandated or recommended linguistic changes (e.g., by journal publishers) may seem to challenge a tradition of academic freedom and where the notion of "authority" that "authorizes" some usages over others has fundamental significance. Finally, since feminist scholars have related language to its context, the sexist language question must be linked with other aspects of professional life. Even if, for example, one introduces a woman scholar at a meeting in gender-neutral language, interrupting her, as one would not interrupt a man, remains a sexist act that undercuts her scholarly presence.

This volume discusses discriminatory language use in the light of current feminist, linguistic, and theoretical thinking and research, identifying problems and suggesting a range of solutions. In this introduction, we briefly review arguments and research concerning sexist and nonsexist language and summarize the debates the subject has engendered within the Modern Language Association. We contend that sexism in scholarly writing not only creates difficulties in communication but also misrepresents teaching and research in modern languages and literature. We point out that resources for unexceptionable language are now plentiful; feminist scholarship, as well as other current writing, offers the scholar many possibilities—*chairperson* is not the cornerstone on which reform must stand or fall. Even a writer with conservative views on language can find acceptable alternatives to sexist wording, and doing so should be as routine as attending to grammar and style.

We disagree with the charge that a call for nonsexist usage constitutes censorship or that planned language change is by definition a form of coercion. Yet scholars' apprehensions about potential censorship and coercion are not frivolous, nor is "academic freedom" invoked as a mere smokescreen to ward off the forces of sexual equality. Though expressions of alarm about curtailing the individual's rights may sometimes have this goal, in principle they reflect legitimate and indeed crucial concerns of any scholar, writer, teacher, or intellectual. Thus at several points in this volume we ask whether and how guidelines for nonsexist usage might appear to challenge linguistic freedom.

The Background

Theoretical writing and empirical research have, over the past two decades, explored the relations among language, sex, and society. Much of this work, especially in the United States, has been shaped by the hypothesis proposed in the 1940s by the linguists Edward Sapir and Benjamin Lee Whorf: that language shapes the perception of reality as much as reality shapes language (see Sapir, "Abstract," and Whorf). In one form or another, this hypothesis underlies much current theoretical work in sociology, anthropology, criticism, and feminist theory. (For an illuminating discussion of the development of the "Sapir-Whorf hypothesis" in the United States and elsewhere, see Newmeyer, especially chapter 5.) Some writing, for example, uses the instability of the linguistic sign (the fact that the relation between words and things is neither inherent nor permanent) to argue that language constructs as well as reflects culture. Language thus no longer serves as the transparent vehicle of content or as the simple reflection of reality but itself participates in how that content and reality are formed, apprehended, expressed, and transformed. For feminists, who seek to understand the nature, scope, and mechanisms of discriminatory social institutions and practices, these issues have become pressing. Thus the sexist language question, seeming at first to represent a practical agenda, is a point of entry into the broader study of women and men as speakers, creators, and bearers of meaning within society and culture. Anyone who explores and seeks to change women's place within texts must confront questions of women's place within both linguistic and material reality.

One fundamental issue involves the inclusion or exclusion of women from that reality. Traditional grammars assert, for example, that the word *man* functions generically to encompass human beings of both sexes:

Man stood upright, and a new day dawned.

Feminists challenge this assertion, pointing out contradictions and ambiguities of what some have come to call "pseudogeneric" usage:

> Man, being a mammal, breast-feeds his young.
>
> When man is depressed, he loses interest in his wife and children.
>
> All men are created equal.
>
> One man, one vote.
>
> All men are human; some men are women.

The use of male "generics" is not free from social and political influences. As Charlotte Carmichael Stopes points out in her 1908 history of the words *man* and *woman* in British charters and statutes, "*man* always includes *woman* when there is a penalty to be incurred [but] it never includes *women* when there is a privilege to be conferred" (5). Similarly, an 1872 feminist tract on the political disabilities of women (preserved in the Fawcett Library, London) observes that "[w]ords [like *he* and *man*] importing the masculine gender [have been held in court] to include women in the clauses imposing burdens, and to exclude them in the clauses conferring privileges, in one and the same Act of Parliament" (qtd. in Kramarae and Treichler, *Feminist* 175). A case in point, detailed by Mary Roth Walsh, was the debate over the admission of women physicians into the Massachusetts Medical Society between 1850 and 1880; opposition rested firmly on the interpretation of *he, man*, and *person* in the bylaws as sex-specific—that is, as meaning "men only" (225–30). During World War I, the US War Department equated *persons* with *men*, preventing women physicians from becoming officers; during the critical shortages of World War II, however—and in response to an intensive lobbying campaign by women physicians—this interpretation was declared "mid-Victorian" and *persons* was taken to include women. Walsh's book takes its title from an ironic and bitter 1946 newspaper advertisement protesting postwar sex discrimination against women physicians: "Doctors Wanted: Women Need Not Apply"; the apparently generic word *doctor* had in fact become sex-specific, once again designating only men.

Like these socially constructed and sometimes socially manipulated generic definitions, the entire process of creating and preserving meanings has been subjected to feminist scrutiny. Dictionaries, where definitions get their passports stamped, yield important information on this subject. Although their editors often claim merely to report usage, not to prescribe it, users regard dictionaries as arbiters of language. Because dictionaries in fact play significant roles as cultural authorities for meaning and usage, feminists have closely examined what they authorize. H. Lee Gershuny demonstrates several ways in which dictionaries, functioning as linguistic legislators, perpetuate the stereotypes and prejudices of their editors, who traditionally have been men ("Public," "Sexism," "Sexist"). Dictionary makers, for example, may select or create illustrative sentences that reflect gender stereotypes prejudicial to women: in the *Random House Dictionary*, Gershuny reports, masculine-gender examples are three times more common than feminine-gender examples; when female sentences do occur, seven out of ten are likely to reflect stereotypes. This tendency is evident not only in stereotypically "feminine" entries like *delicate, emotional, passive*, and *vain* but also in "neutral" entries ("Sexist"). As noted in Paula A. Treichler et al., an eight-volume dictionary of German colloquial usage (Küpper) includes numerous sexist and sexual illustrations, most of them gratuitous. The letter *O*, for example, is introduced by a bright red pair of female lips, puckered in a kissing position to form a circle. Elsewhere, the entry for *Querschießen* 'to shoot obliquely,' 'to throw a monkey wrench,' is accompanied by a photograph of an attractive young woman in a negligee aiming a slingshot into space. Translated, the caption begins: "Quite a lot of imagination is needed to come up with a possible context that might have prompted the lady in the photo above to shoot obliquely." The photo, in other words, is more decorative than illustrative.

The early 1970s were marked by increasing attention to the androcentric features characteristic of both language and the practices of linguistic "authorities." As in the nineteenth century, some women examined religious language, a lively and original area of linguistic activism (e.g., Ruether, *Religion*; *Sexism*). But less attention was focused on the word of God than on the word of man: what Varda One calls "Manglish," Wendy Martyna calls "the he/man approach" ("Beyond"), and Dale Spender calls man-made English (*Man Made*). Varda One's columns about language in the journal *Everywoman* in turn inspired *The Feminist English Dictionary*, edited by Ruth Todasco and subtitled *An Intelligent Woman's Guide to Dirty Words*. The compilers identified six types of "patriarchal epithets" (woman as whore, as whorish, as body, as animal, as -ess, and as -ette). The *American Heritage School Dictionary*, first published in 1972, sought consciously to correct sexist biases (it was the first dictionary to include the

entry *Ms.*); Alma Graham describes the project's goals and methods
("Making"). Related projects and research are reported in Nilsen
("Sexism") and Nilsen et al. *A Woman's New World Dictionary*, edited
by Midge Lennert and Norma Willson, includes such definitions
as *construction* 'a well-paying field of human endeavor not open to
women' and *menopause* 'an archetypal experience exclusive to the
human female.'

Feminist proposals for language change met with some success.
In *A Feminist Dictionary* Kramarae and Treichler offer alternative
feminist definitions for many "standard" words and representations
of women, arguing that when women are taken seriously as linguistically creative speakers, radically different and diverse meanings emerge (see also Treichler, this volume). In reviewing new
words in recent American dictionary editions, Cannon and Robertson suggest that, although traditional stereotypes remain strong,
multiple processes of word formation are influencing the common
language; "the lexical image of women is considerably improving,"
they conclude, "and is beginning to be reflected in positive terms"
(32). But despite these advances, proposals for change have also
met resistance, as Maija S. Blaubergs has documented ("Analysis").
One familiar counterargument is that language is not prejudicial
to women, attitudes are; change the attitudes, and the language
will take care of itself. But the theoretical writing and research of
the last two decades point in the opposite direction: toward the
powerful influence of language on attitudes, on behavior, and on
perception (for further discussion, see Frank's and Treichler's essays in this volume). According to this work, sexist language has
an impact on women—the individuals most likely to feel demeaned
and excluded by it—and language learners in general, for whom
sexist language appears to foster sexist behavior.

A number of theoretical studies suggest ways that language can
reflect, construct, and maintain sexual difference; these include
Maria Black and Rosalind Coward; Deborah Cameron; Suzette
Haden Elgin, "Why"; Gayle Greene and Coppélia Kahn; Alice Jardine and Paul Smith; Cheris Kramarae, *Women*; Sally McConnell-
Ginet, "Language," "Linguistics," and "Review"; McConnell-Ginet,
Borker, and Furman; Kate McKluskie; Toril Moi; K. K. Ruthven;
Dale Spender (*Man Made*); Barrie Thorne and Nancy Henley; Barrie Thorne, Cheris Kramarae, and Nancy Henley; and Mary Vetterling-Braggin. One area of inquiry, articulated by Catherine Belsey
(see especially 43–52 and 103–24), involves the linguistic code itself: how are signs and meanings produced within language and

how do linguistic entities function to represent women? Current work in semiotics, in contrast, looks at "the ways in which systems and codes are used, transformed or transgressed in social practices" (deLauretis, *Alice* 167; and see also Pratt). Some feminists suggest that the distinction between *langue* and *parole* may be useful in specifying concretely what it means to claim that language is "patriarchal" (e.g., Black and Coward; Furman). McConnell-Ginet's research, uniting semantics and pragmatics, attempts to examine both the code and the ways it is used (see, for example, her discussion of *housewife* and *hussy* in this volume as well as her 1983 and 1987 reviews of research).

Feminist theoretical writing from Britain and France and feminist psychoanalytic writing in general have addressed the question of the female subject and its experience within patriarchal social relations, including the way it is constructed and represented in language, speech, and silence (see, for example, Culler; Culley and Portuges; M. Kelly; and McConnell-Ginet et al.; writings in the journals *m/f*, *Camera Obscura*, and *Feminist Review*; and the references cited in Treichler, "Language"). A union of theoretical and empirical perspectives has led to the analysis of such linguistic practices as gossip, storytelling, slang, signifying, and consciousness-raising (e.g., P. Brown; Hall and Langellier; Harding; D. Jones; Keesing; Mitchell-Kernan; Scheman; and Smitherman). The study of the depiction of women in language has yielded several useful generalizations about historical language changes and the ways scholars have analyzed those changes (e.g., Schulz; Rice; Wolfe and Stanley; Baron, *Grammar and Gender*, "Is"; and Wolfe in this volume). In turn, an important question involves the relation between individual linguistic innovations and changes in broader discourse events (conditions for speaking). The work sociologists and sociolinguists have done on natural language illuminates this connection between "microlevel" encounters between individuals and the "macrolevel" contexts (social, cultural, institutional) in which these interactions occur. The findings demonstrate, across diverse settings, that the discourse of individuals is in many ways determined by the authority of institutional practices, which are in turn reconstructed and reinforced by acts of individual discourse. This process becomes especially clear in studies of professions like medicine and law, where the influence of institutional rules on language is fairly specific.

Research on the relation between linguistic behavior and its institutional contexts includes the work of Sue Fisher; Sue Fisher and

Alexandra Dundas Todd, *Social Organization* and *Discourse*; Michel Foucault, *Archeology* and "Politics"; Shirley Brice Heath; James and Lesley Milroy; William O'Barr and Bowman K. Atkins; and Candace West, *Routine*. By analyzing scientific discourse, Ruth Bleier, Donna J. Haraway, Marian Lowe and Ruth Hubbard, Carolyn Merchant, Sue Rosser, and others have shown that many theories—such as conceptions of "the natural"—serve to maintain gender differences. Others have examined relations between gender and race in speaking and writing (Christian; D. Fisher; Hull, Scott, and Smith; B. Johnson; Moraga and Anzaldúa; P. B. Scott; Spillers; Stanback). Another question involves children's language acquisition: how are sexist meanings encoded and how do female children learn to be female speakers? (Goodwin; Wolfe, "Codification"). Still other areas of inquiry include the power and scope of naming (Kramarae, "Proprietors"); the place of gender within specific discourses (e.g., Bleier's study of science or Kessler and McKenna's study of transsexuals); and the examination of the characteristics, production, and reception of women's texts (e.g., Radway, "Identifying").

Empirical research that explores these theoretical notions has been widely reviewed (Berryman and Eman; Frank, "Women's"; Kramarae, *Women* and "Gender"; McConnell-Ginet, "Language," "Linguistics," and "Review"; Shepelak; and Philip M. Smith). A few key studies can be noted here. College students asked to select pictures to illustrate captions like "Social Man" and "Urban Man" were more likely to choose pictures of men only than pictures of men and women; with the "generic" *man* removed from the legends ("Social Behavior," "Urban Life"), significantly fewer students selected pictures of men only (Schneider and Hacker). Studies of grade school and junior high school students consistently reveal that students associated more men-only illustrations with the masculine "generics" than with alternative forms (Harrison and Passero; L. Harrison; Shimanoff). Similarly, researchers found that elementary, high school, and college students interpret job descriptions written with "generic" *he* or *man* as intended for men only (Shepelak, Ogden, and Tobin-Bennett); that gender cues in job advertisements influence the job preferences of high school students (Bem and Bem); and that students make significantly fewer errors in comprehension when coined nonsexist pronouns replace pseudogeneric pronouns (MacKay and Fulkerson). Additional research shows that children's performance in games and tasks is influenced by gender labels (McArthur and Eisen) and by exposure to nonsexist media: after watching a brief TV commercial featuring a woman judge, children more often answered yes when asked whether women can be judges or doctors; and girls of nursery-school age behave more confidently after hearing a story in which a female character plays an essential, active role (Butler and Paisley).

Of particular interest are studies showing that "generics" function differently for women and for men. When children and adults were asked to read sentences containing "generics" ("A working person pays his own way") and then choose a picture to indicate "whom the sentence is talking about," men and boys tended to choose male referents and women and girls to choose gender-indefinite or inclusive referents (DeStefano, Kuhner, and Pepinsky). A series of studies by Wendy Martyna ("What," "Using," and "Psychology") show that women and men differ both in their use of "generic" masculine pronouns and alternatives and in the degree to which they associate these pronouns with concrete images. For women, words like *he* simply do not function to include both sexes; and women are more likely to use *he or she* or *they*. Men are more likely than women to feel included in the category referred to by "generic" *he*; indeed, they are much more likely to see themselves included in sex-neutral sentences referring to a *person* or a *human being*. In general, then, men more frequently use and interpret *he* and *man* as sex-specific than as generic. Women are more likely to avoid using *he* generically. These findings are confirmed and extended by Sniezek and Jazwinski, who conclude that the "masculine bias in our language reflects and reinforces the pattern of male dominance in society" (642; see also MacKay).

Taken as a whole, this body of research supports the hypothesis that linguistic usage shapes and reinforces selected cognitive tendencies, usually those in conformity with widely accepted cultural practices and beliefs. In responding to Schneider and Foss's criticism of feminist linguistic research for adopting such a deterministic view, Shimanoff distinguishes the "strong" version of the Sapir-Whorf position (that language determines thought) from the "weaker" version most feminists adopt (that sexist language reflects and reinforces sexist cultural realities). More recently, scholars in a variety of fields, including the sociology of science, have taken up and vigorously explored the position that language and social relations construct conceptions of material reality (e.g., Knorr-Cetina; Latour and Woolgar). Other studies examine the social construction of sex and gender (Haraway; M. Kelly; Kessler and

McKenna; McHoul; Newton; and Treichler, "AIDS"). The following section addresses some implications of this position, but we conclude here on a cautionary note. While the claim that language shapes notions of reality has powerful appeal, it also means that language can serve to misrepresent or disguise things as they are. The Reagan administration, for example, attempting to justify reducing the federal subsidy to the school lunch program, defined catsup as a vegetable. The quest for nonsexist language runs a related risk: the gender and ethnic balance reflected in publications may obscure the persistence of much social inequality. Diane Savitch, an education historian, sees political dangers in the "cheerful, multiethnic, nonsexist and noncontroversial" world of elementary school readers:

> In their saccharine world, no one suffers unjustly, no one is evil, no one is poor or unemployed, women and minorities are depicted as leaders and achievers in every field. This creates an unrealistic image of a society where all battles are in the past, where racism is history, and where women and minorities have nothing left to strive for. (qtd. in Fiske 22)

We address this problem below in distinguishing between "nonsexist" and "gender-neutral" representations.

Sex and Gender

The terms *sex* and *gender*, which occur throughout this volume, require discussion. They are often used synonymously in contemporary writing to denote biological femaleness or maleness (with *gender* seen by some as merely a way to avoid the word *sex*, which also designates, of course, sexual intercourse and related activities). Others use *sex* for biological characteristics, *gender* for socially constructed ones. Virginia Prince, for example, emphasizing the importance in sex research of distinguishing *sex* from *gender*, defines the terms as follows: "Sex is a fundamental biological characteristic and exists even in bacteria. . . . [T]here are only two sexes: one which makes eggs—females, and one which makes sperm (pollen) —males" (92). "Gender is a cultural phenomenon, and culture in turn is the accumulation of information and behavior patterns that are passed on from generation to generation and which hold societies together" (94). *Male* and *female* thus refer to sex; *girl* and *boy*, *man* and *woman* to gender (see also Oakley; Philips, Steele, and

Tanz; and Rothstein). Finally, *gender* refers to a formal linguistic category involving morphological and syntactic variations in accordance with the grammatical classifications masculine, feminine, and neuter.

But *sex* and *gender* are complex and overloaded terms. The notion of innate biological sex, for example, is complicated by its multiple and often contradictory manifestations. The Johns Hopkins University scientist John Money defines *sex* as a "fundamental distinction found in most species of animals and plants based on the type of gametes produced by the individual—ova by female, sperm by male." In trying to determine how to assign sex to sexually ambiguous infants, however, Money and his colleagues found this definition inadequate, for their analysis had to take into account several measures of "sex": chromosomal or genetic (XX vs. XY), endocrinological (e.g., breast development), gonadal (ovarian or testicular tissue), morphological (structure of external genitals), and nuclear (presence or absence of sex chromatin in somatic cells). In addition, Money wished to consider psychological sex, the individual's self-image, and social sex, the complex of attitudes and expectations that a society attaches to maleness and femaleness. To allow for multiple permutations between biological and social sex, Money decided in 1955 "not to further overburden the word *sex.* . . . Instead, I borrowed *gender* from its sequestered place in grammar and philology, and used it in the term *gender role*" (Money, "Conceptual" 281). *Gender*, in Money's conception, was to be an all-encompassing term, "like a big umbrella that houses all its heterogeneous elements, of which the genital-sexual role is only one" ("Gender" 72); *gender* for him involves both biological and behavioral characteristics, with a person's status as male, female, or "mixed" (Money's term) encompassing legal, genital, vocational, recreational, sartorial, cosmetic, and—we would add—linguistic components.

In a pioneering ethnographic study that explores these questions in everyday life and examines in particular the lives of transsexuals, Kessler and McKenna take the theoretical position "that gender is a social construction, that a world of two 'sexes' is a result of the socially shared, taken-for-granted methods which members [of society] use to construct reality" (vii). In their view, the division of the human species into two sexes is not an "irreducible fact" of nature, unfolding according to a biological blueprint. Instead of being a starting point, a given, biological sex is itself something to be explained; in obviously atypical examples, like transsexuals, biological factors may conflict with social, cultural, or psychological ones, as well as with one another, revealing that sex and gender classification is essentially problematic. Yet the imperative to be either male or female is compelling, and everybody develops numerous ways to identify each individual as one sex or the other.

Kessler and McKenna, like Money, emphasize that social and cultural constructions interconnect with and maintain dichotomous biological sex. Coding individuals into male *or* female across diverse situations, gender as a social construction provides the foundation for biological sex—not the other way around. To underscore this point, McKenna and Kessler use the term *gender* for all aspects of being male or female; they use *sex* to refer to "reproductive or lovemaking activities." The psychoanalyst Jacques Lacan reopened the Freudian debate about the construction of sexual difference ("Freud's sense that sexual difference was constructed at a price and that it involves subjection to a law which exceeds any natural or biological division" [J. Rose 28]). Lacan stressed the crucial function of language in establishing and policing this dimorphic sexual differentiation, classifying all individuals as male or female in their psychic and symbolic lives. The term *sexual difference* captures both the relentless and inevitable evolution of each person into one category or the other and the ultimately fictional or symbolic "difference" that gives *male* and *female* distinctive meanings. (For further discussion, see Mitchell's and J. Rose's introductions to their *Feminine Sexuality*.)

Most social scientists in the United States, including feminist linguists, use the terms *sex* and *gender* in keeping with the biological-social dichotomy (the dichotomy that McKenna and Kessler, Money, and Lacan all seek, in their own ways, to challenge): *sex* refers to a biologically given division between males and females; *gender* to what results as society and culture create boys and girls, men and women, masculine and feminine (see Prince). In feminist writing in this country, the distinction has proved useful. As one scholar notes, *gender* applies

> to the socially imposed dichotomy of masculine and feminine roles and character traits. Sex is physiological, while gender . . . is cultural. The distinction is a crucial one, and one which is ignored by unreflective supporters of the status quo who assume that cultural norms of masculinity and femininity are "natural," i.e. directly and preponderantly determined by biology. (M. A. Warren 181)

Thus Gayle Rubin defines the "sex/gender system" as "the set of arrangements by which a society transforms biological sexuality into products of human activity" (159). As Sally McConnell-Ginet puts it, gender is "the cultural meaning attached to sexual identity" ("Linguistics" 16). Similarly, Joan W. Scott's detailed analysis of *gender* in historical scholarship shows that in theoretically traditional work, *gender* usually serves as a simple synonym for "women" but that in bolder work it "becomes a way of denoting 'cultural constructions'—the entirely social creation of ideas about appropriate roles for women and men" (1056). Scott concludes that the term conceptually links gendered social relations to power in useful ways. But Constance Penley argues that, by reinforcing the biological-social split, *gender* also functions politically to exclude feminist psychoanalytic work; she urges the retention of *sexual difference* (Preface).

In linguistics, *gender* has a specialized formal meaning, one that generally distinguishes grammatical gender from natural or referential gender—a distinction originally made by Aristotle, who classified nouns by their grammatical endings rather than by their referential meanings. *Grammatical gender* is usually defined as a formal, arbitrary marking of morphological forms in keeping with the grammatical rules of a given language. Thus in French the abstract noun meaning "thought" happens to be grammatically feminine, requiring a feminine article and a feminine ending: *la pensée*. *Natural* or *referential gender* designates linguistic forms in keeping with their "real-world" referents: in the sentence "Doctor Lucy Smith places her stethoscope against the patient's chest," the pronoun *her* follows from the sex of the doctor, which we take to be female because of the name Lucy. In English, natural gender generally dictates usage; but there are exceptions, among them conventions governing third-person singular pronouns, the "generic" function of male-sex terms like *man* and its compounds, and the sex marking of certain nouns (*woman doctor*, *waitress*). Thus the rules of traditional grammar would require the male pronoun in this sentence, which does not refer to a specific person: "The doctor places his stethoscope against the patient's chest." When the sex of the antecedent is unspecified, it has long been customary to use the masculine pronoun. As Wilson Follett wrote in *Modern American Usage*, "by a long-standing convention the masculine pronouns serve to denote both sexes after a genderless word" (68). To the grammatical- and natural-gender classifications, Wolfe (in this volume) adds the useful category *cultural gender*. If the sentence about the generic doctor had appeared in a medical textbook, traditional presumptions about cultural gender (most doctors are male) would also have favored the male pronoun, at least until recently.

In *Grammar and Gender* Dennis Baron argues that scholarly discussions about gender have historically been intermingled with attitudes toward the sexes and toward women's status in society; ideas about sex, accordingly, are translated into ideas about language. "This particular type of morphological variation in nouns, pronouns, adjectives, and articles is described in terms of the sexual categories male, female, and neuter, and this fact has colored the way commentators have looked at linguistic representations of reality" (90). "All Nouns the Male, or Female Gender have, As Nature first to things the Sexes gave," wrote James Shirley in 1651 (qtd. in Baron 90). One eighteenth-century commentator contended that grammatical genders function as the "genitals" of language, perpetuating in language human reproductive categories; another proposed the category *imperfect gender* for eunuchs (and for insults). Pronoun use that is now called conventional was historically dictated by the rule that the "most worthy gender" takes precedence in determining pronoun agreement with mixed or indefinite antecedents. Thus male takes precedence over female, and female takes precedence over neuter (because men are "more worthy" than women but women are "more worthy" than animals and other animate nonhuman beings). (See Baron, *Grammar and Gender* 90–97 for a discussion of these views.) Elizabeth Sklar describes the substitution of the term *customary* or *conventional gender* for *most worthy gender* (357). Baron claims, however, that the rule of custom or convention is merely a thin disguise for male superiority; the effect, to render women invisible, remains the same (100).

Thus the terms *sex* and *gender* have a complicated and controversial history, and consistent usage cannot simply be legislated by semantic fiat. In this volume, we have generally followed the widespread pattern of using *sex* to mean the biological categories of male and female and *gender* to designate the cultural and other kinds of identities and attributions associated with each sex. In speaking of gender strictly as a grammatical category, we specify this usage if it is not clear from the context of the discussion.

Male-Dominated, Gender-Neutral, and Nonsexist Language

Judith Hole and Ellen Levine were among the first feminist writers to draw explicit parallels between the current women's movement and its nineteenth-century counterpart: "Both have defined women as an oppressed group and have traced the origin of women's subjugation to male-defined and male-dominated social institutions and value systems" (3). Language, like other social institutions and value systems, does not serve all its speakers equally, for not all its speakers contribute equally to its formulation and maintenance. When feminists charge that language is "male-defined and male-dominated," it is this fundamental difference in contribution and social control that is at issue. Some feminists suggest, further, that the dominant language—created and sustained by white educated men—does not generally incorporate women's experience, nor are women's words and ways of speaking valued (Elgin, "Some"; D. Spender, *Man Made*). Social control is at the core of the sexist language question, and it is the reason that simple individual word changes can never in and of themselves ensure nonsexist usage. For example, recent scholarship on family violence, reviewed by Wini Breines and Linda Gordon, suggests that in cases of incest and child abuse the victims are almost all female and the assailants are almost all male; yet "until very recently," the authors note, "the clinical literature ignored this feature of incest, implying that, for example, mother-son incest was as prevalent as father-daughter incest" (523). Teresa deLauretis comments that these studies—by failing to take gender explicitly into account—"not only obscure the actual history of violence against women, but by disregarding the feminist critique of patriarchy, they effectively discourage analysis of family violence from a context of both societal and *male* supremacy" ("Violence" 14). Such gender-neutral expressions as *spouse abuse* and *marital violence* probably function similarly.

While in the foregoing examples the gender-neutral language appears to be sexist, in that it obscures certain aspects of domestic violence and makes a feminist analysis more difficult, one can argue that gender-neutral language is nonsexist in other circumstances. For instance, although most neurosurgeons, chief executive officers, and professional jockeys in the United States are men, a speaker might use *he or she* to refer to a person in one of these categories to emphasize that such occupations are not barred to women or that women's concerns need to be kept in mind. But another speaker might choose, for rhetorical purposes, to use masculine pronouns, precisely to emphasize male dominance. Are these different choices contradictory? Do they yield clear-cut precedents for usage? As we argue throughout this book, language choices, even in scholarship, are influenced by many considerations, rhetorical purpose and social climate among them. The examples just given reflect attempts to achieve social justice for women. They also demonstrate the difficulty of fully expunging bias in this attempt; as critics of non-sexist language efforts sometimes claim, a bias in favor of women may entail a bias against men. Sometimes an explicit statement of purpose and perspective might suffice to frame the writers' linguistic choices. Obviously in a work of traditional scholarship (as opposed to a polemic, say), care should be taken to avoid bias in either direction. In an earlier draft of this introduction, for example, we used the following two sentences in a summary of conclusions about women's and men's communication:

> Women are more likely than men to have difficulty expressing themselves fluently within dominant or public modes of communication.

> Men have more difficulty understanding what members of the other gender mean.

Stating women's communicative difficulties as a probability and men's as a fact is inappropriate in scholarly writing; we accordingly made the second statement parallel:

> Men are more likely than women to have difficulty understanding what members of the other gender mean.

Another example of bias that is probably inappropriate is cited by Patricia Bell Scott, who contrasts two terms used in contemporary social science research: *maternal deprivation* and *father absence*. Though they point to the same phenomenon, Scott argues, *deprivation* sounds harsher and presupposes a negative impact on the family in a way that the more neutral *absence* does not (88). Adopting parallel usage would represent what Nilsen calls "sex-fair" usage ("Guidelines").

But the "bias" of Breines and Gordon and of deLauretis is different. It represents a reasoned scholarly position that is argued with supporting evidence. It also addresses a particular body of scholarly literature at a particular point in time. Similarly, in Wilkins, Young, and Wellman's interesting exchange on the "political linguistics of race" in the 1980s, Roger Wilkins notes that under Reagan the right has "wrenched the verbal high ground from the left and has turned all the arguments upside down" (63), while David Wellman details the strategies by which it has done so, among them the transformation of *affirmative action* into *reverse discrimination* (bad), which prevents *color-blind hiring* (good), and of *interest groups* into *special interests* (43–62; for details see Wellman; Wilkins et al.).

As Julia Penelope writes:

> We are encouraged to live and work without questioning or challenging the givens of patriarchal consensus reality, and rewarded for appearing to conform to conventional "wisdom," whether it's in our dress or the language we speak. . . . [Thus,] the euphemistic "domestic violence" supplants the more explicit and accurate "wife-battering," "incest" is described as a "family problem"—thereby spreading the guilt between dependent children and male perpetrators and trivializing both the victimization of children and the male predation protected by the family. . . . Language use is, I think, an area in which unconsciousness and ignorance is the preferred state.

This example provides more evidence of a paradoxical aspect of the sexist language question: that in some instances, it is gender-neutral language that obscures the oppression of women and renders sexism invisible. It underlines the difficulty of arriving at simple, unchanging rules for achieving nonsexist writing. The use of gender-neutral language is not sufficient, because gender-neutral language is not synonymous with nonsexist language. Indeed, it was the growing gender-neutral use of *sexism* to mean discrimination against women *or* men that led Andrea Dworkin to adopt the term *woman-hating*; Evelyn Torton Beck uses *Jew-hating* instead of *anti-Semitism* on the comparable grounds that *anti-Semitism* may refer to discrimination against all Semitic groups, including Arabs. Donald Mager notes that some have criticized the term *homophobia* (like *homosexual*) for making lesbians invisible through the conflation of *homo* 'the same' with *homo* 'man.' The philosopher Richard Mohr rejects *homophobia* in favor of *fear of gays*; the use of *homophobia*, he argues, is "morally misleading," transforming bigotry into an abstract clinical illness that relieves the individual of social and moral responsibility (12).

It is important, then, to distinguish between the terms *gender-*

neutral and *nonsexist*. *Gender-neutral* is a linguistic description: a gender-neutral term is formally, linguistically unmarked for gender:
police officer, domestic violence, flight attendant in place of gender-
marked *policeman, wife battering, stewardess*. *Nonsexist* is a social, functional description; a nonsexist term works against sexism in society.
While many gender-neutral terms are consistent with nonsexist
usage, the two are not the same, as the above examples make clear.

The question of what constitutes nonsexist language does not
have easy answers. Should gender be explicitly marked, or should
it be obliterated? This dilemma has created particular problems for
feminists urging the reform of occupational titles in French, Spanish, and other languages in which grammatical gender is customarily marked for nouns, adjectives, and articles, often without regard
to biological sex. In French, *un écrivain* 'a writer' is a male form
and thus, as Monique Wittig claims, it is ungrammatical for a female
writer to call herself *une écrivain*, using the feminine article (*Lesbian*
10–11; for further discussion, see Daly, *Gyn/Ecology* 327; Morris,
"A-mazing" 73; and Wittig, "Mark"). When Queen Elizabeth was
to visit Québec some years ago, a hotel took a new name in her
honor: *La Reine Elizabeth*. But there was a great outcry: although
reine is indeed a feminine noun—and one designating a female
person as well—*hôtel* is masculine. Thus the hotel is today called
Le Reine Elizabeth (Yelin). Some feminists hold that reform requires
the creation of gender-neutral forms, so that *écrivain*, for example,
could take either male or female articles and adjectives. Others
claim that a dichotomy between male and female endings should
be retained or created for all personal nouns and marked according
to the natural sex of the referent. (Thus a female counterpart to
that male deity *le chef* would be created; proposals include *la chefeuse*
and *la cheffe*.) This strategy would, it is argued, linguistically acknowledge women's presence in professions that have traditionally
been grammatically or culturally male. Yet these male-female pairs
do not yield a true generic for reference to a chef of unspecified
sex. Similar disagreements exist regarding other languages. In
Spanish, for example, some prefer the dichotomy *el/la médico* 'the
doctor,' transforming the masculine form into a gender-neutral
term, while others use *la médica* for a female doctor, creating a new
sex-specific form. Complicating the picture are differences in regional preferences that seem unrelated to feminist concerns. German has a more pervasive and productive system of marking feminine
occupational terms: the suffix *-in*. Here, too, there is disagreement
over the preferable strategy for nonsexist usage: should one use
masculine forms as gender-neutral or insist on sex-specific terms?

According to Marlis Hellinger, the Federal Republic of Germany has adopted sex-specific terms for official use, opting for what she labels the "visibility strategy" ("Effecting" 146–52; for further discussion of these issues with reference to several European languages, see Frank, "Sexism").

A final term that merits further comment is *male-dominated*. In this book it specifically refers to institutions that have traditionally been organized and directed by men, with specifiable social, structural, and cultural consequences for women and other subordinate groups. We use it here, in other words, as an empirically verifiable characterization. But it is not used universally in this way. The related term *patriarchal*, preferred by some writers, attempts to characterize abstractly the structures and social arrangements within which various forms of male power over women are elaborated. *Patriarchy* seeks to capture the ideological and symbolic aspects of domination and oppression, as did the earlier widely used term *male supremacy*. Like *sexism*, all these terms refer to systematic and institutionalized beliefs, rules, and practices rather than to the behavior of individuals.

The possibility of systematic social control over language and communication has been explored through research in a number of fields. According to the analysis of the anthropologists Edwin Ardener ("Some"; " 'Problem' ") and Shirley Ardener (*Perceiving*), for example, women, like other subordinate groups in society, may be thought of as "muted." The discussion and study of muted groups, applicable whenever "members of one group are in an asymmetrical power relationship with members of another group" (Kramarae, *Women* 3), provide a valuable way of accounting for women's language and perceptions. This account has several potential implications. Kramarae spells them out as follows: women and men perceive the world differently because of their different experiences and activities, rooted in the division of labor; men's political dominance makes their perceptions dominant, impeding the free expression of women's alternative models of the world; and to participate in society women must restructure their own models to fit the received male system of expression. Kramarae suggests a number of hypotheses that might be explored: (1) women are more likely than men to have difficulty expressing themselves fluently in dominant (public) modes; (2) men are more likely than women to have difficulty understanding what members of the other gender mean; (3) women are more likely to find ways to express themselves outside dominant public modes of expression; (4) women are more likely to state dissatisfaction with dominant public modes of expression; (5) women who consciously and verbally resist the ideas of the dominant group (e.g., women active in the women's movement) will change dominant public modes of expression; (6) women are less likely to coin words that become familiar and widely used; and (7) women's sense of humor differs from men's (*Women* 3–4). We summarize these hypotheses because they succinctly suggest the agenda of much ongoing research on language and professional practices in the humanities, social sciences, and natural sciences. Indeed, questions of language and gender are now addressed in virtually every academic discipline, including anthropology, biology, communication, education, film theory, history, linguistics, literary studies, medicine, nursing, philosophy, psychology, psychoanalysis, and sociology. (The periodical *Women and Language* reflects the disciplinary diversity of this research network.)

Much research remains to be done on the relations among language, gender, and social reality. Studies by Marjorie Harness Goodwin, Patricia C. Nichols, and Marsha H. Stanback, for example, suggest that black girls and women may not relate to language as their white counterparts do and may have different resources for verbal interaction at their disposal. Ongoing cross-cultural research provides important information about the diverse forms and functions of linguistic sex differences (see Philips; Philips, Steele, and Tanz). Further, scholars are only beginning to explore the modes of expression that women have created for themselves outside the dominant mainstream; Pamela Fishman analyzes male and female conversational interaction ("What"), and Carole Edelsky contrasts traditional turn taking in group conversation with more collaborative practices, at which many women seem to excel ("Who's"; "When"). What is needed, finally, is a more theoretical understanding of the way words and meanings are created and maintained, the way some meanings but not others are encoded, heard, credited, and preserved (Bauer; Bickerton; McConnell-Ginet, "Review," "Origins"), and the way constructions of gender come to pervade specific discourses over time (Black and Coward; M. Kelly; Spivak).

Institutional Authority and Debates within the Modern Language Association

We have talked about dictionaries as cultural authorities that legislate as well as reflect language usage. A professional association —particularly the Modern Language Association—may serve a similar function. Recent research suggests that individual linguistic productions are connected to the institutional contexts in which they occur (see Fisher and Todd, *Discourse*). On the one hand, how individuals speak and write in given contexts is part of what defines those contexts (that is, individuals do not merely enact scripts that are already written); on the other hand, institutional discourse, though produced by individuals, exerts strong contextual control over what can and cannot be said. Ray McDermott and Henry Tylbor's essay on this point takes as its epigram a statement from Mikhail Bakhtin: "Language . . . lies on the borderline between oneself and the other. The word in language is half someone else's" (123). For McDermott and Tylbor, this rupture in the relation between language and identity is a self-reflexive interrogation of the scholarly enterprise as well: when scholars speak, which words are theirs and which are someone else's?

Debates on language within the Modern Language Association have frequently been marked by the consciousness that individual scholars are part of a larger institution, the scholarly enterprise in language and literature. This observation brings us to the history of these guidelines. Throughout the 1970s, MLA members regularly expressed themselves on the sexist-language question in letters to the *MLA Newsletter*, *PMLA*, and MLA headquarters. The 1978 annual convention included a series of programs on language and gender, and the following fall the MLA Commission on the Status of Women in the Profession prepared a resolution calling on the association to adopt nonsexist usage as its official editorial policy. Following a preliminary hearing, the resolution came before the Delegate Assembly at the 1979 MLA convention. In the long and passionate debate it evoked, members disagreed on just about every issue: Is *chairman* a noun with no gender or not? Is *chairperson* an "impossible" word? Do constructions like *the scholar . . . he* render women invisible? Can you change attitudes by prescribing linguistic change? Do such prescriptions jeopardize academic freedom? Reflecting on the meeting, the MLA's executive director at the time, Joel Conarroe, remarked:

> It is clear to me that any 115 persons discussing sexist usage are going to have 115 slightly different definitions, each of which is deeply personal and hence "right." As an editor and an advocate of equality, I am aware of the powerful tensions created by conflicting rights—by efforts simultaneously to preserve freedom of speech and to respect the dignity of all our members. The stakes in this debate are high, since whatever we do will have an influence on others. ("Comments" 2)

Throughout the debate, the representative of the Commission on the Status of Women took the position that the issue was not whether particular usages were "sexist"; rather, she said, the resolution called for a stance in principle against discrimination, with definitions and details to be worked out subsequently. The outcome was that the MLA Delegate Assembly recommended that the association "affirm, in statements of editorial policy, a commitment to the use of nonsexist language in its publications and develop guidelines for the use of nonsexist language" (432). In October 1980, the MLA Executive Council approved a revised statement of editorial policy for *PMLA*, effective 1 February 1981: "The MLA urges its contributors to be sensitive to the social implications of language and to seek wording free of discriminatory overtones" ("Statement").

The following year, the MLA Commission on the Status of Women began work on the guidelines for nonsexist usage that find their final form in this volume. Though strongly supported by the MLA staff and many MLA members, the development of guidelines has not been unanimously welcomed, as responses to an announcement of the project in the Spring 1983 *MLA Newsletter* made clear. One MLA member, an editor himself, wrote to warn us that our arguments against "generic" *he* would fail because we would be "encountering an unsurmountable linguistic obstacle in the intuitive 'thinking' process of all native, well-educated English speakers." This comment represents the view of many that attacks on this pronoun best exemplify the folly and futility of proposals for language change. Certainly, this volume underlines the significance that the English pronoun system has for gender issues; probably no single topic is more repeatedly addressed. The writer makes another important point: that a gender-neutral third-person singular pronoun is, indeed, immensely useful and that *he* has been widely accepted for this purpose. We argue, however, that the "generic" use of the male pronoun is no longer—if it ever was—part of the intuitive thinking process of all native, well-educated English speakers. We address these questions more fully in the guidelines themselves.

Another MLA member protested by resigning from the association, expressing a view that demonstrates the strong symbolic meaning that proposals for nonsexist linguistic change can invoke:

> For some years I have seen that once most respected American organ of humane letters, *PMLA*, betray its scholarly purpose more and more openly to the strident polemical ambitions of various currently

fashionable ideologies. I hung on, hoping for a return to policies and ideals answerable to its parent organization's *raison d'être*.

But the Spring 1983 *Newsletter* item headed "Nonsexist Usage in Scholarly Writing" revealed all too starkly the folly of my optimism. . . . [This has] the totalitarian scent of . . . *stylistic* big-brotherhood.

When, if ever, the MLA becomes once more compatible with true academic freedom, I'll gladly rejoin.

Again, although we may not agree with this writer's negative opinion of "currently fashionable ideologies" or his equation of nonsexist guidelines with "*stylistic* big-brotherhood," the question of academic freedom is not trivial, and it is one we will address.

Another writer perceived the call for nonsexist language as part of a frightening pattern of reverse discrimination that seemed to undermine his own professional goals:

Mea culpa! Mea culpa! Here are some sexist thoughts that went through my mind as I stood in front of a departmental bulletin board fat with notices for Fellowships for which I am ineligible to apply because of gender. How am I to get a job? I wish I were a woman. Thirty proposed special sessions at the MLA are, more or less, for women only. One of them is even on this phenomenon: "Feminist Style and Feminist Content in MLA Conference Sessions." The *MLA Newsletter* has news of the new members of the Women's Commission, and the support system for women scholars, and courses on women, plus of course, a call for examples of antifeminist *tone* to be held up to ridicule. . . . How do I keep from being paranoid? Why should I pay for the sins of the last generation of search committees? Grad school admitting committees? Mothers? Why should I even finish my fucking dissertation? Send that paper off? . . . Do my work? Even if all shines, I will still be denied a classroom. Why not retreat into illiteracy, drink beer, make lewd remarks at women in sportscars?

Are you sure what you're doing is good for the human race?

We cite these protests because they are not isolated examples; they illustrate both the deep-seated feelings that many scholars hold about the sanctity of traditional language use and the real-world political significance of the sexist-language question. We believe that they also confirm the need for a detailed scholarly discussion of the issue.

Other members were pleased about the development of guidelines. Some contributed their own experiences. One scholar wrote to say that her published book on popular music used *she* and *her* as the singular sex-indeterminate pronoun:

> I didn't think it'd be such a big deal to do so, because usually I'm referring to how the listener responds to or understands such-and-such, and the listener *c'est moi*. Sometimes I'm even distinguishing how a woman responds from how a man would, so certainly need to use the feminine gender consistently throughout. But I don't believe some of the objections I heard, especially while seeking a publisher: my favorite went something like, "By using the feminine pronoun she flies in the face of thousands (sic) of years of conventional usage, and my girlfriend who's a linguist agrees with me"!!

A number of readers shared examples of sexist and nonsexist usage. One reader referred us to a female author whose book explains computer programming—subroutines, parameters, variables, labels, and so on—by likening it to a knitting pattern, "an explanatory metaphor drawn from a traditionally female domain." Finally, a male reader offered the following general comment on our project:

> It seems to me that the major problem is getting across something that many women need to be told with conviction, and of course more men: that human justice requires equality in *attitude* as well as profession. There is a sense in which people may think they use the "generic he," etc., neutrally, but it is one thing to be a user and another to be someone not considered important enough to be included.
>
> The point that I try to make to people who protest that it seems artificial is that writing demands thought, deliberate care. It is often difficult to make sure that subjects and verbs agree in number, that parallelism is exact, or that in fact our thought proceeds along grammatical and syntactical lines. That *is* the point, that thought must be taken, effort made.

We agree: thought must be taken, effort made, in this area as in other areas of writing. Taking care is part of what scholars routinely do. In turn, their language and writing represent their profession in a variety of ways.

The Social and Professional Context of Scholarly Language

Just as language in general exists within a social context, scholarly language exists within both social and professional contexts. Though scholarly language may sometimes seem to operate autonomously in its own world, it actually serves a number of social functions: (1) it reflects not just the world of books but the world as well, and it is accordingly linked to society in general; (2) it represents the profession formally; and (3) it actively shapes scholars' research processes and linguistic practices.

Scholarly language is neither pure nor objective; rather, its conventions and prescriptions evolve to reflect the attitudes, preferences, and beliefs of individual scholars. When the final volume of the *Oxford English Dictionary* (*OED*) was published in 1928, the publisher's announcement proclaimed the dictionary's comprehensiveness and uniqueness; its historical method, they stated, made the *OED* "a Dictionary not of our English, but of all English: the English of Chaucer, of the Bible, and of Shakespeare . . ." (qtd. in K. M. E. Murray 312). The equation of "all English" with the English of Chaucer, the Bible, and Shakespeare is one that can be contested. Certainly, even for *OED* editor James Murray, the massive dictionary-making project represented a pragmatic compromise between collecting "*all* words" (Murray's original goal) and collecting just "*good* words" (K. M. E. Murray 135). Several studies of the history of English argue that sexist and stereotyped views of women have shaped scholarly conclusions about language development (e.g., Baron, *Grammar and Good Taste* and *Grammar and Gender*; Wolfe in this volume; Wolfe and Stanley); such conclusions, since they are as social and political as they are scholarly, are not irrefutable or immutable, and they should not be used to preserve anachronistic practices.

A profession's language is part of its public representation. Correspondence, guidelines for publication, style manuals, job descriptions, bibliographic practices, letters of recommendation, jargon, brochures, books, conference session titles—all communicate on behalf of the entire profession and help determine how it is perceived. (The press coverage of the annual meeting of the MLA often emphasizes such features of its external representation.) The MLA, moreover, as one of the largest, most heterogeneous, and most influential professional associations, with particular expertise in the area of language use, has a special role in public education. The number of women in the MLA has been rising, and they now account for about 40% of the membership. This increase has coincided with a growing attention to women's concerns: the Commission on the Status of Women in the Profession, the Women's Caucus, the Division of Women's Language and Literature, the Gay Caucus, Women in German, Women in French, Feministas Unidas—all have helped make the MLA more hospitable to women. In turn, women's visibility within the profession has increased through publications, programs, membership on committees, and other activities; so has women's sense of solidarity and their identification with the MLA as a potentially fruitful source of professional support.

That women rightfully belong in the MLA was eloquently articulated by Joel Conarroe, responding to complaints about the 1979 annual meeting:

> One scholar suggested that "programs planned by the division committees have simply gotten lost in the enormous welter of meetings," and another declared her unhappiness with "the proliferation of sections on female this and that, women in X . . . etc." More dramatically, a member wrote to express his views on "the feminist domination of this year's meeting" and on a "feminist 'takeover,'" observations that struck me as wondrous strange. Because feminists, after decades of not really feeling welcome at the party, have set up a lively table near the middle of the room, are they suddenly dominating? Taking over? Approximately a third of our members are women, as are approximately a third of those participating in the Convention—in contrast to a very few years ago, when the percentage of women was much smaller. Because of the strong interest in feminist criticism in the academy we receive scores of requests for sessions, far more than can possibly be accommodated. That several meetings are devoted to the topic is surely not a sign of a takeover but an indication that this area is where energy, as well as research projects, can be found at this particular time. ("Comments" 2)

Against this background, some professional activities and scholarly products take on a somewhat anachronistic flavor. Even a 1981 MLA publication entitled *Introduction to Scholarship* provides an example. This is the latest version of a work initiated in 1952, when the original editor, James Thorpe, noted that the volume

> is about becoming and being a scholar. It is tendered to any members of the scholarly community who would like to read a review of some

current ideas on the aims and methods of scholarship. But it is primarily addressed to students, into whose hands the future of American scholarship will in due course fall. We hope that they will find these essays a useful introduction and a sound orientation. (Qtd. in Gibaldi vi).

The latest collection of essays seems in some respects still to reflect 1952 realities. The contributors make little mention of women or feminist scholarship (out of approximately 160 authors cited, for example, fewer than 10 are women), they chiefly rely on traditional Euro-American sources (though essays on theory and linguistics have been added to the 1981 volume), and they ignore most writing and scholarship by and about black, Hispanic, and other minority men and women; in consequence they seem overall to hold up white males as the role models and authorities for the young scholar. In this instance, the scholarly work is no longer reflecting the field; yet it is certainly representing it symbolically and may well be sending a message to young scholars about what kind of scholarship is practiced and accepted within the profession. This observation is not to chastise the MLA (which, in any case, plans a new edition with broader coverage) but, rather, to point out that even publications prepared by persons sensitive to these issues may emit implicit signals that undermine their explicit intentions.

Feminism and Language Change

As academic women have come of age within the feminist movement and feminists have increasingly entered academia, they have challenged many of the received conventions of the profession within which they live, work, and publish. In the written texts of feminist scholars, for example, we see what Nelle Morton calls "the rising woman's consciousness in a male language structure." The problems and complexities of this tension between feminism and established authority are apparent in the difficulties of constructing an "I" answerable, accountable, to either constituency—an "I" who is both feminist and published (see Culley and Portuges; Gallop, "Writing"; Treichler, Kramarae, and Stafford, *For Alma Mater*). A number of MLA publications, such as *Women in Print I* and *Women in Print II* (ed. Hartman and Messer-Davidow), examine ways in which androcentrism has restricted women's access to print and public expression and maintained male dominance within the profession. Faced with these constraints, women are encouraged to "storm the toolshed" (Marcus "Storming") and to seek new tools (Lorde).

Such action is easier urged than undertaken. Every work of feminist scholarship reflects a small drama of competing loyalties and language enacted at varying levels of self-awareness. There are, for instance, the third-person singular pronouns: *he*; *he or she*; *she*; *she or he*; *she* in alternation with *he* by sentence, paragraph, or chapter; *they*; avoidance of *all* pronouns; *he* with a disclaimer marked by humility, sarcasm, or condescension; or a gender-neutral neologism like *co* or *tey*. Each choice may proclaim a loyalty, a compromise, or a negotiation. All choices have become problematic: none is innocent. The first-person pronouns *I* and *we* also raise questions: for whom do these words stand? Speaking of the "paradox of non-being" for black women, Hortense Spillers cites "the descriptive language of affirmative-action advertisements, or even certain feminist analyses," as examples of texts where the "black female and black male are absolutely equal." As a result, Spillers writes, the "collective and individual 'I' lapses into a cul-de-sac, falls into the great black hole of meaning, wherein there are only 'women,' and 'minorities,' 'blacks,' and 'others' " ("Interstices" 77). The full title of the collection edited by Gloria Hull, Patricia Bell Scott, and Barbara Smith also addresses this paradox of nonbeing: *All the Women Are White, All the Blacks Are Men, but Some of Us Are Brave: Black Women's Studies*. At the 1984 MLA convention, a forum on feminist discourse was entitled "Who Are the 'We'?" Lorraine Bethel titled a poem about black women and the women's movement "What Chou Mean *We*, White Girl?" And how does a woman writer decide which pronoun to use in a sentence like this: *Women have shown that (we/they) can produce challenging scholarship*? The choice between *we* and *they* may be politically difficult, entailing a choice between a feminist and a grammatical convention.

In feminist dedications and acknowledgments, the familiar tributes in male texts to faithful female typists and patient wives are often supplemented or supplanted by thanks to sisters, mothers, daughters and sons, husbands, partners, editors, colleagues, consciousness-raising groups, feminist networks, and the feminist movement. (Janet Radcliffe Richards's explicit denial of a feminist support network suggests that her book *The Skeptical Feminist* is skeptical about feminism as well.) Here too are parodies, like the sociolinguist Betty Lou Dubois's tongue-in-cheek thanks for funding from the National Institutes of Health, citing agency and grant number, to mirror the practices of the male biomedical scientists whose speeches she was studying.

Feminists also use punctuation with varying degrees of daring to make their points. Perhaps most influential are Mary Daly's inventions and Adrienne Rich's hyphenated "writing as re-vision" (Daly; Daly and Caputi; Rich, "When"). More recently, the slashes that characterize Marxist-feminist writing contrast with the nested parentheses and flourishes of feminist psychoanalytic and deconstructive criticism. Italics, long the marker of feminine speech so *exquisitely* perfected by Dorothy Parker, are now often used to highlight particularly outrageous portions of sexist material quoted from male authors. Some feminist titles mock male language, like Scully and Bart's "A Funny Thing Happened on the Way to the Orifice: Women in Gynecology Textbooks." Or they play on words or linguistic structures: Berenice A. Carroll calls her anthology *Liberating Women's History*, and Shirley Ardener entitles her anthropological collection *Perceiving Women*. Ambiguity may bring about subversive infiltration: the title of Mary Daly's *Gyn/Ecology*—a scorching confrontation with various American medical practices—landed the book (as the author had predicted) in some medical libraries. Similarly, her *Websters' First New Intergalactic Wickedary of the English Language*, a reworking with Jane Caputi of Daly's linguistic writings, might be mistaken by some readers for *Webster's*; in fact, the *Wickedary* is a feminist dictionary for *websters* (plural), Daly's term for women who weave words. Some titles are provocative—for example, Anne Koedt's "Myth of the Vaginal Orgasm" and Christine Delphy's "Main Enemy." Others deliberately celebrate maligned aspects of women's existence: thus the journals *Hysteria* and the *Monthly Extract: An Irregular Feminist Periodical*. Names are the focus of usage reform: a woman can now be referred to by her last name only, and the many permutations in use show that her husband's name is no longer her only alternative to her father's. Indexing practices are changing: increasingly, care is taken to categorize index material in a nonstereotypical way that will encourage scholarly access to information about women, ethnic groups, working-class women, and so on (see Berman; Capek; J. K. Marshall; and Searing, *Introduction*). One example of subversive feminist indexing exists in the fifteenth edition of the massive medical textbook *Williams' Obstetrics* (ed. Pritchard and MacDonald)—which, incidentally, contains no pictures of women or babies, only parts, charts, and organs: the index includes the entry "Chauvinism, male," which reads "Voluminous amounts. pp. 1–1190." Perhaps the indexing,

done by a daughter of one of the editors, had some effect, for the
next edition lists only "Variable amounts." Dale Spender's index to
Women of Ideas (and What Men Have Done to Them) reinforces the
book's claims through such entries as "Progress, absurd nature of
concept in relation to women." Ellen Moers's index to *Literary Women*
includes the entry "Advice, masculine," subheaded "bad" and "good."
And, finally, there are neologisms, variant spellings, invented compounds, and other creations. But this creativity is enacted within
diverse social contexts. A given writer may use such words as *womanspirit, herstory, dyke,* and *womyn* in a nonacademic feminist journal,
place them in quotation marks in a feminist academic journal, and
omit them completely in a nonfeminist academic journal.

These practices suggest the particular pressures on feminist
scholars to remain true to the standards, conventions, authoriza-
tions, and rigorous pleasures of their (usually) discipline-based
training and at the same time support the alternatives offered by
a passionate and ideologically committed sorority. Some say that
this goal cannot be achieved, claiming that the term *feminist scholarship* is oxymoronic because anything feminist will automatically
be biased, polemical, and subjective; some feminists claim in contrast that the academy is the enemy, that "the alma mater is a woman
of ill repute" (Kantrowitz 15), and that academic feminists are col-
laborators with the corrupt male establishment. For them "the
wickedness of academic feminism is so obvious as to need no proof"
(Makward 99). Thus, as Ellen DuBois and her colleagues suggest,
it is not surprising that the relations between the academy and
feminist scholarship "are complex and often fraught with tension"
(3).

Whatever one's position, feminists have made themselves felt,
and the entry of women into the academy places pressure on professional leaders and organizers to accommodate them. We have seen
that the sexist-language question has done so, alienating some
members while strengthening the loyalties of others. Journals must
similarly negotiate between the gains and risks of change. When
PMLA published one of its first "theory" articles, the editor felt
compelled to quote the member of the editorial board who had
described it as "touchy-feely stuff" and to suggest that such work
offered readers something of value; his problem was not merely
the article's content or argument, of course, but its stylistic pecu-
liarities (Schaefer 795). As a critical theory perspective has become
more common, journals have had to come to terms with its style
in explicit ways (e.g., by ruling on the use of nouns like *privilege*

and *foreground* as verbs). Similarly, feminist scholarship is more than a matter of content and argument: changes in perspective and worldview bring changes in language. Resistance to nonsexist language is sometimes a resistance to the new worldview it represents. Such resistance may be overruled but should not be discounted as unimportant or ignorant. This book is based on the belief that the connection between language and nonlinguistic reality, though complex and problematic, is unarguable and must be taken explicitly into account in proposals for language change.

The Organization of This Book

In some respects, the traditional language of academic literary and linguistic scholarship conflicts with the realities of a profession in which diversity is thriving. With this book, we seek to encourage a move toward a flexible linguistic repertoire that recognizes many constituencies and welcomes appropriate linguistic alternatives.

The essays in part 1, representing current scholarship on linguistic sexism, illuminate several important problems in identifying sexist language and explore the creation and legitimation of nonsexist alternatives. Sally McConnell-Ginet places linguistic sexism within its cultural and social contexts, examining how meanings are produced, understood, and preserved in the sexual politics of discourse; she moves us away from the notion of "linguistic sexism" as an issue of individual choice (though it may include this) and toward a complex framework where meaning necessarily involves a linguistic community, social relations, and political structures. Paula A. Treichler's essay analyzes the role of authority in the construction and codification of meaning, showing how dictionaries and the process of dictionary making authorize and institutionalize some meanings but not others; using the preparation of a feminist dictionary as an example, she suggests that current feminist discourse, including academic writing, is a rich source for the study of sexist and nonsexist language. Susan J. Wolfe discusses language "as a system of meanings encoded largely by men," examining in her essay a particular subset of men: English language scholars and commentators. Wolfe's essay calls into question the authority— supposedly derived from objective scholarship—that has dictated meanings and usages prejudicial to women and their interests. Moving from theory to everyday practice, H. Lee Gershuny's essay examines sexist and nonsexist usage through a case study of English handbooks, a genre of scholarly writing that is an important "repository of authoritative usage and style." She asks a number of concrete questions about discourse practices in these texts, providing both empirically relevant information about current usage and a useful model for examinations elsewhere—for example, in foreign language textbooks. Francine Wattman Frank reviews the development of guidelines by publishers, businesses, and professional associations as a significant accomplishment of the feminist movement and a successful example of language planning; she discusses the evolution of specific sets of guidelines as well as the development of resistance to them. This essay serves as a bridge to the following section, the guidelines for nonsexist scholarly and professional writing. The essays in part 1 are designed to introduce and amplify the recommendations and commentary in part 2, though each section can be read independently.

The guidelines presented in part 2 offer solutions to sexist usage in general, in scholarly writing in particular, and in associated professional activities. Though we have tried to create a useful reference work by including specific recommendations, we provide not a simple catalog of *do*'s and *don't*s but a more discursive presentation. Above all, we hope to encourage the exploration of alternatives. We hope, too, that attention to prose style will increasingly include the quest for felicitous nondiscriminatory language as a matter of course.

Four bibliographies make up part 3: (1) a list of works cited in this volume; (2) a list of composition handbooks; (3) a list of and about nonsexist guidelines from other professional associations, publishers, and organizations; and (4) an annotated list of selected further readings.

Part One

Language and Sexual Equality

The Sexual (Re)Production of Meaning: A Discourse-Based Theory

Sally McConnell-Ginet

Scholarship on women and language has addressed two main topics: (1) how women (and men) speak (and write); (2) how they (and other gender-marked topics) are spoken of. In each case, feminists have argued, some kind of linguistic sexism is at work. Sexism in how we speak has many aspects. Women's favored styles of language use are often negatively evaluated by the larger community, for example, and women are frequently the victims of male oppression in discourse, suffering interruptions and inattention to their conversational contributions. In more public arenas, similar problems exist on a larger scale: women speaking from pulpits or podiums are still rare, and their writings are viewed as somehow tainted by their sex. Sexism in how women are spoken of manifests itself in a variety of ways, such as "the semantic derogation of women" in the vocabulary and the so-called generic masculines that contribute to women's relative "psychological invisibility."

Extensive annotated bibliographies in Barrie Thorne and Nancy Henley and in Thorne, Kramarae, and Henley attest to the wealth of empirical research on both issues. Later in this essay I discuss specific investigations of the first question—how women speak; Julia Penelope Stanley, in "Paradigmatic," and Muriel Schulz are among those who have studied the second question—how women are spoken of. Each topic has also been explored by many other feminist thinkers: see, for example, Mary Daly; Adrienne Rich, *On Lies*; and the many collections concerned with language from a literary or psychoanalytic viewpoint (including Eisenstein and Jardine; McConnell-Ginet, Borker, and Furman; Abel; Garner, Kahane, and Sprengnether; and Benstock). Other recent writings are cited by Paula Treichler in both "Teaching" and "Language." Kramer, Thorne, and Henley suggest the need for investigating the interaction between language use and what they call *language structure* (our semantic resources), a subject that Kramarae develops somewhat further in "Proprietors of Language." The popular term *sexist language* is generally applied to the second topic, which I call *sexist semantics* for the sake of brevity, but it sometimes is also construed to cover the first, which I call *sexist discourse.* (Some of the papers in Vetterling-Braggin's *Sexist Language,* for example, are more directly concerned with the ways women and men act as speakers than with the ways they are spoken of, despite the book's title.)

My major aim in this essay is to give a brief theoretical account of the roots of sexist semantics in sexist discourse. This way of putting it is, of course, somewhat oversimplified. By *sexist semantics* I mean not only such phenomena as the sexualization and homogenization of words denoting women (e.g., *mistress* and *girl*) and the universalization of words originally denoting men (e.g., *guys*) but also subtler aspects of the relative absence of a "women's-eye view" in the most readily accessible linguistic resources. What I mean by *sexist discourse* also goes beyond the more blatant kinds of male oppression of women in conversation, though I include some examples of these. More generally, I am interested in how sex differences influence both communication and interpretation in discourse.

Whatever we may think of the merits of particular studies, it is relatively easy to see how sexism in a community could have implications for how its members speak and how their speech is evaluated. Because using language is a socially situated action, it is clearly embedded in the same sociocultural matrix that supports sexual bias in the work we do, the wages we receive, the expectations we have of ourselves and others, and so on. What is more difficult to understand is the connections between a sexist society and the semantics of a language; the most familiar theoretical models of linguistic meaning do not illumine the question of how particular meanings become attached to particular forms.

Stated like this, however, the question is misleading, for it suggests that meanings somehow exist independently of their articulation, as though languages merely paste linguistic labels on the semantic furniture of the universe, tagging an independent realm of concepts with sounds (or, in the graphic medium, strings of letters). Not all the possible semantic stock is tagged by a particular language-using community, but no theoretical barrier prohibits its members from adding labels whenever they choose. Or so a common line of thinking goes, a line that I refer to as the *code view* of language (see McConnell-Ginet, "Linguistics" and "Origins"). This view finds popular expression in such comments as "Oh, that's just a question of semantics" (which implies the triviality of the connection between forms and their meanings) or in such familiar adages as "A rose by any other name would smell as sweet" (see McConnell-Ginet's "Origins" for a discussion of this Shakespearean line and its often forgotten context). What the code view fails to address is the significance of the tagging process itself and the possibility that this process shapes and gives coherence to the sometimes inchoate stuff that we seek to wrap our tags around. To understand the source of sexist semantics, the way sexism in society and culture interacts with the system of linguistic meanings, we really need to ask how meaning is produced and reproduced.

The production of meaning designates the processes through which speakers mean something by what they say (or writers by what they write) and through which hearers (or readers) interpret what is said (or written). The reproduction of meaning refers to our dependence, in producing meanings, on previous meanings or interpretations, to our dependence in particular on one another's experience with the linguistic forms being used. I argue that to understand the ways that meanings are produced and reproduced and the significance of sex and gender in these processes, we must consider the conditions of discourse. The key to explaining so-called sexist semantics and, ultimately, to reclaiming the "power of naming" (see D. Spender, *Man Made*) lies in analyzing the sexual politics of discourse. Macropolitical structures play a significant role, of course, in genderizing discourse. Who writes and who reads? Who preaches sermons to large congregations? Who publishes books? Whose speeches are beamed by satellite around the world? Although these are important questions, I will not consider them here but will focus instead on the micropolitics of daily discourse between ordinary individuals. Because most of what we say about daily discourse is more widely applicable, however, this restriction is not so severe as it might seem.

I am indebted to the work of the philosopher H. P. Grice for my basic framework, though I use his ideas in a somewhat special way.

Grice bases his account of meaning on what speakers intend to accomplish by speaking. (See the Grice studies listed under Works Cited and Lewis's and Schiffer's related theoretical analyses, which Bach and Harnish draw on in attempting to develop a general theory of linguistic communication.) The crucial feature of the Gricean account for my purposes is that meaning depends not just on the speaker but on a kind of relation between the speaker and the hearer. It is this potentially social perspective that gives insight into the (re)production of meaning.

What is involved in this account? Grice's explanation goes something like this: in saying *A*, a speaker means to express the thought *B* if the speaker intends to produce in her hearer a recognition of thought *B* by virtue of his recognizing that she is trying to produce that recognition in him by saying *A*. (Grice does not restrict his account to female speakers and male hearers, as the pronouns I have used may imply that he does. I am following many other authors in using both *she* and *he* as "generic" singular pronouns; but since I later discuss in more detail the hypothetical case of a woman talking with a man, the choice of pronouns is not entirely arbitrary.) This back-and-forth intending and recognizing and thinking is, of course, not usually a conscious process. In informal speech, coordination adequate for the purpose is generally taken for granted and not reflected on. The more complex (and the more novel) the thoughts one seeks to express, the more conscious the attention given to the meaning process. There is generally greater self-awareness in writing and reading than in speaking and hearing, because the memory and time constraints are less severe.

In linguistic communication, the speaker typically takes as common ground with the hearer certain beliefs about the language system and, in particular, about familiar connections between linguistic forms (signifiers) and thoughts and concepts (signified). It would seem safe to assume this common ground in most conversations. The assumption can certainly not be maintained, however, in linguistic transactions with very young children. How then do children come to manipulate sounds (and ultimately other means of signaling) to express thoughts? The issue of how much the development of this ability depends on the child's experience and how much it reflects the biologically controlled maturation process does not concern us here. What I do want to stress is that parents usually act as if their child intentionally behaves in certain ways to express thoughts, even though they may well know better.

Let us imagine the bizarre case of a child whose exposure to language involved no social interaction. We might suppose that a loudspeaker intoned English sentences into the nursery and that the child's needs were attended to with no accompanying speech. This child might indeed begin to speak, matching the loudspeaker's output, but there would be no reason to assume that the child *meant* anything by articulating "I love you, Mommy." This child would be like the parrot that produces linguistic forms with no appreciation of how the wider speech community uses those forms.

In contrast, most children in English-speaking families have a radically different experience. When the child produces something like "ma" or "mama"—whether to imitate the language of others or just to attempt vocal control—the parents attach significance to the sounds: they treat the child as if the utterance meant "mama." That is, they begin to make it possible for the child to give this meaning to the sounds by showing that they have attended to those sounds, using the same or somewhat similar sounds themselves in conjunction with such actions as pointing to Mama or having Mama present herself to the child. The crucial thing is that children thus start to participate in a coordinative activity, recognizing their own and others' articulations as somehow the same. The motives they begin to attribute to others' articulations can also serve to guide their own. Let me emphasize that much of this development may well be guided by children's prewired or innate capacities and dispositions, including access to a fairly rich and highly structured conceptual system as well as a natural bent to coordinate their own speech with the articulations of their community. That is, children may have a preexisting stock of concepts waiting to have tags affixed; nonetheless, as tags are placed, some of those concepts are modified or joined with others in various ways that we do not yet clearly understand but that nonetheless result in the production of new conceptual systems. The conceptual systems that children evolve will to a considerable extent reproduce those prevalent in the community.

We cannot, in this essay, follow the child's entire linguistic development. What matters for our purposes is that the child and those around the child manage to *mean* something by what they say because (1) they jointly take the saying to be aimed at triggering a common recognition of thoughts, (2) they jointly take themselves to be relying on shared resources to achieve this coordinated recognition—a common language system plus a certain amount of shared experience. To a considerable extent, the coordination is achieved through the child's adapting to what is customary for the community. Those in the community, however, may also adapt to the child's productions—perhaps accepting novel forms or understanding the child as giving certain standard forms nontraditional meanings. But, by and large, the child and its parents do not endow language forms with meaning by coordinating their uses of them de novo. Rather, the parents (and all the other language users whom the child encounters) exploit the basic consensus achieved in earlier uses, and the meanings the child manages to produce in exchanges basically reproduce those already familiar in the community.

For certain concepts—especially for talking about perceptions of the external world—the reproduction of meaning is probably almost literally that, for the simple reason that children are evidently predisposed to note certain distinctions, to attend to certain sorts of environmental stimuli, and to ignore others. Their innate conceptual systems need only be aligned with the language system in their community. Apparently, for example, children who learn the *up-down* word pair through spatial uses do not need to be taught to apply it to ascending and descending melodies: psychologists have found that even very young prelinguistic infants make this connection between the visual and auditory domains. Nonetheless, most linguistically encoded concepts are not preformed but are produced, in at least their fine detail, as children familiarize themselves with the particular perspectives, beliefs, and practices of the community.

It is by no means clear, for example, that children initially give high priority to sorting people by sex rather than by other characteristics. In languages like Finnish, where *hän* is the only singular third-person pronoun, third-person reference is not differentiated by sex. There is no evidence I know of that Finnish children start by trying to introduce a marking of sex difference here. There is evidence, however, that some English children do not find the *she-he* distinction particularly congenial. Whether or not children find it natural to genderize references to a person—to choose between *he* and *she* even where the sexual information plays no particular role in what is communicated—probably depends on how strongly genderization has figured in their experience. In a household with children of both sexes, for example, the special importance of sex sorting is likely to have established itself fairly well by the time the youngest child is working at pronouns. But some children do resist, perhaps because their rearing has been what Sandra Bem calls *gender-aschematic*. Such children, acculturated into an atypical framework, use the same form for everyone or use the masculine and feminine pronouns in somewhat random fashion, not bothering to attend to the distinction where it does not matter for their purposes. But even they eventually go along with the larger community, and it seems plausible that learning to make the required distinction can serve to heighten the conceptual salience of sex sorting.

The main point here, again, is that endowing linguistic forms with meaning is a socially situated process. The statement applies not just to children learning to communicate but also to more mature speakers struggling to convey increasingly complex thoughts. A major insight of the Gricean perspective is that we can manage to mean much more than what we literally say. How? By relying on what we take to be shared or readily accessible beliefs and attitudes in a particular context.

We can suggest a framework for understanding how cultural biases leave their mark on language systems and, more generally, we can begin to see why and how social inequality results in linguistic inequality. Our focus will be on discourse inequalities created by the sexual division of labor in producing situated meanings. Empirical research on conversational interaction among white middle-class Americans has convincingly demonstrated the influence of sexual stratification on discourse, and I want to extend these results to support an account of how sexual bias can affect the (re)production of meaning.

The major findings on discourse are hardly surprising. Basically, in cross-sex conversation men tend to dominate women in the following ways: (1) they actually do more of the talking; (2) they interrupt women, in the sense of seizing the floor, more often than women interrupt them; and (3) they more often succeed in focusing the conversation on topics they introduce (see, for example, Eakins and Eakins, "Verbal"; Fishman, "Interaction"; Kramarae, *Women*; Swacker; West and Zimmerman; the summary in Treichler and Kramarae; and the many other studies cited in Thorne and Henley and in Thorne, Kramarae, and Henley.) In all these respects, the conversational relation between women and men parallels that between children and adults, employees and employers, and other power-differentiated groups. Not surprisingly, matters are more complex than this thumbnail sketch implies; for example, neither interruption (of which there seem to be different kinds) nor amount of talk is always indicative of control over a conversation, and correlation with sex is affected by many contextual factors. Certainly the proposed picture runs counter to some stereotypes—notably, that women are more talkative than men. If there is any truth to this notion, it may lie in situations other than those on which research has focused to date. For example, female groups may spend more of their time in talk than do male groups. Studies of single-sex conversation do suggest that women regard conversation more as a cooperative enterprise than as a competition, enlarging on and acknowledging one another's contributions, responding to coconversationalists' attempts to introduce topics, and signaling active listening by nods and *mmhmm*s during a partner's turn (see Edelsky, "Who's," and Kalčik). In contrast, men generally view conversation more individualistically and less socially, with each participant's contribution self-contained and the "right" to one's own turn taking priority over any "responsibility" to others during their turns.

To some extent, women and men simply operate with different expectations about how linguistic interactions ought to proceed. For example, men are far less likely than women to give signals that say "I read you loud and clear." This is true not only when they talk with women but also when they talk with one another. A man may interpret another's *mmhmm* as agreement with what's been said, whereas a woman hears another's *mmhmm* as registering comprehension. One young man in a classroom where these differences were being discussed decided he sometimes might be assuming that his girlfriend agreed with him when indeed she was merely signaling that she was still receiving his communication. He resolved to try to distinguish the genuine signals of assent from those of simple connection. When he thought he had an affirmative response, he would stop and say, "Oh, so we're agreed about that." More often than not her reply was "Of course not." (I owe this anecdote to Ruth Borker.) Still, what is involved here is more than different expectations; it is also an exercise of power, whether intentional or not.

Daniel Maltz and Ruth Borker argue that women and men have different models of friendly conversation. Their account draws on such work as Kalčik's study of women's rap groups and Marjorie Harness Goodwin's analysis of directives issued by girls and boys to each other. From a somewhat different perspective, Carole Edelsky contends that in addition to the *singly held floor* that is normative in most conversational studies, there is in some conversations a *collectively held floor* (these are my terms for her "F1" and "F2"); she observes that women participate on a more nearly equal basis with men under collective floor conditions ("Who's"). Undoubtedly, the full account of sexual differentiation in discourse will be far more complex than our current picture. For example, the more inter-active orientation that women and girls have toward conversation does not mean that men and boys have a monopoly on conflict and disagreement—a point the Goodwins make very clear in their in-teresting study "Children's Arguing." Nonetheless, whatever the explanation, the evidence shows that men generally aim at indi-vidual conversational control, whereas women aim at social con-versational collaboration.

Male conversational control and female conversational collabo-ration are, of course, only tendencies: there are women who suc-cessfully interrupt men to steer the conversation in their own direction, and there are men who work at helping their female coconversationalists develop a topic by asking questions, elaborat-ing, or simply by actively indicating their continuing engagement in the listening process. Still, a common pattern involves the man's controlling and the woman's supporting cross-sex conversation. Nor is there any reason to believe that this behavior is somehow biologically rather than culturally produced. Early on, children are identified by others as girls or boys and learn to identify themselves in the same way. Tied to this identification is a process that typically leads them to acquire roughly the practices of linguistic commu-nication that prevail among their same-sex peers (see Goodwin). And linguistic communication, as one kind of social interaction, is embedded in more general political structures that children are, in some sense, being prepared to reproduce. Whatever the precise mechanisms, the net result is that sex is of considerable significance in the politics of talk among adults.

How does inequality in discourse affect what can be meant and by whom? First, men are more likely than women to have a chance to express their perspective on situations, not only because they have more frequent access to the floor but also because they are more actively attended to. This distinction is especially important, since comprehension goes well beyond simple recognition of the linguistic structures used. In other words, where the sexes have somewhat different perspectives on a situation, the man's view is more likely to be familiar to the woman than hers is to him. This observation leads directly to the second point: men are much more likely than women to be unaware that their own view is not uni-versally shared. As a result, women and men may well be in quite different positions regarding what they believe to be commonly accepted (or accessible) in the speech community. This disparity in turn can have important consequences for what each is able to "mean" when engaging in linguistic communication. Why? Because what is meant depends not just on the joint beliefs about the language system and its conventional—that is, standard or established—interpretations but also on what interlocutors take to be prevalent beliefs in the speech community about everything else besides language.

"New" or nonconventional meanings involve a speaker's intending the hearer to infer a purpose to the words beyond that of directing attention to the thought "literally" expressed. Let us take as an example the semantic development of *hussy*, a word that was once merely a synonym for *housewife*. How did it acquire its present meaning? And, once the sexual slur was produced, how was it reproduced and attached to the form so insistently that present generations do not even connect the two words? The example is not in itself important, since *hussy* hardly figures prominently in contemporary discourse, but it is useful for illustrative purposes because its historical development is well documented.

While we cannot, of course, recapture the discourse conditions in which this particular sexual insult was produced, we can sketch what may have happened and reconstruct the course of the word's shift in meaning. It seems plausible that some members of the speech community considered sexual wantonness a salient characteristic of the housewife. Such people could say *huswif* (or, perhaps, the somewhat shortened and familiar form *hussy*) and rely on their hearers to bring that characteristic to bear on interpreting the utterance. Thus they might say something like "What a hussy!" and try to mean just what such a comment conventionally means today. Of course, if they were wrong in supposing that their hearers would recognize this appeal to the negative stereotype, the attempted communication would fail. But the mere fact that the putative common belief was not universally shared would not in itself spell doom. So long as the negative stereotype of housewives was widely known, even hearers who did not accept it could recognize an appeal to it and understand that the term *hussy* was intended as an insult.

A contemporary example of semantic derogation can be found in what some younger speakers are now doing with the term *gay*. Elementary school children who do not connect the adjective with sexuality simply understand it as a word used to belittle. They will, of course, soon learn that *gay* refers to homosexuality and that the belittlement they rightly recognized in older speakers' use of the word is based on attitudes and emotions about sexuality. Often the early connotations will persist and become associated with homosexuality, tending to reinforce the pervasive heterosexism and homophobia in mainstream social groups.

Or consider a somewhat subtler example. A man who means to insult me by saying "you think like a woman" can succeed. He succeeds not because I share his belief that women's thinking is somehow inferior but because I understand that he is likely to have such a belief and that his intention is not just to identify my thinking as an objectively characterizable sort but to suggest that it is flawed in a way endemic to women's thought. The crucial point is that I need not know his particular beliefs: I need only refer to what I recognize (and can suppose he intends me to recognize) as a common belief in the community.

In contrast, it is much more difficult for me to mean to insult him by saying "you think like a man," because to recognize my intention he would not only have to know that my opinion of men's thinking is low, he would also have to believe that I know he so knows (or that I believe he so believes); though such an understanding is not unimaginable in a conversation between old acquaintances, it is quite unlikely in more general communication. And even where the intended insult works, it is construed as something of a joke or as a special usage, unless the stereotype disparaging women's thought (or at least elevating men's) is not familiar to both interlocutors. Thus it is easy to reproduce notions with widely established currency and difficult to produce unexpected or unfamiliar ones. I need not actually believe some commonplace, or even know that my interlocutor does, in order to attribute to him (my choice of pronouns here and throughout this essay is deliberate) the intention to treat it as a view we share. Indeed, even if I explicitly deny that view, I may end up doing so by acknowledging that it is generally believed. Thus, as Finn Tschudi observes, to say "women think as well as men do" is already to acknowledge that the standard for comparison is men's thought. No matter how much I might wish to insult someone by saying that *she* or *he* thinks like a man, I could not so intend without relying on more than general linguistic and cultural knowledge.

There are complications, of course. We may each be aware that the general stereotype is under attack. Until it is decisively destroyed, however, the possibility remains that someone will purport to take it as a shared belief—and thereby succeed in relying on it to convey meaning, unless the "purporting" is exposed. As the stereotype fades, however, the meaning it conveyed may remain but become reattached to the linguistic form as part of its literal meaning. Thus the view of housewives as hussies might not have been robust enough to sustain all the intended uses of *hussy* to insult, but so long as enough of these uses succeeded, subsequent language users could be directed immediately to the insult without a detour through the extralinguistic attitudes. In other words, when enough such insults work in situations that the speakers can take as precedent-setting, where the insult is recognized and associated with the term rather than with the negative view that initiated the term's derogatory connotation, the facilitating stereotype becomes superfluous. One can rely on earlier language experience to re-produce the meaning formerly produced by the stereotype.

This discussion leads to the related issues of what speakers take as background beliefs about the interpretations "standardly" as-signed in the speech community, that is, the literal meanings that can be assumed as "defaults" in talking with others (operative unless something special in the discourse triggers alternative interpreta-tions). One could, once upon a time, call someone a *hussy* and not intend to insult her. One can no longer do so, however, since a contemporary speaker who is familiar with the form can hardly fail to know how it is now standardly taken—and certainly cannot count on an unfamiliar interlocutor to ignore the negative evalu-ation. As we probably all realize, for example, it is becoming harder and harder to make *he* mean "she or he," because only incredibly isolated speakers can have missed the controversy over the so-called generic masculine, the dispute over whether users of *he* in sex-indefinite contexts indeed intend to refer to both sexes and, if they do, how well they succeed in getting their hearers to recognize that intention. (The introductory essay in this volume describes this debate at length.) Given the doubts raised, one cannot say *he* and mean "she or he," because one cannot generally expect hearers to make this identification. Humpty-Dumpty said to Alice, "When I use a word it means exactly what I choose it to mean," but that was, to a considerable extent, wishful thinking. Suppose we intend others to recognize a certain thought or concept just by under-standing the linguistic forms we have used. This intention will be reasonable only if we can expect our listeners to believe with us that the speech community indeed associates that thought or con-cept with those linguistic forms. That is, we must get others to cooperate with us in giving our words the meaning we want. At the very least, our listeners must recognize our intention and help us by acknowledging that recognition.

It may well be that women play a major role in reproducing meanings that do not serve their own purposes or express their own perspectives. They are fully aware that female perspectives are not viewed as commonly held (indeed, are often not recognized at all) and, in the interests of facilitating communication, they allow men to continue to believe that a distinctively male view of things is actually not particular but universal. "This is the oppressor's language," says Adrienne Rich, "yet I need it to talk to you" (*Will* 16). Indeed, some have argued that language is so little "woman's language" that women cannot even manage to mean what they say, much less achieve success in meaning more.

This view has been persuasively elaborated by the philosopher Sara Ann Ketchum. How, she asks, can a woman manage to mean no to a man's "Would you like to go to bed?" She says no with sincerity but he interprets her through a filter of beliefs that transform her direct negative into an indirect affirmative: "She is playing hard to get, but of course she really means yes." But of course she does not mean yes; assent is not what she intends to convey. I would contend that indeed she does mean no, even though she faces an extraordinary problem in trying to communicate that meaning to someone ready to hear an affirmative no matter what she says. (I am not, of course, claiming that one never means yes by *no* but only that one often does not; this is the case we are now considering.) Only if she knows that he will never take her *no* to mean no can she not intend the negation. Yet she still would not mean yes; his refusal to cooperate in her attempts to communicate no might reduce her to a desperate silence, but his unreasonableness, his unwillingness to apprehend her as someone who might mean no, can never compel her to mean yes. Even though what my words mean does not depend solely on my intentions, Humpty-Dumpty is right that it does require those intentions.

Nonetheless, Ketchum's main point certainly stands: meaning is a matter not only of individual will but of social relations embedded in political structures. A positive moral can be drawn from this observation as well: it is possible to produce new meanings in the context of a community or culture of supportive and like-thinking people. I can mean no if my intention is supported by a feminist network that recognizes the sexual double standard and articulates male myths regarding female sexual behavior: I am not a single, isolated individual refusing to submit but, rather, part of a collectivity resisting sexism and violence against women. More generally, women are together challenging the view that "the" culture is what men have told them it is or that "the" language is what is available and what women must reproduce on pain of being condemned to a solitary silence. Rather, women are uncovering the myth of univocality and discovering new voices, their own and their sisters'.

The philosopher Naomi Scheman has illustrated how a feminist community can produce new meanings. In "Anger and the Politics of Naming," she looks at how consciousness evolves—is in some sense created—in a women's rap group: using a mass of internal inchoate stuff, women can work together to form something coherent, to build conceptual structures that allow them both to interpret their own experience and to express that interpretation to others. In other words, they do not just tag preexisting concepts but generate new ones. They are able to think new thoughts, to realize, for example, that they may have been angry without recognizing what they felt. This thought is new not just in particular instances but also in its broader implications—enabling women to interpret an earlier emotion as anger when they did not do so at the time, because their language use did not then offer that possibility. This new interpretation matters because it connects past emotions to the option of purposeful current actions. Women cannot "mean" alone but they can collaborate to produce new meanings and support the reproduction of those meanings in the community.

The research contrasting women's and men's approaches to discourse suggests, in fact, that women may be especially well suited to producing significantly new meanings. Because this possibility depends on the development of a shared new outlook, it might be better promoted in the cooperative mode of discourse than in the competitive, where less attention is paid to the other (and where one extracts meaning by assuming that the speaker reproduces earlier linguistic habits and familiar modes of thinking). It is true, of course, that women will find it harder to express their distinctive perspectives to men than vice versa so long as sexist patterns and practices persist. Nonetheless, women might collectively reshape their conceptual systems, particularly the ways they think about women and men, about individuals and social relationships, and about language and its connection to the individuals and their communities.

Is this possibility what the French feminists mean when they speak of an *écriture féminine*, what English-speaking feminists like

Mary Daly mean when they talk of a "new" gynocentric language? Perhaps, though calls urging women to produce their own meanings are sometimes interpreted as implying that they must leave the old and familiar language to "him." But they cannot begin de novo. Just as the child must start somewhere—and presumably draws heavily on a conceptual structure that is biologically endowed—so must women. It was because the women in Scheman's rap group could assume they all had access to a common language system that they could evolve together views that differed in important ways from familiar interpretations of that system. No matter what women intend to mean by their new language, they can only convey that meaning if they can expect others to recognize the thoughts to which the language aims to direct attention. And if there are indeed new meanings to be reproduced after they are initially produced in specific contexts, then women must find a community both able and willing to apprehend those new meanings.

It is a matter not just of what women manage to mean but also of what all of us, women and men, interpret others as meaning and, ultimately, of what we help or hinder others to mean. As I pointed out earlier, feminist research has established that *he*, no matter what its user intends, is not unproblematically interpreted as generic, and the consequent shift in the community's beliefs about how *he* is interpreted has influenced what one can intend the pronoun to convey. There are now many contexts in which those who are aware of these developments cannot expect *he* to be understood as "he or she," no matter how much they might wish they could. A footnote explaining one's generic intentions does not suffice, since some readers will doubt the sincerity of that announcement and others will forget it. This is not to say that now no one ever means "he or she" by using *he*: my point is just that it is much harder to convey that meaning than it used to be, in large measure because we now know that many earlier attempts were unsuccessful and that many purported attempts were, in fact, spurious. (Martyna provides empirical evidence that the actual use and interpretation of so-called generic masculines are quite different from what grammar books prescribe; see "Beyond"; "Psychology"; and "What.")

Language matters so much precisely because so little matter is attached to it: meanings are not given but must be produced and reproduced, negotiated in situated contexts of communication. Negotiation is always problematic if an inequality of resources enables one negotiator to coerce the other. And because negotiation involves achieving consensus about beliefs and attitudes, it is not surprising that dominant groups have an unfair advantage in working out ways of meaning that are congenial to their beliefs and attitudes. The picture is much more complex than I have indicated here, but the basic point should be clear. Meanings are produced and reproduced within the political structures that condition discourse: though a sexist politics may have helped some men to "steal the power of naming," that power—a real one—can be reappropriated by feminist women and men building new language communities.

From Discourse to Dictionary: How Sexist Meanings Are Authorized

Paula A. Treichler

The term *dictionary* can designate a concrete lexicographic object ("Turning to my *Webster's*, I find that *woman* is defined as an adult human female"); a more broadly institutionalized cultural authority ("As the dictionary makes clear, women are frequently viewed negatively in our culture"); or an abstract repository of linguistically coded entities available in the repertoire of individual speakers (For many English speakers the dictionary entry *woman* is coded *human*, *adult*, and *female*). All these meanings presuppose the conscious or unconscious construction of a set of "definitive" statements commonly thought to be founded on—deduced or extracted from— the study or observation of linguistic and material entities in the "real world." In turn, a dictionary definition places a word within a particular grammatical, cognitive, and material context, thus constraining (dictating) usage, conceptualization, and perception. It is the still, fixed outcome, in other words, of a set of interpretive practices that becomes, itself, interpreted. If discourse is the text from which a dictionary is constructed, a dictionary becomes the text that, in turn, constructs discourse. In this sense a dictionary is any kind of scholarly or authoritative text on words that claims to be based—as most dictionaries do claim—on what is. This equation—provisional and problematic though it may be—is one way of understanding the process through which meanings—both sexist and nonsexist—are authorized.

In this essay I explore the relation between discourse and dictionaries in a specific context: the preparation of *A Feminist Dictionary* (by Kramarae and Treichler). This project necessarily raised questions about how meanings are traditionally authorized, how feminists can intervene in this process, and how any authorization process can work for or against women's interests. In addition to illuminating specific linguistic practices and assumptions, the dictionary project more generally contributed toward an ongoing inquiry into feminist scholarship and the status of knowledge.

I first consider dictionaries as lexicographic objects, summarizing some of the ways traditional dictionaries have sanctioned sexist meanings. Then I briefly sketch the feminist dictionary project: its goals, assumptions, and alternative conceptualizations of *discourse* and *dictionary*. Finally, I note some of the issues involved in the production and authorization of meaning—issues that connect to more theoretical notions of a dictionary—and suggest approaches to examining them in greater depth.

The Authorization of Sexist Meanings

Recent language and gender research indicates a number of ways that conscious or unconscious sexism may enter dictionaries (including historical, etymological, and concise "desktop" dictionaries).[1] The most obvious sexism in dictionaries—certainly the kind most criticized by feminist writers—is the inclusion of negative, stereotypical, and trivializing references to women. This is where much feminist work has concentrated. Ruth Todasco's *Feminist English Dictionary*, for example, subtitled *An Intelligent Woman's Guide to Dirty Words*, was compiled from established English dictionaries —"museum pieces," in Todasco's words, "of an archaic culture"; in identifying "patriarchal epithets," it sought to demonstrate men's prejudiced myths about women and female sexuality and suggested the power of dictionaries to reinforce such means of expression. In "Gender-Marking in American English," Julia Penelope Stanley reports that in standard dictionaries words for women are much more frequent and much more negative than words for men. Feminists have also found androcentric or "male-centered" definitions of words for female sexuality. Thus *clitoris* is sometimes defined as "a failed or vestigial penis"; *Stedman's Medical Dictionary*, for example, describes it as a "homologue of the penis in the male except that it is not perforated by the urethra and does not possess a corpus spongiosum." An important point here is that these definitions are not simply "reflections" of an androcentric culture but ideological constructions of what that culture is to be. As Kate Millet argues in *Sexual Politics*, negative representations of women serve the interests of one group (men) at the expense of another (women). Though the sheer number of such derogatory terms may indeed reflect the mentality of "an archaic culture," their inclusion in a dictionary comes about in part because the editors themselves belong to that culture and make many choices that differentially affect how that culture is to be represented and authorized.

Various selection processes may work to introduce a male bias into the lexicon by valuing the public over the private sphere. Of the more than three thousand works listed in *Dictionaries of the World*, only a handful concern themselves with such traditionally female interests as sewing and fashion (e.g., *The Dictionary of Fashion*). A predominantly male lexicon—military battles, nautical terms, mining and metallurgy, rubber coating and refrigeration—is represented in all the others. Values clearly influence what goes into dictionaries, which dictionaries are published, and which are listed in bibliographies. It has traditionally been the public world of politics, policy, work, and commerce that has seemed to require authorization and community consensus on meaning—as opposed to private activities such as housekeeping and child care (but I discuss below how this situation is changing).

If the lexicon of a standard dictionary consists largely of words for activities, interests, and concerns associated primarily with men, the reason may be not only that men have had greater access to the world's resources but also that the documenters of the world have been largely male. Certainly male dictionary makers have not been reticent in expressing their opinions of women as language users: Samuel Johnson's notorious remark likening a woman preaching to a dog walking on its hind legs—the wonder is not how well she does it but that she does it at all—embodies a common judgment about women as public speakers and foreshadows James Murray's distrust of them as documenters of speech. In his desperation for help with the *Oxford English Dictionary*, Murray did enlist the services of women readers, many of whom derived satisfaction from contributing to this important scholarly project; though Murray was condescending toward them (particularly the "spinsters," into whose lives he believed the *OED* project infused purpose), he found their work efficient and accurate: they were, that is, satisfactory transmitters of the code.

Women's documented contributions to the study of language and the production of dictionaries have been the exception, not the rule. Elizabeth Elstob, author of the first Anglo-Saxon grammar, was one such exception. "I have but one thing more to add," she wrote in her 1715 book dedicated to the Princess of Wales, "that this present, worthless as it is, is the humble Tribute of a Female; the first, I imagine, of the kind that hath been offer'd to Your Royal Highness." Another exception was Janet Taylor, a student of mathematics and navigation who started a nautical academy for merchant service officers and in 1865 published *The Mariner's Friend: Or, Polyglot Indispensable and Technical Dictionary* of nautical and scientific terms in ten languages. A more recent example is Marghanita Laski, who worked on the *OED* supplement; an erudite journalist and book reviewer, Laski responded to the 1958 appeal for help published by Oxford University Press by volunteering to track down the life history of the term *alley cat*. In the end, she contributed more than 100,000 citations from contemporary authors and from particular subject areas, including fashion, food, social life, sewing, embroidery, gardening, and cookery. The existence of such women—and there are doubtless others—is significant, but it does not challenge or change the institutional nature of dictionary making and the authoritative procedures on which it depends. To rescue favorite words the Oxford staff thought were obsolete, Laski was not above including them in the work she herself published and then submitting these uses as citations (see Shenker 91–92). But few women are in a position to authorize their own words and definitions. More commonly women's influence over such activities is cited only when it is negative or aberrant. Thus Harold Whitehall, writing about Cooper's 1565 *Thesaurus*, made this comment:

> The history of dictionaries is larded with strange occurrences: we are not surprised, therefore, that the publication of Cooper's work was delayed five years because his wife, fearing that too much lexicography would kill her husband, burned the first manuscript of his magnum opus. (xxxii)

Nor were only English women chastised for subverting linguistic progress: the Cherokee Indian Sequoyah devoted ten years to creating a writing system for the Cherokee language. Ridiculed and rejected throughout this period, he nevertheless persisted, and by 1819 he had produced the 85 characters of Cherokee. At this point, according to John Howard Payne's contemporary account, "when all his friends had remonstrated in vain, his wife went in and flung his whole apparatus of papers and books into the fire, and thus he lost his first labor" (qtd. in Dykeman 21).

Though dictionary editors claim, sometimes militantly, that they collect words and definitions from diverse sources, their criteria and procedures for identification and preservation (both explicit and implicit) nearly always preclude gathering women's definitions. Definitions for many dictionaries, for example, are constructed from usages found in works by the "best authors"; though what this designation means has been challenged in recent years, it has usually meant "male authors." Admitting some women into this canon or even permitting them to participate in the canonization process reproduces a linguistic class system in which an authorized elite continues to separate, in Nancy Mitford's words, the U from the non-U (see Ross).

One criterion for the lexicalization of a "new word" (legitimation through inclusion in a dictionary) is the number of times it is found in print; given current cultural practices, men's words are far more likely to appear in mainstream publications (see, for example, Barnhart). In addition, few dictionary editors have regular access to print media where women's words would predominate (such as women's periodicals) or where nonstandardized meanings would predominate (such as feminist periodicals).

Dictionary editors typically talk about "backing winners and losers" in the incorporation of new words and meanings. Israel Shenker recounts an example involving *housewife* (34–36). Editors of leading English-language dictionaries were asked in the 1970s whether they would consider revising their definitions of the word in the light of objections by feminists and housewives themselves to the notion of a housewife as "someone who does not work for a living." Feminist writing, in contrast, would more typically define the housewife as the manager of a household—thus one who works inside rather than outside the home. In general, according to Shenker, the editors defended traditional definitions. Some editors made jokes. One said he would consider substituting the notion of a married woman "not gainfully employed." Robert W. Burchfield, the editor of the *Supplement to the OED*, told Shenker that, according to a national census, housewives themselves objected to the label *housewife*. "This wouldn't affect our definition," he said. "We would simply have *housewife* in its traditional definition. But we will react positively to the women's liberation movement, and if they have an alternative, we'll consider it." (The final volume of the *Supplement*, published in 1986, does list the entry *wimmin*, defining it as a semi-phonetic spelling of *women*, adopted by some feminists.) Though the lack of enthusiasm for a feminist definition of *housewife* as "a winner" is of interest, I mention it here chiefly to emphasize that words and definitions are competitive and that acceptance may be a function of special-interest lobbies.

Historical reconstructions of form and meaning may also display the bias of etymologists and lexicographers. One example occurs in the positing of cognates and glosses for attested and unattested forms of many words related to women, including *woman, wife, spinster,* and *widow.* Susan J. Wolfe and Julia Penelope Stanley scrutinized accounts of the hypothesized Indo-European kinship system in this regard and concluded that most etymologies tell us more about the etymologists' worldview (and woman view) than about the Indo-Europeans' languages or their cultural context. "Every word tells its story," as the philologist Max Müller wrote in 1888 (x), but the crucial point seems to be whom it tells its story to. In *Grammar and Gender* Dennis Baron examines in detail the historical accounts of many loaded sex-related words, including *marriage,* which, he notes, has called forth the passions and prejudices of both usage critics and etymologists (45–49). Baron cites Richard Grant White's 1870 rejection of any sentence asserting that women marry men; both etymologically and practically, White maintained, women cannot serve as the subject of *marry* as an active verb but must remain grammatically and socially passive:

> Properly speaking, a man is not married to a woman, or married with her; nor are a man and a woman married with each other. The woman is married to the man. It is her name that is lost in his, not his in hers; she becomes a member of his family, not he of hers; it is her life that is merged, or supposed to be merged, in his, not his in hers; she follows his fortunes, and takes his station, not he hers.   (46)

As Wolfe and Stanley note, along with Baron, this view of man as semantic agent and woman as passive object is also reflected in contemporary linguistics. Emile Benveniste explains that there is no term for marriage in Proto-Indo-European, because "the situation of the man and that of the woman have nothing in common." According to Benveniste, this absence indicates a patrilineal social organization whose terms reflect a basic disparity between men and women: the man "leads" home the woman whom another man has "given" him—the woman enters into "the married state," she does not accomplish an act. The woman does not "marry"—she "is married" (195). (The *New York Times* and some other newspapers maintained this usage convention until quite recently.[2]) Again, Benveniste's interpretation may derive as much from his own cultural and professional conditioning as from the "facts" of the Indo-European lexicon. Wolfe and Stanley, Baron (*Grammar and Gender*), and Carol F. Justus discuss the relation between linguistic evidence and cultural reconstructions.

Not only are etymological data constructed or interpreted to support certain views of linguistic data, but an uneasy and somewhat ad lib relation between the linguistic and the nonlinguistic is often used to justify the status quo. Thus, on the one hand, the "intolerable" homophony of the third-person male and female pronouns in Old English has been invoked to account for the development of a palatalized female form (*she*), while in recent times linguistic convention is called on to show that the pseudogeneric pronoun *he* is not intolerably ambiguous (Wolfe, in this volume; Baron, *Grammar and Gender* 15–20).

Exemplary sentences—both excerpts from published writing (chiefly by male authors, as noted above) and examples concocted by the editors—are often male-biased. H. Lee Gershuny cites "She made his life a *hell* on earth," chosen by the *Random House Dictionary* to illustrate usage of the word *hell* ("Public"). Even in stereotypically "feminine" contexts like cooking, the "she" of the sample sentences fares poorly. The entry for *overdone* provided this sentence: "She gave us *overdone* steak." Though less common today, such sexism persists in some dictionaries.

More subtly, according to Meaghan Morris, a dictionary may also disguise women's power or even their presence. She faults the 1981 Australian *Macquarie Dictionary* (ed. Delbridge) for limited definitions that obscure women's linguistic and political achievements. It defines *sexism*, for example, as "the upholding or propagation of sexist attitudes," a *sexist attitude* as one that "stereotypes a person according to gender or sexual preference, etc.," and *feminism* as an "advocacy of equal rights and opportunities for women." Morris argues that women originally used *sexism* within a broad theory of patriarchy; to say that it means espousing certain "attitudes" that stereotype a "person" is essentially to obliterate its original political meaning. Equating *feminism* with its lowest common denominator ignores both current and historical distinctions among different feminist positions. "While it is true," writes Morris, "that the usages accepted by the *Macquarie* are standard liberal currency today, the

point is that the concepts developed by feminists are not even
marginalised into second place, but rather omitted entirely" ("A-
mazing" 89). Teresa deLauretis makes the same charge about the
term *family violence*; though research indicates that incest, child
abuse, and spouse battering are overwhelmingly committed by male
assailants against female victims, the terms suggest that these are
"family problems" rather than problems related at least in part to
male supremacy ("Violence").

The Discourse Dictionaries Record

My central argument should be clear from this review. When I
speak of the dictionary's authority, I do not mean simply that it
selectively "authorizes" (through lexicalization, dissemination, and
so on) language usage that exists in a culture. Like other scholarship, it also constructs and creates usage. Dictionary editors claim
simply to report usage. But usage itself is a complex notion: not
only is it a function of social, cultural, and situational variables, it
occurs within an intricate network of relationships and idiosyncratic
histories. Further, according to the research cited in the introduction to this volume, usage—and this is certainly true of women's
usage—is itself constrained by social rules and conventions regarding who can speak, whose words will be more heavily weighted,
who will listen, who will record, and so on. Thus, in addition to
the gatekeeping mechanisms in the authorization process I have
detailed, there are differing probabilities about whose discourse
will constitute "usage."

A dictionary, then, is not an isolated institution that functions as
the cultural authority for a given society. Rather, it is constructed
within a given culture, and it may variously embody that culture's
values and practices. There is considerable diversity here, of course.
The term *dictionary*, most readily identified with the *Oxford English
Dictionary* or with the familiar American desktop dictionary, is expected to display authority, comprehensiveness, legislative value,
and scientific objectivity. But the term—which in its most generic
sense means simply "word book"—designates not only the *Oxford
English Dictionary, Webster's New Third International, The Random House
Dictionary, The American Heritage Dictionary*, and other standard contributions to lexicography but also a range of different, often ec-
centric projects, including Gustave Flaubert's *Dictionary of Accepted
Ideas*, Ambrose Bierce's *Devil's Dictionary*, and perhaps even Raymond Williams's *Keywords*.[3] Dictionaries vary in such features as

organization (*Roget's Thesaurus*, for example, follows a semantic category arrangement instead of an alphabetical format), purpose (some dictionaries are essentially glossaries or explications of "hard words" or problematic terms), accessibility (the language in which the book is published affects this), influence (again, the status of the language of publication is critical), and methodology (for example, entries may be primarily qualitative, as in most desktop dictionaries, or quantitative, as in most linguistic atlases and dialect dictionaries). Finally, dictionaries are differently institutionalized. Some are individual and quirky, often short-term products of a single person. In contrast, the *Oxford English Dictionary* involved hundreds of contributors and took 70 years to produce; though money, space, and other arrangements had to be continually and often vituperatively renegotiated, the project came increasingly to be regarded as a unique national resource. *Webster's Third* was estimated to have required 757 "editor years" and to have cost more than $3.5 million (Gove). The first volume of *The Dictionary of American Regional English*, a project conceived in 1889, was published in 1985; it covers letters A through C in 903 pages. The project's resources have, in recent years, been considerable. As the chief editor, Frederick G. Cassidy, notes in his introduction, the sine qua non for the dictionary's success was full-time editorial direction and full-scale funding; the initial volume lists more than 150 staff members and acknowledges widespread support from foundations, government agencies, corporations, and private donors.

In the United States and Great Britain, considerable authority has been vested in many dictionary projects. Despite periodic attempts in these countries to establish governmental or academic bodies as Keepers of the Code, an antiauthoritarian tradition has generally prevailed, with dictionaries—beginning with Samuel Johnson's influential *Dictionary* of 1755—fulfilling this codifying function. Dictionary makers have taken this role seriously. When the final volume of the *OED* was published in 1928 (70 years after the Philological Society [of London] had initiated the project), the Oxford University Press declared the dictionary's "superiority to all other English dictionaries, in accuracy and completeness. . . . [It] is the supreme authority, and without a rival" (K. M. E. Murray 312). Like the *OED*, other English and American dictionaries have sought to document existing language forms; a tradition of lexicographic positivism lays claim to some degree of "scientific objectivity" in this regard, and a seamless methodology often obscures the inevitable editorial bias.

There is no doubt that many dictionaries strive for authority,

comprehensiveness, and so on. The quest for an illusion of authority, indeed, seems to be an occupational disease of dictionary
making:

> To me, making a dictionary has seemed much like building a sizable
> house singlehanded; and, having built it, wiring, plumbing, painting
> and furnishing it. Moreover, it takes about as long. But there can
> be no question that there is great satisfaction in the labour. When
> at last you survey the bundles of manuscript ready for the press you
> have the pardonable but, alas, fleeting illusion that now you know
> everything; that at last you are in the position to justify the ways of
> man to God.   (Cuddon 1)

Yet interestingly—and disturbingly—even when dictionaries explicitly disavow claims of authority and prescriptive definitiveness,
the ultimate outcome for women is the same: dictionaries have
generally excluded any sense of women as speakers, as linguistic
innovators, or as definers of words. Whatever the editors' aims,
dictionaries have perpetuated the stereotypes and prejudices of
writers, editors, and language commentators, who are almost exclusively male. At no point do they make women's words and wom-
en's experiences central. Thus, despite the unique scholarly
achievements and undeniable wit of many of these dictionaries,
they have been produced within a social context that is inhospitable
to women.

A Feminist Position

A Feminist Dictionary, a scholarly project reflecting many contributions and perspectives, represents a different position. As the introduction states, the dictionary is a word book with several purposes:

> to document words, definitions, and conceptualizations that illustrate
> women's linguistic contributions and the ways in which they have
> sought to describe, reflect upon, and theorize about the world; to
> identify issues of language theory, research, usage, and policy that
> bear on the relationship between women and language; to demon-
> strate ways in which women are seizing the language; to broaden
> knowledge of the feminist lexicon; and to stimulate research on
> women and language. The dictionary is intended for feminists, schol-
> ars, feminist scholars, and the general interested reader. Like many
> other dictionaries, it is a compendium of words arranged in alpha-

betical order together with definitions, quoted citations and illustrations, and other forms of commentary. (Kramarae and Treichler 1)

Although *A Feminist Dictionary* acknowledges the situation of women's language and its own production within a system of patriarchal and hierarchical social relations, its authors make several important assertions:

1. They recognize women as linguistically creative speakers— that is, as originators of spoken or written language forms. The identification, documentation, and analysis of women's words and definitions depart from traditional lexicographic practice. Let me return to an earlier example and compare the definitions for the word *woman* in a standard dictionary—the *OED*, say—with those in *A Feminist Dictionary*. Under its first definition of *woman* as "an adult female human being," the *OED* lists 12 usages. Virtually all of them represent views of women that we would now describe as somewhat stereotypical: they depict women in relation or contrast to men, as representative of various traditional (often negative) female qualities, or as sexual; the one exception, in which *woman* is used to mean "one's own woman," is taken from a text in which the woman speaking is a prostitute—one's own woman in a profession dedicated to the service of men. The whole range of meanings, then, depend on men—men's beliefs, comforts, needs, and economic support. In contrast, *A Feminist Dictionary*'s definitions encompass notions of women as autonomous individuals; as distinct from their portrayal by men and male institutions; as confined and imprisoned slaves; as outside the category human; as "the first sex," now reduced from a former more radiant state; and as the embodiment of hope for the future. These usages are more than metaphoric: they are situated in texts that represent various feminist worldviews and give them concrete and sometimes literal meaning.

2. The dictionary also acknowledges the sociopolitical aspects of dictionary making. Criticizing current and past practices that privilege some forms of language over others, many entries question the ways words get into print, the reasons they go out of print, and the politics of bibliography and archival storage, of silence and speech, of what can be said and who can speak. The authors acknowledge the problems inherent in their own selection process and the inevitability of its privileging mechanisms. In the back of the book, they explicitly invite criticism, commentary, and contri-

butions, giving their address and including several blank pages for readers' notes and definitions.

3. *A Feminist Dictionary* draws heavily on excerpted material from feminist publications, many of them virtually inaccessible to the general reader. Women's words become the chief resource for the construction of definitions; acknowledging the incomplete and inevitably partial outcome of this process, the authors suggest other ways that they might have obtained information about words and their meanings. Further, they often stop short of explicit interpretation and offer no "definitions," letting verbatim usages speak for themselves. The focus on women's definitions contrasts with the practice of most other dictionaries, as I noted above in discussing the word *housewife*. Another example of the feminist approach is the way that the National Advisory Committee on Sexual Harassment on campuses constructed its working definition of *sexual harassment* for a US Department of Education report. Responding to questionnaires completed by women students who detailed what the term meant to them, the committee broadened its initial definition to take the varieties of personal experience into account.

4. In relying primarily on feminist rather than mainstream sources, *A Feminist Dictionary* does not seek to capture "an internalized norm" for a given community of speakers. Thus, entries rarely specify "part of speech" (e.g., noun or verb) or linguistic or social status (e.g., standard, obsolete, rare, neologism, or folk linguistics). Labels like *coined, nontraditional,* and *nonstandard* have meaning only in reference to a "real" body of "authorized" words, and, as I have already noted, women have reason to doubt this authorization process. The dictionary also seeks to present rather than to resolve controversy. Definitions of the word *feminist* alone, to return to one of Morris's examples, differ broadly across the women's movement, encompassing the positions of radical feminists, liberal feminists, women of color, Marxists, cultural feminists, and so on. At the same time, the dictionary draws words and definitions from such utopian and science-fiction texts as Monique Wittig and Sande Zeig's *Lesbian Peoples: Material for a Dictionary*, Marge Piercy's *Woman on the Edge of Time*, and Suzette Haden Elgin's *Native Tongue*, thereby blurring the line between words that "are" and words that "might be."

5. The dictionary represents not just feminist usages but also traditions of feminist conceptualization. This policy raises the question of the relation between a book about words and a book about the world. As I noted above, some etymologists use the word *marriage* to reinforce a prescription for women's passivity. The *OED*,

however, generally defines *marriage* as a union between two persons whom it implicitly defines as equal (the condition of being a husband or wife; the relation between married persons; spousehood; wedlock). Many of the feminist dictionary definitions of marriage challenge this notion of equality: "Leave matrimony alone, Girls," advised the nineteenth-century writer Fanny Fern. "It's the hardest way on earth of getting a living." Feminist writers have consistently put forward the idea of marriage as "woman's trade"; also important is the view (going back at least to the eighteenth century) that marriage is "legalized prostitution." Though at least one *OED* definition refers to marriage between "contracting parties" and though a number of the citations involve economic aspects of marriage, the notion of marriage as women's profession is entirely absent (*marriage bawd* and *marriage broker*, two terms hinting that marriage is an economic exchange, are characterized as "opprobrious").

6. Whereas several previous feminist dictionaries criticize the negative view of women embodied in traditional dictionaries, *A Feminist Dictionary* tends to emphasize women's definitions of themselves. In the dedication to one of her novels, Fanny Fern, who disavowed membership in the established male literary fraternity, pictured her book being read in a cozy family setting around the fire. Midway through the nineteenth century, using a metaphor particularly appropriate to the concerns of this essay, she told her women readers, "Should any *dictionary on legs* rap inopportunely at the door for admittance, send him away to the groaning shelves of some musty library, where 'literature' lies embalmed, with its stony eyes, fleshless joints, and ossified heart, in faultless preservation" (qtd. in Baym 33). *A Feminist Dictionary*, likewise, does not use male authority as its constant reference.

A feminist dictionary can be a significant scholarly and political intervention. Kramarae and Treichler's is proving controversial, and no doubt it should be, for the authors have never claimed that their motives are pure or their methods objective. Yet my argument in this essay is not that dictionaries are constructed in selected and biased ways that may ultimately be sexist or nonsexist. Rather, it is that there are important relations between dictionary making and theoretical questions involving lexical definitions and the delineation of concepts: the construction of a "real" dictionary invokes the abstract construction of a dictionary from discourse and the ongoing interplay between discourse and dictionary as we use language in our "real lives."[4]

Taking a term like *women*—perhaps the abiding point of inquiry and renewal for a feminist dictionary—we might entertain the following questions. Where do meanings come from? What does "a meaning" formally consist of? What is its linguistic and material history? In what and whose texts does it figure? Whose texts does it circumvent or undermine? Does a meaning exist if no dictionary affirms it? What is the relation between the lexical entries of an individual speaker and those of the culture as a whole? Between meanings in "the culture as a whole" and its subcultural discourses? In what form do lexical disjunctions occur? What strategies come into play when meanings and countermeanings clash? What are the function and value of semantic intervention? Who may intervene? How does the weight of prior discourse constrain the production of future meaning? Whose discourse? Whose future? How does meaning constrain usage? When we consciously or unconsciously produce meaning, where do our data come from: introspection, eternal verities, lived experience, empirical research, cultural productions, theories of how the world works, dreams, other speakers, other texts? What authorizes a given usage at a given moment? Whose interests do particular meanings and usages serve? Who may authorize meanings? Who may interpret them? Whose interpretations are authorized? What are the consequences—economic, symbolic, legal, medical, social, professional—of given meanings? What are the consequences if meanings are not fixed, are seemingly limitlessly inchoate? Does any given meaning construct or entail the potential existence of its opposite? Can one circumvent such binary oppositions? From what position does one propose and authorize new definitions without thereby reproducing the apparatus of authority and false universality? What can be the claim of "new" meanings within a system of social arrangements and material conditions that privileges "old" meanings? On what grounds can these questions be addressed?

Authorization and Its (Dis)Contents

The preceding questions deliberately conflate several universes of inquiry to emphasize the heterogeneity of theoretical concerns raised—not resolved—by the production of a feminist dictionary. Any dictionary, says Erica Reiner, editor of the *Chicago Assyrian Dictionary*, is in dialogue with what precedes and follows it: "We stick out our necks, and then somebody comes along ten years later and corrects the guess. I don't think corrections will come out unless we say something. One writes a dictionary *against* something—

against an accepted opinion" (qtd. in Shenker 41). One also writes a dictionary *for* something, and thus a feminist dictionary seeks to be a strategic act on behalf of women's interests.

This is not to say that such a dictionary is not also and equally a constructed linguistic universe. But this universe has never been constructed before: by drawing discourse from new places, seeking less camouflaged, interpretive practices, and addressing a feminist linguistic community, the dictionary points out—and the Indo-European root *deik* has yielded both *deixis* 'point to' and *dictio* 'dictionary'—that dictionary making can yield a distinct and rather unexpected outcome. *A Feminist Dictionary* does, I think, challenge many instances of the linguistic coding practices pervasive in the culture; and one hopes it will provide strategic authorization for alternative and nonsexist meanings. But most interesting, perhaps, it avoids privileging the binary division between male and female that pervades Western discourses about women (see Nelson, "Envoys"; Wittig, "Mark"). This division, as feminist theorists have noted, is likely to be represented linguistically not even as *male* versus *female* but as *male* versus *nonmale*. By starting with feminist discourse, we can begin to look in some depth and detail at what the now unescorted term *female* may entail. Once this shift is made, the term *nonsexist* itself begins to come apart. For it is a word whose meaning is rigidly situated in relation to dictionaries we know well and to familiar "sexist" texts, traditions, and social arrangements. Of course the pervasiveness of those arrangements and their power to dictate and authorize are undeniable, so that the term *nonsexist*, their mirror, mirrors what is. Even the phrase *nonsexist guidelines* is, in this sense, a capitulation. But with a different linguistic universe, a different dictionary—whose touchstone is a word like *feminist* or *female* or *women*—we can envision considerably more freedom. Again, putting women at the center of discourse, taking them seriously as its authors, radically shifts our perspective on the production and authorization of discourse.[5]

What I have been emphasizing here is that many feminist definitions differ in content from those found in standard "man-made" dictionaries. But a feminist dictionary with feminist content—seeking to honor "authorings" by women—does not circumvent questions of authority and authorization. Like all scholarly projects, it is inevitably implicated in what can broadly be called the politics of authorization. In concluding, I want to return to this question of authority and the dictionary's function—figurative or actual— as an object in the "real world."

The role of authority in the authoring and authorization of discourse is not well understood and has generally not been directly addressed by scholars in linguistics, semantics, or philosophy, whose discussions of meaning—as Mary Louise Pratt, among others, points out—have tended to be idealized and abstract, giving little attention to the contextual and cultural circumstances in which speakers use and interpret language. The widespread scholarly conception of language as a fluid and democratic exchange, Pratt writes,

> brings before us the persistent and terribly misleading metaphor of the linguistic marketplace, a kind of verbal utopia where a mythical free enterprise of words prevails, all voices vying equally to be heard. . . . An account of linguistic interaction based on the idea of exchange glosses over the very basic facts that, to put it crudely, some people get to do more talking than others, some are supposed to do more listening, and not everybody's words are worth the same. (13)

In this literature the word *bachelor*, for example, is repeatedly analyzed as a technical, "definitive," and purportedly universal concept, without regard for its sociocultural status (e.g., its connotations in comparison with *spinster*), for the authority of given scholars to authorize particular definitions on behalf of all human beings, or for the real consequences of authorizing given definitions. But these issues have been pressing concerns for feminists and feminist scholars, who are crucially interested in how definitions come about and are used and abused: how discourse, that is, relates to dictionaries and how dictionaries shape discourse. The series of questions in the preceding section suggest some possible approaches, based on current thinking and research, to a better understanding of how meanings—sexist, nonsexist, scholarly, popular, individual, cultural, and so on—are authorized.

One project involves the exploration of current feminist discourse. The term *discourse* refers to language use, both written and spoken, but further implies some form of dialogue—language in action within a specific context and set of social arrangements. (For a more detailed discussion of what *discourse* means, see Treichler, "Wall.") Though discourse draws on and provides evidence for an abstract, received code or system, the notion of discourse necessarily involves specific settings, fields, or repertoires: conversational discourse, feminist discourse, medical discourse, legal discourse, same-sex discourse, scholarly discourse, breakfast-table discourse, and so on. The term is useful because it can refer both to the general and to the specific, to the abstract and to the local, to writing and to speech. This consideration subverts any global notion of "usage" and requires us to embed our study in particular settings and circumstances. For example, many feminist academics control a range of written and sometimes competing lexicons (see, for example, Bart, "Being"; Frye, *Politics*; Gallop, "Writing"; Leffler, Gillespie, and Lerner; and both the introduction and the guidelines in this volume). The same feminist scholar might, depending on circumstance and setting, write the following sentences:

1. Women are seeking to reclaim their own history.
2. Women are seeking to reclaim our own history.
3. Womyn are seeking to reclaim our own herstory.

Although the first sentence expresses a feminist sentiment, its lexical and grammatical forms are conventional. The second is essentially equivalent in meaning to the first; but the shift from *their* to *our*, inserting the writer into a collectivity of women, creates a shift from third to first person, which some journal editors would find unacceptable. The third, displaying unconventional spelling and a feminist neologism in addition to the shift in person, goes even further in challenging the rules of what Baron calls "grammar and good taste." Indeed, challenge to tradition is at issue here, and these three sentences, accordingly, do not "mean the same thing." The disruption of conventional language is intended to signal a disruption of conventional society, or at the least to authorize a different relation to that society. These three examples could well have appeared, respectively, in *PMLA*, in *Signs*, and in *Sinister Wisdom*. Numerous other features of these publications would document the existence of the linguistic continuum I am suggesting here. Arriving at an understanding of both formal variance and the shades of meaning implied by the choices speakers make might help us better comprehend how authority interacts with a speaker's aims and intentions and how important it is in influencing choices among variant usages.

One key to feminist academic writing involves the writer's negotiation with authority—not only as prescriptivism or authoritarianism (the issues usually addressed in discussions of dictionaries) but as the right to author (see Gilbert and Gubar, *Shakespeare's Sisters*). The philosopher Naomi Scheman and the linguist Sally McConnell-Ginet ("Origins" and this volume) have both stressed the importance of the feminist movement in authorizing women to produce and articulate new meanings and in interpreting what those new meanings are. But see Jane Gallop on the feminist scholar as the (constrained) child of both a paternal and a maternal text ("Writing").

A second project involves the dissemination of feminist concepts. What happens to feminist definitions when they leave the feminist linguistic community? Most feminists have experienced the shock of semantic disjunction that occurs when one attempts to articulate to an "outsider" a concept shared within one's own circle. On a micropolitical scale, such a disjunction may need to be negotiated between couples, colleagues, friends, and small groups. How does authority within relationships affect these negotiations? Is external authority (e.g., the citation of a scholarly or feminist publication) brought into the negotiation? The role of authority in usage is also related, of course, to the conditions and power relations of speaking and understanding. Authority is not merely a feature that a speaker or hearer brings to an interaction but also, at least in part, something that is constructed within the discourse and that emerges from it. Accordingly, authority may shift with the topic, for men continue to be seen as the "experts" in some domains, women in others. In scholarship this division may occur as well, with men generally authorized to produce abstract and theoretical meanings and women to produce interpretations connected to feelings and human relationships. (See Carroll, "Politics"; Gilbert and Gubar, "Sexual" and *Shakespeare's*; Kamuf; and Meese on what Carroll calls the "class system of the intellect." Marcus, in "Still Practice," suggests that male critical theorists are drawn to feminist theory because it offers a body able to nourish their own disembodied abstractions.) Or established male scholars may lend their own names and authority to feminist thinking, thus making it intellectually "respectable." As Elaine Showalter points out regarding the field of literary theory, what happens then is that subsequent scholars cite those male authorities rather than the feminists whose ideas these authorities wrote about ("Critical"). (Of course, she also notes, many male critics have remained oblivious to feminist criticism for fifteen years—feminist criticism seeming to exist in its own time and space.) Balsamo claims that the major texts of postmodernism cite almost no feminists but nonetheless outline a conception of contemporary culture that feminist writing has, in many respects, been articulating for more than a decade.

A third area of inquiry might trace in detail the macrodevelopment of feminist linguistic innovations. How does an innovation travel within the subculture? What happens when it moves into popular culture? Feminist linguistic innovations in speech and writing are potentially a rich source for studying the formation of English words, an area of current research that raises a number of intriguing questions about the creation and lexicalization of words and meanings (see Bauer). We might ask how, where, and under what circumstances feminist innovations arise. What are the morphemes that cease or continue to be productive within feminist writing? For example, the journalistic coinage *suffragette* initially designated a member of the women's suffrage movement, the feminine suffix *-ette* intended by the press to demean and trivialize; but when the radical suffragists took up the word, it came to refer to the most militant wing of the movement. The feminists as a whole never adopted the suffix; in contrast, they widely—though not universally (see Brooke)—use the prefix *woman* in words like *womanspace* and *womanspirit*. Bauer notes that the status of the user may be important to the life of a word; does "status," obviously related to "authority," also influence words formed within the relatively nonhierarchical and democratic feminist movement? How does a new word travel? Who puts it in quotation marks? At what point and for whom does a word like *herstory* lose its novelty and gain acceptance as the name of a special kind of enterprise? Similarly, how widely used are gender-marked terms like *woman doctor*? What words have feminists created to name concepts previously unnamed? In this context, Gloria Steinem describes words like *sexism* and *sexual harassment* as significant feminist contributions to the language. "Fifteen years ago," she writes, "we just called it 'life' " (149). Betty Friedan, in *The Feminine Mystique*, calls women's mysterious dissatisfaction with domesticity "the problem with no name" (11–27). Twenty years later, in the light of additional data and further conceptualization, Marilyn Frye refined Friedan's definition:

> [*The Feminist Mystique*] locates the problem *in women*. . . . Because [Friedan] focused on women only of a certain race and class, and because she did not have a global or a radical perspective, she did not see that all women, even those who perforce have a lot more than domesticity to cope with, "want something more" and that this wanting . . . is not a problem. A book about *the problem* would have to be a book about men, not about women. (*Politics* 42)

Frye's conceptual analysis of the term *male chauvinism* is a starting point for that project. Another concern is the depoliticization of feminist innovations that move into the general speech community; examples already given include *sexism* and *family violence*.

A fourth area of inquiry involves the formation of concepts. How do conceptualization and reconceptualization occur? Gregory L. Murphy and Douglas L. Medin, cognitive psychologists, have for some time been exploring how concepts are acquired; recently they have asked what makes a conceptual category coherent. Virtually all current accounts of concepts rely on some notion of similarity among the entities that a given concept comprises (see Medin and Smith's review of existing models for understanding concepts— the classical, the prototype, and the exemplar). But this notion is inadequate, Murphy and Medin argue, because, in failing to link concepts to general world knowledge, it fails to identify constraints on concepts. (Thus there may be widespread agreement that all trips include the feature of motion, but this attribute does not distinguish trips from many other concepts that also feature motion.) Their proposed approach focuses instead on individuals' theories about the world and attempts to specify connections between theoretical and conceptual knowledge. This emphasis seems to me to have interesting implications for understanding sexism as part of a body of theoretical knowledge that would tend to generate sexist rather than nonsexist definitions and etymologies. In turn, this understanding could guide the construction of nonsexist definitions.

Linda Coleman and Paul Kay, discussing prototype semantics, cite the familiar riddle about the young man who is involved in an auto accident that kills his father. He is rushed to the emergency room of a hospital; the surgeon, on entering the room and seeing the patient, exclaims, "Oh my god, I can't operate—he's my son." How is this situation to be explained? The answer, of course, is that the surgeon is the young man's mother, and the riddle works because the listener's conception of *surgeon* rules out the female gender. Coleman and Kay argue that the issue is not linguistic but social: the minority of surgeons who are women. But I think it bears closer investigation, for in fact the history of medicine is a history of passionate debate over how the words *doctor, surgeon,* and so on are to be defined. Within this history, we find not only a refusal to authorize constructions like "the surgeon . . . she" ("the surgeon was his mother") but also a repeated marking of the noun as feminine (*doctoress, woman surgeon, gal surgeon*), so that in effect it becomes a new and lesser noun. I would argue that Coleman and Kay's distinction between typicality (most surgeons are male) and prototypicality (surgeons are male) breaks down where definition and conceptualization are protected and legislated by those in authority.

The category *woman*, for example, is being intensively explored from many directions within feminist scholarship. One line of argument goes that the word itself—especially the singular form with a capital *W*—carries with it a universalizing and homogenizing cultural tradition: "We have learned that one becomes a woman in the very practice of signs by which we live, write, speak, see. . . . This is neither an illusion nor a paradox. It is a real contradiction—women continue to become woman" (deLauretis, *Alice* 186). Whenever men have encountered this word, it has become the site for idealized and ultimately confining definitions—definitions that have been translated into the specialized discourses of medicine, law, and so on, frequently with real consequences for women (see, for example, Walkowitz; H. Rose).

A fifth and rather intriguing project might involve constructing a feminist version of the distinctive-features framework of linguistics. In a much cited article, "The Traffic in Women," Gayle Rubin briefly discusses this framework, which, it seems to me, would provide an interesting way of analyzing such immensely problematic and complex concepts as *woman, femininity*, and *feminism*. It would enable us to categorize definitions, to understand the crucial operating feature(s) of these concepts, not for eternity but in given situations. It might also enable us to predict co-occurrences of forms in discourse. Susan Wolfe, in this volume, discusses the generation of anaphoric pronouns within transformational grammar, where *he* automatically replaces a noun if the masculine gender is taken to be the "general feature" of human nouns. Wolfe points out that Meyers sees these rules as an example of sexism in society's use of language but not as a product of sexism in linguists' formulation of rules. In "Generics" Stanley talks about the acceptance of maleness as an inherent semantic feature; Wolfe, in this volume and elsewhere, talks about "cultural gender." Obviously, multiple identities require description. A grid of features might enable us to specify what is operative in a given situation. Different features might be crucial depending on who is doing the defining and for what purposes. The following persons might have very different priorities in their definitions of *female*, for example: a midwife or obstetrician at the moment of delivering a baby, a baby's mother or father, a geneticist, a horse breeder, an anthropologist, a fashion designer, an Olympic coach, an editor with the *New York Times*, a female impersonator, someone talking (knowingly or unknowingly) with a transsexual, a biographer of Jane Austen, a lawyer arguing before a female judge, Dustin Hoffman creating the title role of *Tootsie*, Elaine Showalter writing about Dustin Hoffman creating the role of Tootsie, and so on. Thus in one situation the existence of a penis or a vagina might be an important factor, but in another—say, talking unknowingly with a transvestite—other features (clothes, hair, makeup, voice, ideology, behavior) might be the telling gender signal. Here we may recall the scene in *Huckleberry Finn* where Huck, disguised as a girl, gives away his sex when he catches a ball of yarn tossed into his lap by clamping his knees together, not by spreading his knees, as a girl would, to catch it in the skirt of her dress. In Margaret Atwood's novel *The Handmaid's Tale*, which depicts an environment so toxic that many fetuses are nonviable "shredders," the crucial feature of a baby is not sex but humanness. In that world the ability to reproduce healthy children becomes a woman's one sure hope of continued existence. Several contributors to Tony Larry Whitehead and Mary Ellen Conaway's collection about sex and gender in cross-cultural fieldwork note cultures and cultural situations where sex and gender are *not* particularly relevant. Mary Poovey describes how women in mid-Victorian Britain were legally categorized by sex and property rights ("Speaking"). Single women could own property but could not engage in sexual activity with men; married women could have sexual relations but could not own property. Prostitutes, who could both own property and perform sexual acts, became a "border case"— a case, that is, that contradicts existing conceptions and dichotomies. In this instance, Poovey argues, prostitution generated an enormous discourse designed to repair this contradiction and reinstate a stable conception of womanhood; and female sexuality in this discourse became "a site of intense contestation." Such detailed semiotic analyses move us away from the sex-gender breakdown and encourage a less constrained process of ongoing, situationally dependent construction and deconstruction.[6]

A sixth area to explore more fully is the ease with which language lets us universalize. Many of us have learned to appreciate the multiplicity of definitions of *woman*, but within that concept are other terms that we more easily reduce and universalize. In recent years, for example, scholarship and theoretical writing have constructed a category called the *Third World Woman* (see Mohanty). We have all encountered the stereotype: a poor and uneducated woman, largely ignorant of her civil and legal rights, sometimes locked in revolutionary struggle (her contribution invariably seen as manual rather than intellectual labor), and oppressed by structures and institutions beyond her control (most commonly, female circumcision and, in some Arab countries, the veil). The "experts" responsible for this definition include colonial and imperialist Western governments, Western-trained cultural anthropologists, Western-trained authorities on economic development, and Western feminist scholars. For the rest of us, trickle-down images prevail and encourage us to evaluate institutions like the veil and the harem according to a traditional Western understanding of oppression. Third World women are thus among the groups who we believe, with Marx, "cannot represent themselves—they must be represented." Leila Ahmed, however, suggests a different understanding: "Although universally perceived in the West as an oppressive custom, [the veil] is not experienced as such by women who habitually wear it. More than anything perhaps, it is a symbol of women being separated from the world of men, and this is conventionally perceived in the West as oppression" (523). She elaborates:

> To continue to think about the Middle East's segregated societies in terms of [received ideas about oppression] is confining to feminist thought in that it imprisons us in the constructs that men have imposed on reality. Such constructs . . . disguise and conceal aspects of Islamic societies that feminists might view as sources of women's strength and perhaps mobilization. (527)

She provides another example:

> Even the harem, always so negatively perceived in the West as a place of confinement, is also, positively, a space for women forbidden to the male. The very word "harem" is a variant of the word "*haram*," which means "forbidden" (and also "holy"), which suggests to me that it was women who were doing the forbidding, excluding men from their society, and that it was therefore women who developed the model of strict segregation in the first place. Here, women share living time and living space, exchange experience and information, and critically analyze—often through jokes, stories, or plays—the world of men. (529)

A seventh issue is the possibility of continuing to develop a feminist semantics. Feminist scholarship, theory, and activism call into question the idea of presiding expertise—of uncompromised positions of authority from which definitions can legitimately and unproblematically be authorized (see Penelope). A crucial feature of the feminist movement is its commitment to the grass-roots articulation of lived experience. A feminist process of discovering meanings, a feminist semantics, requires that women be queried directly. It makes this demand in at least two ways. First, it argues for the authenticity of lived experience, for definitions created out of experience by those who have the experience, and asserts the right of each individual to have a hand in how he or she is to be defined. Second, it challenges the notion of overarching, monolithic, timeless, context-free categories and concepts: there is no essential core of features or qualities that make up the category *woman* and can serve to police its boundaries. Rather, *woman* is repeatedly a function of the discourse in which the term is produced; it may "refer to" or "describe" a particular social or historical being only as it arises out of that discourse. The definition process, in other words, is inevitably contextualized. The "authorization" of definitions therefore calls for theoretical knowledge grounded in lived experience, contextual specificity, and an awareness of the nature and history of particular discourse production.

Finally, Hilary Putnam's notion of the "division of linguistic labor" provides a useful perspective on linguistic authority. Putnam, a philosopher, asks just what it is that language tells us about reality. (Linguists, including Meillet, Jespersen, and Sapir, explore this question as well; see Jespersen, *Language* 253–54, for example. See also Pamela Fishman's feminist analysis of the "division of conversational labor" ["Interaction," "What"].) For many terms, Putnam suggests, a division of linguistic labor is at work: "What I refer to as an 'elm' is, with my consent and that of my linguistic community, what people who can distinguish elms from other trees refer to as an elm" (274). Usage in a given field thus depends on each individual's consent to, and cooperation with, the reality articulated by "relevant expert[s]" (275). This linguistic division of labor, Putnam suggests, is quite possibly a linguistic universal, for we cannot even imagine "a world in which every one is an expert on every topic" (266). In a broad sense, this formulation enables us to conceptualize the influence of authority on language and to understand, in turn, why any widespread challenge to authority and expertise is bound to have linguistic repercussions—as "nonexperts" seek to wrest from the "experts" the power to articulate reality and monitor patterns of denotation. Putnam elsewhere discusses the denotative power of terms created by medical experts, such as *multiple sclerosis* and *polio* (328–34). His analysis suggests a useful way for feminists to examine controversial words and usages, for nowhere are "contests for meaning" more evident than in the area of women's health. For many decades of the nineteenth century, for instance, the concept of *neurasthenia* was vigorously and emotionally debated by physicians, scientists, women, and others (Sicherman). Today the word *labor*, together with such words as *childbirth*, figures in a struggle between organized medicine—particularly gynecology—and the women's health movement. In 1920 a landmark paper by the obstetrician and gynecologist Joseph DeLee introduced a definition of the birth process as pathological and abnormal. (We do not call it normal, he told his colleagues, when a baby's head is crushed in a door and the infant dies of cerebral hemorrhage; yet "when a baby's head is crushed against a tight pelvic floor, and a hemorrhage in the brain kills it, we call this normal" [40].) In particular, DeLee's definition, which authorized forceps delivery, essentially medicalized childbirth, on the one hand identifying the process as interesting to organized medicine and on the other hand providing the theoretical grounding for both a technical and a nontechnical lexicon that defines birth as abnormal (see Poovey, "Scenes," for a discussion of physicians' debates on this subject). Today that lexicon is being challenged. The language of gynecology textbooks, charged Gena Corea in 1977, defines the female body as hostile territory and the medical staff as a kind of SWAT team, trained for swift and aggressive intervention. And many of these texts, according to Diana Scully and Pauline Bart, fail to incorporate Kinsey's research on female sexuality, let alone Masters and Johnson's. Indeed, an index entry reads as follows in the 1976 edition of *Williams' Obstetrics* (ed. Pritchard and MacDonald): "Chauvinism, Male. Voluminous amounts. pp. 1–1190."[7] Such subversion—even from the marginal position of the feminist indexer—bears watching, for it is a struggle for the right to create and define that has important material consequences both for women and for medicine. But this current feminist challenge to a culturally sanctioned division of linguistic labor (which grants physicians, as experts, the right to the definition process) needs to be described and interpreted within the notion of a linguistic class system and a set of existing (though rapidly changing) material conditions. Whose words are of value? Whose carry economic weight? Whose control the resources that authorize medical treatment? As I argue in discussing Charlotte Perkins Gilman's story "The Yellow Wallpaper," a theoretical understanding of authority and power is critical to this process, as is information about doctor-patient interactions and economic contingencies (Treichler, "Escaping" and "Wall"; see also Martin). Only such an analysis will enable us to understand why, as Sally McConnell-Ginet suggests, the woman who calls her gynecologist by his first name is committing a revolutionary act ("Address" 34).

I have discussed dictionary making not only to describe concrete ways in which selected meanings are "authorized" by those in "authority" but also to suggest that authority may be central to the way we construct and interpret concepts and use them in discourse. The production of a feminist dictionary—which gives unique prominence to women as creative language users—links the notion of authority to that of "authoring." I have argued that this issue is relevant to our understanding of how meanings—both sexist and feminist—travel between discourse and dictionary and have pointed out a number of ways in which this question might be fruitfully investigated.

Notes

[1] Dictionaries are commonly classified as etymological, historical, foreign-language, new-word, hard-word, specialized, and concise. The concise dictionary is a particularly American creation, differing in kind from its English predecessors. It is more "democratic" in being typically a single volume, modestly priced (nowadays usually available in paperback), with functional, idiomatic definitions directed toward usage. Harold Whitehall's sketch of dictionary history attributes this format to the large immigrant population in the United States, to the system of widespread popular education, and "to the vast commercial opportunities implicit in both of these" (xxxiii). See Zgusta; Sledd; and Sledd and Ebbitt for further discussion.

[2] In June 1986, the State Supreme Court of Maine ruled that women as well as men can commit rape and that males as well as females can be rape victims. The *New York Times* headlined this story "Woman May Be Rapist, Maine High Court Holds."

[3] For at least a century in Britain, the term *dictionary* signified one thing only: Samuel Johnson's *Dictionary* of 1755. According to Whitehall, a bill was once thrown out of the British Parliament because a key term was not "in the Dictionary" (xxxii). As James Murray told the story in a 1900 lecture, however, the minister requesting a definition of an agricultural *allotment*, not then known to English law, was told to "look in the Dictionary." When his questioning persisted, he was further instructed: "Johnson's Dictionary! Johnson's Dictionary!"; amid laughter in the House, he at last subsided into silence. Indeed, notes Murray, *allotment* in this particular sense is *not*

to be found in Johnson's Dictionary. "But the replies . . . are typical of a large number of persons, who habitually speak of 'the Dictionary,' just as they do of 'the Bible,' or 'the Prayer-book,' or 'the Psalms'; and who, if pressed as to the authorship of these works, would certainly say that 'the Psalms' were composed by David, and 'the Dictionary' by Dr. Johnson" (5–6).

The term *dictionary* derives from the Medieval Latin word *dictionarium*, a nominalization formed on the participial stem of *dicere* 'to say.' Dennis Baron has suggested to me that *dictionary* might literally be best interpreted to mean a "thing of saids," though others render *dictionary* as a repository or housing for sayings, speaking, and words. The broad meaning "word book" appears in the *Random House Collegiate*, the *Encyclopedia Brittanica*, and elsewhere. In his 1900 lecture, Murray noted that

> it would have been impossible to predict in the year 1538, when Sir Thomas Elyot published his "Dictionary," that this name would supplant all the others, and even take the place of the older and better-descended word *Vocabulary*; much less that *Dictionary* should become so much a name to conjure with, as to be applied to works which are not word-books at all, but reference-books on all manner of subjects. . . . (18)

I cannot resist adding that it would doubtless have been impossible for Murray to predict that his own dictionary, fondly termed GOD (great Oxford dictionary) by some of its readers, would be fully computerized by 1989, all 16 volumes accessible on three compact disks (Clines). The acronym for the massive multimillion-dollar task of bringing the *OED* into the computer age is OEDIPUS, the last four letters standing for integration, proofing, and updating system; and to the dictionary itself, no longer GOD, the project staff have given the name *Oedipus Lex*.

⁴ In a useful commentary on this problem, George Lakoff and Mark Johnson claim that the following assumptions underlie most discussions of meaning by linguists and philosophers:

> Truth is a matter of fitting words to the world.

> A theory of meaning for natural language is based on a theory of truth, independent of the way people understand and use language.

> Meaning is objective and disembodied, independent of human understanding.

> Sentences are abstract objects with inherent structures.

> The meaning of a sentence can be obtained from the meanings of its parts and the structure of the sentence.

> Communication is a matter of a speaker's transmitting a message with a fixed meaning to a hearer.

> How a person understands a sentence, and what it means to *him*, is a function of the objective meaning of the sentence and what the person believes about the world and about the context in which the sentence is uttered. [The emphasized male "generic" *him* is in the original.] (196)

Lakoff and Johnson argue against this "objectivist" position. Their alternative seeks to link the meaning of a sentence to a conceptual structure
that is in turn grounded in our subjective experience of, and interaction
with, the world. Yet, like the tradition they challenge, they also assume
the existence of a "natural" world that structures our conceptualizations
and understandings. This position seriously underestimates the degree to
which language is permeated by other language as well as by experience.
Three general sources for the study of words and meaning are Keith Allan
(vols. 1 and 2), Laurie Bauer, and Milroy and Milroy.

[5] For example, the entries under *lesbian* in *A Feminist Dictionary* explore
the political, social, cultural, ideological, and sexual meanings and implications of this term for women, for feminists, and for lesbians; the authors
cited are not primarily concerned with lesbians' sexual preference for
women, which is viewed as merely one—and not always the essential—
aspect of being a lesbian. In standard dictionaries the definition of the
term begins and ends with the sex of a lesbian's object of desire. But *A
Feminist Dictionary* cites Monique Wittig's argument that the concept *lesbian*
escapes the ubiquitous man-woman dichotomy because lesbians have opted
out of the patriarchal culture that defines and maintains that opposition
("One" 53; see also Judy Grahn). This decision to place women at the
center of discourse has been, to date, the least comprehensible characteristic of *A Feminist Dictionary* for reviewers unfamiliar with, or unsympathetic
to, feminist writing and thinking. Some, indeed, completely miss the point.
Anthony Burgess, for example, reviewing the book in the *London Observer*
(27 Oct. 1985) under the headline "Penile Servitude," sees the dictionary
as "battering at the supposed male stronghold of language." But Burgess
sets the authors straight: "Language is arbitrary and inert, as Saussure
taught us, and it is probably bisexual." He concludes, "You can hear the
snapping of the *vagina dentata* on every page." Barbara Smith commented
as follows in the *New Statesman* (3 Jan. 1986):

> *A Feminist Dictionary* does not deal in sterile signs, but the living, evolving
> language of feminism. . . . Anthony Burgess in the *Observer* . . . has wonder-
> fully fallen into the trap laid for his ilk: *A Feminist Dictionary* surely was written
> by feminists for feminists about feminism, and therefore he is excluded. . . .
> He sees the book as "a manifold gesture of hate" with "the snapping of the
> *vagina dentata* on every page." *A Feminist Dictionary* is not the OED refashioned
> with a labyris dripping Y chromosomes, and the *vagina dentata* is a *male*
> invention. . . .

[6] Such an analysis need not be merely an academic exercise. In an essay
assessing Britain's social policies toward Gypsies, Roy Todd discusses the
impossibility of defining the Gypsy (or traveler) population in monolithic
or essentialist terms. The search for an adequate definition reveals "the
disparity between Gypsies' own definitions and those commonly offered
by lay members of the settled community; and the complexity of the task
of adequately encompassing the distinctive features of Gypsy culture" (181).
Todd then shows that any given feature, no matter how seemingly essential—whether Gypsy ancestry, self-employment, traveling, or mastery
of Gypsy languages or cultural practices—will only function in specific

contexts to distinguish Gypsies from non-Gypsies. No single feature, in other words, is essential to the distinction, a fact that has a number of policy implications.

[7] As noted in the introduction to this volume, the 1980 edition was evidently improved, for the index entry for *male chauvinism* reads merely "variable amounts." By the 1984 edition (ed. Pritchard et al.), the term *male chauvinism* is not indexed, and at least some additions to the text itself seem to be more "feminist" in tone.

[8] An earlier version of this essay was presented at the Linguistic Society of America symposium Sexism, Semantics, and Discourse. Baltimore, 28 December 1984. At a number of points I draw on the introduction to *A Feminist Dictionary*.

The Reconstruction of Word Meanings: A Review of the Scholarship

Susan J. Wolfe

In discussing verbal messages, sociolinguists customarily distinguish between *use*, the form the speaker (sender) adopts, and *code*, the rules that underlie the form and allow the hearer (receiver) to interpret it. An individual's use of a word or construction in a situation does not imply that the form is characteristic of a group of speakers or that the pattern of the group is responsible for the form. Hence sexist usage does not presuppose that language itself—the code—is sexist. It is clear, for example, that an individual can refer to a woman as a dog without a lexicon that lists "unattractive woman" as a possible definition for *dog*. But it is equally clear that viewing the way language is acquired tends to blur the distinction between code and use.

Language learners, after all, must infer the rules governing language from the messages they hear, and, as Elizabeth Closs Traugott points out, their "imperfect" language learning may bring about changes in the language itself: "The fact that each generation, or rather each child, learns language anew and makes its own hypotheses about the patterns of the language is the main cause for language change. . . . Children have the capacity, in other words, to 'restructure' the language—that is, to reanalyze it and develop new sets of patterns" (9–11). Children's need to infer underlying rules from the messages they receive provides a possible concrete explanation for language change and appears to support the case for distinguishing linguistic phenomena from the speech events in which they occur. Frank Parker, who ascribes language change to problems in transmitting clear messages, is among those who study language through speaker-hearer interactions and argue that the grammar of a language "does not have an autonomous existence apart from the speakers of language." His position, though at odds with the conception of language as largely innate and independent, offers us a way of accounting for language change. Over time, Parker suggests, the grammars of individual speakers are transmitted to new speakers. In this process, individual speakers do not have direct access to the grammars of other speakers; rather, they construct their own new grammars by making hypotheses about the utterances they hear (3). Naturally, some of these hypotheses may be incorrect; children may perceive a sexist usage to be part of the code of English and incorporate it into their grammars. It is thus possible for a sexist comparison (e.g., of a woman to a dog) to generate a sexist lexical entry (definition) that becomes part of a grammar and, by extension, enters the code of an entire linguistic community.

The Male Bias of English

The English language indeed seems to have evolved through the perceptions of its learners. As Dale Spender notes, feminists concerned with linguistics hold that a language can be constructed with a male bias (*Man Made*), and Michael J. Schneider and Karen A. Foss maintain that English is such a language. Schneider and Foss attribute sexism in English not merely to the speakers but to the rules of English syntax and semantics: "English is biased in favor of the male in both syntax and semantics" (1). A salient example is the rule requiring the masculine pronoun in reference to an antecedent of unspecified sex (such as *a professor* or *everybody*). This convention implies that women are inferior or subordinate to men, as does the systematic assignment of negative or pejorative connotations to words denoting women (compare, for example, the connotations of *courtier* and *courtesan, master* and *mistress*).

The existence of sexism in language is not surprising to those who recognize language as a system of meanings encoded largely by men. As Dale Spender comments, women have been excluded from the construction not only of many cultural forms but of the disciplines that study such forms: "It is a mark of the sexism of linguistics as a discipline that in all the research which has been done on the history of the language the question of the role played by women in its production and development has received virtually no attention; indeed, such a question has not even been asked!" (*Man Made* 32)

The question of sexual inequality in language should hardly be considered trivial by those who have dedicated themselves to the study of language and its expression in literature. The relevance of sexist usage, even to literary criticism or linguistic theory, has been substantiated by Dwight Bolinger. He contends that it is inconsistent to analyze form independently of content, particularly in disciplines devoted to studying the "meanings" of terms and sentences (and, by implication, the "meanings" of literary works). In his 1973 presidential address to the Linguistic Society of America, Bolinger urged linguists distressed about sexism in society to extend their social conscience to their profession. Asserting that "truth is a linguistic question" for those who accept responsibility for language use, he further asserted that the current linguistic interest in meaning extends naturally to the issue of how well meanings fit facts. Hence, he argued, linguistics ought to be concerned that "women are taught their place, along with other lesser breeds, by the implicit lies that language tells about them" (541–42).

Bolinger's claim that linguistics has only recently become involved with the question of meaning should not be taken as a comment on the past several centuries. Not until the advent of structural linguistics and early transformational linguistics did language study purportedly become divorced from the study of meaning in context, thereby eliminating from its consideration such irrelevant factors as usage and social contexts. Indeed, English prescriptive grammarians of the eighteenth and nineteenth centuries deferred to social realities both in using the English language and in describing its grammar (Bodine; Stanley, "Sexist").

To document that these grammarians equated gender with biological sex, Julia Penelope Stanley cites the formulations of Michael Maittaire, "The gender signifies the kind or sex"; Lindley Murray, "Gender is the distinction of sex"; and R. Harrison, "Nouns have properly two GENDERS; the *Masculine*, to denote the male kind; and the *Feminine*, to denote the female." Hence, Stanley argues, prescriptive grammarians used the words *man, men, mankind,* and *he* literally, to refer to male persons ("Sexist" 801–02). Terms of male reference understandably predominated in English grammars because women were all but excluded from the educated audience for whom prescriptive grammars were written. Discussions of learning and language use, such as this passage from John Fell's 1784 *Essay towards an English Grammar*, were both directed toward a largely male audience and assumed to describe the writings of men: "Many wise and learned men have made use of our language in communicating their sentiments to the world, concerning all the important branches of science and art. Some men, whose writings do honour to their country and to mankind, have, it must be confessed, written in a style that no Englishman will own" (vi–vii). The notion of male superiority not only accounted for prescriptive grammarians' own use of masculine terms but informed their discussions of grammatical gender in language. These writers theorized that terms applicable to both sexes should be considered masculine because the male was the nobler sex; hence, they argued, terms for the divine being were regarded as masculine, except among languages spoken by "idolatrous" peoples:

> Beings superior to man, although we conceive them to be of no sex, are spoken of as masculine in most of the modern tongues of Europe, on account of their dignity; the male being, according to our ideas, the nobler sex. But idolatrous nations acknowledge both male and female deities; and some of them have given even to the Supreme Being a name of feminine gender.   (Beattie 137)

> The gender of words, in many instances, is to be determined by the following principle of universal grammar. Those terms which are equally applicable to both sexes (if they are not expressly applied to females), and those plurals which are known to include both sexes, should be called masculine in parsing; for, in all languages, the masculine gender is considered the most worthy,* and is generally employed when both sexes are included under one common term. Thus *parents* is always masculine.   (G. Brown)

Goold Brown footnotes *Hermes* (written by James Harris, another male grammarian) as an authoritative source for the belief that God is a masculine term because the male is the more worthy sex:

> *"The Supreme Being (*God* . . .) is, in all languages, masculine; inasmuch as the masculine sex is the superior and more excellent; and as He is the Creator of all, the Father of gods and men."—*Harris's Hermes*, p. 54.

As Stanley points out, the early treatments prescribing the masculine gender for terms of general reference based their rules on

what their authors regarded as the natural distinction between the
sexes and the rightful preeminence of the male ("Sexist" 804–05).

The influential grammarian Otto Jespersen observed that social
stereotyping by sex was largely responsible for the perception that
many common nouns or terms of general reference were masculine
or feminine; hence such nouns, "though possessing no distinctive
mark, are as a matter of fact chiefly or even exclusively applied to
one sex only, because the corresponding social functions have been
restricted either to men or to women. This is true of *minister, bishop,
lawyer, baker, shoemaker,* and many others on the one hand, *nurse,
dressmaker, milliner* on the other." Jespersen went on to note that
words of common sex seemed to assume lesser importance when
marked as feminine: "When it is desired to restrict common-sex to
one sex, this may be done in various ways, thus *man-servant* or
*servant-man, maidservant, servant-girl, a he-devil, a she-devil, her girl-
friends, a poetess* (but it is a higher praise to say that Mrs. Browning
was a great poet, than to call her a great poetess)" (*Philosophy* 232).
Unfortunately, Jespersen failed to explore fully the ramifications
of his parenthetical remark, the implication that female reference
alone is associated with negative connotations.

Jespersen did observe, however, that *widower* and *bridegroom* were
the only male words derived from female words (in contrast to
heroine, duchess, and scores of other female words with a male base),
and he saw the disparity as "a natural linguistic consequence of the
social preponderance during many centuries of men" (*Essentials*
190–91).

Other early twentieth-century grammarians did not share Jespersen's perception of English as a language that reflects male social
dominance. Most of them simply described the use of generic *he*
as "correct" on the basis of number concord, a practice that has
persisted among modern grammarians. Paul Roberts, for instance,
terms the use of singular pronouns to refer to indefinites "conservative": "The tendency for the meaning to dominate is strongest
in the use of *they* (*them, their*) in reference to an indefinite pronoun:
'Everyone averted their eyes.' Conservative usage prefers 'Everyone
averted his (or her) eyes' " (20). Roberts's account does, however,
allow for the possibility of the feminine pronoun, if only parenthetically.

More recently, grammars based on transformational theory have
"generated" anaphoric pronouns by means of replacement rules,
stating that the pronoun *he* can almost always stand for a common
noun referring to a person because all such nouns share a single

semantic feature. The shared feature may be termed either *male* or *masculine*, on the grounds that human nouns in English are "generally" masculine. Walter E. Meyers, for example, in a handbook that uses transformational rules to teach prescriptive grammar, explains that *masculine* is the "general feature" of human nouns: "For human nouns, *masculine* appears to be the general feature, *feminine* the special one: that is, unless a human noun is specifically marked *feminine*, the noun phrase of which it is the head noun is replaced by *he, his,* or *him*" (113).

Though Meyers might be hard pressed to locate a generative treatment of pronouns explicitly identifying the feature *male* or *masculine*, his applied rule appears to have a solid foundation in the assumptions of theorists. The examples offered by Tanya Reinhart suggest that males are the referents of most common nouns and indefinite pronouns; subsequent references to such antecedents are most often masculine pronouns (115–35). Quoting from linguists and philosophers of the past two decades and supplementing their examples with her own, she provides sentences in which masculine pronouns refer to *candidate, businessman, psychiatrist, employee, student, anybody remotely connected with the assassination, worker, anybody over 60,* and *nobody,* as in "You should give nobody matches near his child's crib" (119). When feminine pronouns do appear in examples, they refer to *actress (who kissed Brando), every daughter of every professor,* and *a pregnant girl.*

Stanley J. Cook and Richard W. Suter, in their descriptive grammar of Modern English, observe that the use of masculine pronouns to refer to indefinite antecedents, though perhaps "sexually biased," is acceptable Standard English:

> All right, what about the practice of using masculine *his* in a sentence where sex is not specified but the antecedent is singular and human? It is true that sentences like "Each person has his own desk" and "Everyone likes to be his own master" can seem awkward and sexually biased. But . . . Standard English has accepted such sentences without reservation for years. Rather it is a matter of questioning social and political values. If a person writes sentences like those just given, he or she might be considered chauvinistic or socially unaware by some, but not unintellectual or illiterate.   (147)

Though obviously aware that the use of masculine pseudogenerics is a *form* of sexism, these authors seem unaware that the Standard English rule is the *product* of sexism.

Meyers concludes that the generic use of the masculine pronoun is prescribed because "in English, we often speak as if the person referred to were male unless we have information to the contrary" (36), a habit Stanley attributes to the predominance of men in most occupations and socially prominent and powerful positions:

> Those nouns that refer to powerful and prestigious social positions and occupations carry [+male] as their inherent semantic feature, e.g., *doctor, lawyer, judge, chairman*. Such nouns are understood to refer to males unless a special "female marker" is added, either as a prenominal modifier, e.g., *lady doctor, female surgeon* ... or as a feminine suffix, e.g., *waitress, authoress*. ... Only a few human nouns in English carry [+female] as an inherent feature (or [−male], as [some] would mark them), e.g., *nurse, prostitute, secretary, mother*. ("Generics" 1–2)

Elsewhere, I have extended Stanley's analysis to other European languages in which usage reflects the assumption that most agents are male and are therefore to be marked grammatically as masculine:

> It would appear that in the actual use of agentives, several modern Indo-European languages—French, German, and Russian—though said to have "grammatical" gender and concord, do not differ from English, said to have "natural" gender. All four languages automatically assign masculine readings to agentive nouns which designate roles normally performed by males. A word denoting the roles of "doctor" or "judge" will be masculine in either system of gender-marking, because males enact those roles. Cultural assumptions about appropriate male and female roles determine gender-marking as clearly as do reproductive functions. (Wolfe, "Gender" 786–87)

Such languages, I argue, have "cultural" gender rather than grammatical or natural gender.

English Pronouns

Historical linguists have also relied on natural distinctions between the sexes to explain the forms of English pronouns. The pronominal system of English has clearly undergone historical change. It has, for example, lost the distinction between singular *thou* and plural *you*, a process still under way in a number of other European languages, such as Spanish and French. The Old English first-person dual forms *wit* 'we two' or 'us two' and *uncer* 'my and one other person's' have long since been lost. Losses not infrequently alter pronominal paradigms.

Changes in the forms of individual pronouns, however, appear to be rare enough to warrant comments (Strang 236). Hence Jespersen attributed the substitution of Scandinavian third-person plural pronouns (*they, them, their*) for the native English forms (*hie, him, hira*) to the extraordinary influence of Scandinavian settlers on the people of Northern England (*Essentials* 212). But to account for the loss of the Old English feminine nominative *heo* and its ultimate replacement by *she*, historical linguists point to a psychological need on the part of English speakers. Phonetically distinct forms, according to this argument, are necessary to reflect the natural distinction between the sexes. From the twelfth through the fourteenth century, over two dozen orthographic variants of the feminine nominative appeared, among them *hi, ho, hy, he, sche, scheo, ssche, che, xe, ye* (C. Jones 128). Commenting on the profound disturbance in *they* and *she*, Barbara Strang, for instance, describes the masculine-feminine and singular-plural distinctions as "fundamental to the working of the language." She appears, however, to regard sexual differences as the primary reason for these distinctions:

> As a result of phonological change considerable areas of the [South] had come to have the same form for the feminine singular, and almost all the country except the [Southwest] and [West Midlands] to have it also for the plural. Yet the distinctions between *he, she*, and *they* were then, as now, fundamental to the working of the language (when, in one of the best-known [Middle English] love-poems, the lover says of his lady "He may me blisse bringe," the danger of misunderstanding is evident). (236)

Pyles likewise finds the possibility of ambiguity in sexual reference "intolerable": "The feminine pronoun had a variety of subject forms, one of them identical with the corresponding masculine form—certainly a well-nigh intolerable state of affairs, forcing the lovesick author of the lyric 'Alysoun' to refer to his sweetheart as *he*, the same form she would have used in referring to him" (171).

Mossé has also examined the [š] variants of the feminine nominative singular, attributing the Northern *schō* to the influence of the Old English feminine demonstrative *sēo*:

> The *schō* type . . . of the Northern dialect and of Scots is perhaps the form taken in Middle English by the Old English feminine de-

monstrative *sēo*, then *sīo* with a displacement of accent (*s'io* > *si'o* > *sj'o*) which would have facilitated the palatization of *s* to *sh* ([s] to [š]). But it must be remarked that the Old English feminine pronoun *hēo* could very well, by an analogous process (*h'io* > *hi'o* > *hj'o*), arrive at the same palatization." (56)

This explanation fails because it is morpheme-specific; other Old English words similarly formed (*seolc* 'silk' and *heorte* 'heart') did not undergo the hypothesized palatization.

Mossé, like Strang and Pyles, attributes the form *she* to the "very great ambiguity" resulting from the homophony of the feminine nominative pronoun with another pronominal form. But he stresses the similarity between the pronunciation of the feminine pronoun and that of the third-person plural pronoun:

> The *schē*, *shē* type . . . is essentially that of the East Midlands. It is found as early as the *Peterborough Chronicle* under the form *scǣ*. This is the type which is met, to the exclusion of all others, in the common literary language, in the second half of the 14th century (*Mandeville*, Wyclif, Chaucer, Gower). The origin of the *schē* form is obscure and very controversial. It is not impossible that it goes back, just like the other two, but by a somewhat different process, to the Old English feminine 3rd person *hēo*. . . . It is only necessary to remark that in certain dialectal areas of type 1 (*hēo/hō*) there was a homophony between the 3rd singular feminine pronoun and the 3rd plural (*hī*, *hē*, *hēo*) which resulted in a very great ambiguity. (56)

Finally, a generative historical account of the same process explicitly identifies the need for distinctions involving "sex and animateness" in English grammar as a constraint on the direction of grammatical change: ". . . it might be possible to explain the direction of these pronominal changes in terms of a general instruction to the grammar to the effect that *superficial case-marking forms may be deleted just so long as distinctions involving sex and animateness are not impaired*" (C. Jones 132).

It seems remarkable that ambiguity of reference (whether the ambiguity would have existed between the third-person feminine and third-person plural forms or between the feminine and masculine forms of the pronoun) is offered by linguists as adequate to explain the *she* forms of the feminine nominative. As Julia P. Stanley and Susan W. Robbins note, the pronoun *he* has served a dual function, replacing either a male antecedent or a common noun or pronoun of indefinite reference (81). Yet while linguists and grammarians have argued that the ambiguity between pronouns referring to females and those referring to males must have been "intolerable," they have accepted without question the potential ambiguity of generic uses of *he*. Noting this discrepancy, I have suggested elsewhere that linguistic analyses of the changes in the Middle English feminine pronoun, like the shifts themselves, may have been motivated by sexist assumptions. I theorize, for instance, that the constraint Charles Jones postulates for English grammar —that "distinctions involving sex and animateness" may not be "impaired" through changes in grammatical forms—was one imposed by speakers, not by the structure of the language, and that male speakers were in a position to issue what Jones terms "an instruction to the grammar":

> Such analyses show that the patriarchal paradigm determines which explanations historical linguists will offer for grammatical changes, just as the paradigm directs changes in the grammar itself. Jones ignores the fact that *speakers* of Middle English provided "a general instruction to the grammar," and that they were probably male speakers. Yet surely the "disruption" of the nominative case of the feminine pronoun—resulting in some two dozen orthographic variants before the general adoption of the maximally distinct [š], while the masculine pronoun retained the same form—is some indication that those who controlled linguistic shifts were also those who wielded cultural power. (Wolfe, "Constructing" 331)

If this hypothesis is correct, we can conclude that sexist attitudes have helped shape interpretations of grammatical change no less than they have determined prescribed usage (cf. Baron, *Grammar and Gender*).

Semantic Change

Sex marking or sexual reference, which has figured strongly in discussions of English pronominal reference, is often mentioned in conjunction with semantic change as well. Historians of the English language commonly cite, for instance, the sexual specialization of the noun *girl*, which once signified "a child of either sex." They less frequently observe that nouns, once they become female-specific, usually acquire debased or obscene connotations:

> Again and again in the history of the language, one finds that a perfectly innocent term designating a girl or woman may begin with

totally neutral or even positive connotations, but that it gradually acquires negative implications, at first perhaps only slightly dispar- aging, but after a period of time becoming abusive and ending as a sexual slur. (Schulz 165)

Schulz claims to have located approximately a thousand words and phrases that describe women in sexually derogatory ways, and she explains the large number of these slurs by noting that female terms undergo pejoration while corresponding male terms do not (I have already referred to the contrasting semantic developments of *cour- tesan* and *courtier*, *mistress* and *master*).

The ubiquitous deprecation of female terms suggests that Schulz has succeeded in establishing a connection between a semantic fea- ture (female) and a semantic process (pejoration), a discovery with important implications for scholars studying semantic change. Per- haps it is not surprising that grammarians and lexicographers have overlooked the systematic relation between female reference and disparagement; they may simply have taken for granted the neg- ative connotations of female terms.

The unconscious sexism of diachronic linguists may have con- strained both their methodology and their findings (Wolfe, "Con- structing"; Wolfe and Stanley). In attempting to reconstruct the Proto-Indo-European language by comparing cognate forms in the ancient written languages of Europe and India, they naturally had to reconcile apparent differences among the senses and forms of related words. Benveniste observes that the difficulties involved in this task are formidable but not insurmountable:

> Even within the corpus of a single language, forms of the same word can be divided into distinct groups which seem hardly recon- cilable. Thus from the root **bher-*, represented by *fero* in Latin, three separate groups of derivatives have evolved which form as many lexical families: (1) *fero* 'to carry' in the sense of gestation, from which *forda* 'pregnant female' is derived, linking up with *gesto*; (2) *fero* 'carry' in the sense of 'bring about, involve, entail' is used with reference to manifestations of chance, hence *fors*, *fortuna* and their numerous derivatives, which also include the notion of 'fortune, riches'; (3) *fero* 'carry' in the sense of 'carry off' forms a group with *ago* and can be defined as referring to seizure and booty.
>
> If we compare with this the forms derived from *bhar-* in Sanskrit the picture becomes still more varied. To the senses just listed we must add those of 'to carry' in the sense of 'support, take care of,' hence the derivatives *bhartr-* 'husband'; from 'carry' in connection

with horse riding comes 'ride,' etc. Thus one only has to study in detail one of these groups to see that in every case they constitute a coherent lexical unit hinging on a central notion, readily supplying institutional expressions.   (173–74)

Benveniste's account suggests that reconstructed meaning and reconstructed form are mutually dependent and that both rely in turn on the scholar's ability to perceive "a central notion" or semantic relation. But, as Wolfe and Stanley point out, similarities in meaning must seem "plausible" if a historical linguist is to infer an etymological relation. When the central notion of two Proto-Indo-European roots is obscured, linguists may assign them different sources. Thus the two **magh*[1] roots postulated for Proto-Indo-European—the one giving rise to terms denoting "power" (English *might*, Old Persian *magus* 'member of a priestly caste,' *magi*, and *magic*), the other meaning "fight" (surviving only in *amazon*)—may have been distinguished solely because linguists were unwilling to connect terms for power with the word *amazon*. If this conjecture is correct, the Proto-Indo-European lexicon needs to be reexamined (235–36).

Equally important, the reconstructed vocabulary of the Indo-Europeans has provided the most important data in the reconstruction of Proto-Indo-European culture. Because Indo-European terminologies of kinship have appeared uniformly patrilineal, patriarchal, and patrilocal (the bride leaving her family's household to join her husband's), historical linguists have concluded that Indo-European society was, like the culture of ancient Rome, uniformly patriarchal as well. But anomalies in the reconstructed lexicon suggest that these scholars may have overlooked or misinterpreted data that did not conform to their preconceived notions of prehistoric Indo-European culture (Wolfe, "Constructing").

There are, for example, no cognate terms for concepts basic to the institution of marriage; terms denoting "husband," "wife," and "marriage" are lacking. But historical linguists argue that the absence of such cognates provides additional evidence for the antiquity of the institution:

The term which we translate by 'marriage' is only valid for the woman and signifies the accession of a young woman to the state of legal wifehood.... That is why there is, properly speaking, no Indo-European term for 'marriage.' As Aristotle observed for his own language, "the union of man and woman has no name...." In fact,

the expressions encountered today are all secondary creations; this
is true of Fr. *marriage*, German *Ehe* (literally, 'law'), Russian *brak*
(derived from *brat'sja* 'carry off'), etc.   (Benveniste 193–95)

Linguists have also deduced that the absence of a term for biological paternity indicates the importance of the male parent among
those who spoke Proto-Indo-European. But, as I noted in an earlier
essay, "[w]hatever the source of *pəter, its correct interpretation
seems to have excluded biological paternity. The term designated
'father' only in some uncertain mythological and (later) classifica-
tory sense." (" 'Sister' " 259). While most scholars no longer argue
that *pəter denoted actual kinship, some speculate that invocational
uses of its derivatives in ancient languages may be traced to a
common Indo-European mythological use of the name for "father"
(e.g., Benveniste 170–71). Thus, they interpret the term as proof
of the importance of the male parent, affirming his mystical status
as clan progenitor.

Benveniste's analysis of the word for "father" leads to an explanation of the "broad" meaning of the term *brother*, denoting "a
member of the brotherhood," those who shared common descent
from a mystical father (179). Here Benveniste uses the nonexistence
of a term for a biological male sibling to argue for the relative
importance of a brother among the Indo-Europeans. But I have
come to a different conclusion:

> In fact, *phrātēr* does not mean the consanguineous brother; it is
> applied to those who consider themselves as descendents of the same
> father. . . . In light of these facts, *bhrātēr denoted a fraternity which
> was not necessarily consanguineous. The two meanings are distin-
> guished in Greek. *Phrātēr* was kept for the member of a phratry,
> and a new term *adelphós* (literally 'born of the same womb') was coined
> for 'blood brother.' . . . Henceforward, the two kinds of relationships
> were . . . polarized by their implicit reference: *phrātēr* is defined by
> connexion with the same father, *adelphós* by connexion with the same
> mother. Henceforth, only the common maternal descent is given as
> criterion of fraternity.   (" 'Sister' " 260–61)

As I pointed out here, the hypothesized progression of the system
of Indo-European kinship from one based on mystical relationships
to one based on biological maternity is counterintuitive. Moreover,
it ignores the apparent relation between the Greek terms denoting
uterine kinship and the Sanskrit terms of similar meaning, a con-

nection discussed by W. B. Lockwood. Lockwood observes that the Sanskrit compound *sagárbhyas* 'full brother' is a related form and notes that it is possible to relate the Sanskrit verb *gárbhas* 'to do' to Greek *delphús* 'womb' (from which *adelphós* is derived) through regular sound changes; he finds that both terms for "brother" provide evidence of matriliny in "Indo-European antiquity":

> Gk *adelphós* (Homer *adelphéos*) . . . has been dissimilated from **hadelpheós*. The prefix is IE **sm̥-* 'one.' . . . The basic sense of the compound is therefore 'belonging to one womb.' It is a formation of Indo-European antiquity, from a time when society needed a term for 'uterine brothers and sisters,' i.e. not the children of parents, but the children of a specific mother. (185)

Less than one page later, though, Lockwood too concludes that "Indo-European society was . . . markedly patriarchal, the wife entering the husband's family," on the grounds that terms for the wife's relatives, unlike those for the husband's, are varied and indefinite (185–86). Similar cultural reconstructions are virtually uncontested by scholars studying Indo-European languages and cultures. Discrepancies between such interpretations and the underlying data suggest that sexist biases may have prevented historical linguists from envisioning an ancestral culture radically different from their own and thus blinded them to the correlation between cultural change and semantic change among the Indo-Europeans.

More significant for the discipline of linguistics as a whole is the possibility that sexist bias may cause linguists to skew their analyses to fit preconceived notions of how languages ought to work. Perhaps, for instance, Proto-Indo-European roots have been divided not only because they derived from different sources but because on occasion their common sources were not "easily reconcilable." Or perhaps sexism, rather than any "natural" relations, has shaped English pronoun usage. A discipline that aspires to scientific rigor cannot afford to incorporate observer bias unreflectively into its descriptions of language or to adopt models that incorporate the biased politics of their creators. We all know how difficult it is to acknowledge, let alone transcend, our own linguistic preconceptions and practices. At best we can only strive for linguistic objectivity and hope that to some degree we can achieve it. To do so is to benefit linguistic scholarship. To fail to recognize the problem is to fail to do scholarship of any sort.

Note

[1] Throughout this essay, I use an asterisk to denote a reconstructed form (e.g., *magh). Reconstructed forms that appear outside quoted material are those of Szemerényi.

English Handbooks 1979–85: Case Studies in Sexist and Nonsexist Usage

H. Lee Gershuny

As scholars and teachers we are bearers of culture. Our writing and instructional material identify what is significant, valuable, and aesthetically pleasing in both literature and language usage. We are thus as concerned about nonsexist usage in textbook writing as we are in scholarly writing.

Functioning as a repository of authoritative usage and style, the ubiquitous English handbook is our most important text selection. It influences students' writing throughout their formal education and beyond. Its statements and illustrations, like the dictionary's, are often perceived as the final arbiter of usage—an authority even higher than that of the instructor. The community of handbook writers and selectors therefore needs guidelines to ensure that an *awareness* of linguistic stereotyping informs the actual usage in these texts and extends the meaning of "good" English to language that does not demean or degrade anyone because of gender, race, ethnicity, age, class, or sexual preference. My discussion of stereotyping in recent English handbooks (1979–85) is based on the following questions:

1. Does the handbook include a general discussion of the social implications of language?
2. To what extent is linguistic sexism treated as a topic?
3. What nonsexist alternatives are recommended or used in illustrative material?

4. To what extent does the illustrative and explanatory material reflect sexist assumptions or stereotypes?
5. How can English handbooks effectively present nonsexist usage?

Since English handbooks are commissioned by publishers and since many publishers voluntarily adopted nonsexist guidelines fairly early on (e.g., Holt, Rinehart, and Winston; Houghton Mifflin; Macmillan; and McGraw-Hill), we might expect handbook authors to show an awareness of the social implications of language, the structural and semantic patterns of linguistic sexism, and the nonsexist alternatives available in academic and popular writing. We might also expect a current handbook to adopt a descriptive stance—that is, to describe what is now acceptable in standard usage—instead of prescribing antiquated grammatical conventions that have little regard for common usage or cultural diversity.

But such a stance is not what we generally find. Handbooks first responded to publishers' guidelines by including illustrative material featuring women, ethnic groups, and racial minorities. An informal survey of several college handbooks published between 1972 and 1975 determined that their examples tend to balance the use of feminine and masculine nominals in generally unstereotyped contexts but that no specific mention is made either of nonsexist language as an option within standard usage or of the problems surrounding the pseudogeneric *he* and *man* (Gershuny, "Sexism"). More recently, the third edition of William Strunk, Jr., and E. B. White's *Elements of Style* was criticized for its sexist illustrations and ineffective treatment of the pseudogeneric *he*—both in violation of the publisher's guidelines for nonsexist usage (Worby 1979). Thus, despite the numerous guidelines of professional organizations and publishers and nearly twenty years of research documenting the pervasiveness and damaging consequences of linguistic sexism, consciousness-raising is still needed. It is crucial especially for those who monitor and teach usage to recognize nonsexist language, and nondiscriminatory language in general, as the preferred standard.

Attention to the Social Implications of Language

Most English handbooks do not examine the social implications of language. At most, they discourage dialect, jargon, and nonstandard usage as ineffectual and inexact in writing. In a section called

"Consideration," however, Frederick Crews addresses "linguistic *consideration*, or regard for your reader's feelings" (3rd ed. 191).[1] In addition to weighing the appropriateness of slang and other nonstandard usage, he cautions students to be sensitive to language that could be construed as racist or sexist (3rd ed. 191; 4th ed. 219). In the same section, he recommends avoiding offensive language, including "slurs and stereotypes" and sexism in "names, titles, and common gender":

> Racial slurs like *nigger, honky,* and *wop,* and demeaning stereotypes like *pushy Jew* and *dumb Swede,* are inexcusable. And sexually biased phrases such as *lady driver, schoolgirl gush, female logic,* and *typical male brutality* mark their user as a prisoner of condescending stereotypes. (3rd ed. 193–94; 4th ed. 219–21)

Even though Crews encourages students to be "linguistically considerate" in order to communicate effectively, he does not explain the relations among language, thought, and culture. In both the 1980 and 1984 editions of his book the need to avoid "slurs and stereotypes" is essentially limited to writing inoffensively.

Treatment of Linguistic Sexism

Even when current handbooks do discuss linguistic sexism, they seldom list either *sexism* or *nonsexist usage* in their indexes. As a result, the issues, labels, and symbols that feminist linguists have challenged and changed become invisible, subordinate to other subjects, or trivialized as unimportant to language usage in general. Rarely is there any treatment of labeling or semantics except as part of a section on denotative and connotative meanings. The explanation and grammar of nonsexist usage are likely to be included under "diction" and "pronoun agreement." Instructions on the salutations in business letters and the choice of examples throughout the text can also reflect an author's attitude toward discriminatory language.

Connotation

To demonstrate how the same behavior could elicit descriptive terms with opposite connotations, one handbook contrasts negative adjectives for feminine subjects with positive adjectives for masculine subjects:

> He is ambitious; she is pushy.
> He is tough-minded; she is ruthless.
> He is foresighted; she is calculating.
> He is firm; she is stubborn.
> He is self-respecting; she is egotistical.
> He is persistent; she is nagging.   (Heffernan and Lincoln 137–38)

The paragraph following these illustrations emphasizes that prejudices can be reflected in word choices and urges students to treat their subjects fairly. But the authors do not mention the double standard operating in sexist gender semantics, where *he* is often called *ambitious* or *firm* but it is almost always *she* who is *pushy* or *nagging*. Illustrating the concept of connotation with positive-masculine and negative-feminine pairs demands a more extended discussion of the generally negative overtones of feminine terms— whether structurally marked, like *poetess* and *majorette*, or semantically marked, like *secretary* and *prostitute*. When examples reflect traditional male prejudices, failure to elaborate on the structural and semantic double standard misleads students and leaves sexism unchallenged. Students may conclude that word choice is simply a matter of individual conscience with no connection to biases embedded in culture and language.

Pronoun Agreement

Handbooks are most likely to comment on sexist language in their sections on the reference of pronouns. These frequently include short discussions of the pseudogeneric masculine singular pronouns and the problem of pronoun agreement when the antecedent is a word of unspecified sex, like *everyone*. The handbooks base the following recommendations for nonsexist alternatives on the range of actual usage:

1. Treat *everyone* and *everybody* as singular and use *his or her* to refer to this antecedent: "Everyone in the cast had to furnish *his or her* own costume" (Heffernan and Lincoln 134).[2] But frequent use of such *either-or* pairs is sometimes discouraged as awkward and monotonous (Flachmann 112).
2. "Use *she* whenever the indefinite pronoun is more likely to be

female than male." Crews makes the recommendation in his third edition (195) but changes it in his fourth: "Use *she* whenever you are sure the indefinite person would be a female (a student in a woman's college, for example)" (221). The revised rule seeks to obviate the tendency to stereotype sex roles, as in the use of *she* with the antecedent *nurse* and *he* with *doctor*.

3. Avoid using as antecedents singular pronouns designating persons of unspecified sex, such as *each* and *everyone*. Thus the sentence "The cast *members* each had to furnish their own costumes" is preferable to one beginning "Each of the cast members" (Heffernan and Lincoln 314).

4. Avoid using as antecedents singular nouns designating persons of unspecified sex; substitute plurals: "*Students* must show *their* permits to register" (McMahan and Day 81).[3]

5. "Omit the pronoun altogether when it isn't essential: not *Everyone needs his vacation* but *Everyone needs a vacation*."[4] Crews gives this recommendation in his third edition (195) but modifies it in his fourth to deal with awkwardness rather than with the pseudogeneric *his*, here replaced by *his or her own*: "Omit the pronoun altogether wherever you can do so without awkwardness: not *Everyone needs his or her own vacation* but *Everyone needs a vacation*" (221).

Handbooks that recognize the problems posed by the pseudogeneric masculine pronoun usually recommend options 1, 3, and 4. The nonsexist alternatives and examples presented and the manner in which the discussion is cast all affect students' responses and understanding. Handbook writers and composition instructors need to be aware that prescriptions for sexist usage can be subtly disguised in a variety of ways. An authority who appears to adopt a descriptive stance on usage by presenting nonsexist alternatives to discriminatory wording may nonetheless convey a quite different message. The following passages from Fear and Schiffhorst, while implying both prescriptive and descriptive views, uphold "traditional" androcentric standards as "correct":

Indefinite antecedents such as *a person, each, neither, either, someone, anyone, no one, one,* and *everybody* almost always take singular pronouns. . . .

INCORRECT: When a person is confused, they should ask questions.

CORRECT: When a person is confused, *he* should ask questions.

Although a person could as easily refer to a female as to a male, traditional usage requires the masculine pronoun form. But many writers now avoid such usage. In very informal business situations, they often use the plural form *they* for *he*, or, in formal situations, use both the masculine and feminine forms (*he or she*). Perhaps the safest method is to recast the sentence.

CORRECT: When confused, a person should ask questions. (69)

Diction

A few handbooks discuss nonsexist usage under both pronoun agreement and diction. Those that provide alternative solutions to the pronoun problem usually do so in the section on diction or in a glossary of usage. Some warn readers against sexist references and give examples of nonsexist terms that contrast with sexist ones. Coulthard, for example, gives this advice on using appropriate words:

> Avoid sexist references. Many readers are offended by general references such as "man" or "mankind" and by masculine pronouns and male occupational terms used to refer to both men and women. Such expressions result from habit and long practice, and while usually no offense is intended, these references are nonetheless discriminatory and likely to alienate a number of your readers.
>
> Sexist nouns and pronouns almost always can be avoided without creating awkwardness or resorting to such self-conscious, unpleasant terms as "personkind" or "chairperson," as these examples illustrate:
>
> SEXIST: If mankind is to survive, we must develop new forms of energy.
> NONSEXIST: If humanity is to survive, we must develop new forms of energy.
>
> SEXIST: Man is a strange animal.
> NONSEXIST: Humans are strange animals.
>
> SEXIST: Most congressmen were off campaigning for reelection.
> NONSEXIST: Most members of Congress were off campaigning for reelection.
>
> SEXIST: Outgoing chairman Janice Wellborn turned the gavel over to the newly elected chairman, Nate Hampton.
> NONSEXIST: Outgoing chairwoman Janice Wellborn turned the gavel over to the newly elected chairman, Nate Hampton.
>
> SEXIST: If the reader wants to review the main ideas of a theme, he can look back over the topic sentences.

NONSEXIST: If readers want to review the main ideas of a theme, they can look back over the topic sentences. (302–04)

The following material from the 1980 edition of McMahan and Day takes a similar approach in contrasting pseudogeneric *man* with gender-neutral alternatives:

The generic *man* (as the term is called) is supposed to include both sexes—all human beings. But unfortunately the same word, *man*, also means simply a male human being; thus the term is ambiguous. Sometimes it includes both sexes; sometimes it doesn't; and sometimes nobody can tell whether it does or doesn't. Also, *man* is another word, like the generic *he*, that eclipses the female. To avoid this subtle sexism, use *person* or *people* when you mean a person or people, not just males.

SEXIST: We want to hire the best *man* we can get for the job.
FAIR: We want to hire the best *person* we can get for the job.

A number of compound words using the word *man* can be avoided with little difficulty:

Avoid	**Prefer**
chairman	chairperson, chair, moderator
congressman	representative, senator
councilman	council member
fireman	fire fighter
foreman	supervisor
mailman	mail carrier
mankind	humanity
manpower	work force
manmade	artificial, manufactured
policeman	police officer
salesman	salesperson (211)

Business Letters

Handbooks that include sections on business letters usually cite *Ms.* as an appropriate form to use in addressing a woman.[5] Hans P. Guth recommends checking to see whether a woman indicates her preference "in the signature line of her own correspondence" (2nd ed. 498). For the salutation of a letter to someone whose surname is unknown, William Herman suggests *Dear Sir or Madam, Dear Sir, Dear Madam,* or *Gentlemen*; he recommends *Miss, Ms.,* or *Mrs.* before a woman's name typed below her signature. He does not discuss titles in the salutation when the addressee's name is known. Celia Millward, though she and Herman have the same publisher, does not recommend including a title before the name typed below the signature. Both handbooks give a married woman the option of typing her husband's name, preceded by *Mrs.*, below her signature. Thus they skirt the salutation problem and leave to the letter writer the choice of using *Ms.*, *Mrs.*, or *Miss* in the closing.

H. Ramsey Fowler, in contrast, not only suggests general salutations such as *Dear Sir or Madam* and *Dear Smythe Shoes* (the company name) but advocates *Ms.* in salutations when a woman has no other title, "when you don't know how she prefers to be addressed, or when you know that she prefers to be addressed as *Ms.* If you know a woman prefers to be addressed as *Mrs.* or *Miss*, use the appropriate title" (522–24). McMahan and Day recommend only *Ms.*, not even offering *Miss* and *Mrs.* as options. Authors that do not mention the salutation problem usually include only sample letters addressed to *Sir* or *Mr.*, thus ignoring the sexist language issue and the existence of women in the business world (e.g., Heffernan and Lincoln 508–13).

Illustrative Material

McMahan and Day underscore their view of linguistic sexism as a serious issue by choosing sexism in children's textbooks as the topic for a sample research paper. Other authors scatter nonsexist illustrations throughout their books: "My sister wants to become a commercial-airline pilot because she is hung up on planes" (Heffernan and Lincoln 129); "Since the beginning of the women's movement, females have become more inclined to share the expense of a date" (Flachmann 53).

The following sexist illustration appears in Watkins and Dillingham under "Pronouns: agreement, reference, and usage," just two pages before a discussion of indefinite pronoun agreement that recommends avoiding both sexist usage and "ridiculous alternatives": The *writer* finished *his* story" (56). No specific writer is identified, and since male authors predominate in literature courses, referring to "the writer" with a masculine pronoun maintains a stereotype. A revision exercise in the same section presents a similar stereotyped context: "No matter what the detergent commercials say, no woman is really jubilant at the prospect of mopping their [sic, to be corrected to *her*] dirty kitchen floor" (61). Handbook writers generally draw on the writing of both women and men for illustrations, though most citations have male authors.

Guidelines for Authors and Reviewers

In general, handbooks should address the issues and sociolinguistic problems raised by sexist usage and linguistic stereotyping both in the appropriate sections on grammar and in separate sections dealing with labeling, semantics, or the interaction of language and culture. The following recommendations for promoting nonsexist usage are meant to guide those who write English handbooks as well as those who select them for instructional purposes:

1. Index discussions of nondiscriminatory alternatives to sexist and other forms of stereotyped usage.
2. Illustrate principles of effective writing with lively, nonsexist, and unstereotyped sentences.
3. Cite unbiased passages by both female and male writers from a variety of ethnic and racial backgrounds.
4. Explain nonsexist usage from the point of view of descriptive linguistics. Avoid prescribing traditional sexist usage as the "correct" standard.
5. Suggest topics for essays and term papers that deal with sexism and linguistic stereotyping in general.
6. Enlarge diction sections to include nonsexist alternatives to objectionable wording.
7. Enlarge connotation sections to recognize the double standard in semantically and structurally marked gender terms. Positive and negative connotations can be easily illustrated by contrasting pairs of feminine and masculine words. For example:

seamstress	tailor
spinster	bachelor
hostess	maitre d'
lady judge	judge
stewardess	steward
majorette	drum major
governess	governor

8. Deal with the salutation problem in sections on business letters. Mention *Ms.* as an option many women prefer. Suggest a range of nonsexist greetings. When the gender and surname of the addressee are unknown, the possibilities include *Dear Subscriber, Dear Colleague, Dear Entering Student, Dear Reader, Dear Friends*; when the name is known but not the gender, *Dear Professor Smith* and

Dear Robin Smith are among the alternatives. Another solution is to omit the salutation entirely.

Notes

[1] The handbooks cited in this chapter are listed in the second bibliography in part 3 of this volume; they are not included in the first bibliography, Works Cited.

[2] This recommendation also appears in Hodges and Whitten 74; Watkins and Dillingham 58; Crews, 3rd ed. 195; Crews, 4th ed. 221; and Guth, 1st ed. 70–71.

[3] This recommendation also appears in Coulthard 334–35; Watkins and Dillingham 58; Crews, 3rd ed. 195; Crews, 4th ed. 221; and Guth, 2nd ed. 71.

[4] This recommendation also appears in Fear and Schiffhorst 69.

[5] *Ms.* is recommended by Guth, 1st ed. 414–16; Hodges and Whitten 515; McMahan and Day, 1st ed. 322–23; and Watkins and Dillingham 150.

Language Planning, Language Reform, and Language Change: A Review of Guidelines for Nonsexist Usage

Francine Wattman Frank

A lively debate over the question of sexism and language has punctuated the current feminist movement, both in the United States and abroad. Consequently, discriminatory usage is now widely recognized as a significant issue. Feminists point to both subtle and nonsubtle uses of language as offensive to women in general, and numerous empirical studies confirm this perception. As a result of these studies and, more important perhaps, as a result of changing attitudes in contemporary society, a variety of groups, among them large publishing companies and professional and scholarly associations, have taken the position that sexist language, whether deliberate or unintentional, has no place in a society committed to equality of professional opportunity. Accordingly, a number of these organizations have drafted guidelines suggesting alternatives to traditional sexist usage. Some guidelines simply recommend these alternatives, while others, such as those of the American Psychological Association, more forcefully state that "authors . . . are expected to avoid writing in a manner that reinforces questionable attitudes and assumptions about people and sex roles" ("Guidelines for Nonsexist Language" 2). Whether or not these groups will publish manuscripts that disregard the implications of such language use depends on the commitment and vigilance of their editors.

Some scholars consider this particular concern about language exaggerated. They fear that the preoccupation with sexist usage and the preparation of guidelines will destroy valuable stylistic devices that they view as inherently useful or beautiful. Their belief that traditional forms should be preserved leads them to oppose all activities that might bring about change.

The issue is a serious one. Indeed, a set of guidelines published by a major scholarly association and aimed at eliminating sexist practices in professional writing may well influence language use. The guidelines should, if they are successful, play a role in defining appropriate usage in this area in much the same way as the style sheets of various publishers have defined acceptable forms. This act of prescribing usage is actually a "treatment" for language, a way of remedying what many perceive as a language malady. The medical notion of prescription lends itself nicely to the notion of planning: one speaks of a "treatment plan" prescribed according to a diagnosis of the problem. The treatments prepared for sexist language are examples of what is known in linguistics as language planning.

Language Planning, Reform, and Change

Since little information is available, outside linguistic circles, about what language planning means and what it implies, the subject merits discussion here. In its widest sense, language planning focuses on identifying language problems. From this perspective, language problems occur in the broad context of communication and include the relation between the language code and other social patterns. Language planning often involves work of national relevance, such as fostering a particular variety of language, as Israel did, or rejecting a colonial language, as many developing nations have done, and selecting a national language from several indigenous languages. But it does not deal exclusively with problems of such magnitude. Language planners are also engaged in studying a more general phenomenon, the demands modernization makes on language. A major task of language planning today is to identify specific aspects of society that require planned action regarding language resources. One common example is the need for terminology to accompany new technologies. The critical point here is that language problems must be seen within their social and political context. Language is in fact a key resource that can be manipulated for different goals. Although various groups may focus on language as a means of achieving their own political, social, or economic ends, the planning process requires that, in seeking solutions to language problems, they consider alternative objectives, methods, and strategies. In weighing these alternatives, planners use their best knowledge to forecast consequences.

The drafting of guidelines for nonsexist usage is an activity decidedly within the scope of language planning. It aims at reconciling the current commitment to equal opportunity with linguistic traditions long held to be unchangeable. The fact is that the structure of contemporary society is no longer congruent with stylistic preferences that ignore the presence of women in a multitude of areas or that demean women by making them the object of casual humor. Modernization, then, is making demands on language. Just as the development of computer science has necessitated an expanded technical vocabulary, so too do social changes require transformations in traditional language usage. While recent work on language planning deals more with national and international issues involving multilingualism than with attempts to modify usage in a single language, the literature in this field does contain discussions relevant to nonsexist reform. In an unusual attempt to provide a theoretical framework for prescriptive linguistics, Donald G. MacKay proposes a cost-benefit-analysis approach to predicting the success of language prescriptions, taking as his example a hypothetical rule requiring "the substitution of singular *they* for prescriptive *he*" (349). He also comments on the implications of nonsexist reforms for language planning (362).

It is a truism that language continually changes. Much of this change occurs as speakers become influenced by new products, new technologies, and new alliances; but not all such change is spontaneous. Language planning is at work in the political arena as it is in the advertising world. Expressions gain currency overnight, and idioms that are marginally acceptable one year often become fashionable and witty the next. Like other planned solutions to language problems, the drafting of a set of guidelines on nonsexist language is designed to bring about change, a specific kind of change. A principal objective is to foster the adoption of stylistic devices that are compatible with the goal of social justice. To illustrate the importance of language in the shaping of a just world, the following section briefly examines the way language functions in society.

Language and Its Functions in Society

As a number of linguists have observed, language combines the functions of a mirror, a tool, and a weapon. In a very real sense, it does reflect society. Indeed, some scholars suggest that all relationships are essentially linguistic, because it is through language that people come to understand not only their similarities, differences, and roles but social reality itself (this argument is discussed in the introduction to this volume and in Treichler's essay, as well as in Belsey's *Critical Practice*).

Language is also a tool. Human beings use it to interact with one another, and such acts as requesting, persuading, inquiring, challenging, defending, and retreating are generally carried out through speech. Conversation is, in William Labov and David Fanshel's words, "a means that people use to deal with one another. In conversation, participants use language to interpret to each other the significance of actual and potential events that surround them and to draw the consequences for their past and future actions" (30). The true action in any exchange is what speakers intend, that is, how they mean to affect listeners, to move them, and to cause them to respond.

Depending on one's perspective, however, language can be a weapon as well as a tool. Members of society generally share a community of interest. They tend to form groups and to seek the confirmation of their perceptions of reality by various means. One of these, labeling, can clearly serve as a tool to clarify individuals' positions regarding one another and to delimit their mutual duties and obligations. But labeling often becomes a weapon. Dominant groups—that is, groups that enjoy the privileges of power—frequently use their position to legitimize their own value system. One way they do this is to label others "deviant." Thus we find that Hitler labeled Jews "creatures," a term that justified treating them like parasites and vermin. White racism justified slavery by declaring all blacks "inferior" and justified the destruction of Native American cultures by calling Indians "savages." Some factions in the United States today justify discrimination against gays by classifying them as "deviant" or even, in response to the current AIDS crisis, as "diseased" or "contaminated." The irony of this process is that those who are stigmatized may come to accept their labels as their reality.

The question of how language relates to reality has long been a subject of controversy among linguists. The so-called Sapir-Whorf hypothesis, for example, which stresses language as a determinant of thinking, has been largely discredited in its strong version (see the introduction to this volume, which discusses the hypothesis in the context of contemporary thought in several disciplines). Few would suggest that sexual or racial inequality exists because of language use. Nor would many argue that banishing sexist and racist labeling would in itself result in a just society. At the same time, it is clear that language not only reflects social structures but, more important, sometimes serves to perpetuate existing differences in power; thus a serious concern with linguistic usage is fully warranted.

Language Change and Social Change

The proposed reforms of sexist phenomena in our language are based on two premises. One is that language is, as Edward Sapir put it, "a guide to 'social reality.' " The other, a modified version of the Sapir-Whorf hypothesis, holds that language influences our worldview and "powerfully conditions all our thinking about social problems and processes" ("Status" 68).

Early in this century, in 1906, Antoine Meillet pointed to the role of social factors in language change: "the only variable element to which one may appeal to account for linguistic change is social change, of which variations in language are merely the consequences . . ." (17; my trans.). In general, subsequent generations of scholars did not heed Meillet, and linguistics during the first half of the twentieth century is characterized by skepticism about social explanations for linguistic change. The skepticism has been largely overcome by recent work in sociolinguistics that has firmly established the significance of social factors in language change (see, for example, Labov, *Sociolinguistic* and *Locating*). Here, in contrast to studies of language planning, the focus is on the specifics of linguistic change in such areas as phonology, grammar, and the lexicon. In proposing "some general principles for the study of language change," Uriel Weinreich, William Labov, and Marvin I. Herzog argue that "linguistic and social factors are closely interrelated in the development of sound change" (188).

Language Attitudes and Language Reform

The recent appearance of guidelines for nonsexist usage exemplifies the complexity of the relations between social phenomena and linguistic change. Julia Penelope Stanley points out that the proposals embodied in the guidelines do not call for actual changes in the English language. Apart from suggestions on pronoun use, most deal with lexical matters and pertain to the usage of existing words, such as *man, poetess,* and *spokesman* ("Gender-Marking" 74). The pervasive resistance to these suggestions reveals attitudes toward prescriptive language rules. Roger T. Bell notes that these rules "embody formulations of attitudes to language use which, even if ignored in practice by users, are indicators of social views of 'correctness' that influence such behavior as stereotyping and hypercorrection . . ." (90). Later in his study, he observes that

> the attempt to include social factors in the mechanisms of linguistic choice has also thrown up three key issues: the means available for the correlation of linguistic and, what had previously been termed "extralinguistic" phenomena, the problem of relating linguistic form to social function, and the degree to which attitudes of users are seen to be important factors in their linguistic behavior. (216)

The question of attitudes is perhaps most relevant to the study of nonsexist guidelines. Since prescriptive rules embody attitudes, persuading people to "violate" some of these rules to achieve nonsexist usage involves changing their attitudes toward sexist language as well as toward other forms of sexist behavior. A great deal of sociolinguistic research demonstrates correlations among language, attitudes, and behavior. Although most of these studies concern attitudes toward speakers of other languages and dialects or toward stigmatized forms of pronunciation and grammar, some findings seem applicable to the new lexical usage encouraged by nonsexist language reforms.

In his essay "Language, Speech, and Ideology," David Smith argues that recent research on language attitudes assumes "a direct concomitant, if not causal, relationship between attitudes and behavior." He continues:

> It follows from this assumption, from the standpoint of the pragmatics of communication, that change in behavior will inevitably be attended by change in attitude. Whether the most "practical" and "workable" means to accomplish change, therefore, is to force behavior change and thus create dissonance necessitating a change in attitude, or to change attitude (perhaps by pointing out existing dissonances) is a debatable question. (97)

Smith proposes a sociocultural framework for examining some concepts crucial to sociolinguistics and includes among its components a language system and a parallel ideological system. The ideological system, "realized behaviorally as a set of esthetic-ethical judgments," consists of a "cosmology," or a "set of beliefs concerning how things are"; a value system; and an attitude system that "serves to arrange and relate values and beliefs to each other and to behavior" (106). According to Smith, both the ideological and the language systems are culture systems, hence "adaptive, learned, conventional, and largely unconscious" (108). The adaptive quality of these systems and their attendant survival value imply that

> emotional commitment to established patterns of behavior is apt to be profound, not just because of some ethnocentric notion that this is the only, or best way to do something, but because doing it this way has important survival value. It, therefore, becomes incumbent upon the culture-change broker to demonstrate that his suggested changes will not jeopardize the survival of those who are being asked to change. (108)

Smith claims that his model may hold "clues as to what is the least traumatic avenue to behavior change" (109). Thus, fostering awareness of "existing dissonances" would be preferable to forcing behavioral change.

When we review empirical research on the relation between changes in attitudes and changes in behavior, the implications for the study of nonsexist guidelines become clear. In an article on sexist language and attitudes, Kristine Falco refers to Martin Fishbein's conclusion that knowledge of a person's attitudes has little value in predicting behavior (291). If anything, people seem more likely to bring their attitudes into line with their behavior than to modify behavior in accordance with their attitudes (Fishbein 477). Citing additional evidence that behavior change can cause attitude change, Falco concludes that "it thus appears that the most efficient means to our end is to tackle sexist *actions* rather than sexist *attitudes*" (291). Research on verbal behavior, for example, shows that people asked to write in support of something they oppose or to give speeches they disagree with tend to change their opinions to favor the views they express. These and similar findings for other types of behavior led Falco to surmise that feminists may be on the right track in seeking behavior changes in many areas, including language usage, and "assuming that attitudes will change thereafter" (292).

The evidence Falco cites seems to contradict Smith's conclusion that the most effective and "least traumatic" approach is not to force behavioral change. In attempting to apply the findings of sociological and psychological research to sexist language behavior, we once again confront the relation between language on the one hand and society and thought on the other. Language reflects attitudes, but precisely how does it affect them and what happens when it is both the object and the instrument of the desired change? Nonsexist language guidelines may conflict with traditional usage, which reflects in a number of overt ways the traditional sexist bias of society. Some of this usage is supported by prescriptive language rules, which, as we have noted, indicate beliefs about correctness and formulate attitudes toward language use. Emerging views about the equality of the sexes and an increasing awareness of injustice to women have created pressures for change in both attitudes and behaviors. As a result, language use that accords with sexist behavior becomes an object of attack itself, another manifestation of behavior in need of change.

Relations among attitudes, language, and behavior are illustrated by the drive for equal employment opportunity. One may wish to persuade employers to hire women for certain positions previously occupied only by men; evidence indicates that if employers actually do hire women, they will change their attitude toward hiring women. Language use related to employment includes the common expression *the best man for the job*. Will getting employers to substitute *person* for *man* in that phrase help change their attitudes or hiring behavior? The least one can say is that using *the best man* is incongruous with affirmative action toward sexual equality in employment. As Falco points out, "there should be more studies to see if language change can directly affect attitudes" (292). In the meantime, she suggests, "we can pay close attention to our own speech habits . . . and continue to demand changes in the media, believing that as verbal behavior changes, the attitude changes we desire will follow" (294).

Proponents of guidelines for nonsexist writing share Falco's belief and act accordingly, but they also believe that the social changes underlying the adoption of the guidelines, along with the social pressures created by the guidelines themselves, can accelerate the usual slow pace of language change in response to societal change, creating a sort of snowball effect. Insisting on nonsexist usage may be equivalent to forcing behavioral change, the expedient David Smith finds inadvisable; men may see it as a threat to their traditional power in the domain of public communication, whereas discussion of the inequities, the "dissonances" in the existing system of usage, may be less disruptive. As Falco indicates, however, it would probably also be less effective. Many have indeed interpreted the adoption of guidelines as a threat, not only to the power of men but to the cultural traditions represented by the English language.

Historical Precedents for Language Reform

Among the precedents for current attempts to rid language usage of objectionable elements are periodic campaigns by language academies, governments, and other official bodies to defend a particular language from the invading hordes of foreign words. But these efforts, designed to prevent language change that is already occurring, have generally not succeeded. Although appeals to patriotism and refusals to admit the intruders into official dictionaries may have killed off a few stray words, popular usage has generally gone its own way and embraced words that met felt needs. "Language purification" campaigns, then, might be described as attempts to point out the dissonances the foreign words create and to stimulate linguistic resistance to these words. Some of them— for example, the French government's most recent drive—have been reinforced by penalties, but they have not usually been accompanied by sanctions, such as a refusal to publish material containing the condemned words. On the contrary, the media have often been the chief "culprits" in promoting the imports.

Pronouns of address may provide a more promising field of inquiry in this respect. The now classic work of Roger W. Brown and Albert Gilman established that pronoun systems are susceptible to change in response to social and political factors. As for conscious efforts to reform pronoun usage, however, several historical examples have been ultimately unsuccessful. Modern Italian has three pronouns of address: the informal *tu* and the formal *lei* and *voi*. Some speakers make a three-way distinction that includes *voi*, the historically older form, along with the more modern *lei*. In a study of contemporary rules of address in Italy, Elizabeth Bates and Laura Benigni note that "Mussolini tried unsuccessfully to impose a universal reciprocal *voi* during his 20-year regime. We were unable to determine any remaining effect of this historical effort in our interviews" (280). Starting from the premise that *lei* represented an outmoded class structure, Mussolini's campaign to eliminate its use included such measures as posting slogans (e.g., *Date del voi!* 'Use the *voi* form!') and having telephone operators monitor pronoun use in order to offer the same advice.[1]

Brown and Gilman concentrate on the formal and informal pronouns of address, exemplified by French *vous* and *tu*, which they abbreviate V and T. They describe the situation in revolutionary France as follows:

> The Committee for the Public Safety condemned the use of V as a feudal remnant and ordered a universal reciprocal T. On October 31, 1793, Molbec made a Parliamentary speech against V. . . . For a time revolutionary "fraternité" transformed all address into the mutual *Citoyen* and the mutual *tu*.   (264)

In their discussion of the specific choice of *tu* over *vous*, Brown and Gilman conclude that "the answer lies with the ancient upper-class preference for the use of V. There was animus against the pronoun itself" (265).

English pronouns became the focus of controversy even earlier, when Quakers in the seventeenth century adopted the practice of addressing everyone as *thou*. The pronoun *thou* subsequently disappeared from English usage, and Brown and Gilman comment that "the forces at work seem to have included a popular reaction against the radicalism of Quakers and Levelers and also a general trend in English toward simplified verbal inflection" (266).

The Controversy over "Generic" Usage: Early Commentary and Suggestions for Change

The question of gender and generic usage in English is examined in detail in the introduction to this volume and in Susan J. Wolfe's essay, as well as in the guidelines (pt. 2). The brief treatment here merely considers the subject in relation to language reform. In discussing sex-indefinite *they* and *he*, Ann Bodine points out that though the early English grammarians regarded the masculine gender as "worthier" than the feminine and paid great attention to details of usage, they did not proscribe singular *they* (134–35). Apparently the earliest work to authorize generic *he* was Kirby's 1746 grammar, where rule 21 states that "the masculine person answers to the general Name, which comprehends both Male and Female; as any person, who knows what he says" (qtd. in Bodine 135). The attack on singular *they* did not begin in earnest until the end of the eighteenth century, when it began to appear in examples of "violations" of the rule for pronoun agreement. Bodine reports that "prior to the nineteenth century, singular 'they' was widely used in written, therefore presumably also in spoken, English. This usage met with no opposition" (132–33).

Although the success of the grammarians in the educational establishment has undeniably affected today's written English, many authors continued in their "erroneous" use of *they* right into the twentieth century. Casey Miller and Kate Swift cite examples from well-known writers, including George Eliot, John Ruskin, George Bernard Shaw, Lawrence Durrell, and Doris Lessing (*Handbook* 47–48). Many who do avoid singular *they* in their writing are likely to use it in informal speech. A number of feminist writers on this subject note the 1850 Acts of Parliament Abbreviation Bill, which prescribed concise language in Parliamentary statutes and which, among other measures, sanctioned the generic use of *he*:

> Be it enacted, That in all Acts to be hereafter made Words importing the Masculine Gender shall be deemed and taken to include Females, and the Singular to include the Plural, and the Plural the Singular, unless the contrary as to Gender or Number is expressly provided. (*British Sessions Papers* 1850; qtd. in Baron, *Grammar and Gender* 140)

Similar statements are found in leases and other legal contracts today but, as Miller and Swift point out, the generic function of these terms "was often conveniently ignored. In 1879, for example, a move to admit female physicians to the all-male Massachusetts Medical Society was effectively blocked on the grounds that the society's by-laws describing membership used the pronoun *he*" (*Handbook* 45). And Dennis E. Baron notes that although the 1850 Abbreviation Bill treats gender and number together, it does not treat them identically—"for though the inclusiveness of number is reciprocal . . . that of gender is not: the feminine does not imply the masculine" (*Grammar and Gender* 140). Bodine claims that, as far as the development of pronoun usage is concerned, "intentionally or not, the movement against sex indefinite 'he' is actually a counter reaction to an attempt by prescriptive grammarians to alter the language" (131).

Unlike the pronoun *he*, the word *man* did start out as a general term for human beings regardless of sex, but Old English also had separate sex-specific terms: *wif* for woman, and *wer* or *carl* for man. The compound term *wifman* 'female person' is the origin of today's *woman*, but both the simple and the compound terms for man were all but lost as *man* came to take on its sex-specific meaning, thus creating the androcentric ambiguity of the modern word. According to Miller and Swift,

> by the eighteenth century the modern narrow sense of *man* was firmly established as the predominant one. When Edmund Burke, writing of the French Revolution, used *men* in the old, inclusive way, he took pains to spell out his meaning: "such a deplorable havoc is made in the minds of men (both sexes) in France. . . ."   (*Handbook* 12)

It is also relevant to remember that the framers of our Declaration of Independence and Constitution were almost certainly using *men* in its sex-specific sense. (As the Supreme Court justice Thurgood Marshall pointed out in 1987, the bicentennial of the United States Constitution, *men* was used in a color-specific sense as well, to mean "white males" only.)

The "unfortunate" absence of a common-gender singular pronoun has long been deplored by writers on the English language, including some of the prescriptive grammarians who insisted on the use of *he*. Specific objections to the "generic *he*" and conscious attempts to find an alternative usage seem to date from the mid–nineteenth century. Reviewing the proposals for an epicene pronoun—a pronoun form to refer to either sex—Baron cites the following comments of H. W. Fowler and F. G. Fowler in their 1924 book, *The King's English*, on the preference of the nineteenth-century novelist Susan Ferrier for *one . . . their, each . . . their*, or *him or herself*: "the particular aversion shown to them [generic masculines] by Miss Ferrier . . . may be referred to her sex, and, ungallant as it may seem, we shall probably persist in refusing women their due here as stubbornly as Englishmen continue to offend the Scots by saying England instead of Britain" ("Epicene" 84–85).

According to Baron, the earliest "public call" for the creation of a common-gender pronoun is an anonymous item in the "Contributors' Club" section of the November 1878 *Atlantic Monthly* asking that "the eminent linguists leave the spelling reform and such trifles long enough to coin us a word." Baron reports that "the sole response in the same section of the *Atlantic* is an argument for

singular *they*, *their*, and *them* on the analogy of *you*" ("Epicene" 85).
(Other early commentaries suggested extending the use of *one*.)
Singular *they* has continued in use despite the grammarians, and it
has many advocates among today's feminists. Nevertheless, as Baron
points out, "neologism had its attractions" (86). The most widely
known is probably *thon*, coined by the lawyer and composer Charles
Crozat Converse in 1884. A blend of *the* and *one*, it actually appeared
in Funk and Wagnalls's *Standard Dictionary* in 1898 and in later
editions through 1964. It also appeared in Webster's *Second New
International Dictionary*. Baron comments as follows on the neologisms:

> The early pronoun proposals generally lack the feminist motivation
> of the most recent ones, although reactions against earlier epicene
> pronouns often reveal a spirit of antifeminism. All the neologists,
> and even some of their opponents, recognize a semantic gap in the
> language that needs to be filled. . . .　(87)

The glossary appended to Baron's article (88–96) lists in chronological order some thirty-five suggestions for common-gender pronouns, from *ne*, *nis*, *nim*, probably coined about 1850 and suggested
again in slightly altered form as *ne*, *nis*, *ner* in 1974, to the 1978
form *hir*. A fairly steady stream of inventions from the 1880s to
about 1940 seems to have been followed by a period of inactivity,
corresponding to a lull in the women's movement; in the 1970s,
the neologisms began again in earnest, this time with a clear feminist
bent. (See Baron, *Grammar and Gender* 205–09, for an even more
comprehensive chronology of proposals for an epicene pronoun.)
　　There is evidence that the relation between "generic" masculine
terms and the status of women was an issue before the onset of
the current feminist movement. Baron cites a 1934 reference to a
new set of pronouns, *she*, *shis*, *shim*, proposed at a women's conference some years earlier by a speaker who "pointed out that the
tyranny of man appeared no less in the laws of grammar than in
the laws of the land" ("Epicene" 92). Another indication is the
complaint Stephen Leacock made in 1944 about the "perpetual
extension of the use of *his* or *her* where we used merely to use *his*
when I was young. In those rude days women didn't count for so
much as now. . . . But the women's vote has set up a sort of timid
deference that is always afraid of omitting or insulting them" (qtd.
in Baron, "Epicene" 85). Mary Beard took an opposing view when
she contended that

the ambiguous usage of the word "man" by men who discuss human affairs ... gives them a peculiar advantage of self-defense if the charge is made that they are not remembering women at all when they speak or write of "man" or "men," for they can claim that they are using these words in their generic sense.   (47)

Agent Nouns

Agent nouns, especially those denoting occupations and professions, are a major concern of guidelines for nonsexist usage, which generally recommend sex-neutral terms without the suffix *-man*. Along with *he* and *man*, these nouns are probably the most controversial of the proposed reforms. By now, for example, most of us have participated in disputes over the term *chairperson*.

Miller and Swift offer a concise review of the history of these nouns in their book *Words and Women*, where they point out that many "agent nouns are, in their ultimate origins if not in their immediate past histories, both gender free and sexless" (45). They refer readers to the *Oxford English Dictionary*, which notes that the former restriction to males of agent nouns formed with *-er* is now "wholly obsolete" and that by the fifteenth century *-ster*, which was originally a feminine suffix, "no longer had an exclusively feminine sense." As for *-ess*, although it was used freely in coining words in the sixteenth and seventeenth centuries, according to the *OED*, "[m]any of these are now obsolete or little used, the tendency of modern usage being to treat the agent-nouns in *-er*, and the substantives indicating profession or occupation, as of common gender ..." (qtd. in Miller and Swift, *Words* 49).

Despite these changes, when H. W. Fowler published his *Dictionary of Modern English Usage* in the 1920s, he was, according to Miller and Swift, "convinced that 'feminines for vocation-words are a special need of the future.' He called them 'sex-words' and hoped that new coinages like teacheress and singeress would find acceptance." Fowler also "rebuked women writers who would not accept the designation *authoress* as he thought they should" (*Words* 45–46).

The Feminist Movement:
Protest against Sexist Language

The reawakening and growth of the feminist movement in the late 1960s and 1970s rekindled interest in the question of language and gender. Women's speech and the reflections of sexism in the English language became the foci of increasing attention among both scholars and the general public. Analyses of what Muriel R. Schulz labeled the "semantic derogation of women" in the lexicon joined discussions of the sexist "pseudogenerics." The spurt of neologisms to replace "generic" *he* has already been mentioned. Most of those listed in Baron's 1986 chronology date from the 1970s and 1980s (*Grammar and Gender* 205–09).

One important target of the feminist attack on sexism was the textbooks used in American schools; they were criticized for their stereotyped representation of the sexes and for their use of language that tended to make women invisible except in roles like mother, daughter, homemaker, and perhaps teacher and nurse. An early example of such criticism is Marjorie B. U'Ren's 1971 essay "The Image of Women in Textbooks," which reports that girls and women were either absent or stereotyped in some thirty elementary school textbooks then in use in California.

In their 1977 book, *National Politics and Sex Discrimination in Education*, Andrew Fishel and Janice Pottker explain how the feminist movement came to focus on sexism in education and turned to the federal government out of frustration with the hostility or lack of interest at the local and state levels. They see the Women's Educational Equity Act, approved by Congress in 1974, as "one of the first successful attempts on the part of women['s] groups to use the congressional process to achieve a legislative objective that benefited their own special concern . . ." (67). During the hearings held in 1973 before subcommittees of the Senate and the House of Representatives, extensive documentation was offered on sex bias in textbooks and other aspects of education. These hearings brought the issue to public attention. Fishel and Pottker comment that the record of the two hearings, which exceeded a thousand pages, "constituted the most comprehensive reference sources available at the time that documented the discriminatory treatment received by women in elementary and secondary education" (78).

As finally approved, the 1974 act authorized funding for several types of activities, including the "development, evaluation, and dissemination of curricula, textbooks, and other educational materials" (84). In their discussion of the problems and politics involved in the passage of the act and the low level of funding for its implementation, Fishel and Pottker conclude that "the formation of an effective women's lobby on education issues constitutes a legacy that may be, in the long run, a more important end product on this issue than the actual passage of the Women's Educational Equity Act itself" (91).

Spanning the period from 1970 to 1976, the history of Title IX, as outlined by Fishel and Pottker, is longer and far more complex than that of the Women's Educational Equity Act. The proposed legislation was first approved in June 1972 and went into effect on 1 July of that year, but regulations were not published until 1974. Although the most controversial aspect of Title IX concerned women's sports, the question of curriculum and textbooks also figured in the debate. The draft document included a requirement that schools and colleges review textbooks for sex bias (Fishel and Pottker 111), but before it was released for public comment, this item was deleted by Casper Weinberger, who was then secretary of health, education, and welfare. Although the matter of textbooks came up again during the ensuing discussion, the final regulations, which went into effect in July 1975, did not cover educational materials.

Textbooks and Public Pressure

A review of the Congressional testimony on the Women's Educational Equity Act and Title IX reveals that local groups were already exerting pressure on publishers to eliminate stereotyping in textbooks. For example, *Dick and Jane as Victims: Sex-Role Stereotyping in Children's Readers*, a 1970 report prepared by Women on Words and Images, is based on a study of 134 elementary school readers in use at that time in New Jersey. A later summary of the report cites some of the findings: the ratio of boy-centered to girl-centered stories in the books was 5 to 2, men as main characters outnumbered women 3 to 1, and 6 times more biographies were about men than about women (Women on Words, "Look" 160). Among the sexist characteristics of the books was the frequency of stories in which girls were demeaned as a class. The authors comment, "The readers give boys the ammunition, if society hasn't done so already, to attack girls as foolish, vain, silly, dumb, boring, no good at games and sports, etc., ad nauseum. Boys are never ridiculed as members of the group 'male' " (169). In another study Marsha Federbush documents sex discrimination in mathematics books, concluding that "textbook companies want business, and they are not eager to be accused of discrimination. . . . When told of their book's inadequacies, some indicate . . . that they will make the necessary changes in future editions" (181). Federbush suggests that local committees be formed to review textbooks and other material, that school systems refrain from purchasing discriminatory books and inform publishers of this policy, and that "a set of guidelines . . . be drawn up and presented to companies to use as directives to authors and artists preparing new books" (182).

In a useful analysis of approaches to combating sexism in language, Maija S. Blaubergs describes three major positions on the issue: (1) since sexist language merely reflects societal sexism and sex-role stereotyping, direct changing of the language is neither desirable nor feasible; (2) irrelevant references to sex or gender are at "the root of the problem of sexist language" and their substitution by neutral terminology is important in itself; (3) traditional usage tends to render women invisible and "emphasis on feminine terms will enhance females' self-concept. . . ." Blaubergs notes that "all three approaches are theoretical, albeit also political, stands" ("Changing" 259). The earliest items listed in Blaubergs's bibliography date from 1970 and 1971. (They include Densmore's "Speech Is the Form of Thought," Faust's "Words That Oppress," Kidd's "Study of the Images Produced through the Use of the Male Pronoun as the Generic," Varda One's "Manglish," and Strainchamps's "Our Sexist Language.")

It is difficult to single out any specific incident or activity that decisively influenced publishers to adopt and implement guidelines for nonsexist language usage. Certainly, the studies cited in this section played a part. At least one publishing house indicated to me that its editorial policy reflected the preferences of local and state textbook committees, some of which had adopted nonsexist usage as a criterion for book selection. According to a 1987 article in the *New York Times*, this criterion remains in force; the author quotes the head of one textbook committee as saying that "the first thing we look for is ethnic and gender balance, even above educational considerations" (Fiske 22). (It should be noted, however, that some local committees have campaigned for a return to "traditional" values, including traditional roles for women.) It has also been pointed out that publishers' textbook divisions employ a considerable number of women as editors, including many who share feminist concerns about sex bias in education; their presence must have created a favorable climate, or even pressure, for adopting the guidelines.

Guidelines for Nonsexist Usage

Although the literature dealing with language planning has largely ignored the question of nonsexist language reform, it does provide an appropriate context for discussing the guidelines for nonsexist usage. The following analysis of the goals and content of the guidelines makes use of the classification system Heinz Kloss proposed for identifying government attitudes toward specific languages in multilingual societies (79–80; for a discussion of this system see Bell 182). These attitudes range from recognition as "sole official language" to proscription. The adaptation of Kloss's proposal presented here refers to usage rather than to language and provides a framework for classifying the status of both traditional usage and nonsexist reforms:

> *Sole official usage*: granted the status formerly accorded traditional terms such as "generic" *man* and *he*.
>
> *Joint official usage*: considered by some groups to be as acceptable as the alternatives; some organizations, for example, allow both the "generic" terms and new usages like *chairperson*.
>
> *Regional official usage*: endorsed by "local" sectors of society, such as feminists who use only nonsexist alternatives for biased wording and publishers who follow nonsexist editorial guidelines for certain types of publications.
>
> *Promoted usage*: preferred by official bodies.
>
> *Tolerated usage*: "neither promoted nor proscribed by authorities—its existence is recognized but ignored" (Bell 182); new usage in this category would not be rejected by editors but, in contrast to usage with joint official status, would not be formally or officially recognized.
>
> *Discouraged usage*: disfavored by editorial policy; the *New York Times*, for example, in its pre-1986 refusal to use *Ms.* and its insistence on the "generic" use of *man*, has placed the reforms in this category, while publishers with nonsexist guidelines discourage traditional usage.

The goal of feminists active in the campaign for language reform is to raise the status of nonsexist usage throughout society to that of sole official usage and to demote traditional usage to discouraged status. Currently, nonsexist usage is at an intermediate stage. Depending on the group one is concerned with—whether all writers of English in the United States, some governmental and publishing bodies, or feminists—it varies from discouraged to joint official usage, reaching the sole official stage in only a few limited contexts. By adopting guidelines, publishers and other groups place nonsexist usage in the category of promoted or regional official usage.

Form and Content

Nonsexist guidelines have been adopted by a variety of organizations, including textbook divisions, professional societies, publishers of newspapers and magazines, and special groups such as religious bodies. The form of the guidelines ranges from a single sentence to an entire handbook. In the first category is the recommendation that currently appears in *PMLA*, the journal of the Modern Language Association. The "Statement of Editorial Policy" printed at the beginning of each issue ends with this sentence: "The MLA urges its contributors to be sensitive to the social implications of language and to seek wording free of discriminatory overtones."

Most guidelines are short booklets with general introductions, specific examples of offensive usage accompanied by brief explanations or comments, and suggested nonsexist alternatives. Guidelines produced by textbook publishers often go beyond issues of language usage to include such matters as appropriate illustrations and balance in the content of the text. They may concern discrimination against minorities as well as gender bias, and at least one, the 1981 guidelines Houghton Mifflin issued under the title *Eliminating Stereotypes*, deals with the treatment of disabled persons, older persons, and other stigmatized groups.[2]

Specific Recommendations

Existing guidelines reflect a remarkable consensus in the changes they consider necessary to achieve nondiscriminatory language. In general, they discourage usage that ignores or demeans women, reinforces bias and stereotypes, or focuses inappropriately on gender. They usually refer to problems caused by ambiguity and stereotyping, and those adopted by the American Psychological Association distinguish between sexism in designation and in evaluation. Most of the guidelines make the following recommendations:

> Use true generics or sex-neutral terms when reference includes both sexes—for example, *poet* and *nurse* for both sexes, *chair* or *chairperson* instead of *chairman*, *worker* instead of *workman*, *humanity* or *human beings* instead of *mankind*, *the average person* for *the man on the street*.
>
> Use parallel or symmetrical expressions for both genders—for example, *men and women* or *husbands and wives* instead of *the men and their wives*; *Lytton Strachey and Virginia Woolf* instead of *Lytton Strachey and Mrs. Woolf*; *King and McEnroe* instead of *Ms. King and McEnroe*. Some guidelines also recommend attention to order in expressions such as these to ensure that men do not always precede women.
>
> Treat women and men as individuals instead of defining them solely

by their relationship to others—for example, *Jane Russo*, not *Mrs. Louis Russo*; *Mr. and Mrs. Rosen* or *Louis and Jane Rosen*, not *Mr. Rosen and his wife*; *Mary and Joseph Smith*, not *Mary Smith and her husband, Joseph*.

Use neutral references rather than biased or stereotyped terms—for example, *woman* instead of *gal* or *chick*; *drive*, not *masculine drive*; *house or office cleaner* or *domestic worker*, not *cleaning lady*; *feminist*, not *libber*.

Use an alternative to the "pseudogeneric" *he*, *his*, or *him* when referring to a person of unspecified sex. For example, omit the possessive *his* or replace it with an article where appropriate: *The good teacher respects students* instead of *The good teacher respects his students*; *The writer tells the reader* instead of *The writer tells his reader*. Other alternatives include recasting the sentence in the plural, using the second person *you*, or using both feminine and masculine forms such as *he or she*.

Guidelines developed by professional associations and journals share the concerns of those adopted by book publishers but tend to be shorter. Some of them, such as those of the American Psychological Association, are based on or accompanied by studies carried out by specially appointed committees, and their examples reflect the subject matter of the profession in question. While the publishers' guidelines are often prescriptive, officially requiring nonsexist usage in their textbooks, the professional guidelines, like those of the National Council of Teachers of English, are more likely to promote nonsexist usage without making it mandatory. The guidelines issued by special groups follow a pattern similar to the others, ranging from one- or two-page formats to substantial manuals. Newspapers usually include the issue of sexist usage in their style manuals. Finally, general handbooks of nonsexist usage, such as the one by Miller and Swift, are available for individual writers who wish to avoid discriminatory language.

Responses

Responses to the guidelines have ranged from enthusiastic acceptance to accusations of censorship and tampering with the English language. Negative comments, especially those in the media, have frequently taken the form of ridicule and satire. The vehemence of some of these remarks can be explained by the relation between attitudes and behavior change discussed earlier, in particular by the attitudes reflected in prescriptive grammar. It is clear that, for some people, the guidelines represent a threat to established values as well as to traditional language usage (D. Smith).

Blaubergs classifies the arguments advanced against the changes proposed in the guidelines, in particular arguments about the use of "generics," as follows: (1) since the degree of sexism in a culture does not necessarily match the degree of sexism in its language, changing language will not change the culture; (2) the issue is trivial; (3) nonsexist prescriptions are coercive and violate freedom of speech; (4) "sexist" language is not really sexist; (5) word etymologies demonstrate that perceptions of sexism are wrong; (6) so do other forms of authority; (7) change is difficult and impractical; (8) historical and literary tradition must be defended ("Analysis" 136).

The cross-cultural arguments, Blaubergs points out, are based on a misunderstanding of the relation between the proposed reforms and the Sapir-Whorf hypothesis: "Whether language merely reflects existing societal practices or contributes significantly to them, sexist language by its existence *reinforces* . . . sexist thinking and practices" ("Analysis" 137). The claim that women may be more oppressed in a society whose language lacks gender distinctions does not affect the validity of proposals for changing language usage that is itself sexist.

Some feminists as well as antifeminists find the issue trivial. They generally describe the concern about sexist language as "silly" or as diverting attention from the "real" inequalities in society. But the very prevalence of this argument indicates that the concern is not trivial. The Ad Hoc Committee on Sexist Language of the Association for Women in Psychology makes this statement:

> The major objection, often even to *discussing* changing sexist language, is that it is a superficial matter compared with the real physical and economic oppression of women. And indeed, women's total oppression must end; we are not suggesting any diversion of energies from that struggle. We are, however, suggesting that this is an important part of it.

Freedom-of-speech arguments often accuse the proponents of guidelines of wishing to impose censorship. The following example, protesting NCTE's guidelines on nonsexist usage, is from a 1976 contribution to the Forum section of the *English Journal*: "Indeed, the committee would, in effect, blacklist those authors who do not adhere to its suggestions for nonsexist language" (Alter 12). A similar complaint about guidelines appeared in the *Washington Post*:

> It seems that a multitude of terrorized individuals and institutions (including State legislatures) have set about mangling perfectly neuter and valid words like *foreman* and *motorman*. . . . The principal counterfeiters—let us be frank about it at the outset—are the less sensible activists of the women's rights movement; the users are those who are cravenly intimidated by them.   (Friendly)

Activists in the women's movement must have been surprised to discover that they had the power to terrorize and intimidate state legislatures. Blaubergs comments that most arguments in the freedom-of-speech category do not object to the right of journals and other publications to require writers to follow a manual or a set of requirements involving other aspects of form and style. Censorship complaints are rarely voiced except when those guidelines include nonsexist usage.

Arguments that the guidelines reflect a misunderstanding of language—that the use of "generics" and other so-called sexist terms is not really sexist—are closely related to arguments that cite word etymologies or appeal to authority in general. Some critics declare that nonsexist intentions must inevitably produce nonsexist results. As the American Psychological Association notes, however, "imprecise word choices . . . may be interpreted as biased, discriminatory, or demeaning even if they are not intended to be" ("Guidelines for Nonsexist Language" 488).

Blaubergs points out that those who defend traditional usage by focusing on the history of words like *man* and *mankind* have themselves been criticized for relying on inaccurate or incomplete data and for selectively denying changes in word meanings. While they insist on the "original" meaning of *man*, for example, they do not advocate returning to the historical meaning of *girl* as a young person of either sex. Other appeals to authority go beyond word etymologies, extending to the entire realm of prescriptive and traditional usage. (For further discussion, see Wolfe's essay in this volume and Baron's *Grammar and Gender*.)

Instead of dismissing proposed language reforms as trivial or denouncing them as coercive, some critics claim that the recommendations are too difficult to carry out and that certain features of language, such as the pronoun system, are particularly resistant to change. The linguist Robin Lakoff, though she is herself a critic of sexist language, finds this area "both less in need of changing and less open to change than many of the other disparities." Although she recognizes that the use of pseudogeneric *he* is not trivial for many people, she says, "I feel in any case that an attempt to change pronominal usage will be futile" (45).

A number of writers justify their use of "generic" *he* or *man* by disclaiming sexist intentions. One representative example in a widely used introductory linguistics book appears in a footnote to the sentence "Man's curiosity about himself led to his curiosity about language":

> In English and in many (most?) other languages, the masculine forms of nouns and pronouns are used as the general, or generic, term. We would have liked to avoid this but found ourselves constrained by common usage. Had we said "Woman's curiosity about herself . . . ," this would have been interpreted as referring only to women. Using the word "man" . . . we are sure that the interpretation will be "man and woman." Wherever "man" or "mankind" or a similar generic term is used, the reader is asked to consider these general terms embracing the whole of humanity, unless of course the meaning can specifically be related to the male members of the species. (Fromkin and Rodman 17)

This passage, reminiscent of the parliamentary bill that declared *he* to be generic, reflects a view shared by many who sincerely oppose sexism but view traditional usage as a constraint that cannot be violated without sacrificing good style. As Blaubergs notes, some guidelines do permit authors this escape hatch ("Analysis" 144). In addition to the examples she cites, the following statement appears in the 1977 *Wiley Guidelines on Sexism in Language*, which contains detailed suggestions for nonsexist usage: "To avoid problems of repetition or inept wording, some authors use the generic *he* freely and add a general footnote . . . explaining that masculine pronouns are used for succinctness and that they are intended to refer to both males and females." After providing several examples of acceptable disclaimers, the guidelines conclude with a warning: "Although the avoidance of sexist language can be a literary problem, and good, strong English may sometimes demand the use of impersonal pronouns, text footnotes or prefatory notes should not be used as a cure-all for sexist writing" (n.p.). (McConnell-Ginet's essay in this volume makes a similar argument.)

The final type of argument Blaubergs analyzes claims that the

proponents of change would destroy our cultural heritage by rewriting literature to conform to the new nonsexist standards. These
arguments, which are closely related to those defending the purity
of the English language, rarely include specific examples. A special
case, which receives only cursory attention from Blaubergs, has
been the object of impassioned debate in one sector of the population. It concerns attempts to change the traditional texts of the
English versions of the Bible, as well as the wording of hymns and
prayers, to render them gender-neutral. Feminist criticism of traditional biblical texts and feminist versions of the Bible date back
to the nineteenth century. In 1876 Julia Smith produced "the first
feminist Bible and the first English translation of the whole Bible
by a woman" (Kramarae and Treichler, *Feminist* 68), and Elizabeth
Cady Stanton's *Woman's Bible* appeared in 1895 and 1898 (see Wel-
ton for a description of Stanton's project). Recently, Jewish women
have attempted to reinterpret the Torah to include the perceptions
of women (see Heschel for extensive discussion).

Some recent advocates of change attribute the sexist language of
many biblical passages to the translators and claim that it may not
faithfully represent the original text (Trible discusses the language
of the Old Testament and its translations); but beyond the question
of translation, the wording inevitably reflects the patriarchal Judeo-
Christian society of its creators. Although critics accuse the refor-
mists of demanding a "sexless" or "neutered" Bible, the revision
of religious texts has gained surprising momentum. Many religious
denominations have devoted serious discussion to the issue and
have adopted sex-inclusive versions of hymns, liturgies, and prayers. Among the most notable modifications is the deletion of sex-
specific references to God. The pronoun *he* may be replaced by a
repetition of the noun; a reference to God the *Father* may be extended to God as *Father and Mother*, or a genderless noun may be
substituted. Also common is the replacement of the word *man* with
a true generic. (For an extensive discussion of sex-inclusive language in religious texts, see United Presbyterian Church; "Linguistic Sexism"; Russell; and Miller and Swift, *Words* 17–82, 146–48.)

Consequences

Although much of the criticism described above occurred soon after
the guidelines first appeared in the 1970s, similar arguments are
still being advanced today. It is therefore legitimate at this point
to ask what effect the guidelines have had on usage. The answer

must be a provisional one, for it is still too early to attempt a definitive evaluation of their success. The results to date appear to be mixed. A preliminary examination of books for schoolchildren published since the appearance of the guidelines indicates that the new policies have succeeded in eliminating much of the most blatant sexist usage. Robert L. Cooper, who studied the use of androcentric generics in a variety of American publications (including magazines, newspapers, science magazines, and the *Congressional Record*), found "a dramatic decline in the rate of androcentric generics from 1971 through 1979" (19). His limited sample indicated that "the form least resistant to change was *man*" (19). The decline in the use of "generic" *he* indicated that writers adopted solutions like pluralization in preference to those involving two pronouns, such as *he or she* (17). Other signs of success include the widespread adoption of the title *Ms.* and the changes in occupational titles. (Baron suggests, however, that no accurate information exists about the usage of *Ms.*; despite its acceptance in some contexts as a marriage-neutral title for a woman, it also seems to be used to distinguish perceived feminists from other women ["Is it [mIs] or [mIz]?"].)

Evidence of success in eliminating sexist usage in textbooks needs to be evaluated critically. Diane Ravitch raises the worrisome possibility that, "by eliminating sexist references in content as well as language, and failing to deal overtly with the issue of sexism, textbooks are presenting a different but just as unreal a world as before" (qtd. in Fiske 22). It should be kept in mind, moreover, that many of the older texts are still in use, so that it may be some time before all schoolbooks reflect the suggestions in the guidelines. Finally, we do not know whether current efforts to restore "traditional" values to education will succeed in reversing some of the progress made thus far. One fundamentalist religious group succeeded in persuading at least the lower courts that some books "undermined parental authority and promoted feminism and other causes that were contrary to their religious beliefs. . . . The judge ruled that children could be excused from reading anything that offended their religious values" (Fiske 22).

At the college level, results of the guidelines are less obvious. While some texts have been written or revised to conform to nonsexist usage, the choice is typically left to the author. More disturbing are cases of blatant sexism found in books published recently. For example, in Steven Schmidt's *Creating the Technical Report*, published in 1983 by Prentice Hall, the use of column headings and subheadings is illustrated by a chart classifying secretaries as blonde, brunette, redheaded, and bald. To counter any unlikely claim that the designations are intended as generic, an example of informal art elsewhere in the book shows a man writing and a woman typing. The typist is shown leaning forward so that every curve of her body is accentuated, in a posture in which it is probably impossible to type. While it is to be hoped that this book is an unfortunate exception to the general trend in textbook writing, complacency is obviously not in order.[3]

In the world of commercial publishing beyond the realm of textbooks, nonsexist usage is not at all the norm. The guidelines we have examined are generally not used in the trade-book divisions of the publishers that have adopted them for textbooks; usage in trade books seems definitely to be left to the authors. In contrast, some university presses have internal rules on nonsexist usage, with editors generally responsible for ensuring gender-neutral language, and many scholarly journals, as I have mentioned, have adopted nonsexist guidelines. These policies have had a notable effect on the language of scholarly writing in the past ten years. In a recent essay, Alleen Pace Nilsen describes the development of the *NCTE Guidelines for the Use of Nonsexist Language in NCTE Publications* and recounts her experience in using them as coeditor of *The English Journal.* According to Nilsen, she and her coeditor "promised to make the journal a model of *inconspicuous sex-fair language:* ("Guidelines" 42). She provides examples of original copy considered sexist alongside the edited versions to illustrate some of the problems the editors encountered and the ways they solved them. Nilsen concludes that "[u]sing sex-fair language requires skill as well as commitment" (51). She suggests a "need for research and development of training materials to teach committed people how to be successful in using sex-fair language" (52).

Usage in the mass media varies. Although there is a trend in favor of nonsexist usage, some prestigious publications, such as the *New York Times,* have stubbornly resisted it. Until 1986, in fact, a woman could not be given the courtesy title *Ms.* in the *Times,* no matter what her own preference might be. Thus Sandra Gilbert's 1984 review of Janice Radway's *Reading the Romance* refers to the author throughout as "Mrs. Radway"—a designation that neither feminist scholar would have used on her own and that certainly jarred feminist readers. In reports of sports events during those years, a woman's surname is preceded by *Miss* or *Mrs.* in contexts where only the last name is used for a man. In the sports section of 3 July 1983, for example, the following headlines appear on page 1: "Miss Navratilova Takes Fourth Wimbleton Title" and "Emotion Rules the Way Martin Lives and Works" (referring to Billy Martin, the manager of the New York Yankees). In the first story, all tennis players are initially given their full names—for example, Martina Navratilova and John McEnroe—but further reference distinguishes between the sexes, using "Miss Navratilova" and "McEnroe." In June 1986, however, the *Times* announced that *Ms.* would henceforth be used as a title for a woman, thereby joining many other publications in referring to women as autonomous human beings, independent of marital status. And shortly thereafter the paper gave the names of women athletes the same status as those of men.

In view of the negative responses to the guidelines cited earlier and the persistence of sexist practices, it was surprising to discover, in a 1982 article by Sol Steinmetz, general editor of *The World Book Dictionary*, that "the feminist campaign against sexism has made a triumphant breakthrough in the area of language." Steinmetz reviews the major proposals for reform and describes the resistance as "surprisingly mild, confined mainly to facetious comments in the press on the proliferation of 'person' compounds . . . and the elimination of 'man' in occupational titles. . . ." He comments that "one vainly looks in recent books on language for a serious discussion of the subject" and cites a recent discussion of "language changers" that fails even to mention antisexist reforms. His explanation for this silence is "that the matter has been settled already in the minds of most people," that "the antisexist movement has made remarkable inroads in the language," and that "the 'King's English' will no longer be his exclusive domain" (8).

A more sober appraisal of the situation today suggests that these cheerful views were premature. The silence that Steinmetz refers to may reflect not writers' acceptance of feminist reforms but their view of the matter as trivial or as best left unpublicized. But should opponents awaken to the possibility of moderate feminist success, their protests might well increase. In fact, in a review of Mary Vetterling-Braggin's *Sexist Language* that appeared only a few months before Steinmetz's article, Roger Scruton labels feminist linguistic reforms a "tasteless assault on the language" and finds "something shrill and hysterical" in the Modern Language Association's decision to remove all "irrelevant" uses of gender from its publications. About the same time, Brigid Brophy reviewed the British edition of Miller and Swift's *Handbook of Non-sexist Writing* in the *London Review of Books*, presenting an amalgam of the familiar arguments against guidelines. She accuses the authors of a "tin ear and insensibility to the metaphorical content of language" and claims that the "assaults by pressure groups of equal ineptitude" are designed to nag writers and editors into "acts of censorship or pledges of self-censorship." She advises writers and editors that they "should not give way, and they need experience no crisis of conscience because, if they yielded, they would accomplish nothing whatever for the cause of sex-equity." Similarly, John Simon refers to Miller and Swift's book as "A Handbook for Maidens" and concludes that "by allowing irresponsible alterations in the language, we are not only losing the necessary touch with the glories of our literary past, we are also inviting a linguistic turmoil that must lead to the breakdown of everyday communication in the not so distant future" (31).

After a brief lull, the issue of sexist usage again became the focus of media attention in May 1985, when the *New York Times* editorial page and letters to the editor section, as well as William Safire's column "On Language," commented on an attempt by a regional official of the US Department of Education to get the University of California at Berkeley to change the wording in one of its catalogs. The offending words included *man, mankind,* and other "generic" terms. The university resisted and passed the list of objections to a professor of journalism who consulted a group of 15 journalists before replying. His report, stating that the challenge to the "generics" is "political, not linguistic or logical," characterizes *ombudsperson* and *freshperson* as "barbarisms" and the expression *his or her* as "cumbersome and unnecessary." Safire quotes the professor's report approvingly, concluding that although "sexism is *wrong,*" "the imposition of language change by government fiat, rather than by spirited private debate, is—as the Secretary of Education likes to say—intrusive, meddlesome, unwarranted and wrong" (11). Language planning by the federal government is apparently not well received in this country.

The official in question did have some defenders, among them a writer who, in a letter to the *New York Times* published the same day as the Safire article, admits that neologisms may be "awkward at best" but concludes that "given a choice between the risk of a little phonetic barbarism and the fact of a language that in a few simple nouns and pronouns minimizes (if not oppresses) about half our fellow human beings, who can choose?" (Rousmaniere). But the influence of William Bennett, the secretary of education at that time, made it unlikely that colleges would be given further official advice regarding the language in their publications. As it stands, institutions like the University of California can continue to use the traditional "generics" and offer courses called "Of Molecules and Man: A View for the Layman"—unless, perhaps, their own students or faculty members protest.

While feminists may take encouragement from the undeniable victories that the campaign against sexist language usage has scored, the undertaking is ambitious, and much remains to be done. As Steinmetz points out, success would mark the first time since the eighteenth-century prescriptivists that "a small but vocal group of activists" had achieved a major reform in usage (8). In contrast to the prescriptivists, who were basically elitist in presuming that their rules embodied the ultimate authority on linguistic "purity," the feminists are conducting a popular movement against authority in the name of fairness and equity. Accomplishing their objectives would represent a remarkable achievement indeed.[4]

Notes

[1] I owe this information about Mussolini's efforts at linguistic change to Robert J. Di Pietro.

[2] *Eliminating Stereotypes* represents not only economic, ethnic, and cultural variety but also diverse household arrangements—families with untidy living rooms, for example.

[3] *Creating the Technical Report* was brought to my attention by Patricia H. Whiting, a faculty member in the College of Engineering at West Virginia University. She wrote to the publisher detailing her objections to instances of sexism in the text.

[4] An earlier version of this essay was delivered at the Tenth World Congress of Sociology in Mexico City, July 1982, and published under the title "Language Planning and Sexual Equality" in Hellinger 231–54.

Part Two

Guidelines for Nonsexist Usage

Paula A. Treichler and Francine Wattman Frank

Preface

The essays in part 1 of this book provide a theoretical and empirical foundation for reforming sexist scholarly writing practices. They are recommended both for those who wish to know more about the underlying cultural issues and for those who are not convinced that sexist language is a problem. Publishers supportive of non-discriminatory usage may find it helpful to refer resistant authors to these historical and reflective analyses. But editors and writers seeking practical solutions to biased wording may go directly to the guidelines themselves.

The guidelines advocate nonsexist alternatives to sexist usages. At present, it seems reasonable to expect scholars as a matter of course to seek to avoid sexist language as conscientiously as they seek to avoid imprecision, inaccurate citations, and infelicitous wording. An irony of the past two decades is that many scholars in literature and linguistics, whose professional lives testify to the significance of language and linguistic detail, have resisted non-sexist language proposals and indeed have claimed that the sexist language problem is trivial. This argument is now often based on a new claim: that the problem has been solved. But neither claim is true. Sexist language is not trivial; and it continues to be pervasive.

Nonsexist writing may not come naturally. We agree with the writer who considers it

> unrealistic to assume that writers with good intentions will sponta-
> neously use nonsexist language effectively. Good intentions are no
> substitute for craft. Like all first-rate writing, nonsexist writing re-
> quires skill placed in the service of an educated eye. But we needn't

> exaggerate the degree of skill required. A practiced pen is needed;
> genius is not. (Shear 19)

We recognize, of course, that the conventions of individual presses and publishers may conflict with some alternatives mentioned here. It is unlikely, for example, that leading academic journals within the next few years will embrace the use of the pronoun *they* with a singular antecedent; despite its historical validity and common use in oral and informal written communication, *they* in this context is widely condemned. Many scholarly journals, however, are now open to some unconventional usages if the author can make a good case for them (e.g., *he or she* or even generic *she*, with an antecedent of unspecified sex).

In the first section of the guidelines we discuss "classic" sexist language practices that continue to occur despite widely publicized objections. We analyze them in some detail and with special attention to scholarly and professional writing. Our goal is not to provide a narrowly prescriptive catechism. Many excellent guidelines and handbooks are now available that identify common problems and offer solutions in formats designed for easy reference (see pt. 3). Rather, we wish to explore these pervasive abuses in depth. We agree with Donald G. MacKay that the "fundamental aim of prescriptivism is to predict which among a set of alternative forms or rules will prove most useful for future speakers to learn and use in some (usually formal) context" (350). Accordingly, our recommendations take the multiple functions and contexts of scholarly and professional writing into account. In the second section, we focus on some of the special concerns of scholarly writing, particularly in literary and linguistic fields—not only writing associated with research and interpretation but also such efforts as the compilation of dictionaries and handbooks. Again, we seek alternatives that acknowledge these concerns and do not oversimplify them. In conclusion, we briefly note other areas of professional life where sexist language may be a problem (e.g., in pedagogical practices and in interactions with the public).

The guidelines are therefore organized around (1) common problems of linguistic sexism in writing, including scholarly and professional writing, and (2) special concerns about sexist usage in scholarly writing and related professional activities. We have tried not to address any problem under more than one heading, though some overlapping occurs; readers should consult the index to locate sections that interest them. The discussion of each major problem is followed by a succinct summary of recommended usage. While most of our recommendations fall within the bounds of conventional good usage, they do not bear an official MLA endorsement. Moreover, we have not confined ourselves to those that conform to MLA's current editorial practices; instead, we identify and discuss nonsexist alternatives for a wider range of scholarly and professional publications, citing some usages that lie outside a strict prescriptivist tradition and giving the reasons for our preferences.

The guidelines are intended for students, teachers, and scholars in the humanities; for editors at presses and journals; and for those who teach and write in the sciences, social sciences, and professions. We illustrate our discussion predominantly with authentic examples from recent scholarly and professional writing and from literary publications like the *New York Review of Books*, the *Times Literary Supplement*, and the *Women's Review of Books*; for some usages, however, we have had to create examples, to draw on sources outside the modern languages, or to rely on feminist journals like *Sinister Wisdom* and *Heresies*, whose editorial practices yield nonsexist writing alternatives not (yet) accessible through more conventional publications. To reflect current scholarly practices fairly, we have for the most part chosen examples published after 1975; by then many publishers and professional associations had adopted policies or guidelines for nonsexist writing, so we would not expect to find earlier types of blatant sexism after that date. Work since 1975, in fact, offers evidence of considerable creativity, for many scholars who have adopted standard nonsexist writing practices have also devised their own alternatives to traditional conventions and representations of sexual difference.

Because our examples are not uniquely good or bad but merely illustrative of current usage, we do not identify authors or titles; instead we cite only the information that seems pertinent to our topic, usually the year of publication and the journal title or generic type of publication. We do not indicate an author's sex unless it is directly relevant.

Finally, to make clear the parallels and connections between linguistic sexism and linguistic discrimination of different kinds, we also cite and discuss various other types. Arguments about some of these are by now well articulated—one thinks particularly of writing about race—and there is considerable material to draw on. In other areas, however, attention to biased language is just developing (a criticism of terms related to mental or physical disabilities, for example, is certain to affect the language substantially), and we do no more than sketch questions about some usages. Gender remains our central concern in these guidelines; other perspectives deserve books of their own. Our point is that these issues intersect, illuminating once again the social and cultural complexity of language and its defiance of the quick fix.

Common Problems of Sexist Usage

The problems most commonly identified in discussions of sexist usage and guidelines for nonsexist usage still occur widely, and good solutions are not always obvious. We therefore discuss them here at some length, noting their special implications for scholarly writing. We begin with the most notorious of these discriminatory practices, the use of male-specific words as generics.

"Generic" *He*

A *generic* term is one that is intended to function universally rather than specifically. Because sex marking is prominent and sometimes obligatory for English nouns and personal pronouns, it is not surprising that discussions of sexism in language have generally focused on the injustice, ambiguity, and incongruity created by traditional "generic" uses of words in these grammatical classes. All nonsexist guidelines, for example, debate the legitimate scope of the pronoun *he* and the meanings conveyed by allegedly generic *man*. These usages, which Robert L. Cooper and others call *androcentric generics*, are highly resistant to change because they occur in many contexts and perform many functions in English and because many writers consider them integral to "correct" English. Calls for change may seem on the one hand to require complicated acrobatics and on the other to threaten fundamental and accepted standards for good writing. We argue that the problems caused by false generics by now far outweigh their convenience and that many graceful solutions are available, some of them quite simple. Indeed, we suggest, convoluted alternatives almost always signal a deeper problem and the need for further analysis in the writing or editing process. At the same time, appeals to "tradition" ignore the dependence of English on multiple traditions, including a strong populist countertradition that recognizes such usages as *for you and I*, *between the three of us*, and *everyone enjoyed their new nonsexist handbooks*. The term *traditional*, however, usually refers to the prescriptive tradition constructed and upheld by usage experts, strict-constructionist grammarians, and many literary scholars and professional writers. But traditional grammar can change its precepts, as is evidenced by the currently acceptable use of *none* with a plural verb, as in *none are wearing suits*. Commenting on *none* as a singular pronoun, Claire Cook notes that

> many English teachers, especially in the past, have insisted that it can have no other meaning, classing it with such invariably singular indefinite pronouns as *everything*, *nobody*, *anyone*, and *each*. Most contemporary grammarians, however, contend not only that *none* can be plural, meaning "not any ones," but that the sense is more commonly plural than singular. (83)

In opposition to the traditional endorsement of the so-called generics, we argue that a number of these terms raise theoretical, linguistic, and semantic problems; that they frequently and inaccurately imply a white male norm; and that satisfactory stylistic alternatives, many within the prescriptive tradition, are increasingly plentiful. (For empirical research on generics, see the introduction to this volume; for common critical responses to proposed reforms, see Frank's essay.)

The Controversy

Of all the problems identified as examples of sexist usage, the "generic" *he* is perhaps the most common. This usage has been the prime target for feminist reform (and number one on what the columnist and language commentator William Safire calls the "feminist hit list" ["Hypersexism" 10]). Widespread discussion and criticism have focused attention on generic *he* and made it a sensitive index to social change. One measure of this sensitivity is the coexistence of competing pronominal forms, not only in the culture at large but often within a single speaker's repertoire. This phenomenon is particularly evident in speech, where ongoing conflict among competing forms cannot be disguised by subsequent editing. For example, the competition between conventional usage and newer forms is apparent in this female medical student's description of a small-group exercise at a 1979 women's conference:

> Then each of us gave the list to the person on our right and he
> evaluated each item on the list according to what he or she had
> observed—well, obviously, it would be "she" in a women's group.

The student's confusion illustrates Catherine Belsey's point that
ideological self-consciousness (here, probably a newly found awareness of gender in the context of "women in medicine") may disrupt
the smooth operation of previously accepted linguistic conventions
(*Critical* 42–43). In 1980 the director of a major institute within
the National Institutes of Health, a distinguished male scientist,
found himself in a similar predicament in talking to a group of
medical school deans, all but two of whom were men. Describing
the ongoing search for an executive director, he said:

> The executive director plays a crucial role at the NIH and so it's
> very important that he—he—she—he/she—he or she—be a top sci-
> entist and also be able to work with all the institute directors.

In this rather complicated example, it seems likely that linguistic
convention (the widely accepted use of *he* in such contexts), personal
experience (acquaintance with previous male executive directors),
and covert gender (the assumption that the next executive director
would also be male) were all at work in encouraging the speaker
to use the male pronoun to refer to the executive director. Moreover, since he was a man speaking largely to men (the two women
in the group sat at some distance from him and remained silent
throughout the meeting), the circumstances would not discourage
the use of *he*. But the speaker was also an employee of the federal
government, which by this time had mandated gender-neutral job
descriptions and occupational titles; as a highly placed administrator at the NIH, acting in an official capacity, he probably felt responsible for upholding "policy," including the use of gender-neutral
language. The force of these competing claims was apparent in his
speech.

A vigorous exchange in the journal *College Composition and Communication* illustrates the widespread self-consciousness and strong
opinions held about the male third-person singular personal pronoun. Opening the exchange from a feminist perspective, Mary K.
DeShazer condemns the widespread use of "generic" *he* in composition texts on the grounds that this usage excludes women
("Sexist"). In response, the composition authorities A. M. Tibbetts
and Charlene Tibbetts defend *he* as an acceptable generic: "widely
accepted standards of *good usage*," they write, can be defined as

"being what good writers write. . . . Our own sampling of good
writers shows general acceptance of the generic pronoun" (485).
They approvingly cite, for example, the usage of *he* by a respected
male scientist writing in *Newsweek* about being a scientist, then
criticize a composition textbook for recommending alternatives to
generic *he*:

> The authors have to wrestle so hard with the language to produce
> a mainly *he*-free text that you are constantly aware of the strain.
> Instead of attending always to their excellent ideas, you are diverted
> occasionally by the battle going on: How, you wonder, are they going
> to manage this particular *he*, which is about to pounce snarling from
> the darkness of the next sentence?   (487)

They argue that "the English teaching profession and NCTE have
consistently come down on the side of good usage being what good
writers write" (485). DeShazer counters that "by publishing guidelines toward nonsexist language, NCTE and other organizations as
well as many publishers have strongly encouraged competent writers to modify their usage and so avoid sexism and sex-stereotyping"
("Reply" 490). The Tibbetts's astonishing vision of feminists waging
guerrilla warfare against bestial pronouns in the jungles of language disguises the weakness of their argument. In a period of
linguistic transition, there are sure to be "experts" on both sides—
Stephen Jay Gould, for example, an eminent scientist and writer,
consistently challenges conventional assumptions about what is "generic" (*Mismeasure* 16). Moreover, the rejected composition text,
the Tibbettses tell us, was written by two "intelligent" and "skillful"
authors who are also presumably in other respects "good writers."
So their criterion for proper usage seems questionable, for here
"good writers" disagree. The exchange demonstrates the vehemence of arguments over a "mere" linguistic convention. Similar
exchanges in the *Newsletter of the American Anthropological Association*
(Gregerson 8–9) led the editorial board to call a moratorium on
letters about sexist language. K. E. Thomas, meanwhile, traces the
sexist language theme through a decade of letters to the London
Times. Betty Lou Dubois and Isabel Crouch surveyed several years
of English language use, both oral and written, to determine the
results of "the great 'he/she' battle" ("Linguistic" 35). They conclude
that the range of gender-neutral alternatives they found and the
many examples of inconsistent usage and hypercorrection "illustrate the state of linguistic disruption which is a natural by-product
of change and one in which we currently find ourselves" (35).

What is the origin of this disputed use of *he*? According to common wisdom, pronouns substitute, or stand in, for antecedent nouns or nominal phrases and exemplify a general grammatical process of substitution (identified by Bloomfield 249–63 and further described by Lyons 2: 657–77 and by Jacobs and Rosenbaum 121–26). When the noun in question identifies a human being, the substitute word is a personal pronoun marked for "humanness." (The plural personal pronoun *they*, however, is not so marked; it can substitute for a plural noun denoting persons or things.) English personal pronouns are marked for case (*she* versus *her*), for number (*she* versus *they*), and for person (*I* versus *she*). In some languages, it is obligatory to mark all personal pronouns for sex; in contemporary English, only the third-person singular pronoun in reference to a human being retains an obligatory and dichotomous marking of female or male. As Suzanne Kessler and Wendy McKenna note, this linguistic dichotomy reinforces, and is reinforced by, our deep-seated cultural belief that sexual identity is "naturally" and immutably either male or female; but their ethnographic study of transsexuals challenges this belief, revealing a broad range of signals that one "reads" in attributing a sex to a person. With transsexuals, both signals and readings are destabilized, and this disequilibrium, as one would expect, is reflected quite clearly in the pronoun system. Transsexualism generates profound pronoun disturbance, and some people may refer to a transsexual with such mixed forms as "he–she–it."

When a singular antecedent of unspecified gender refers to one of a group that includes both sexes, speakers have traditionally had the choice of using *he* or *she* or the "ungrammatical" *they*. As we noted earlier, the English Parliament in the nineteenth century sought to resolve this problem by decreeing that in its acts the masculine pronoun would henceforth be used in such instances but would be understood as having a female as well as a male antecedent. However convenient this solution, it ignored another long-established tradition in which *he* was virtually always sex-specific and *they* was commonly used when the sex of the antecedent was unknown. Casey Miller and Kate Swift cite the following examples:

> Each of them should . . . make themself ready. (William Caxton)
> God send everyone their heart's desire. (William Shakespeare)
> If a person is born of a gloomy temper . . . they cannot help it.
> (Lord Chesterfield)   (*Handbook* 44–45)

Although many educated speakers and writers today would not accept this use of *they*, others point to its history, widespread popular usage, and pragmatic value. We are not concerned here with its current status (though we discuss this point below), but we want to emphasize that male generics have a more unstable and fragmented history than present-day authorities on grammar suggest (see Miller and Swift, *Handbook*; Baron, *Grammar and Gender*; and Wolfe in this volume). Studies also indicate that the "generic" status of male terms is far from universally reflected in usage: the pronoun *he* and the noun *man* and its compounds occur much more frequently as sex-specific or ambiguous expressions than as true generics (Graham, "Making"; Martyna, "Beyond").

Associated Problems

There are sound reasons to avoid using *he* to mean "he or she." For many speakers and listeners, it no longer functions (if it ever did) as a true generic: it simply does not do the job. Rather, the pronoun *he*—far from representing its antecedent in a gender-neutral or gender-inclusive way—identifies an apparently neutral antecedent as male. Thus, research indicates that in the following sentence the masculine pronouns would transform the potentially gender-inclusive antecedent "assistant professor" into a man:

> The assistant professor should learn about the tenure process before he goes through it.

For many speakers of English, the pronoun *he* simply cannot shed its male identity. In view of this social reality, the use of *he* as a generic becomes a form of social injustice. The lexicographer Alma Graham puts it this way:

> If you have a group half of whose members are A's and half of whose members are B's and if you call the group C then A's and B's may be equal members of group C. But if you call the group A, there is no way that B's can be equal to A's within it. The A's will always be the rule and the B's will always be the exception—the subgroup, the subspecies, the outsiders.   (Letter)

In literary studies, certain abstract entities—"the reader," "the interpreter," "the native speaker of English"—are conventionally invoked to represent a disembodied individual consciousness that interacts with texts (or language, or the world) through certain specifiable processes, experiences, and procedures:

> Dryden's reader is more than just a composite of Dryden's tastes and prejudices, he also represents a class of intellects and has an intangible aesthetic life. (*PMLA* 1979)

> In the unlikely event that a speaker of English wished to look up the definition of "horse" in a good dictionary, what is it that he should expect to find? (*Lingua* 1980)

> The interpreter is led, then, to draw inferences concerning those semes that have been singled out. He is led, in other words, to take the various semes as the starting points for new semantic representations. (*New Literary History* 1984)

> [O]ne may conclude that the speaking figure becomes a simple referential element and is disconnected from the discourse, which is supposed to come from his lips and mind. He is not a person anymore but must be seen as a locus—we would like to call it a locutory locus. . . . [T]he speaker is not speaking, but allowing the flow of words to go through his lips; he is not implicated in it, and as such, his words are representative not of him, but of a higher degree of knowledge. (*Semiotica* 1985)

The argument runs that "generic" *he* is justified in such contexts because entities like "the reader" have no concrete status as actual persons. Being disembodied, they have neither one sex nor the other, and it would therefore be inappropriate, even bizarre, to concretize them through the use of, say, *he or she*, or even plural *they*. But as these quotations illustrate, the male pronoun may also be problematic, though for different reasons in each example. In the first, the critic discusses Dryden's conception of the reader, a composite figure who to some degree evidently embodies many of Dryden's own qualities. The male sex reference that this resemblance implies creates an ambiguity about whether "the reader" is a true generic here. The second example presents a "speaker of English"—that staple figure of American linguistics—not carrying out the usual abstract linguistic introspections but actually looking up a definition in a dictionary: the concreteness of this image (however "unlikely" the event) complicates our ability to make a generic or gender-neutral interpretation. In the third example, *he* refers to an unambiguously abstract antecedent. But the problem it raises is even more fundamental. The convention of the abstract "inter-preter" presupposes a view of literature in which encounters be-tween texts and human consciousness operate according to universal rules of perception, deduction, and so on. The use of the male pronoun as generic not only reinforces the common identification of men with intellect but also suggests male interpretation as the gold standard of universal thought. The final example makes ex-plicit the assumption that "the speaking figure . . . is not a person anymore" but rather a "locutory locus" through which words flow. But this intensely abstract conception of language production is given lips and a mind, a jarring incongruity. In addition, the point of this conception is to dissociate the speaker from the spoken: although human beings speak and listen, believing that their lan-guage originates within them, they are in fact mere loci (like bodies inhabited by alien pods), conduits for the discourse of the age, which originates elsewhere. Here, then, there would seem little problem in presenting the human figure, real and concrete, as either male or female; the abstract linguistic function would pre-sumably not be impaired or compromised by the sex of its human shell. But some recasting of the passage may be necessary to achieve a smooth revision:

> One may conclude that the speaking figure becomes a simple ref-erential element and is disconnected from the discourse, which is supposed to come from the lips and mind. He or she is seen no longer as a person but as a locus—we would like to call it a locutory locus. . . . Though the words flow through the speaker's lips, the speaker is not truly speaking or implicated in them; indeed, the words do not represent the individual speaker but a higher degree of knowledge.

Or:

> One may conclude that individual speaking figures become simple referential elements, disconnected from the discourse supposed to come from their lips and minds. The speaking figure is not a person anymore but must be seen as a locus. . . .

In her 1978 book *The Resisting Reader*, Judith Fetterley eloquently challenges the conventional notion "that literature speaks universal truths through forms from which all the merely personal, the purely subjective, has been burned away. . . ." This pretense, she argues, helps keep "the design of our literature unavailable to the consciousness of the woman reader. . . ." If such a reader is to retain her own reality, she must resist the false universality these texts offer and become a "resisting reader" (xi). Notions of universality are socially and historically constructed, often promoting the interests of some groups over others; but as the construction process fades from view, its legacy of universality comes to seem natural. As Belsey points out, the tensions over androcentric language arise from the feminist challenge to the "naturalness" of using male-marked linguistic forms to refer to males and females (42–43). The sexist language controversy illuminates its own ideological underpinnings.

Accordingly, as more and more women become vocal readers, writers, interpreters, and translators, the "generic" *he* comes to seem increasingly inappropriate. Its incongruity is a second major reason for avoiding the usage. Consider, for example, this opening sentence from the review of a novel:

> A novelist's vice usually resembles his virtue, for what he does best he also tends to do to excess.   (*New York Times Book Review* 1981)

"The novelist's" virtues and vices are detailed for several lines, followed by two paragraphs referring to Hardy and Dickens; then readers learn that the novelist being reviewed is Toni Morrison. It is no longer a semantic surprise that women write; grammar should no longer mark them as exceptions.

Another example of incongruity, provided by Miller and Swift (*Handbook* 49), comes from an article about a forum on southern writing that featured the speakers Eudora Welty and Robert Penn Warren:

> Each author also presented an evening of readings from his own works.

Here the antecedent *each author* has dictated the use of a singular male pronoun to serve both sexes. This makes even less sense than "generic" usage, because, as Sally McConnell-Ginet has noted, *he* is virtually always coded as sex-specific when its antecedent is a particular individual ("Linguistics" 8). Such sentences intensify the sense of incongruity.

In the following passage from a *New Yorker* profile of Chris Evert, the author shifts from a sex-specific pronoun for a particular female tennis player to a generic pronoun for "a top-class player," with the sex of the specific individual dictating the sex of the generic:

> Some friends of mine used to wonder how she [Chris Evert] could concentrate so long on staring the ball into her racquet and manage at the same time to watch where her opponent was moving. They finally agreed that a top-class player can tell from an opponent's first few steps after she hits the ball what she will be doing, and they came to believe that there is also a kind of instinctive sense, which operates even when a player's mind is fixed on the ball and which informs her where her opponent is. (*New Yorker* 1986)

This usage avoids the sense of incongruity noted in the Toni Morrison example but seems to limit the reference to top-class women players, just as a story about Jimmy Connors that referred to a top-class player as *he* might seem to refer only to men. If the author does not intend such specificity, a recasting of the passage is indicated. But it must be done with care. Here a simple shift to the plural produces other flaws:

> They finally agreed that top-class players can tell what opponents will be doing from their first few steps after they hit the ball: they also came to believe that a kind of instinctive sense informs players of an opponent's whereabouts and operates even when their mind is fixed on the ball.

Note the confusion created by the three potential antecedents of *they* (*my friends, top-class players, opponents*). Note also that, while *their first few steps* easily replaces *her first few steps*, *their mind is fixed on the ball* is a bit awkward. Because the wording is figurative, one could perhaps justify linking plural *their* with singular *mind* in this context, but in other examples a singular noun would be clearly unacceptable:

> Their nose was burned in the noonday sun.

> Their mind was all awhirl.

In shifting to the plural, then, one has to make sure not only that there is no ambiguity about the antecedent of the newly introduced *they* or *their* or *them* but that the shift to the plural pronoun does not entail other shifts that raise additional editorial problems. In this passage an alternative solution is clearly in order:

They finally agreed that the first few steps an opponent takes after hitting the ball can tell a top-class player what movement to expect in the opposite court. They also came to believe that even when the player's mind is fixed on the ball, a kind of instinctive sense registers the opponent's whereabouts.

In the next example, conversely, male pronouns highlight the incongruities of traditional assumptions. In a 1971 review of Kate Millett's *Sexual Politics* for a feminist journal, the author uses pronouns to suggest that Millett's intended audience is the male "reader" but that the book challenges the link between *the reader* and *he*:

> Millett never suggests that hers is a sufficient analysis of any of the works she discusses. Her aim is to wrench the reader from the vantage point he has long occupied, and force him to look at life and letters from a new coign. (*Aphra* 1971)

Readers and writers are not the only participants in academic life who have been considered "generically" male. For many decades, such nouns as *candidate, administrator, student,* and *professor* have also conventionally called for masculine pronouns:

> In a student's major field, where there is greatest need for specialization, he might be expected to take such noncourse courses. . . . (*Profession 78*)

A teacher at a college or university, though not at a high school or grade school, is also treated as male:

> The English teacher is asked to publish critical studies of Chidiock Tichbone that earn the approval of his peers. . . . (*Profession 78*)

As a result of social changes and institutional as well as disciplinary pressures (such as affirmative-action guidelines for the preparation of job descriptions), pronoun usage is in flux and may be inconsistent, even in print. These examples, both from the same page of *Profession 78*, reflect an intermediate stage in which "generic" *he* coexists with gender-neutral usage:

> Many of us still see him or her as the traditional student of the sixties. . . .

> I tried to describe the background which a freshman student was likely to bring to his English class.

Some authors may initially use *he or she* to establish their gender-inclusive intention and subsequently shift to "generic" *he* for convenience. But even this practice may seem to reflect sloppiness (just as inconsistent spellings would) rather than sensitivity toward sexism. The following passage, describing procedures used to compile dictionary entries, exemplifies a mixture of usages that is not entirely successful:

> We allocated the contributor in question a certain number of words . . . and provided him or her with a detailed "briefing." . . . Within certain limits, however, the contributor was free to decide how the material could most effectively be organized; whether, for example, if he had been given 100 terms and 10,000 words, to write 100 entries of 100 words each [or 10 entries of 1,000 words each]. . . . In every respect, indeed, contributors have been allowed the maximum freedom. . . .   (*Dictionary of Modern Thought* 1977)

When *he* is retained as a generic but used in alternation with gender-neutral generic forms, the writer's motives are often unclear. Here is another example:

> Every case of inquiry in the human and cultural disciplines, of which semiotics is a part, involves the practical accomplishments of an observer artfully engaging in the embodied objective practices of his or her discipline.
>   The semiotician produces the history and the meaning he wishes to found his historical semiotics on.   (*Semiotica* 1985)

The author may have intended to introduce an *observer* as a gender-neutral term by using *his or her*, so that thereafter *he* and *his* would be understood generically. But because the pronominal reference to *he* occurs in a new paragraph with a new antecedent—*the semiotician* instead of *an observer*—the reader may be puzzled: are *an observer* and *the semiotician* different, and if so are observers both male and female while semioticians are only male? Or is the variation "just" sloppy writing?

When a passage uses different forms to refer to persons of unknown sex, it is important to edit carefully to avoid unconscious or accidental stereotyping. For example, a lengthy booklet prepared by the housing division at a midwestern university refers to "the student" as *he* throughout, except in contexts like the following: "Should the student change her mind, she must petition for a new room prior to the second week of the term." The statement was probably not meant to imply that women students can't make up their minds, but it nonetheless had that effect.

A third reason to avoid using *he* as a generic pronoun is that it often creates or compounds ambiguity. Even sex-specific pronouns may be ambiguous, of course, in certain sentences: In "Superman said that when he saw Lois she was leaving," we infer that *she* does not refer to Superman; but in "Superman said that when he saw Martin he was leaving," we do not know whether *he* refers to Superman or to Martin. When "generic" *he* is used, ambiguity multiplies. Here is an example:

> The depressed person often becomes aware of strong feelings of self-dislike; he feels worthless and guilty about his shortcomings. He believes that nothing he can do will alleviate his conditions. . . . Crying spells may set in, the person loses weight, finds himself unable to go to sleep. . . . Food no longer tastes good, sex is not arousing, and people, even his wife and children, become wholly uninteresting. (Psychology textbook 1975)

This passage appears to begin with a generic use of *he*, referring to the gender-neutral *depressed person.* But when *his wife and children* appears in the last line, the pronoun must be reinterpreted as masculine. The question is, What *is* the antecedent meant to be? Is this passage intended to apply to men only? Perhaps only to married men with children? Or would it hold for depressed persons of either sex, married or single? The generic raises special problems of this sort in scholarly scientific writing. Herbert Posner, an epidemiologist, argues that the ambiguity of masculine generic language makes it scientifically unacceptable; it should not be retained simply because it is conventional in scientific and medical journals. Recommending that scientists clarify the terms of their analysis, Posner urges that "generic" usages be discontinued in favor of the "unambiguous reporting of the sex of human beings" (175).

For all these reasons, then—injustice, incongruity, and ambiguity —it makes sense to avoid the false generic use of the male singular personal pronoun. What are the alternatives?

Alternatives

The following sentence illustrates a traditional "generic" use of *he*:

> The assistant professor should understand the tenure process before he goes through it.

This statement is generic in two senses. *The assistant professor* is intended to represent assistant professors as a class ("The assistant professor is a faculty member with probationary status"), and the statement as a whole, expressing a general rule, is semantically "lawlike" (see Dahl 99; Allan 2: 134–42). Not all alternative statements are equally effective in preserving meaning, and some are stylistically superior to others. The following list includes possibilities to be considered as well as some to be avoided.

1. Recast the sentence in the plural

Changing singular noun phrases and pronouns to plurals is often the most painless way to avoid male "generic" pronouns in everyday writing:

> Assistant professors should understand the tenure process before they go through it.

This version preserves the lawlike quality of the original statement. But the plural can be a problem if one intends to emphasize the rights and responsibilities of the individual:

> A faculty member will be given access only to specified portions of his file.

Solutions may require minor changes in the wording of the original:

> Faculty members will be given access only to specified portions of their own files.

> Assistant professors should understand the tenure process they will each go through.

> Assistant professors should determine the unique requirements of their individual departments as they prepare for tenure.

The last example illustrates a problem with recasting in the plural that we noted above, the introduction of ambiguity when a sentence contains more than one plural noun. The problem would be compounded if the sentence read as follows:

> Assistant professors should get to know the senior faculty members of their departments as they prepare for tenure.

Reordering offers one solution:

> As they prepare for tenure, assistant professors should get to know the senior faculty members of their departments.

Deleting the pronominal clause would also suffice:

> Assistant professors preparing for tenure should get to know the senior faculty members of their departments.

The following example, where the "offending" masculine pronouns occur in a relative clause, requires a somewhat different solution:

> *singular*: A faculty member who spends all his time with his colleagues may find he can only talk shop.

> *plural* that avoids *he* but introduces ambiguity: Faculty members who spend all their time with their colleagues may find they can only talk shop.

> *plural* with deletion of ambiguous *they*: Faculty members who spend all their time with their colleagues may only be able to talk shop.

a. In most written contexts, avoid *they* with a singular antecedent

Because the use of *they* with a singular antecedent is widely condemned within the scholarly community, we do not advocate its use in writing. Many alternatives to generic *he* are available that do not offend traditionalists. Just as the goal of precision in writing calls for rejecting the use of *he* to refer to an antecedent that may be female, it precludes the use of *they* to refer to a person of unspecified sex:

> An assistant professor needs to learn about tenure if they want to succeed.

The problem with *they* construed as singular is not merely that the usage offends some readers; it is also that such a construction may make the antecedent of the pronoun ambiguous:

> The assistant professor who repeatedly loses tenure battles may conclude they are worthless [*they* = *assistant professor*? or *tenure battles*?].

b. Take care in using singular *they* colloquially

In informal speech, many people are comfortable using *they* with a singular antecedent, particularly with a sex-indefinite pronoun like *nobody* or *everybody*. For such speakers, constructions like the following make intuitive sense:

> Everyone should introduce themselves to their colleagues.
>
> Anyone can dress as they please.
>
> Nobody dared voice their real thoughts.

And sometimes this structure finds its way into print:

> Everyone else is, in an introductory text of this sort, to be absolved to their own temporary good fortune.   (Textbook 1978)

So do ludicrous instances of "correct" usage, like this example from an article submitted to *Ms.* magazine's "No Comment" column:

> If anyone believes that "the Safe Period does not work for everybody," he can be assured that the Ovulation Method will give him the certainty he seeks and which he was unable to find in the Rhythm Method. . . .

The controversy over singular *they*, as we have noted, reflects both the persistence of a once widely accepted tradition that prescriptive grammarians have banished from formal written English during the last two centuries and an ongoing tension between spoken and written language conventions. Starting from the premise that prescriptive *he* is inadequate and that changes are in order, MacKay discusses the possibility of developing prescriptions for singular *they*. He concludes that "singular *they* may well expand under increasing political pressure to use alternatives to prescriptive *he*, but the present findings suggest some fundamental limits to such expansion in formal contexts" (364). More likely to succeed are "context-restricted prescriptions," whereby *they* would refer to indefinite pronouns and corporate nouns (such as names of cities), and "multiple-choice prescriptions," allowing a variety of solutions, depending on the context (365). In some settings, where *between he and I* and comparable acts of linguistic violence are committed hourly, the use of *they* with a singular antecedent may not even be noticed.

2. Shift the person of the pronoun to the first person (*I* or *we*) or to the second person (*you*)

Sometimes it is appropriate to shift to the first person to avoid pseudogeneric *he*. For example, the sentence

> An associate professor should help his junior colleagues understand the tenure process.

could be revised to read:

> As associate professors, we should help our junior colleagues understand the tenure process.

or

> As an associate professor, I try to help my junior colleagues understand the tenure process.

Sometimes, it is possible to shift to a second-person generic *you*. A sentence like

> The student should return his or her examination to the instructor's mailbox by noon Wednesday.

is less awkwardly rendered as an imperative (with *you* as the understood subject):

> Return your examinations to your instructor's mailbox by noon Wednesday.

Though some may not feel comfortable using generic *you* in scholarly writing, this usage does work for others. In this example the essay writer, a feminist scholar, addresses her readers somewhat conversationally:

> You can determine [the different influence of the two authors] by comparing the number of printings of Ware's book (1) with the number of printings of Firestone's (9). . . . (*Communication* 1985)

Although *you* is too familiar a form to use in many contexts, in a publication like a "survival handbook" for beginning faculty members, the second person may be appropriate:

> As an assistant professor, you should understand the tenure process before you go through it.

And reflexives are less cumbersome with the second person:

> As an assistant professor, you should find out for yourself the requirements for tenure.

3. Use *he or she* or *she or he*, but avoid repeating such phrases

" 'He' deserves to live out its days doing what it has always done best," argues the psychologist Wendy Martyna, "referring to 'he' and not 'she' " (qtd. in Miller and Swift, *Handbook* 47). As Francine Frank observes in her essay in this volume, proposals for an epicene pronoun (one with a single form for either sex) have a long history in linguistic scholarship and usage criticism. Dennis Baron summarizes them chronologically (*Grammar and Gender* 190–216); significantly, however, his chapter on the 150-year search for a word to replace the masculine pronoun is called "The Word That Failed." Alternatives that have had some limited success are *he or she* and its variants.

He or she is often substituted for *he* in reference to someone of unspecified sex:

> The assistant professor should understand the tenure process before he or she goes through it.

Many writers and editors would prefer using the plural in a sentence like this. But when it is important to preserve the focus on the individual, then *he or she* is certainly acceptable:

> Every reader responds to this scene in his or her own way.

This strategy, which is now common in scholarly writing, need not be unduly cumbersome or obtrusive:

> The analyst is part of the history he or she writes.   (*Semiotica* 1985)

In the following sentence, however, with its somewhat complicated syntax, the use of *his or her*, while not causing misunderstanding, may nevertheless contribute to it:

> The [Indo-European] lexicologist or historical anthropologist with a kinship specialty will fail to confront Szemerényi's opus only at some jeopardy to his or her scholarly accountability.   (*Language* 1980)

In this example, the use of *his* alone might be more ambiguous, because the antecedent might momentarily seem to be Szemerényi rather than the lexicologist. Although *his or her* is less likely to be misunderstood in this way, since Szemerényi's sex is known, it is still theoretically possible to misread *his* as referring to Szemerényi and *her* as a generic pronoun referring to the lexicologist. In such contexts, the use of alternative pronouns may require simplifying the passage:

> Szemerényi's opus is crucial to our understanding of Indo-European kinship; any lexicologist or historical anthropologist who ignores it jeopardizes his or her scholarly accountability.

While the occasional use of *he or she* is generally accepted, its repeated appearance on a page is almost always objectionable. The following revision of the above example is no improvement:

> If the Indo-European lexicologist or historical anthropologist with a kinship specialty wishes to keep himself or herself up to date, he or she will fail to confront Szemerényi's opus only at some jeopardy to his or her scholarly accountability.

In the following example, the pronouns seem to be mechanically generated:

> Satisfaction with relationships is dependent upon the manager's style of communication, his or her personal attributes, and his or her managerial competence.   (Author's abstract in a *Women and Language* bibliography 1984)

It is often possible to delete such repetitions:

> Satisfaction with relationships is dependent upon the manager's style of communication, personal attributes, and managerial competence.

A feminist scholar, however, might wish to retain one set of alternative pronouns, even at the expense of efficiency, precisely to emphasize the presence of women in a field from which they have been excluded:

> Satisfaction with relationships depends on the manager—his or her style of communication, personal attributes, and managerial competence.

Nonsexist usage may function to call attention to, and therefore challenge, the apparently seamless operation of linguistic and social custom. Those who wish to achieve this goal can do so by slightly varying accepted patterns—for example, by using *she or he* instead of *he and she*:

> The truly great mathematician does not despair when she or he is not understood.

The repeated use of *he or she* or *she or he* in a longer passage is obviously intolerable:

> The assistant professor should understand the tenure process before he or she goes through it. He or she should obtain a summary of written criteria and procedures from his or her department head. He or she may also find it useful to talk with a well-informed and trusted senior faculty member in his or her own department. He or she may want to share experiences with other assistant professors in his or her own department and elsewhere in the university. The point is that he or she should take active steps to educate himself or herself about the official tenure process before he or she goes through it.

Such passages can easily be corrected by shifting to plural nouns and pronouns or by recasting in the first or second person. We provide a more sophisticated revision below, under solution 11.

4. Alternate masculine and feminine pronouns in appropriate contexts

Alternating gender pronouns, if done carefully, is occasionally an effective solution to the sexist language problem. Recent revisions of Spock's baby-care manual use masculine and feminine pronouns in alternate chapters, as the preface explicitly notes. And while not recommended for written English, the following usage by a male keynote speaker was an effective rhetorical device at a 1979 medical conference:

> When you are selecting an outside curriculum consultant to evaluate your medical school's curriculum, you need to ask some fairly obvious questions: Is he an expert? Is she an M.D.?

Here the alternation is designed to emphasize that women as well as men are qualified to be hired as consultants. But if care is not taken and such usage appears to be random, the reader will miss the point, and the text may accidentally display sex-stereotyped usages. McConnell-Ginet describes listening to a lecture on good teaching in which the speaker used *he* with sex-indefinite referents like *the good student* and *a conscientious professor*. The pronoun seemed intended as generic until the speaker said, "When a student finally gathers courage to ask a question, don't intimidate her." McConnell-Ginet remarks that though the speaker might not have consciously wished to express gender stereotypes, they were nevertheless evident in this pattern of language use. ("Feminism" 169)

5. Avoid alternative-gender forms requiring slashes or parentheses

The alternatives to generic *he* cited in Clarence L. Barnhart's 1980 *Dictionary of New English* include *s/he*, *he/she*, *him/her*, and *his/her* (Cannon and Robertson 25–26). Other alternatives are *(s)he* and *he(she)*. Barnhart's usage data suggest that *s/he* is not widely accepted: it does not have a clear counterpart in the spoken language, and it does not yield parallel possessive and objective cases as *he/she* does. The use of parentheses, as in *he(she)*, brackets women as a kind of afterthought. All such forms are difficult to pronounce and awkward in the possessive. Writers of administrative manuals or other quasi-official documents may give priority to achieving accurate and legally inclusive language and devote little consideration to style. But even in such contexts passages like this one are no pleasure to read:

> The assistant professor should understand the tenure process before s/he goes through it. S/he should obtain a summary of written criteria and procedures from her/his department head. S/he may also find it useful to talk with a well-informed and trusted senior faculty mem-

ber in her/his own department and with other assistant professors in her/his own department and elsewhere in the university. The point is that s/he should take active steps to educate her/himself well before the official tenure process begins.

We recommend avoiding such uses of slashes and parentheses. They cloud the issue, obscuring the complex relations between pronouns and antecedents that need to be thought through. While they may look like a quick "gender-neutral" cure for sexist language, they not only prove ineffective but discourage the writer from seeking better alternatives. Are there circumstances in which *he or she* (or *she or he*) would not be as appropriate or useful as *s/he*? A federal unit (say, the army), directed to recast all its official documents in gender-neutral language but given no budget to do so, might decide that the best way out was to insert an *s/* manually before every *he* until the texts could be reprinted. But in ordinary circumstances, any context where *s/he* is appropriate is likely to be equally hospitable to *she or he*. According to Barnhart, *he or she*— and again we would add *she or he*—has become the most common and readily accepted replacement for *he*.

6. Use "generic" *she* in special circumstances

She has traditionally been used primarily in contexts where the antecedent is clearly female.

> The turn-of-the-century Mount Holyoke student knew she wanted an education.

> The professional female athlete of today assumes she will be treated professionally.

The choice of a feminine pronoun in such sentences seems clear-cut. Yet the following statement, made by a New York State legislator during an abortion debate and cited in the feminist literature (e.g., Kett and Underwood 18), uses a masculine generic:

> Everyone should be able to decide for himself whether or not to have an abortion.

As we have noted, what seems to be generic usage is often an expression of cultural gender, that is, cultural expectations embodied in linguistic form:

> The teacher who trains her students to read well will be rewarded in heaven.

Presumably cultural gender also dictates the pronoun in the following sentence:

> An autobiography coming into a library would be classified as nonfiction if the librarian believed the author, and as fiction if she thought he was lying. (University press book 1957)

Here the librarian is assumed to be female and the author is assumed to be male. Whether or not this usage reflects cultural gender, one might argue that it efficiently differentiates the two different antecedents in the sentence (using *he or she* for both would, of course, create ambiguity). But the writer could accomplish the same task and break with prevailing gender stereotypes:

> An autobiography coming into a library would be classified as nonfiction if the librarian believed the author, and as fiction if he thought she was lying.

Yet this sentence seems to reflect another set of stereotypes: that women lie and men make judgments. It seems best to avoid "generic" pronouns altogether. The sentence can make its point without referring to the librarian or the author:

> An autobiography coming into a library would be classified as nonfiction if it was perceived to be true and as fiction if it was perceived to be a lie.

But since many stylists advise avoiding the passive voice in most contexts (see 11a below), the following alternative might seem preferable:

> When an autobiography comes into the library, the librarian classifies it as nonfiction or fiction, depending on whether or not the author seems to be telling the truth.

Some writers use generic *she* politically, to challenge the convention of generic *he*:

> The assistant professor should understand the tenure process before she goes through it.

This device may be effective when it clearly contests cultural gender expectations (though, as we note below, it should be used with caution). The linguist Sally McConnell-Ginet often uses the pronoun *she* with such antecedents as *the linguist* and *the speaker*. In her essay in this volume, for example, she describes the crucial feature of H. P. Grice's account of communication, that meaning depends not just on the speaker's intention but on the social relationship between the speaker and the hearer:

> Grice's way of putting it goes something like this: in saying *A*, a speaker means to express the thought *B* if the speaker intends to produce in her hearer a recognition of thought *B* by virtue of his recognizing that she is trying to produce that recognition in him by saying *A*.

As she notes in her essay, McConnell-Ginet is following other authors in using both *she* and *he* as "generic"; at the same time, by linking *she* to the speaker and *he* to the hearer, she prepares the way for her discussion of such a conversational situation later in the essay. She has defended this usage to journal editors on the grounds that her central concern is language and gender and, specifically, questions of meaning and interpretation when gender comes into play. In the example just given, she is discussing what happens to what women mean in a male-oriented linguistic community where their listeners are men. Elsewhere, McConnell-Ginet uses *she* generically, to reinforce the necessity of including both sexes in linguistic analysis:

> The shift is from a focus on the individual speaker/hearer, who possesses a particular (socio)linguistic identity, to her social relationships and interactions with others as those are realized in language use. ("Linguistics" 17)

The argument that such usage is generic usually rests on three assertions: (1) that if *he* can be intended to include women, *she* can just as easily be intended to include men; (2) that in fields and traditions of discourse where *he* has been virtually universal, men are already and inevitably "understood" to be present; and (3) that a particular rhetorical or persuasive point can be made with generic *she*. The first assertion may be appropriate as a political position, but it does not justify the use of generic *she* in nonsexist scholarly or professional writing. Clearly one cannot argue that *he* is unacceptable as a generic, whatever the writer's intention, and then condone generic *she* in analogous contexts. The second assertion seems to us a more plausible basis for a female generic, so long as it is seen as a historically and contextually bound device—that is, as serving at the moment to redress a tradition of omission. The third, which is essentially McConnell-Ginet's strategy, may be effective for writers willing and able to articulate their intentions. But while this usage of *she* may be warranted in special circumstances, some readers interpret it not as generic but as sexist (or "reverse-sexist"), and we do not recommend it.

In the following example, a different author links pronoun choice and real-world statistics:

> Throughout this book I refer to teachers, researchers and other professionals as "she" unless the context is masculine. As the teaching profession is overwhelmingly female and I am a female researcher it seems a perverse form of false consciousness to use "he" except where absolutely necessary.   (Book on classroom interaction 1976)

Although this decision challenges the convention of generic *he*, such usage may reinforce cultural gender expectations. The author uses statistics—semireferential gender—to justify her departure from the conventional usage of the male generic; while there may be strategic reasons for using the pronoun *she*, the grounds advanced here are questionable. Because pronoun usage constructs and reinforces as well as reflects reality, the statistical dominance of men or women in a profession does not in itself warrant a stereotypical pronoun choice.

One makes linguistic choices in a social and institutional context, and in that context the choices themselves may make statements. Some writers use pronouns deliberately to undermine the statistics of a profession. Others choose pronouns that reflect their own sex. But these choices may carry different and indeed conflicting connotations for writer and reader. In a paper submitted to a male philosophy instructor a female graduate student used the pronoun *she* throughout with the antecedent *the philosopher*. Because *she* has no established generic status in the academic world at large, the instructor found it "distracting" to read; he gave her a B with the option of revising and resubmitting the paper for a more "careful" reading. For him, we presume, the pronoun *she* simply did not work as a generic and registered as a usage equivalent to *ain't*; further, he may have concluded that the student was more committed to politics than to philosophy. But the student's intentions were different. She wished to emphasize that *he* did not function for her as a generic and that she thus felt excluded by much philosophical writing; instead of using *he or she* or a plural, however, she chose a form that would subvert *he* and at the same time mark her own inclusion within this professional field. She decided not to revise the paper; and when final papers were submitted at the end of the term, a number of students used *the philosopher . . . she*.

This incident suggests another feature of the politics of language change: when one wishes to engage in linguistic innovation, it is sometimes prudent to do so as part of a collective action; because innovation takes place within a context of established institutional practices, the decision to challenge them may incur penalties. Individual writers who depart from traditional stylistic conventions may consequently discover, for example, that publishers will reject their manuscripts. In making decisions about usage, one may attend to this reality or ignore it, but it is a reality nonetheless.

7. Edit out the personal pronoun

One can sometimes eliminate a troublesome personal pronoun by restructuring the sentence with an adjective or noun clause introduced by a gender-neutral relative or indefinite pronoun. For example, the sentence

> The assistant professor will be ahead of the game if he learns about the tenure process before he goes through it.

can be revised to read

> The assistant professor who learns about the tenure process in advance will be ahead of the game.

Another possibility is

> Whoever seeks tenure should learn about the process before going through it.

The following revisions recast the sentence to eliminate the personal pronoun without introducing a subordinate clause:

> An assistant professor should learn about the tenure process before going through it.

> The assistant professor should learn about the tenure process well in advance.

When a long passage is rewritten to expunge all problematic pronouns, however, it may sound strangely mechanistic and disembodied. Here, as elsewhere, the choice of the appropriate nonsexist alternative requires care and awareness of style.

8. Use *one*

Carolyn G. Heilbrun opened her 1984 MLA presidential address as follows:

> One—that wonderfully neuter, transcendent, hegemonic one—always begins a presidential address by referring to past presidents.   (281)

In some contexts, *one* can be used as a gender-neutral alternative to the false generic *he*:

> As an assistant professor, one should learn about the tenure process before one goes through it.

> One should learn about the tenure process before going through it.

One is more common in British usage, where it is often used nongenerically to refer to oneself as the speaker or writer:

> One feels a real need here for political analysis of the tenure process.

9. Avoid revisions that distort the original meaning

When revising another's work to eliminate a pseudogeneric *he*, take care to preserve the author's meaning. In the following example, taken from a 1986 set of nonsexist guidelines, the recommended change fails to do so:

> *Condemned usage*: The professor who gets published frequently will have a better chance when he goes before the tenure board.

Recommended usage: The professor who gets published frequently will have a better chance when faculty tenure is granted.

The following revision retains the sense of the original:

The professor who frequently gets published will have a better chance before the tenure board.

In the next example (one introduced earlier) eliminating the male generics without distorting meaning is more complicated:

The depressed person often becomes aware of strong feelings of self-dislike; he feels worthless and guilty about his shortcomings. He believes that nothing he can do will alleviate his condition. . . . Crying spells may set in, the person loses weight, finds himself unable to go to sleep. . . . Food no longer tastes good, sex is not arousing, and people, even his wife and children, become wholly uninteresting.   (Psychology text 1975)

One solution here is to recast the paragraph in the plural, changing *wife* to *spouses*. But the result seems odd:

Depressed people often become aware of strong feelings of self-dislike; they feel worthless and guilty about their shortcomings. They believe that nothing they can do will alleviate their condition. . . . Crying spells may set in, the people lose weight, find themselves unable to go to sleep. . . . Food no longer tastes good, sex is not arousing, and people, even their spouses and children, become wholly uninteresting.

People does not function as the plural of *person* in all contexts. Here the switch from *the person* to *the people* fails to convey the original meaning because the plural, when unmodified, has an indefinite or universal connotation. In addition, *spouse* still carries a more technical sense than *wife* or *husband* (cf. *sibling* in contrast to *brother* or *sister*). Preserving the sense of the original calls for further changes. But even when these changes are made, the passage is far from perfect. As we noted above, the correction of sexist usage often points toward other problems—here, for example, a lack of parallelism in the series. While our focus in this volume is limited to sexist usages, we might nevertheless emend this passage as follows:

> Depressed people often develop strong feelings of self-dislike, worth-
> lessness, and guilt. They believe nothing they can do will alleviate
> their condition. . . . They may experience crying spells, lose weight,
> and have trouble sleeping. . . . They no longer enjoy food, sex, or
> other people, not even members of their family.

Although recasting the passage eliminates the "sexist language,"
the underlying ambiguity, as discussed earlier, remains unresolved:
the male terminology of the original clouds the facts of depression
and creates a serious problem of interpretation. To clarify such
material, one must know what the original means. Is this description
valid for any depressed person, or does it apply only to men (or
perhaps only to married men)? While the context of the passage
might answer such questions, it might not affect the incongruity
of the sentences in question.

10. Preserve the flavor of the original

Nonsexist guidelines sometimes appear to emphasize content and
ignore style. One set of guidelines, for example, disapproves of the
following sexist piece of advice:

> Act like a lady and think like a man.

The guidelines advocate revising it to read as follows:

> Act and think sensitively and clearly.

The new version is really a replacement rather than a revision; it
paraphrases the content, sacrificing the original language. Paraphrasing is sometimes the best course, but it may also fall flat, like
the botched punch line of a joke. Here the original sentence is less
a serious piece of advice than a pithy and even an ironic motto—
a motto whose irony does not go unappreciated by the many women
who post the longer version in their offices:

> Look like a girl, act like a lady, think like a man, and work like a
> dog.

We would certainly argue that such stereotypical values do not serve
women well in the workplace; yet the self-conscious appropriation
and public posting of these clichéd expectations for "working women"

depend on the language itself and the punch line. The paraphrase, sounding more like Marmee's advice to the girls in *Little Women*, misses the point:

> Act and think youthfully, sensitively, and clearly, and work very hard.

Editing another's work involves a problem similar to that of translating across languages. One must attempt to grasp the author's intention and, as far as possible, convey the tone or flavor of the original while eliminating objectionable wording (and perhaps even improving the prose if it is flat or awkward). If this solution proves elusive, one may simply retain the original but use quotation marks or italics to mark the questionable or ironic wording. In an essay on speech-act theory, for example, Mary Louise Pratt discusses the notion of an authentic self that is fully realized through speech:

> It's all a matter, as Austin loved to say, of a man's [sic] word being his bond. (8)

Pratt chooses to retain the precise wording of the aphorism; the public-school code it invokes helps support her larger argument that the Ideal Speaker for speech-act theory is a British cricket-playing gentleman. Elsewhere in her essay Pratt uses quotation marks to highlight a problematic phrase:

> [O]ne is reminded of the recent press conference in which the rape and murder of four unarmed American nuns in El Salvador was described by Secretary of State Haig as an *"exchange* of fire." (13–14)

Quotation marks serve a similar purpose in the following example, where paraphrase would fail to capture the series of stereotypes that in the critic's view the character of Toni Morrison's Sula defies:

> For black audiences, [Sula] is not consciousness of the black race personified, nor "tragic mulatto," nor, for white ones, is she "mammie," "Negress," "coon," or "maid." (Spillers, "Hateful" 1984)

Cora Kaplan uses quotation marks to register her disapproval of an adjective others have used:

> [Women's literary texts] express the politically "retrograde" desires for comfort, dependence and love. . . . (155)

Preserving the flavor or style of the original is often a problem in editing literary writing, as in the following example:

> Nobody who remembers his Kierkegaard will have the slightest difficulty comprehending these goings-on.   (*Atlantic Monthly* 1980)

Some types of revision we have already mentioned would remove the male pronoun while adequately paraphrasing the content of this sentence:

> *Shift to plural*: Readers who remember their Kierkegaard will not have the slightest difficulty comprehending these goings-on.

> *Omit the pronoun*: Nobody who remembers Kierkegaard's work will have the slightest difficulty comprehending these goings-on.

> *Shift person*: Those of us who remember our Kierkegaard will not have the slightest difficulty comprehending these goings-on.

But an effort to preserve the idiomatic flavor of the original may call for a more creative approach:

> No Kierkegaard devotee will have the slightest difficulty comprehending these goings-on.

In the following example, the male pronoun is used ironically to emphasize the maleness of a conference program on sociobiology to which only one female speaker had been invited:

> Each speaker seemed especially anxious to have his version of the history of science adopted, so that the legitimate lineage could be established. (The one woman who was invited . . . was assigned the task of discussing sociobiological implications for philosophy of mind! . . .)   (*Signs* 1981)

Though traditionally the *his* in this passage would be interpreted as "generic," the author's sex-specific usage emphasizes that the masculine possessive does not apply to women and is therefore *not* gender-neutral; the sentence duplicates and thus unmasks what the author views as sociobiology's male-centeredness and ideological presumption of male dominance. The specific "real-world" reference she adds indicates that there was actually only one female speaker. The use of *he or she* in this instance would have disguised that imbalance. This example also shows that restoring a purely sex-specific meaning to *he* may lead to greater effectiveness and clarity of style.

11. Avoid introducing stylistic flaws

Using nonsexist language does not require the suspension of normal critical faculties. Earlier, to illustrate the excessive use of alternative gender combinations, we quoted a passage that mechanically reproduces gender-neutral linguistic forms with little attention to good sense. The following revision preserves nonsexist language but avoids needless words by eliminating pronouns and making minor changes in structure:

> Before going through the tenure process, the assistant professor should understand what it involves. It may be useful to obtain a summary of the department's written criteria and procedures from the head, to consult a well-informed and trusted senior colleague, and to talk with other assistant professors within and outside the department. The point is that one should prepare for the tenure review far in advance.

Editorial efforts to clean up sexist usage *and* to reduce the clumsiness of repeated gender-neutral expressions often result in better writing.

a. Take care in shifting to the passive voice

One common way to avoid a pseudogeneric *he* is to recast the sentence in the passive voice, but like the use of *he or she*, this strategy can produce less than felicitous results:

> The tenure process should be understood well before the assistant professor goes through it.

> Well before the tenure process begins, it should be understood by the assistant professor.

Often wordy and awkward, passive constructions also tend to remove a clear sense of voice and presence. Style guides invariably recommend the active voice as more forceful and direct and describe only a few circumstances that warrant the passive. In general, then, we do not suggest using the passive voice to achieve nonsexist language if a more concise and graceful solution is available, as there usually is:

> Assistant professors should understand the tenure process long before they go through it.

> Well before the tenure process begins, the assistant professor should know what it involves.

b. Avoid needless reflexives

Reflexive pronouns add complexity to writing; the struggle to make them gender-inclusive can ruin a sentence. This example is from an article about New York City yuppies who, having grown up on TV dinners, now seek real American home cooking:

> The yuppie, in the insecurity that's the flip side of dull arrogance, will darkly conjure up someone else, someone better, someone born of a real mom who baked real strawberry-rhubarb pie, and wonder why he himself or her herself was cheated. (*Village Voice* 1985)

With the grammar corrected, the problematic clause would read:

> The yuppie . . . will . . . wonder why he himself or she herself was cheated.

The error would probably not have occurred without the reflexives ("why he or her was cheated" is unlikely), but even the grammatical version of the sentence is awkward. One alternative is to avoid reflexives:

> In the insecurity that's the flip side of dull arrogance, the yuppie will darkly conjure up someone else . . . and will feel cheated.

Similarly, the sentence

> An assistant professor should educate himself about the tenure process before going through it.

could be rewritten as

> An assistant professor should study the tenure process before going through it.

12. Avoid needless correction of appropriately used sex-specific pronouns

In reference to specific individuals, *he* in English is unambiguously marked for males and *she* for females; therefore, the sex-specific use of gendered pronouns is appropriate and natural. Hesitating over sex-specific usage may signal hypercorrection or confusion about what a given individual's sex is, as in the transsexual example cited earlier. In the late 1970s one academic department instituted a "gender-neutral" policy for letters of recommendation for graduate students: as notes accompanying the letters explained, the writers were asked to use initials instead of a student's first name and to use the masculine pronoun for subsequent references. But faculty members obviously, and understandably, found it difficult to refer to a woman as *he*, and many a letter went out with an obtruding *s* clearly visible under the correcting fluid (McConnell-Ginet, "Linguistics" 8).

Hypercorrection involves overgeneralizing a usage rule to cover instances where it is inappropriate. Often occurring during periods of linguistic transition and competition, it is currently a common phenomenon in pronoun usage. Recommending a shift from the male pronoun *he* to a plural, for example, one published set of guidelines offers the following example of bad and improved sentences:

Condemned usage: He is expanding his operation.

Recommended usage: They are expanding their operation.

Do the two sentences have the same meaning? On the face of it, the statement seems to be about a specific individual's actions:

Dean William Marmaduke is doing so well that he is expanding his operation.

In this context the plural would make no sense and indeed would be incorrect as it is in the following sentence:

Dean William Marmaduke has done so well that they are expanding their operation [presuming that they = Marmaduke].

Here, pronoun reference to a particular individual, properly sex-specific, is treated like a generic and wrongly "corrected." Third-person pronouns change in number and gender to match their antecedents:

> The dean is expanding his empire.
>
> The dean is expanding her empire.
>
> The college administration is expanding its empire.
>
> The college administrators are expanding their empire.

Of course, some sentences in which third-person pronouns and their antecedents agree in number and gender are nonetheless problematic. In the following example, a sex-specific usage of the feminine pronoun occurs with the antecedent *chairman*:

> A chairman of twenty years told me that I was the first one in fifteen years to come to her campus to talk to her. (*Profession 78*)

We discuss problems associated with *chairman* and related words at greater length in a later section. The point here is that the cultural gender acquired by some nouns may have diverse linguistic consequences. As the last citation shows, not all speakers code *chairman* as male, so that constructions like *chairman . . . she* do not strike everyone as incongruous. Yet a female judge told the *New York Times* in 1984 that she was addressed as "Sir" at least once a day: "for many people, the combination of *Judge* with *female* simply doesn't compute" (Loftus; and see Copleman).

Sex-specific usage does not invariably depend on the absolute knowledge of genuine "reality." Kessler and McKenna explain that, in writing about transsexuals, they use pronouns to accord with the gender impression conveyed by each individual:

> Throughout this book, the gender pronoun we use for an informant (whether the informant is a professional, an "everyday" person, a transsexual, or anything else) refers to the attribution that we made in interacting with the person. (19)

Gender-specific pronouns are objectionable, of course, only when they are meant to apply to both sexes, as in this "lawlike" sentence:

> When a dean expands his operation, he expands his ambition as well.

In such contexts, as we have noted, one can preserve the generic meaning in a nonsexist form by recasting the sentence in the plural:

> When deans expand their operations, they expand their ambitions as well.

13. Avoid incongruity and inconsistent correction

In the current state of flux, self-consciousness about gender-marked language is common. There is a tendency, perhaps more common in speech than in writing, to correct inconsistently, to use both sex-specific and gender-neutral language in reference to the same subject. The results can be ludicrous, as the following sentences illustrate (in each example, the speaker is a male physician addressing a class of male and female medical students at a midwestern university):

> Every medical student should decide for himself or herself whether to wear a coat and tie in the hospital setting.

> The patient who is anxious often keeps jiggling his trouser leg or his dress during the interview.

There might be circumstances in which either of these sentences would be appropriate, but taking into account the predictability of gender-marked dress in the American Midwest, we are inclined to attribute these statements to an uneasiness with changing language norms. The following variations convey the intended meanings while eliminating the incongruity:

> Medical students can decide for themselves whether to dress formally in the hospital setting.

> Patients who are anxious in their interviews often keep fidgeting.

Those who experience words like *chairman* and *fellow* as coded for male would find sentences like these incongruous:

> The department chairman who becomes pregnant will find few precedents for maternity leave.

> If the Fellow accepts appointment for at least six months, her air fare will be paid in addition to the stipend.

But those who experience such nouns as true generics (coded for either male or female) would find the following incongruous:

> If the Fellow accepts appointment for at least six months and is accompanied by his wife, his wife's air or rail fares will also be paid.   (University notice 1983)

In the next example, from the *New Yorker* profile of Chris Evert we cited earlier, the mix of the sex-specific *she* with the noun *frontiersman* might also strike some readers as incongruous:

> During both the warmup and the match itself, she [Evert] reminds one of a frontiersman sighting down the barrel of his rifle at a distant object when she fastens her eye on the approaching ball. . . .

Such gender contradiction might be deliberate, since one could argue that a male image for Chris Evert is not incongruous but admirable. It would nonetheless be desirable, for the sake of those who would find the male noun and pronoun intrusive, to consider potential revisions:

> She reminds one of a sharpshooter sighting down the barrel of a rifle at a distant object when she fastens her eye on the approaching ball.

> She fastens her eye on the approaching ball as if she were sighting down the barrel of a rifle at a distant object.

14. Avoid ambiguity; clarify the terms of analysis

The epidemiologist Herbert Posner recommends dropping generic language in scientific writing in favor of unambiguous language. Writers should clearly signal this policy (1) by frequently using *male* and *female*, even if the terms seem irrelevant in a given instance, (2) by confining *man* and *men* to their sex-specific sense and making this usage apparent (e.g., by mentioning women early on), and (3) by avoiding third-person singular pronouns that do not refer to sex correctly. These practices will clarify the terms of analysis.

As we have noted, confused or ambiguous personal-pronoun usage sometimes reflects confusion or ambiguity about sex and gender. Thus pronouns are sometimes used to insult those who differ from the gender stereotypes (a homosexual man, for instance, may be referred to as "she") or to deprive them of their identities. Kessler and McKenna quote a male-to-female transsexual who wrote to them about how her transition from "Paul" to "Rachel" was treated by those she worked with at a university science laboratory:

> One department head, a rather rigid ex-naval officer, had always disliked me. My advisor once told me that genuine talent threatened him. With my transition he refused to use feminine gender pronouns in relation to me. The secretarial pool and students were supportive enough to discourage this, an act of untold courage for which I will eternally be grateful. However, even a year later when he absolutely had to speak of my accomplishments to strangers, as he advertised the department, he would refer to me as "he" and use my old name. (Kessler and McKenna 210)

Ambiguity may result when a text shifts between generic and sex-specific referents, a shift that may occur in either direction. The following passage, for example, moves from discussion of a videotaped "real" medical encounter between a patient and a male medical student to reflection on the relative powerlessness of medical students in the medical hierarchy:

> It appears that the medical student's role in this encounter was to "practice" his skills with a "real" patient; it was not assumed that the information he obtained might have clinical relevance.
> The medical student, then, though encompassed by the profession, does not yet fully embody it; his actions are minimized in terms of his impact on the actual delivery of care. Perhaps precisely because medical students often have little apparent "real" impact, most studies of medical professionalization focus on residents or mature physicians. (Essay in a sociolinguistics anthology 1984)

The first paragraph refers to an actual medical student who happens to be male; the new paragraph appears to be speaking of a medical student generically—a transition signaled by *then* but confused by the continuing use of *his* to refer to "the medical student." In the end, the message is ambiguous about whether the second reference is to the individual medical student under discussion or to medical students in general. A shift to the plural in the new paragraph would be an improvement:

> Medical students, then, though encompassed by the profession, do not yet fully embody it; their actions have a minimal impact on the actual delivery of care.

This simple change in number, however, still leaves some confusion because it posits a generalization too soon; even in the next sentence the transition to plural is somewhat jarring. A more workable solution is to rewrite the sentence so that the transition is more explicit:

> We can conclude in this case that the medical student, though encompassed by the profession, does not yet fully embody it; his actions have a minimal impact on the actual delivery of care. Perhaps because, like this student, medical students in general have little apparent "real" impact. . . .

An even more explicit transition would be still better:

> If this case is representative, then, we can conclude that medical students, though encompassed by the profession, do not yet fully embody it; their actions have a minimal impact on the actual delivery of care.

Many solutions are clearly available. The main point is that removing the surface "sexist language" flows easily from making an effort to think genuinely about the referent (just as drawing on diverse resources in other dimensions of writing can yield graceful and unobtrusive solutions).

It is not impossible for a scholar who initially resists nonsexist usage to come to recognize the validity and feasibility of this goal. We close this section with just one example. The opening page of a 1976 essay in *PMLA* entitled "Reading Criticism" included the following sentence:

> It is difficult to separate the critic's anxiety about what he has written from his manifest reluctance to be read.

Cary Nelson, the author of this essay, describes the evolution of his views and practices over the subsequent ten years as follows:

> In 1975, when I was completing this essay, there was already widespread debate about the use of nonsexist language. That year, my

own university distributed a memo (in response to a request from its Committee on the Status of Women) requiring that sex neutral titles and explicitly inclusive pronouns be used in campus communications. No comparable demand was made of scholarly publications. At the time, I felt that distinction valid. Usages like "he or she" seemed awkward, an intrusion in the highly cathected and idealized domain of writing. In this particular essay, however, I was aware that my first generic *he* was itself quite awkward, since it referred specifically to the critics I quoted at the opening of my essay, one of whom was a woman. But I could see no solution to the problem. Shortly after the essay was published, the MLA Commission on the Status of Women in the Profession wrote to the *MLA Newsletter* to say, in part, that the author of the essay apparently considered himself to be engaged in a radical project but the traditional use of the generic *he* proved otherwise, an argument that was particularly telling. In a later issue, a conservative letter appeared attacking the Commission on this issue in terms I did not admire. About the same time, I began to use "he or she" in the classroom, feeling that references, say, to class assignments should acknowledge both male and female students. I believed, improbably, that this unstable separation between speech and scholarly writing would hold forever, that I would never adopt epicene pronouns in my writing. Within a few years, however, my convictions, held with such certainty, began to change. Now I find the generic *he* awkward; I cannot read it without being distracted. Two points seem worth noting in this little narrative: first, our convictions about usage and the probabilities of language change are often entirely transitory; second, where issues of sexual difference traverse our investments in our own prose, positions may be particularly irrational. (Letter)

Other Pronouns

Pronouns other than *he*, of course, may cause confusion because of shifting referents, and in some contexts even the use of *we* and *you* can be discriminatory.

Ambiguities

In the following example, from a feminist essay on science, *we* occurs with a confusing succession of possible antecedents, shifting back and forth between apparently generic and sex-specific usages:

> Science is a human construct that came about under a particular set of historical conditions when men's domination of nature seemed a

Summary of Recommendations

"Generic" *He*

Here and elsewhere in these guidelines, we recommend shifting or recasting passages to avoid discriminatory overtones while preserving the meaning. Although writers who attempt to follow this advice may initially find themselves revising language that appears to convey a sexist message, practice in taking care can lead to a better solution—one in which it will have become natural to select among nonsexist alternatives without having considered the formerly prevalent sexist expression.

The following list summarizes the possibilities and pitfalls to consider in editing out the pseudogeneric masculine pronoun:

1. **Recast the sentence in the plural, using *they*, but avoid *they* with singular antecedents.**

2. **Shift the person of the pronoun to the first person (*I* or *we*) or the second person (*you*).**

3. **Use *he or she*, or *she or he*, if no smoother alternative suggests itself; but avoid repeatedly using such combinations in a passage.**

4. **Alternate feminine and masculine pronouns in appropriate contexts.**

5. **Avoid alternative-gender forms requiring slashes and parentheses.**

6. **Use generic *she* in special circumstances.**

7. **Edit out the personal pronoun.**

8. **Use *one*.**

9. **Preserve the meaning of the original.**

10. **Preserve the flavor of the original.**

11. **Avoid introducing stylistic flaws.**

12. **Avoid needless correction of appropriately used sex-specific pronouns.**

13. **Avoid incongruity and inconsistent correction.**

14. **Avoid ambiguity; clarify the terms of analysis.**

positive and worthy goal. The conditions have changed and we know now that the path we are travelling is more likely to destroy nature than to explain or improve it. Women have recognized more often than men that we are part of nature and that its fate is in human hands that have not cared for it well. We must now act on that knowledge. (Anthology on feminism and biology 1979)

Although the passage clearly seems to implicate male scientists in the will to dominate nature, it is unclear whether the human hands that hold nature's fate include women's and whether *we* in the final sentence means "women," "feminists," "the authors," or "the human race." Here, again, the surface language cannot be repaired until the terms of the analysis are understood.

One could revise by differentiating the genders more strictly and eliminating the questionable *we*. This approach creates a less wordy and more consistent reformulation of the entire passage (though because of the ambiguity of the original it is impossible to tell whether the new version fully conforms to the authors' meaning):

Science has been socially constructed under a particular set of historical conditions in which men's domination of nature seemed a positive and worthy goal. Conditions have changed, and it is now clear that this quest for domination is more likely to destroy nature than to explain or improve it. Women, more often than men, have seen themselves as part of nature and have recognized that nature, in male hands, has not been well cared for. They must now act on that knowledge.

As we noted above, a shift in person is sometimes an appropriate way to avoid an ambiguous *he*:

Third person: The scholar typically learns to respect the original texts he works with.

First person: As scholars, we typically learn to respect the original texts we work with.

Second person: As a scholar, you should learn to respect the original texts you work with.

But the first- or second-person pronouns alone do not guarantee gender neutrality. In the following example, the masculine simile *ad man* serves to identify both the referent and the reader (the addressee) with maleness:

The stance of an advocate, like the stance of an ad man pushing a brand name, necessitates making the most of whatever distinguishes your product from another.   (Literary text 1977)

And as the above passage on feminism and science suggests, *we* may be a problem as well as a solution when the writer fails to distinguish between referents. In a letter to the editor, two traditional (female) prescriptive grammarians begin the paragraph using *we* to mean themselves as writers; by the end of the paragraph, however, the first person plural has apparently expanded to include virtually all reasonable speakers of the English language except "militant feminists":

We hope that the editor of the *New England Journal of Medicine,* as well as the editors of all similar publications, will not be cowed into making a capricious change in usage. Those who exclude themselves when the generic "he" is used may do so at their own pleasure. Our position, we realize, will not endear us to militant feminists, but we ask only that they react with reason rather than raw ire. Since a certain amount of stability and conformity is required for a language to maintain its communicative effectiveness, gratuitous tampering is to be discouraged. So feminists, please, leave our language alone!   (*New England Journal of Medicine* 1978)

Perhaps these writers would contend that *our* in the last sentence refers only to themselves, though this seems a rather idiosyncratic stance toward English and hardly one that justifies the broader claims the passage makes about what is required for "a language" to remain effective. Ironically, the final phrase here invokes Robert A. Hall, Jr.'s 1950 book, *Leave Your Language Alone,* which argues forcefully for a descriptive approach to language, forsaking the prescriptive high road to claim instead that language as commonly spoken is okay.

We, You, and the Feminist Movement

The use of *we* has been important in feminist discourse. Linked to the antecedent *women,* it has served to signal some degree of female or feminist solidarity:

Women have had the power of naming stolen from us.   (Feminist theory book 1973)

Before the feminist movement, a woman writer would probably not consider any pronoun other than *they* in the following sentence:

> Women, especially, need to understand the tenure process before they go through it.

Today, the sentence might well appear with the first-person plural pronoun:

> Women, especially, need to understand the tenure process before we go through it.

Traditional grammar holds, of course, that a pronoun must agree with its antecedent in person, number, and gender, and the use of the first-person plural pronoun to refer to a third-person plural antecedent violates that tradition. Feminist scholars who do not want to challenge conventional usage on this point might prefer a phrase such as *we women* or *as women we* in the last example:

> As women, we have a special need to understand the tenure process before going through it.

The use of the first person and the third person in reference to *women* may vary even within a single work, depending on the particular female constituency designated. In this example an author uses the first person plural several times:

> [T]he effort to gain political power explains only one of the reasons that feminists avoid public criticism of each other. A second is that we are always seeking ways of working together. . . . There is another reason, a cultural one, why many women are not disposed to argue with or criticize each other. Simply stated, we have been conditioned not to argue. (*Journal of American Folklore* 1975)

Here the author's use of *we* identifies her as a woman and a feminist. Yet, on the same page, she disclaims membership in a different group of women, referring to them as *they*:

> For one thing, many women do not know the terms and functions of logic and argumentation; they have never learned them. (*Journal of American Folklore* 1975)

The use of *we* and *us* within the women's movement has its critics even among feminists. Women of color have repeatedly challenged the readiness of white middle-class women to generalize about women and to use *we* in statements that disguise the diversity of female interests and positions. A number of essays asserting this diversity from the perspective of black women appear in *But Some of Us Are Brave* (ed. Hull, Scott, and Smith). Mary Berry's foreword, for example, notes a number of scholarly books about "women" that are exclusively about white women (e.g., Chafe's *American Woman*). In contrast, the "Black Feminist Statement," by the Combahee River Collective, begins by defining exactly who is speaking:

> We are a collective of Black feminists who have been meeting together since 1974. . . . As Black women we see Black feminism as the logical political movement to combat the manifold and simultaneous oppressions that all women of color face.   (Hull, Scott, and Smith 13)

Meaghan Morris recounts a lecture given by the American feminist Mary Daly in Sydney in 1981 in which Daly talked about her books *Gyn/Ecology* and *Pure Lust* ("A-mazing" 79–80); in Morris's words, Daly's lecture style, focusing on shared knowledge of her work and her goals, functioned "like the Communion Service," ritually reuniting "speaker and hearers in an affirmation of their common identity." According to Morris, "the *we*-ness of the address was ruptured, however, by a woman who called out 'Mary, you're not speaking to *me*' " (79). Some members of the audience then became for Daly a *you*, separated from the shared *we* of her discourse.

As feminist discourse comes to encompass the voices of women of diverse classes, different national and ethnic groups, women of color, women from Third World populations, women with a variety of political agendas, the notion of a shared, worldwide, collective feminist identity becomes increasingly difficult. "Who Are the 'We'?" asked an MLA forum on feminist discourse. For some, the fragmentation of individual and group identity meshes with a vision of postmodern society for which no single "master narrative" is possible. Thus Donna Haraway asks, "[W]ho counts as 'us' in my own rhetoric? Which identities are available to ground such a potent political myth called 'us,' and what could motivate enlistment in this collectivity?" ("Manifesto" 73).

Given these sensitivities about the use of the first person plural, one should unequivocally specify whom it encompasses rather than let readers decide this question for themselves. A writer who belongs to different groups and uses *we* in more than one sense must make sure that each referent is clear. In her 1984 presidential address to the Modern Language Association, Carolyn Heilbrun skillfully interweaves extracts from Helen Vendler's 1980 presidential address with her own comments as MLA president, as a member of the profession, and as a woman, establishing from the outset that she is representing more than one constituency:

> You will already have guessed that I am going to speak tonight not just as the president of the MLA but as a woman president, to ask what effect the fact that women are one third of our membership, and more than a third of our professional colleagues, has had or is likely to have on our association and our profession. I speak both to women and to men. I speak to men about their inevitable problems with "revolutionary reaction and reappropriation" where they might have expected "gratitude and imitation." I speak to women of the need we have long felt to articulate—and here again I borrow Vendler's words, though from a different occasion—our "own balance between danger and decorum in imagery of rebellion (which usually lost) against tradition (which usually won)."

Here the possessive *our* in the first sentence refers to the MLA members—the *I* and *you* that make up the unstated *we*. In the sentences that follow, Heilbrun signals that she is about to shift the sense of *our*, distinguishing male members of the association—*they*—from female members like herself, the new referents of *we* and *our*. While this shift was undoubtedly obvious when Heilbrun delivered the speech, standing before the audience as a woman president, sensitive grammarians who read the address and who have difficulty linking a first-person pronoun to a third-person antecedent might assume that *we* and *our* continue to refer to the entire membership. For the most part, however, Heilbrun keeps the meaning of *we* clear through such constructions as *we women*: "Today, we women speak of the body but not alone of childbearing"; "We women in the MLA are now in a retrospective mood. Some of us are full professors. . . ."

Some writers use the pronoun *we* with an antecedent like *women* in positive contexts and *they* in negative contexts. The following examples, derived from one cited earlier from the *Journal of Amer-*

ican Folklore, may be effective in making political statements; but such judgmental shifts are not, in general, recommended:

> Women have made original contributions to scholarship and have had significant impact on our fields.

> Women have played it safe in scholarship and have had little impact on their fields.

Note that these sentences are different from the following two, which are restrictive in their references:

> Women who have made original contributions to scholarship have significantly affected our fields.

> Women who have played it safe in scholarship have had little effect on their fields.

There is nothing wrong with using *we* to indicate a specified collectivity:

> As women who support the Equal Rights Amendment, we have different views about equality than do women who are against it.

Our point, rather, is that the use of *we* will not produce a magical unity:

> As women, we must support the Equal Rights Amendment and defeat the male-dominated forces who are against it.

But women are also among those who oppose ERA.

The second person may be appropriate when the relationship between the author or speaker and the audience is fairly clear and when that relationship warrants direct address. If, for example, the following sentence, quoted earlier with a first-person plural subject, occurred in a keynote address at a women's conference, *you* could replace the *women-we* structure:

> You, more often than men, have seen yourselves as part of nature and have recognized that nature, in male hands, has not been well cared for. You must now act on that knowledge.

But is the speaker in a position to direct women listeners to act? If the speaker is female (the original text, quoted above, was written by women), her failure to include herself in the agenda suggests that she is above doing what she prescribes for her audience. If the speaker is male, it seems quite odd for him to tell women to save the world. What will his role be? Does his maleness make him unfit to participate in this salvation?

Summary of Recommendations

Other Pronouns

1. **Make shifts between generic and nongeneric usage explicit.**

2. **Make shifts between antecedents explicit.**

3. **Clarify the referents of *we*, *our*, and *us*.**

4. **Avoid judgmental shifts from *we* to *they*.**

5. **Use the second person advisedly.**

Man, Its Compounds, and Other False Generics

"When I speak of mankind," says a male character in a Steig *New Yorker* cartoon, "one thing I *don't* mean is womankind" (qtd. in Miller and Swift, *Handbook* 26). But rarely are the so-called generic nouns used with such explicitness. More often terms like *man, mankind*, the suffix *-man*, and other *man* compounds are ambiguous, paralleling and reinforcing the use of generic male pronouns to disguise, obscure, or trivialize the presence of women.

The Myth of Generic *Man*

As the philosopher Janice Moulton argues in her essay "The Myth of the Neutral 'Man,' " the use of generic *man*—whatever the author intends—is *not* interpreted as gender-neutral (102). One feminist writer asks us only to imagine this sentence to be aware of how mythical is the claim that *man* is "generic":

When the first ancestor of the human race descended from the trees, she had not yet developed the mighty brain that was to distinguish her so sharply from all other species.   (V. L. Warren 473)

Marilyn Frye, like Moulton a philosopher, puts it this way:

The confusion of "man" with lower case "m" and "Man" with upper case "m" is revealed when the attitudes with which a man meets a lower animal are engaged in the male man's encounter with the female man.   ("Male" 15)

Such an encounter was vividly described by a male writer-surgeon in a 1981 symposium on the scientific essay as literature:

The central issue in man's evolution was bipedalism. When man thrust himself erect, he truly became *Homo erectus*: for he discovered front-to-front copulation. And woman in her turn was rewarded by orgasm, unknown to all other species.

Only the male man, one concludes, is *Homo erectus*; the female man is happily appreciative of this new angle.

Apart from discussions of evolution, nowhere is man's province staked out more definitively as the male man's territory than in writing about language:

The Sapir-Whorf hypothesis is concerned with the possibility that man's view of his environment may be conditioned by his language.   (Sociolinguistics text 1983)

Anthropologists have long noticed that control over language is the essential base on which authority rests and that the exclusive manipulation of words must remain with the one in power if he means to stay in power. Even more so, the right to speak may become a duty to speak so as to prove the master's dominion over words. Pierre Clastres argues: "the man in power is always, not only the man who speaks, but the sole source of legitimate speech."   (*Semiotica* 1985)

In the following passage, the author deliberately subverts the uncritical male generic usage of the preceding examples:

[M]ost people agree that . . . the ability to use language is an adaptive characteristic that has helped mankind to climb the evolutionary ladder. Whether it has helped womankind is another matter. . . . (Book on language and gender 1986)

Such self-consciousness is rare, for the confusion of "generic" *man* with male *man* is built in on the ground floor. Many dictionaries— for example, *Webster's Collegiate*—define *man* as "a human being, especially an adult male human being" and cite the capacities "for articulate speech and abstract reasoning" as distinguishing characteristics; in *Webster's* entry for *woman*, no cross-reference to *man* permits her to share in these attributes.

Children begin to interpret *man* as male at an early age, even in the face of countervailing influences. In her research with school-children Carole Edelsky observed this process at work in a second-grade classroom:

> The students were all sitting on the floor while a few (one at a time) talked about some projects they were working on. . . . Sean reported that he was learning, from two books he was reading, about growing bacteria. He showed one of the books and talked about an experiment he was planning to do and that others could do also. Then he showed a two-page spread of all the recent scientists (according to this book) who had worked on bacteria. Nicole asked: "Why aren't there any girls in the picture?" The students are noisy and the teacher says: "Nicole, say it again." Nicole: "Why aren't there any ladies—why aren't there any women in the picture?" (With each self-correction, it was quieter and she was more deliberate. She probably had these words ordered because the teacher very deliberately tries to defeat sexism in classroom materials and in classroom activities such as the rules for lining up, and would be unlikely to say *ladies* herself.)
>
> Sean answered: "Because bacteria are 'friends of man.' " The teacher asks: "Do you think 'friends of man' means men only?" Sean: "Yes." The teacher asks about six other students what they think. The girls asked say it means both "women and men." One boy agrees; another agrees with Sean that it only means "men." Teacher: "How about 'Dogs are man's best friend?' or 'a giant step for mankind?' " Sean: "Only men." The teacher goes back to the topic of bacteria and the pictures of men in the book. Sean: "It's only men because only men are scientists." ("Observation")

The sense in which an author uses *man* is often unclear, as in this example from a 1974 book review:

> The swaggering braggard who emerges from the Carlos Baker book and from most of the other lesser biographies may shock literary men and some journalists with finer feelings, particularly the ladies, but while Hemingway was swashbuckling around, he put some hair on the chest of literature. (*Manchester Guardian* 1974)

Is "literary men" generic, or are "the ladies" included only among the "journalists with finer feelings" and not among the "literary men"?

The *man* in the following comment about Mary Shelley is also potentially confusing:

> The boldness with which she once pursued metaphysical speculation now seems, first of all, a defiance of one's proper place—here man's in relation to God but also, by extension, woman's in relation to the family.   (*PMLA* 1980)

In this example, the special problems of literary criticism are apparent, for the author may be self-consciously and ironically mixing the generic with the nongeneric to contrast the relationship between man and God with that between woman and family. The apparent loftiness of generic *man*, in other words, is deliberately deflated by the more narrowly generic *woman* that follows. That *she* is the subject of the relative clause points to a possible sex-specific meaning for *man*. The author's awareness is thus a critical factor in finding appropriate nonsexist language. In technical terms alone, however, the juxtaposition of an apparently inclusive generic *man* and a sex-specific generic *woman* clouds the intended meaning of *man*. The use of plurals would clearly convey a sex-specific meaning: ". . . here men's in relation to God but also, by extension, women's in relation to the family." If the intended meaning is generic, substituting *the individual's* for *man's* would eliminate the ambiguity.

A deliberate interplay between generic and sex-specific *man* is apparent in this feminist discussion of the dualism of precybernetic machines:

> [B]asically machines were not self-moving, self-designing, autonomous. They could not achieve man's dream, only mock it. They were not man, an author to himself, but only a caricature of that masculinist reproductive dream.   (*Socialist Review* 1985)

Gender-Marked Compounds

Feminists have given much attention to discouraging the use of such gender-marked compound words as *manpower*, *chairman*, and *manmade*, and it is in this area, perhaps, that they have had their most consistent and widespread success. Many state and federal government agencies, for example, have officially adopted gender-neutral job titles, substituting *firefighter* for *fireman*, *police officer* for *policeman*, *flight attendant* for *steward* and *stewardess*, and so on. Many organizations routinely find substitutes for such words as *manpower* (Miller and Swift suggest *personnel, staff, work force, available workers,* or *human resources* [*Handbook* 29].) At the same time, this is the area of language most readily caricatured by critics of language change. *Personhole cover* as a substitute for *manhole cover* is a favorite proposal among these critics. Some researchers distinguish between compounds in which *man* occurs as a stressed syllable (e.g., *mánpower*) and those in which it is unstressed (e.g., *cháirman*). They argue that listeners do not perceive unstressed *-man* as a male gender-marker. Others argue (1) that these words appear in writing as well, where stress is irrelevant, and (2) that change has an important symbolic function in asserting women's presence.

There is considerable variation in the ways speakers use and interpret these terms, particularly those, like *chairperson*, that are seen as feminist coinages. Many women prefer the title *chairman* to *chairperson*; though this choice is often taken as a rejection of feminist beliefs, it may signal a desire to avoid a term so demonstrably populated—to use Mikhail Bakhtin's phrase (254)—with the intentions of others. A speaker's usage patterns are often difficult to determine precisely. For example, a woman researcher presenting statistics about women in higher-education administration explained that her graph did not include "the women chairmen." Is *chairmen* used as a true generic—restricted here to chairmen who happen to be women—or is *women chairmen* a compound that contrasts with *chairmen*, a term restricted to men? At an annual conference, a woman who chaired the women-in-medicine section of a medical organization introduced her successor as "our past vice-chairperson this year and our new chairman." One would need more data to determine whether this speaker was using the forms *chairperson* and *chairman* in random variation or in complementary distribution, equating *chairperson* with second best (in the context *vice-*) and *chairman* with the top office (which she herself had held). In contrast, a male committee chair, in an academic program where all the committees were chaired by men, said, with no apparent self-consciousness, "I've sent copies of the document to all the committee chairpeople." He apparently had replaced *chairman* with *chairperson*, *chairmen* with *chairpeople*, and used these forms regardless of sex or power issues. These examples return us to our distinction between *gender-neutral* linguistic forms and *nonsexist* language.

As McConnell-Ginet has pointed out, one speaker can make *chair-person* in reference to a woman sound like an insult while another can make *chairman* welcoming and respectful. The gender-neutral usage of the committee chair just quoted appears to be nonsexist as well.

The *Person* Alternative

Person is currently a serviceable noun to indicate an individual of either sex. It has come to function in recent years as the most frequently recommended gender-neutral replacement for *man* in many contexts (Cannon and Robertson, for example, note the current linguistic productivity of *-person* in many compounds). The noun *person* has functioned generically for many years, of course, as in the standard disclaimer of fiction and films: "Any resemblance to persons living or dead is purely coincidental." And in Evelyn Waugh's prefatory "Warning" in *The Loved One, person* refers explicitly to either sex:

> If in the vast variety of life in America there is anyone at all like any of the characters I have invented, I can only remind that person that we never met, and assure him or her that, had we done so, I would not have attempted to portray a living individual in a book where all the incidents are entirely imaginary.

Legal documents and detective fiction have traditionally applied so-called generic terms explicitly to either sex—in law to close loopholes, in detective stories to complicate the question of whodunit. Legal documents typically use male terms, with footnotes indicating whether both sexes are included. Marcia Muller's 1983 novel *The Cheshire Cat's Eye* illustrates detective fiction's typical attention to the sex of pronouns. Shortly before his death, the murder victim tells the detective that he was on his way to meet someone—someone who is now suspected of killing him. The detective reports this conversation: "He said that the person he was meeting was unreliable because he had a drinking problem." "He?" asks a colleague. "Figure of speech," says the detective; "Actually, I think he said 'the person'" (67–68). In contrast, Robert B. Parker's detective, Spenser, uses gender-neutral language to make social commentary. In *A Catskill Eagle* Spenser reports that he "called Ives on the number he'd said was always manned. He'd misstated slightly. This morning it was womaned" (185). Later in the book he tells a rich man why he came to borrow money from him:

> "I took you at your word, sir."
> "Many people say that. You seem actually to do it. I don't assume you take everyone at his word."
> "Or hers," I said. "No, sir. Just people who can be taken at their word."   (276–77)

When individuals or specific aggregates of the population are referred to, *person* or *people* can be appropriate:

> At the turn of the century, men moved to the cities in growing numbers.

> At the turn of the century, people moved to the cities in growing numbers.

In the following sex-specific example, the equivalent references to Prospero as a *person* and to Gonzalo as a *man* affirm the usefulness of *person* as a replacement for *man* in designating an individual:

> Consistently it is Gonzalo, the man of patient faith, who endures trials. . . . Prospero, also, is a person of faith. . . .   (*PMLA* 1983)

But *person* does not carry the cosmic connotations of "generic" *man* and cannot always substitute for it:

> Man stood upright and a new day dawned.

> A person stood upright and a new day dawned.

> People stood upright and a new day dawned.

Some writers find *human beings* a reasonable alternative in this context; others would use *humankind, Homo sapiens,* or *the human animal*:

> Human beings stood upright and a new day dawned.

This example shows that the surface revision of sexist writing may mar the rhythm of the original. Some writers view this price as well worth the gain in clarity and equity. Others may not be willing to make the sacrifice; we suggest that they seek a new way to formulate their meaning, one both aesthetically pleasing to them and free of discriminatory overtones.

Person is given a more generic status in Marge Piercy's science fiction novel *Woman on the Edge of Time*; the noun, designating either sex, yields the third-person epicene pronoun *per*:

> We could tell person intended to speak to more of you. . . .
>
> At first we were trying to save per.   (315)

But *person*'s generic function is not written in stone. Despite our claim that *person* can replace *man* in some contexts, its history gives pause. Although *person* is currently considered the prime gender-neutral alternative to *man* in everything from government documents to jokes, it has in the past been restricted to certain subsets of human beings. In British English, it customarily designated a working-class woman, especially a young one, in complementary distribution with *lady*, used for a middle- or upper-class woman. (Robin Lakoff's insights suggest that in many American contexts *lady*—e.g., *cleaning lady, bag lady*—has acquired the working-class connotations of British *person*.) As Cheris Kramarae and Paula A. Treichler note in *A Feminist Dictionary*, in the United States *person* has historically meant a male human being with various legal and moral rights and responsibilities typically denied to females—those qualities, indeed, taken to define *personhood*. It is ironic, the authors observe, that the right-to-life movement willingly defines fetuses as persons (thereby making abortion murder) but refuses to advocate adoption of an equal-rights amendment that would define women as persons under the Constitution. For decades, for example, *person* was a battleground for women physicians seeking opportunities in the armed services, and it was not, in fact, until World War II that the relevant official documents explicitly defined the word so that women physicians would have equal opportunities and benefits (Walsh 225–30).

Other False Generics

The following example illustrates an ambiguous use of *boy* that parallels the use of "generic" *man*:

> [W]ith younger people you really don't know what they will do.
> Maybe the new boy will continue to do metaphysical poetry....
> (*Profession 79*)

Is *boy* intended here for a young person of either sex, or is it only
the new boy (not the new girl) who will do metaphysical poetry?
Generic *boy* finds its brother in generic LAD, an acronym used by
linguists in the 1960s and early 1970s to designate the Language
Acquisition Device—a model for the hypothetical young first-
language learner, whose gender, in journal articles, was invariably
male (see Levelt for characteristic usage).

Woman has also been described as a false generic, appearing in
some contexts to encompass all women but in fact referring only
to some women. Alice Walker suggests, for instance, that the *women*
in *women's studies* is not readily applicable to black women:

> It is, apparently, inconvenient, if not downright mind straining, for
> white women scholars to think of Black women as *women*, perhaps
> because "woman" (like "man" among white males) is a name they are
> claiming for themselves, and themselves alone.   ("One Child" 44)

Walker's observation has implications for language use. While white
middle-class American women, for example, increasingly designate
a married woman by her given name and surname (Jane Joseph)
rather than by her husband's name (Mrs. John Joseph), this practice
is not necessarily the preference of Afro-American women, whose
history denied them the legal right to that designation. What signifies bondage to one woman may mark freedom to another.

Finally, some terms that do not appear generic nonetheless disguise heterogeneity—words like *tradition*, *history*, and *culture*, which
scholars often use automatically. Though many feminist coinages,
described below, are designed to call attention to how these terms
function, there seem to be infinite ways that language can reflect
social hierarchy, cultural presence and absence, conceptions of self
and other. The calling into question of many heretofore commonly
used expressions comes with larger shifts in social organization:
demographics, the makeup of professions, the growing voices of
the silent and oppressed. Like an influx of speakers of a different
language, these shifts create many points of tension. No recommendations for language change can—or should—fully anticipate
the future. The linguistic strategies we suggest in this volume reflect
greater awareness of these issues and the reasons for choosing some
terms over others.

Summary of Recommendations

Man, Its Compounds, and Other False Generics

1. **Do not use *man* "generically."** *Man* no longer functions generically for many people, and instances of ambiguous usage are too common to justify a continued effort to have it refer to either sex. The term *man* should be defined exclusively as an adult male human being.

2. **Signal that you are not using *man* generically.** Because of the long-standing confusion between "generic" *man* and male *man*, it is, for the present, helpful to let readers know how you are using the term. We repeat Posner's recommendations for signaling sex-specific usage, cited more fully above: (1) use the terms *male* and *female* frequently, even if not deemed relevant in a given instance; (2) if *man* or *men* is used in the sex-specific sense, use *women* early on; and (3) use only pronouns that indicate sex correctly.

3. **Whenever possible, use true generics in place of *man*.** Numerous alternatives to *mankind* are available, including *humankind, human beings, women and men, people, humanity,* and, where appropriate, more specific designations such as *our ancestors, eighteenth-century society, Homo sapiens, the human animal, farmers,* and *rural populations*.

4. **If you choose to use a male generic, signal your awareness of its problematic status.** In the following passage the author contrasts women's verbal proficiency in most areas of language with their general failure to master "the arcane dialect of the masculine ruling class." The "vast mass" of women's writing, she argues, most of it in the form of letters, diaries, and other occasional writing, "was not set down in the hope of immortality." She continues:

   > Most of it does not assume the posture of the writer addressing (his) public but remains the unaffected discourse between self and self or self and a familiar friend. (*Tulsa Studies in Women's Literature* 1982)

   The parentheses prevent an automatic identification of the word "writer" with maleness, at the same time emphasizing that most writers who self-consciously wrote for the public were male.

continued

5. **Avoid expressions you dislike.** "I prefer not to use 'human-kind,'" wrote an author to the MLA editorial staff during the copyediting of an article for *PMLA*. "I never use it and find it a clumsy word. Surely, 'mankind' need not be abolished from the face of the earth. It's generally in use throughout the Middle Ages and Renaissance." No doubt some other alternative could have been found, however—say, *humanity*, *human beings*, *we*, or *people*. For common but widely disputed terms, it may be helpful to spend some time identifying alternatives you find acceptable. On occasion, of course, an author and an editor may be unable to negotiate perfect agreement; but such is life, and an impasse does not invalidate the effort.

6. **Try to respect others' preferences.** When members of a group specify how they wish to be designated, take their arguments seriously and, if possible, respect their preferences. If a particular usage irritates you, try to find a reasonable alternative. Many writers are more comfortable with *chair*, for example, than with either *chairman* or *chairperson*.

Feminist Alternatives and Related Innovations

Out of the feminist critique of "he/man language" have come many proposed alternatives (Martyna, "Beyond"). Numerous neologisms, for example, serve to challenge or replace traditional nouns and pronouns that are considered inherently sexist or falsely universalizing in other ways.

Variations in Use and Acceptance

Some of the alternative terms, like *chair* or *chairperson* for the traditional *chairman*, have been widely adopted and discussed. Others, like *herstory* for *history* (*his story*), rarely occur in traditional academic journals, except in quotation marks as examples of feminist usage. Feminist coinages are common in nonacademic feminist publications, however, as in this passage, which addresses the invisibility of black women and black lesbians within the generic category *feminist*:

This invisibility is perpetuated by the lack of a significant body of literature reflecting a Black feminist or Black lesbian-feminist ideology, as well as by the silencing of the herstory of woman-identified relationships in Africa.   (*Heresies* 1981)

A writer's use of a word like *herstory* may vary depending on whether the target publication is a traditional academic journal, an academic feminist journal like *Signs*, a feminist journal like *Heresies*, or some other medium (for further discussion see the introduction to this volume and Treichler's essay). Even the same essay may introduce feminist alternatives in some contexts but not in others. A paper read and distributed at a 1983 speech communication conference uses a standard spelling of *women* on the first page— "I examine women's music and social change in this paper"—but an innovative spelling later, along with a nontraditional compound noun:

Disappointingly for the lesbianfeminist, the vision of the Women's Liberation movement continued to envision wimmin's primary relationships being with men.

Herstory is perhaps the best-known example of a more general feminist linguistic strategy designed to raise consciousness about the ubiquitousness of the male presence in language. This strategy involves replacing occurrences of obviously male-gendered terms such as *man* and *he* with their feminine or generic counterparts. Other terms are identified as sexist because of their linguistic roots: some feminists reject the term *seminal*, for example, because it praises originality on the basis of a relation to *semen* 'seed'; instead they might use *originative, germinal,* or the coined feminist adjective *ovular*:

In her ovular work, Michelle Rosaldo indicated the importance of the value which attaches to [the public and to the private] sphere. . . .   (Anthology on feminist social theory 1983)

Many of the ideas [in this paper] originated in the context of a germinative discussion.   (*Heresies* 1980)

DuBois's classic reading of the African-American predicament is posed in the opening chapter of this germinal piece.   (Essay in literary criticism 1987)

Feminists object to *seminal* not merely because it has a "male origin" but because that origin is equated with creativity and value. (Some people do not use the term *denigrate* on the grounds that it literally means to "blacken" [someone's name or reputation] and thus associates blackness with unworthiness.) This process of replacing objectionable terms sometimes violates received notions of what we "know" about etymologies and semantic functions of words: feminist neologisms include *himmicane, hersterectomy, womage,* and *efemcipated,* as in Bina Goldfield's *Efemcipated Handbook,* an explicitly consciousness-raising exercise that mechanically replaces *man* with *fem* in hundreds of English words. The strategy essentially involves the assertion of feminist words and meanings in defiance of scholarly authority (though, as suggested elsewhere in this book and in Baron's *Grammar and Gender,* the legitimacy of established derivations may also be questioned): *herstory* therefore designates not merely an alternative version of *his story* but a different kind of narrative—one told by women about women (and men)—and its etymological "incorrectness" is irrelevant to its users. Though many of these coinages are primarily playful or illustrative, they usually incorporate political insights: *himmicane* pointed to the convention of naming *hurricanes*—destructive acts of nature—for women and treating them metaphorically as female; here the feminist argument brought about change, and male and female names are now alternated. Similarly, the following example challenges a term that seems to embody received masculine values:

> How important it is for us to recognize and celebrate our heroes and she-roes.   (Maya Angelou; qtd. in Orr 15)

A large group of words like *patronize, patriot,* and *virtue* have etymologically male roots, often from Greek or Latin, but usually go unchallenged, presumably because their sex-specific origins are no longer apparent. Indeed, people who would avoid an explicitly masculine phrase like *love of fatherland* might use *patriotism* instead. Terms such as *patriarchy* and *androcentrism,* however, are considered useful in feminist writing precisely because they suggest masculinity that has been institutionalized in law, governance, tradition, and language. With somewhat more imagination, Barbara Smith borrowed from art history the term *ithiphallic* 'having an erect penis' and used it to describe a certain genre of masculine prose ("Wordplay"). Donald N. Mager points out that the phrase *lesbians and gay men* is increasingly preferred over *homosexuals,* in part because the root *homo* 'same' is seen as connected to, and thus masculinized by, *homo* 'man.' Some women reject the word *testimony* because of its etymological association with *testes* (coupled with the Islamic practice of regarding women's statements under oath as less valuable than men's) and coin words like *ovarimony* instead.

We do not recommend flight from accepted lexical items simply because they are suddenly identified as contaminated. Resistance to words derived from Greek and Latin is especially ironic, for although by Virginia Woolf's day these languages could be seen as accoutrements of male privilege, they had been denounced in earlier centuries as feminizing influences that threatened to destroy the robust masculinity of Anglo-Saxon English. The point is that any term may come to be seen as problematic after its etymology and other associations are articulated in contemporary discourse: the word *choice*, for example, was extensively analyzed in the Sears discrimination case (see Rosenberg). Once a word has been challenged, it becomes harder to use it innocently and to disregard the objections raised in the relevant literature.

Like the lexical coinages discussed above, alternative spellings often have political functions: the spelling of *women* as *womyn* or *wimmin* is not merely the application of a simpleminded desire to "rid the language of men" but rather a graphic representation of a separatist political stance. (*Wimmin*, however, is included in the final volume of the supplement to the *Oxford English Dictionary*, published in 1986; see Shepard.) Many feminists use these innovative options strategically and somewhat self-consciously. For example, the author of an essay in a scholarly journal places *herstory* in quotation marks:

> We may choose to call [attention to] "herstory" but we ought also to see how clearly our alternative version of history is related to the other forms which tell the story of exploration, conquest, colony, and empire from the point of view of the subject peoples. (*Tulsa Studies in Women's Literature* 1982)

A different author writing in a less academic feminist journal omits the quotation marks:

> [T]his Women of Colour issue is herstoric in Canada. (*Fireweed* 1983)

Many terms given currency by the feminist movement, of course, have been widely adopted within society at large: *sexism, misogyny, chauvinism, feminism.* Other terms have arisen primarily out of feminist scholarship. The literary scholar Ellen Moers, perceiving a gap in the scholarly lexicon, invented the term *heroinism* to refer to the self-conscious woman who becomes a professional author. A number of reviewers in the mainstream press cited this word to mock or otherwise criticize the book (Michael Wood headed his review "Heroine Addiction"), thus revealing their reluctance, perhaps, to give women the power to name and define. Even Maureen Howard's choice of words, in charging that Moers sometimes "postures unbecomingly," reinforces a conclusion that Moers's gender was not irrelevant to her critics' evaluations. As a term, *heroinism* is not much used, except possibly by some feminist literary scholars. In fact, some feminist writers would not use *heroine* at all, because of its potentially trivializing suffix. One alternative is *hero*. Another, for those uncomfortable with the masculine connotations of *hero*, is an appropriate synonym—say, *protagonist, model,* or *central character*. A third possibility is to create, as Maya Angelou does in the example quoted above, a lexical innovation like *she-roe* or *hera*. Though such casual innovation is outside the bounds of the conventional Anglo-American prescriptive tradition, it occurs regularly in Afro-American speech and writing (see, for example, Gates, "Blackness"; Mitchell-Kernan; and Smitherman).

Adrienne Rich's *re-vision* ("When")—roughly designating the process by which women awaken to the political realities of their lives and, awakened, see texts with new eyes and write from a fresh perspective—was introduced into the wider feminist community, where it has flourished, undergoing continual "re-vision" itself. This comparison is not to equate the two terms but, rather, to suggest their differing receptions—the mainstream press highly judgmental of Moers and willing to entertain her arguments and language only piecemeal and grudgingly, the feminists catching up Rich's word and putting it to use as a contribution to a larger collaborative enterprise. The term *gynocritics*, fostered by Elaine Showalter, falls somewhere in between. While it is seen as a more academic and hence less broadly liberating term than *re-vision*, it goes beyond *heroinism* in its applicability, designating for many feminist literary scholars a kind of analysis that "begins at the point when we free ourselves from the linear absolutes of male literary history, stop trying to fit women between the lines of the male tradition, and focus instead on the newly visible world of female culture" ("Toward" 131).

Mary Daly, originally trained as a theologian, has contributed puns, analyses, and linguistic innovations that have enriched the lexicon of both academic and mainstream feminism. Indeed, it was she who dubbed the mainstream the *malestream* and exposed what she termed the *methodolatry* of the patriarchal academic establishment, a form of tyranny that

> hinders new discoveries. It prevents us from raising questions never asked before and from being illumined by ideas that do not fit into pre-established boxes and forms. The worshippers of Method have an effective way of handling data that doesn't fit into the Respectable Categories of Questions and Answers. They simply classify it as non-data, thereby rendering it invisible. (Daly, *Beyond* 11).

In the name of creative thought, she calls on feminist scholars to commit *methodicide* by killing the patriarchal disciplines (*Beyond* 7–12). Some of her terms seek to reclaim and honor qualities that have stereotypically been assigned to females and judged negative: *hag, crone, spinster.* Similarly, Alice Walker offers *womanism* as a unique name to honor black feminism:

> Feminism (all colors) definitely teaches women they are capable, one reason for its universal appeal. In addition to this, womanist (i.e., black feminist) tradition *assumes*, because of our experiences during slavery, that black women already *are* capable. (Letter)

Walker took *womanist* from a black folk expression used by mothers to their daughters: "You acting womanish," that is, like a woman. She comments, "I share the old ethnic-American habit of offering society a new word when the old word it is using fails to describe behavior and change that only a new word can help it more fully see" (Letter).

Other Innovative Language

Language that is initially innovative may, through repeated use, unself-consciously enter the lexicon. In a 1984 newsletter, a man who uses a wheelchair describes a visit to Nicaragua during which a contingent of American activists with disabilities took a "wheel around town." There is considerable debate about the language associated with handicaps, and opinions differ among those who have disabilities as well as among those who do not (sometimes called "temporarily able-bodied," or TABS by the disabled community). Should people with disabilities be characterized with words like *blind*, *deaf*, and *mute*? Debra Connors reports that soon after she began to lose her vision, she was asked to join a support group of disabled women: "What do you mean *disabled*? *I'm* not disabled. I just can't *see*, that's all!" (92). Should negatively charged expressions be expunged: "blind as a bat," "deaf to the country's wishes," and so on? Kirsten Hearn, in a letter to the British feminist magazine *Spare Rib*, gave the term *handicappist language* to everyday phrases that take their meaning from "normal" sensory abilities: "I see what you mean" to mean "I understand," "What is your view?" or "What is your stand?" to mean "What is your opinion?" or "What is your position?" The word *disability* itself encompasses what Anne Finger calls "a laundry list of disabling conditions":

> Disability, we are told, does not just mean being in a wheelchair. It also includes a variety of conditions, both invisible and visible. These include being deaf or blind, having a heart condition, being developmentally disabled or being "mentally ill." While this is necessary to an understanding of disability, thinking about disability only in medical or quasi-medical terms limits our understanding: disability is largely a social construct. (293)

Connors elaborates on this point:

> *Disabled, handicapped, differently-abled, physically or mentally different, physically challenged, women with disabilities*—this is more than a mere discourse in semantics and a matter of personal preference. *Disabled women* is the term which most accurately characterizes our position in American society. Sexism and able-ism work in concert to disqualify us from vast areas of social life. Our unique set of barriers is further compounded by discrimination based on our race, age and sexual preference. Objectified as women and as medical, social work and charity cases, disabled women have been deeply invalidated as human beings. We have been disabled by our society. No euphemism will change this. (82–83)

Though the history of "disabled people has yet to be written," Finger suggests that they evidently had a more routine presence in earlier rural and village societies than they do today. Industrialization created formal structures into which one had to "fit." Those who did not—those "disabled" by increasing standardization—found life more difficult. Finger traces the language that captures this change:

The word *defective,* for instance, was originally an adjective meaning faulty or imperfect: it described one aspect of a person, rather than defining that person totally. By the 1880's, it had become a noun: people were considered not merely to have a defective sense of vision or a defective gait—they had become totally defined by their limitations, and had become *defectives.* A similar transformation took place a few decades later with the word *unfit,* which also moved from being an adjective to being a noun.   (285)

Conceptualizing disability as a social construction facilitates action and activism. A Berkeley car dealer some years back promised the Center for Independent Living two vans fully equipped for persons with disabilities; but when the vans were delivered, they didn't work. Disabled protestors picketed the dealer in their wheelchairs, carrying signs reading, "THIS GUY SELLS LEMONS TO CRIPPLES." The vans were replaced. *Crippled,* obviously, was a strategic political choice made by those with the right to choose. In most contexts, *crippled* has been replaced by *disabled, handicapped,* or a more medically specific phrase, like *spinal cord–injured.* Some now advocate replacements for *disabled* and similar terms; the most widespread substitutes are *differently abled* and *physically challenged.* But Karen Lindsey questions the euphemistic quality of much "politically correct language":

[S]ome of the new language that has arisen simply cosmeticizes reality. "Differently abled" makes people sound as though they belong to another species—as though they fly, or breathe with gills. "Physically challenged" sounds like handicaps are exciting adventures. The phrases attempt to deny the basic fact that there is something that most people can routinely do that people with disabilities can't— seeing, hearing, walking, etc.   (16)

The current debate about terms for persons with disabilities may seem irrelevant to, say, the eighteenth-century scholar who would not mind using a decent substitute for *mankind* but would rather be hit with sticks than use *humankind.* But language is informed by such questions as how people see history or, more accurately, how their present perceptions shade their vision of history. In *Genesis and Development of a Scientific Fact,* the philosopher of science Ludwik Fleck compares anatomical illustrations from several distinct cultures and historical periods but notes that actually it "is only theories, not illustrations, that can be compared" (35). Mary Douglas discusses the institutional context in which textbooks are revised every decade. New editions are necessary not only to incorporate the latest advances in the field but also, and more commonly, to modernize the slant, the feeling:

> In the intervening years, some slogans have become visible, some words have become empty, and others too full, holding too much cruelty or bitterness to modern ears. Some names count for more, and others that count for less are due to be struck out. The revisionary effort is not aimed at producing the perfect optic fit. . . . [W]hen we look closely at the construction of past time, we find the process has very little to do with the past at all and everything to do with the present." (Douglas 69)

The various innovative terms we have discussed can contribute toward this "revisionary effort."

Gender Marking and Related Usage

Markedness may refer to formal differences that distinguish between pairs of words—for example, the suffixes in *widower* as opposed to *widow* and in *lioness* as opposed to *lion*. Typically such marking is asymmetrical, with the unmarked term considered neutral, general, and standard, and the marked term considered deviant. The concept of markedness also encompasses a judgment (sometimes intuitive, sometimes founded on knowledge of patterns in many languages) about which member of a pair is the "base" and which is the "derivation" from the base. In English the word *countess* is said to derive from *count*, rather than the other way around. While a conception of formal markedness may be useful and plausible in linguistic analysis, semantic markedness, which is independent of formal marking, is "a complex and controversial subject." According to John Lyons, "semantic marking is a matter of degree" (*Semantics* 1: 311). Thus, though *count* is unmarked in relation to *countess*, it cannot substitute for its marked counterpart in the same way that *lion* can substitute for *lioness* or *dog* for *bitch* (the last pair is marked semantically but not formally). In many languages, the male term is the unmarked one and, in contemporary English, *man* is regarded as the generic unmarked term, *woman* as the marked term. According to Lyons, however, except for its use as "a generic referring expression," the degree of markedness is less than that of many other word pairs: "If 'man' is said to be unmarked in relation to 'woman,' it must be recognized that this is so only in highly restricted circumstances" (*Semantics* 1:

Summary of Recommendations

Feminist Alternatives and Related Innovations

1. **Routinely adopt conventional nonsexist alternatives to terms found objectionable.** Considerable effort has been expended, for example, on identifying or creating rational, plausible gender-neutral job titles. Abandoning *waitress* does not entail substituting *waitperson*; *waiter* will do. There is no excuse at this point for rejecting nondiscriminatory titles that already exist in the standard vocabulary.

2. **View the more radical feminist lexicon as a resource and draw on it according to your needs.** It would be inappropriate for us to make specific suggestions for using innovations designed, in part, to challenge existing practices. The decision to adopt or forgo them should depend on the nature and purpose of the project: Are traditional terms suitable? Is there value in calling attention to terminology? Are the coinages theoretically necessary or justifiable? How much effort will be required to use them?

3. **Explain or justify your use of any nonstandard alternatives.** Many feminist innovations—structural inventions, idiosyncratic spellings, and neologisms—have by now acquired distinct meanings and connotations that figure significantly in ongoing debates. Thus they are often central to an author's argument. But if the terms have originated outside mainstream English-language writing—in European discourse, in feminist journals, or wherever—an author may encounter an editor unfamiliar with them and may have to demonstrate their theoretical importance. Readers, too, may need some background information on a particular usage.

4. **Try to understand and respect the objections of groups to the ways in which they are conventionally labeled.** Seek out intelligent and sensitive alternatives that both you and they can accept. The term *persons with disabilities*, for example, avoids the euphemistic quality of *persons who are physically challenged* as well as the problem raised by totalizing terms like *the disabled*, which identify individuals exclusively by their physical disadvantages.

309). One cannot say "The men in the next room," in other words, to refer to a group of women and men. We have discussed some of the consequences of this asymmetry.

Feminine Suffixes

One well-known form of gender marking in English is the feminine suffix. This usage conforms to the tradition in which male forms are unmarked and generic while female references must be marked. But the use of feminine suffixes with agent nouns to distinguish men from women has long been a controversial practice. This analysis is from 1911:

> The discrimination between the sexes in all that is worth having or being is so unfairly partisan as almost to give the impression that the distribution of our English affixes is the outcome of a misogynist's spleen. For a woman, equally with a man, may be an imbecile, a convict, a liar, a thief, or a fool, without any terminological inexactitude. But when we come to the other side of the shield, she may not be a hero, a benefactor, an administrator, a prophet or a poet, because these things are masculine prerogatives, and the courage and ability of women must be otherwise expressed. We do not speak of a servantess, a drunkardess, an incendiatrix, or a pauperine; these attributes are not worth claiming a preemption for. But everything denoting prominence or superiority must carefully distinguish between the real thing and its mere imitation. "Master" must not mean "mistress," nor "manager" include "manageress." There is a world of difference between "governor" and "governess," and between "adventurer" and "adventuress." One would think that heroism, like cowardice, would be the same in essence whether displayed by a woman or a man; but while this is tacitly admitted in the case of the vice, with the virtue it is otherwise. Cortez and Pizarro may be heroes; Joan of Arc is but a heroine. If a woman conducts a paper, we call her an editress; if she writes a book she is dubbed "authoress," her best work thus receiving only that "comparative respect which means an absolute scorn." And, lastly, you may, if you feel so disposed, speak of a woman as a devil—one of Shakespeare's characters does so—but you cannot under any circumstances speak of her as a god. Only men can be gods. So that, to sum up, the shame and the dishonour of Adam may be shared by Eve, but in his honour and glory he must stand alone.   (Beanland 207)

Because of their negative connotations, feminine suffixes are no longer routinely added to nouns as women move into various professions, but a few usages are commonly retained—*actress* and *waitress*, for example. Yet feminist linguistic activists contest even these terms. Some years ago *flight attendants* became the official designation for the airlines' employees formerly known as *stewardesses* and *stewards*, though the older terms are still in common use colloquially. In many restaurants, the term *waiter* is used for both men and women (and a restaurant occasionally creates a hypercorrect form like *waitperson*). In London, there is a move to have theaters and theatrical agencies remove *actress* as an official designation and use *actor* or *female actor* instead; in this country, too, many women who perform in the theater refer to themselves as *actors*. The goal in these cases is to remove the formal marking that distinguishes a position held by a man from an equivalent position held by a woman. At times, however, a sex-specific designation may be appropriate: for example, a casting agency may hold auditions for female parts and therefore wish to advertise for *female actors*— the dropping of the suffix necessitating an alternative form of gender marking. But the burden is on the language user to justify the need to take sex into account.

Ever since feminine suffixes were consciously introduced on a large scale, purportedly to create appropriate occupational titles as women moved into new fields, there have been objections. When women physicians began to be called "doctoresses," for example, they claimed that the title was a lesser one, designed to set them apart from the real doctors, the men: they noted as evidence that the designation was also applied to abortionists, witches, nurses, and doctors' wives. When one medical school announced that a woman's MD degree would confer on her the title of *doctoress*, the tumultuous protest precipitated a crisis that ultimately forced the school to close (for further discussion see Walsh). Thus these suffixes have long been opposed, particularly in the United States.

The following examples were therefore rather surprising to find in a 1980 volume of literary criticism published by a university press:

> Mrs. McIntyre, like her estate manageress, is seen to be a stranger to a particular area of experience.

> A bull rams her; a Negress smashes her; she is captured and shot by a criminal.

The archaic *manageress* is unnecessary; if the sex of the estate manager is required, "female estate manager" or "woman estate manager," though wordier, is all right. Stating the woman's name would be another alternative. The use of *Negress* suggests a racial as well as a sexual stereotype; in 1980 it was certainly inappropriate, considering that in 1969 the *American Heritage Dictionary*, reflecting long-standing sentiment, said the word was "now often considered offensive." *Black woman* would have been a more suitable term for the critic to choose, especially as *black* is used elsewhere in the essay. If both *manageress* and *Negress* reflect the vocabulary of the text being analyzed, a conscientious critic can indicate this fact without adopting those usages. One solution is to refer to the original words in quotation marks:

> Johanna is not amorous, she is not even the stock "coy shepherdess" in her refusal of Raimond.   (*PMLA* 1976)

Quotation marks can communicate a scholar's awareness that a term is stereotypical, sexist, or otherwise problematic. They may also, of course, simply mark reference to a term. In any case, while preserving the lexical context of the discussion, the quotation marks signify that the words enclosed are the original author's and may no longer be appropriate.

Other Forms of Asymmetrical Usage

Language may be marked for gender in a variety of ways. In the following passage, a critic's modern paraphrase of what seems to be a view expressed in a nineteenth-century novel, the stereotyped notions of women are reinforced by the adjectives *good* and *personal* in contrast to the male-oriented noun *objectivity*:

> Good women are too personal; they need more objectivity; their sense of fair play revolves too much around their immediate family, not around mankind in general.   (*PMLA* 1976)

Similarly, women's interest in the "immediate family" is unfavorably contrasted with a more abstract interest in justice for "mankind in general." The next example, from the review of a book on Thomas Carlyle and his circle, also uses stereotypically female adjectives to refer to the woman but only nouns to refer to the man. While not intrinsically prejudicial, adjectives can dilute the force of nouns and make them seem less fundamental and substantive (an eighteenth-century essay describes man as noun, woman as adjective—i.e., a mere modifier of man):

> Tom is something of a tyrant, as well as a martyr to his Aryan hierology . . . but the sweet intelligent Jane is only conventionally submissive. Her letters survive and are drawn on to show a bright gossipy talent. (*New York Times Book Review* 1981)

Although the author does refer to both Carlyles by their given names, instead of calling the husband "Carlyle" and the wife "Jane," the juxtaposition of *sweet* and *intelligent* converts the description of the woman into a stereotype, as does the choice of *gossipy* to describe (and belittle) her talent. This is a book review, of course, and the reviewer is presumably influenced by the tone and perspective of the author of the biography. But wherever the language originated and whatever the judgment about Thomas and Jane Carlyle, the reviewer need not have reproduced commonplace sexist stereotypes. In contrast to these female-associated terms, some male-associated adjectives have come to function as positive metaphors; "Seminal Semantics," for example, was the headline for Lorna Sage's review of Jacques Derrida's *Dissemination*. In a related vein, attempts by male scholars to express positions sympathetic to feminism often generate quite strange language. The following example is from an essentially positive review of Dale Spender's *Man Made Language*:

> Here's another propaganda book written by a woman identified as an "Australian feminist," a modestly kinky thought. (*Communication* 1983)

Feminists have long been aware that verbs, which generally designate action, may be marked for sex; witness this parenthetical commentary in an 1861 feminist discussion of women's rights under the law:

> If the husband absconded without making sufficient provision for his wife, she is permitted (!) to use her own property and earnings, or the earnings of her minor children, to secure a support.

The distinction between active and passive voice in English encourages some degree of sex-linked correlation in writing. (See, for example, Treichler's 1980 linguistic analysis of active and passive voice in Kate Chopin's novel *The Awakening*.) We noted in our introduction that the verb *to marry* did not conventionally take a female subject until recently: women did not marry, they were married to men.

Like adjectives, verbs and verbals, especially those describing women's use of language, often reinforce negative stereotypes about women, as in this review of a feminist book:

> [The authors'] emotional force is not addressed positively to the inherent dignity of women. . . . It is largely misdirected into a sterile, inter-female yammering against men. (*Times Literary Supplement* 1982)

Terms like *yammering* (*gossiping* is probably another) illustrate what has been called *gender deixis* (see McConnell-Ginet's "Review Article"): though not formally marked for gender, such words point to a feminine subject.

In an early study of the captions of *New Yorker* cartoons, Cheris Kramer [Kramarae] found that students could readily identify the sex of the speaker from the language of the caption: swearing, sports, and slang pointed to male speakers; diminutive words like *itsy-bitsy* and phrases like *oh, dear* and *we've been gossiping* pointed to females. (Kramer emphasized that these gender-attached terms bore no relation to real speech but merely reflected easily recognized stereotypes.) Precisely this point is highlighted in the following example, in which the writer signals awareness of sex-stereotyped labels by using quotation marks:

> Men have "stories" or "yarns"; women "gossip" or "clothesline."
> (*Journal of American Folklore* 1975)

Asymmetrical usage is another form of markedness: just as the title *doctor* alone has tended to mean "male doctor" while a female doctor must be specially designated, women of color have charged that much feminist writing reproduces implicit norms of race if not of sex. In the following example, parentheses are used ironically to suggest how the adjective *white* is virtually always "understood" in conjunction with the word *feminist*:

> Mary Helen Washington . . . documents other omissions and also discusses the dangers of tokenism in the new (white) feminist rewriting of literary history; she is currently compiling an anthology of literary criticism by black women. (Anthology on women's scholarly publishing 1981)

A pervasive and subtle form of asymmetrical usage is the different meaning attached to a word when it refers to a woman instead of a man. The following entries from Kramarae and Treichler's *Feminist Dictionary* illustrate this disparity:

IMPOSING: When used to describe a male, retains its customary English meaning [of impressive], but when used [by males] in reference to a female, it always means battle-ax.   (John Leo 1984)

RUTHLESS: "A man has to be Joe McCarthy to be called ruthless. All a woman has to do is put you on hold."   (Marlo Thomas 1980)

Another widespread example of asymmetrical usage is the hyphenation of terms designating ethnic groups—for example, *Afro-American*, *Asian-American*, and *Mexican-American*. "Mainstream" white writing often assumes itself as center, considers its own tradition as "tradition," and uses modifiers only to mark the productions of other groups. In the scholarly writings of these groups, however, *Euro-American* (or *Anglo* or some similar term) is routinely used to refer to the "mainstream," thus marking this tradition as only one of many and distinguishing among groups in a more balanced way.

Asymmetrical usage is also evident in the historical linguistic process Muriel Schulz has dubbed the "semantic derogation of women" and Robin Lakoff has identified as a significant feature of English in keeping woman in her place. This process acts on pairs of sex-marked words that are approximately parallel in meaning and value; over time, through changing usage, the female term of the pair undergoes semantic derogation and becomes negative, disparaging, sexual, or less important than the male term: *governor* versus *governess*, *master* versus *mistress*, *dog* versus *bitch*, and so on. A recent example, provided by Nancy Hall Rice, involves the slang word *hoser*. This word entered the lexicon of college students in the United States by way of *SCTV*, the satiric Canadian television equivalent of *Saturday Night Live*, where it was used among male comics to refer to males and to mean something like "beer-drinking lout." Rice found, however, that some of her students at a midwestern university were using *hoser* in a new sense, applying it to women to mean "sexually promiscuous."

Naming and Labeling

Names, titles, and naming practices are sensitive indexes to a host of cultural, social, legal, historical, and political realities. Una Stannard's *Mrs. Man* remains a state-of-the-art exploration of naming.

Not unexpectedly, feminist scholars have identified a number of problems in this area, including asymmetrical usage, diminutive or unprofessional designations, and incongruous or anomalous references.

Asymmetrical usage may manifest itself in the different treatment given the names of female and male writers: *Miss Austen* versus *Dickens*, *Mrs. Woolf* versus *Leonard Woolf*. A surprising example appears in a 1986 review of a book about Phillis Wheatley—surprising in the degree of insensitivity a contemporary scholar can show toward current debates and practices about women's names. With an air of considerable self-congratulation, the reviewer refers to Wheatley, a black poet, as "the famed Phillis" and "Ms. Wheatley" (while referring to male writers by their surnames). The commentary disparages Wheatley's poetry ("everything turns to oatmeal under her vaunted 'genius' "), but one can make critical judgments without resorting to racist and sexist flippancy.

The nonprofessional designation of female authors in contrast to the use of full names or last names for male writers is a related problem: *Jane* (for Jane Austen), *Virginia* (for Virginia Woolf), *Dorothy* or *Dottie* (for Dorothy L. Sayers). Once again, the problem resides in asymmetrical usage. If it would be inappropriate to refer to Nathaniel Hawthorne as *Nathaniel* or *Nate*, it would be inappropriate—overfamiliar or condescending—to refer to Dorothy Sayers as *Dorothy* or *Dottie* (as one of her biographers did).

First names are a particular convenience, of course, in articles about, say, Virginia and Leonard Woolf, Dorothy and William Wordsworth, Percy and Mary Shelley, Nathaniel Hawthorne and his daughter Una. Although first names are workable if usage is kept parallel (*Percy* and *Mary*, but not *Shelley* and *Mary*), we recommend varying the devices needed to keep references clear. Once the two names have been introduced, an article on Virginia Woolf with passages about Leonard Woolf might include the following variations:

This time Virginia went unaccompanied by Leonard.

This time Woolf went alone (not even Leonard Woolf accompanied her).

This time Woolf went unaccompanied by her husband.

This time Woolf went to her meeting unaccompanied.

In contrast, if the name *Wordsworth* has been used throughout an essay to designate William Wordsworth as its subject, it would be awkward if a section on his sister, Dorothy, then referred to her as *Wordsworth*. Our recommendation would be to use *Dorothy Wordsworth, William Wordsworth, his sister, her brother,* and so on, as necessary to avoid ambiguity.

A case in point is Mary Poovey's 1980 essay on Mary Shelley, in which she uses first names sparingly, usually coupled with the surname, and only as necessary to distinguish Mary Shelley from Percy Shelley; first names may be used when both Shelleys figure in the same sentence:

> The puzzle Shelley presented to her contemporaries is well worth our consideration. . . .   (332)

> Shelley combines this model with the notion (implied by the poetry of Wordsworth, Coleridge, Byron, and Percy Shelley) that an individual's desire, once set in motion, has its own impetus and logic. . . .   (334)

> Like Percy Shelley's version of this scene in "Mont Blanc," Mary Shelley's image suggests an inhumane icy nature. . . . Yet, unlike her future husband, Mary Shelley does not temper this presentation of nature by claiming for the imagination a saving supremacy. . . .   (336)

> Twice Shelley insists on Percy's role in her project. . . .   (345)

In some circumstances, involving large families or multiple characters with the same name or complex intimate interrelationships, first names may be the only graceful way to keep individuals apart. In the last example, Percy Shelley is called by his first name only because the two names are nearly adjacent. The third example addresses a different problem: that of married women's names. Here, the name *Mary Shelley* is used for the still unmarried Mary Wollstonecraft Godwin because it is under this name that she came to be known as a writer and it is her writing that concerns this essay (as opposed to, say, a biographical essay). As we note below, a critic might come to a different decision about *Elizabeth Barrett* versus *Elizabeth Barrett Browning*, whose writing appears under both names. Finally, using a surname (with no first name) to designate a woman but not a man with the same last name, as Poovey does in the Shelley essay, can often foil the tendency to turn male names into touchstones and symbols, as this hypothetical example does:

> Hope springs eternal, and on that first day I still believed that a budding Wordsworth or Shelley might emerge from the unpromising array that filled my classroom.

Still another problem is incongruous or anomalous usage introduced into feminists' reviews of feminist works. For example, a
feminist review of Janice Radway's *Reading the Romance* was edited
to refer to Radway as "Mrs. Radway." Equally anomalous or anachronistic may be Euro-American or feminist-centered usage (e.g.,
Ms. Austen, Ms. Curie). Some black women (e.g., Davis 15) have
forcefully argued that the rejection of the title *Mrs.* by white middle-
class feminists is not necessarily shared by black women, who were
traditionally denied the right to take their husband's names: Mrs.
Booker T. Washington, as Cheryl Clarke et al. note (128), took that
name and used it with pride. Some research may be necessary to
find the reason for a woman's name preference. Professional women
may use multiple names over the course of a lifetime. Here we
discuss naming practices; elsewhere we discuss the problems of
citing and indexing a person with multiple names.

The most common reason for a woman's name change is marriage or divorce. If a woman scholar establishes her professional
reputation under her birth name (a term now widely preferred to
maiden name), she will often retain that name throughout her
career to avoid confusion. If she marries, she may or may not adopt
her husband's name in her nonprofessional roles (such a name
change derives from custom, not law). If she has published under
her married name and at some point decides to resume her birth
name (perhaps after a divorce), she can aid readers by signaling
the change in a uniform way or using a transitional form for some
period of time. Madelon Gohlke Sprengnether, for example, first
published under Gohlke, her married name. When she decided to
return to Sprengnether, her birth name, she continued for a time
to use Gohlke as a middle name. Such a tactic enabled her to use
the name she wanted without relinquishing an established identity.
In contrast, she might have decided to introduce Sprengnether so
that it preceded Gohlke, thus retaining for a time her usual place
in bibliographies; when readers had become familiar with the new
middle name, she could have dropped Gohlke.

Adopting a hyphenated name after marriage has the advantage
of preserving identity and alphabetical order in bibliographies:

Sally Marie Smythe
Sally Smythe Jones
Sally Marie Smythe-Jones

And it also permits a return to the birth name without a change
in established alphabetical place:

Joan Kelly-Gadol → Joan Kelly

Of course, it is important that the hyphen be included consistently, so that the name will always be alphabetized in the same place. This seems obvious, but the failure to hyphenate consistently is one of the common problems reported by official record keepers (who sometimes discover they have created two files for the same person).

When an author's name changes over time, the date of publication of a given work is often a sufficient indication of which name is currently in use and should be considered primary (for historical figures, biographical information may be needed). But the feminist movement has generated other types of name change where primacy is less clear. In the early years of the women's movement, as in the suffragist movement, professional women (including academics) sometimes adopted movement names in addition to the names under which they were already publishing. Thus in the 1960s and 1970s Jo Freeman used the name Joreen for her women's-liberation pieces; the two names were not always cross-referenced, for they appeared in different contexts. Another academic, a biologist, uses three personae [we give her a pseudonym here]: in scientific publications, she is S. Jackson Phillips; in her professional life at the university, she is Sue Jackson-Phillips; and in feminist publications, she is S. Sue Jackson. To some degree this practice parallels that of writers who use different pen names for different genres: the professor and literary critic Carolyn Heilbrun publishes detective novels under the name Amanda Cross (as the poet C. Day Lewis and the Oxford scholar J. I. M. Stewart published their detective fiction under the respective names Nicholas Blake and Michael Innes). Cheris Kramer, a sociolinguist, changed her last name to *Kramarae* in the early 1970s to incorporate *Rae*, her mother's name; in order to retain *Kramer*, her married name, without appearing simply to add to it the Latin possessive case ending *ae*, she changed the *e* in *Kramer* to *a*. Because Kramarae is the primary name, Kramer citations typically include the notation [Kramarae] or [*see* Cheris Kramarae].

Because the feminist movement encourages creative naming, some authors have chosen imaginative names for themselves. One feminist cartoonist uses the pseudonym *bülbül* to protect her family from the repercussions of her politics; it is the Hungarian name of a small bird that symbolizes freedom. Some feminists use only a single name: Brooke, Starhawk. The Berkeley feminist Laura X adopted a name modeled on that of Malcolm X: women, she argues, are slaves within a patriarchal society, as black men and women were slaves within a racist society; the X signals women's anonymous identities, always subsumed under the names of their husbands and fathers. Here, as with Malcolm X or feminist columnist Varda One, we recommend treating the name as a single unit (and alphabetizing it as Laura X rather than as X, Laura).

Feminist scholarship is cross-cultural and interdisciplinary, and encounters with "non-Anglo" names are therefore inevitable. Obviously, it is important to be attentive to unfamiliar spellings, diacritical markings, and the diverse naming practices of other cultures (Islamic, Hispanic, and Asian cultures, for example, typically have conventions different from those of Anglo-American names). Any comprehensive handbook of style provides guidance.

Sometimes the adoption of nonsexist usage is thwarted by contravening forces, as in the directive sent to public information officers in the state of Pennsylvania: "If you use Ms. for a female, please indicate in parentheses after the Ms. whether it's Miss or Mrs." Further evidence that sexist practices die hard is provided in another example. In 1988, all deans, program directors, and department heads at a large midwestern university received from the chancellor's office an updated policy statement prohibiting discrimination based on sex or physical handicaps. One dean had copies of the memo sent to selected members of his staff; in accordance with common administrative practice, he listed the recipients on the top of the memo as follows:

> Dr. SMH
> MHP
> Adele G
> Ellen C
> Roger J
> Dr. SJR
> Dr. EQW

SMH, SJR, and EQW are men with PhDs. Adele G and Ellen C are women with PhDs. MHP and Roger J are a woman and a man without PhDs. The designations appear to represent a hierarchy, whether conscious or not. Titles are not ordinarily used with initials in office correspondence, but since they were used for some individuals, they should have been used for all: thus the five staff members with doctorates should have been titled Dr., and MHP and Roger J should have been titled Ms. and Mr. As Adele G put it in a note to the dean's office, "The differential use of titles for Drs. SMH, SJR, and EQW versus Adele G and Ellen C is a form of sex discrimination. However small, it does reinforce stereotypes potentially harmful to some of us."

In *A Feminist Dictionary* Kramarae and Treichler define *naming* as a "fundamental process for identifying, defining, and conceptualizing experience." Both names and labels function to represent phenomena, and in many cultures, names have intrinsic power. Name-avoidance taboos are common and sometimes extend even to words that sound like the taboo names. Women and other subordinate groups are characteristically named and labeled by others, with little opportunity to name themselves. As women literary scholars point out, names and labels for women's writing often serve to belittle it. Bonnie Costello, for example, cites the labels male critics have given Marianne Moore's work: "genuine," "gossipy," "fussy." Her poetry, says T. S. Eliot, is "feminine," and R. P. Blackmur says it shows a "chastity" of taste, a "genuineness"; John Crowe Ransom, meanwhile, praises Moore for displaying less "deficiency of masculinity" and hence more "intellectual interest" than other women writers (222). These labels stereotype women's writing as inferior, Costello argues, and they have become so pervasive that even a feminist critic like Suzanne Juhasz can call Moore's writing "spinsterly" (223). Bonnie Zimmerman suggests that similar "perceptual blinders" have prevented feminist literary critics from acknowledging lesbianism and lesbian writers. Ellen Moers, for example, recognizes that the term *lesbianism* has been used as a slur against a number of unmarried women writers; Zimmerman points out, however, that Moers vigorously defends them against this heinous charge but never questions the charge itself or explores what their experience as women loving women might have meant in their work or their lives (180).

Similar labels have affixed themselves to other women's literary traditions. Tey Diana Rebolledo, for example, comments that, as recently as the early 1980s, Chicana poetry was sometimes called "tortilla poetry" or "adobe poetry"—allusions to earlier images in Chicano poetry of men making revolutions while women stayed at home and made tortillas (143). Similarly, in characterizing contemporary American Indian women's poetry, Patricia Clark Smith describes an older genre of "eagle feather poetry," primarily a product of white missionaries' "renditions" of American Indian poetry. The scope and function of labeling that diminishes women writers and women characters are discussed extensively by Nina Baym; Hazel Carby; Barbara Christian ("Shadows," *Black*); Sandra Gilbert and Susan Gubar (*Shakespeare's*); Carolyn Ruth Swift Lenz, Gayle Greene, and Carol Thomas Neely; Deborah McDowell; and Claudia Tate. Feminist linguistic and theoretical writing on signification and discourse discuss "naming" in more detail (see especially Black and Coward; Cameron; McKluskie; and Morris, "Amazing"; in this volume McConnell-Ginet's and Treichler's essays note further research).

Inevitably, linguistic usage carries signals about a speaker and helps shape the attitudes of a hearer. At the same time, language is action that constructs and codifies positions. Scholarly writing has traditionally embodied and thus reinforced stereotypical attitudes toward the sexes. Much past practice has been unconscious; but today efforts to avoid or counter sex stereotyping in language must often be conscious. Lakoff, Schulz, and others, for example, have written about *women, girls,* and *ladies,* three female-marked terms that reflect distinctly different assumptions. In the following sentence, marriage is viewed as the key to female adulthood:

> The author attaches little importance to Edward's partially concurrent affair with Lady Farness, except to emphasize that all three were married women, the Prince being incapable of falling for unmarried girls. (*Saturday Review* 1975)

In the next example, the humor derives from the one female label, "weather girls":

> Everyone—from clowns and announcers to masters of ceremony and weather girls—comes equipped with miles of smiles. . . ." (*PMLA* 1976)

In contrast, this author undermines sexist labeling by indicating awareness of it:

> . . . for Shelley wants most of all to assure her reader that she is no longer the defiant, self-assertive "girl" who [lacks] proper humility. . . ." (*PMLA* 1980)

The quotation marks signal recognition of a stereotype and simultaneously suggest its undesirability and inappropriateness.

Syntactic Constructions

Ideas about gender may be deeply inscribed in discourse. Examining syntactical and semantic structures in ethnology, Claire Michard-Marchal and Claudine Ribéry find dramatic differences between the ways men and women are depicted as subjects of discourse. Men are agents of action, genuinely "animate" beings; women are passive caretakers, objects. The following sentence, from a 1936 essay by Claude Lévi-Strauss, is an example:

> The whole village left the next day in approximately 30 canoes, leaving us alone with the women and children in the abandoned houses.   (Qtd. in Michard-Marchal and Ribéry 64)

The authors further illustrate this point with typical sentences from other ethnological and linguistic studies:

> When they hunt, the men meticulously explore the forest in order to systematically exploit all resources.
>
> The men leave the job of gathering to the women.
>
> The men are the masters of the forest because they master it.
>
> The women reign over the camp because they are wives and mothers.   (61)

Here men are constructed syntactically as agents: they have intentions, goals, and systematic activities; they act on their environment. The women are passive: they do not act on their environment; even when they reign, they merely "are." The syntax is reinforced by the gender-linked verbs and nouns *explore, exploit,* and *master.* Without knowledge of the society, we are not able to suggest accurate nonsexist alternatives. In the second sentence, however, *women* could easily be the agent: *Women have the job of gathering* or, in line with the first sentence, *Women ingeniously gather and prepare food and other resources.* Revision of the final sentence would depend on the significance of women's "reigning" over the camp and its relation to marital status. What, for example, is the role of unmarried women or widows without children? And if "reigning" depends on marriage, the fourth sentence might read: *Revered as wives and mothers, the women reign over the camp.*

The original sentences demonstrate not merely stereotypes about gender but the interaction of the language system with widespread, often implicit, notions of what the world is like. To illustrate this interaction of language with ideology, McConnell-Ginet cites the following pair of sentences:

Men can care for children just as well as women [can].

Women can care for children just as well as men [can].   ("Linguistics" 22n11)

Subjects in a study designed by Finn Tschudi found the second sentence distinctly bizarre. Formally unremarkable, the comparative *just as well as* structure fails only because it violates the way the equation normally conveys information, with the "inferior" term on the left, the "superior" term on the right:

I think I write just as well as Joyce Carol Oates does.

There are, of course, an infinite number of sentences in English that may function in a "sexist" way in specific circumstances. Here we merely note briefly some additional syntactic constructions that feminists have questioned. One kind involves *agent deletion*—for example, through passive constructions. In an essay subtitled "Some of Our Agents Are Missing," Julia P. Stanley and Susan W. Robbins describe "truncated passives" as an important category of English syntactic construction that obscures relationships and erases responsibility. While the passive voice often functions in this way, such constructions, argue Stanley and Robbins, are especially used against the powerless, including women. In the sentence "Many women suffer from untreated menopause," for example, the phrase *untreated menopause* implies that menopause needs to be treated and that women have failed to seek treatment. Daly points out that a sentence like "Estrogen replacement therapy is required" similarly functions to disguise who requires it, what the replacement is, and in whose interests this treatment is given (*Gyn/Ecology* 257–58). The phrase *estrogen replacement therapy* is a nominalization of a process: the therapy entails a physician's replacing a woman's natural estrogen with synthetic estrogen. Like other nominalizations, a complex noun phrase that compresses a set of relationships sacrifices information for the sake of brevity.

Semantics can also erase responsibility. A 1985 newspaper article about the building of a tunnel in Japan is illustrative:

> For thousands of tunnel hands—all of them men, superstition having kept women out—there is the added worry of layoffs.

The sentence technically points to "superstition" as the "agent" that kept women out of the tunnel. But whose superstition? The men's? The women's? Management's? The culture's?

Agent deletion is one special syntactic form of ambiguity in English. The use of false generics, which we discuss at length in an earlier section, is another major source of ambiguity that has concerned feminists. As McConnell-Ginet points out, ambiguity is also a source of play, of politics, of complexity in language. But "the politics of ambiguity is vitally important: who interprets and who evaluates?" (qtd. in Kramarae and Treichler, *Feminist* 44).

Syntactic stereotyping occurs on the surface of sentences as well. In many expressions that explicitly refer to both sexes the male term traditionally goes first (as in *males and females*): These expressions belong to a larger category of collocations that include irreversible binomials such as *good and bad* and *great or small*. In describing the preferred sequence of these expressions, John Lyons credits Yakov Malkiel with pointing out that "it seems to correlate quite well with what, on other grounds too, we might describe as a hierarchy of semantic preference" (Lyons 1: 276). Another explanation for the order is that the unmarked form usually precedes because it is shorter than the marked term. The expression *ladies and gentlemen* might seem to fit this explanation, but *gentlemen* is itself a marked term and the expression is most often used in direct address where the conventions of politeness call for "ladies first." The sometimes conflicting basis for the order facilitates change, and today many writers are deliberately reversing these supposedly fixed expressions, especially where the basis of sequencing is sex. The result is to make linguistic usage more flexible:

> . . . a model for the frontier that encompasses three paired frontier images of women and men. (*Journal of American Folklore* 1975)

Comparative constructions, including similes and metaphors, often reveal their authors' underlying assumptions about sex-linked behavior and characteristics. The following example appears to signal the author's conviction that men, the reference group, have used scholarship for political purposes, a practice considered objectionable:

> Women, just as much as men, must be careful not to use the guise of folklore scholarship to try to further political ends, worthwhile though those ends may be. (*Journal of American Folklore* 1975)

Here a book reviewer's simile communicates a negative view of women:

> Like a woman telling a joke, Miss Waugh starts with the punch line and asks us to be patient while she fills in. (*New York Times Book Review* 1975)

In the next passage, the comparison between the lot of a professor and that of a movie hero combines with sex-marked labels (which may well be used ironically) to create a male image of academe:

> In an ever-expanding economy and birth-rate, professoring turned out to be a hot profession. . . . It was as in a movie of the thirties . . . where the hero had chosen to marry not the rich bitch but the good poor girl, and then discovered that she was really a millionairess in disguise. (*Profession 79*)

Later in the same article, graduate assistantships are referred to as "sort of the football scholarships of the learned clerks." A comparably "male" metaphor occurs in this example:

> While Hemingway was swashbuckling around, he put some hair on the chest of literature. (*Manchester Guardian* 1974)

In an essay about tradition in women's literary criticism, a male author chooses to use what he evidently considers a female metaphor:

> In the beginning was an aborted word. The first example of a woman's literary criticism in Western tradition, or more accurately the first miscarriage of a woman's criticism, occurs early in the *Odyssey*. (*Critical Inquiry* 1983)

Further consciousness-raising is needed. In an essay on graduate study the author, after criticizing another writer for appearing "to confine the mentor-ward involvement only to the situation of two males," proposes to "discuss young professionals independent of sex." In accord with this intention, the author uses *he/she* as a generic pronoun but reverts to stereotypical male identification in comparing the relationship between graduate students and their advisers to that between "Courtier and Lord" and in contrasting the scholarly community with "hearth and home," thereby placing the male academic world in conflict with a traditional female domain (*Communication Education* 1979).

The whole issue of gender marking is addressed in two satiric pieces by proponents of nonsexist language. In "A Tale of Two Sexes," a deliberately overdrawn satire about life in a corporate office, Bobbye D. Sorrels reverses existing conventions to show a top executive named Ms. Janesdaughter issuing orders of the following sort to her male assistants: "The chairwoman of the board is coming over too, so be sure the board room is in top shape. Although the chairwoman of the board is only a figurehead, he is married to the mayor and we want to impress him because of her" (*Nonsexist* 10). In a satire also designed to shock and thereby to challenge linguistic "tradition," Douglas R. Hofstadter begins with the premise that English is marked for race but not for sex: terms like *chairwhite* function as "generics," courtesy titles indicate whether or not black persons are employed (*Nrs.* versus *Niss*), white people are universally addressed as *Master*, and many terms contain "the time-honored colored suffixes 'oon' and 'roon,' found in familiar words such as *ambassadroon, stewardoon,* and *sculptroon*" (163). Hofstadter uses this "natural" division to demonstrate the absurdity of charges by "black libbers" that such language is "racist." Hofstadter's point, obviously, is that a systematic division by race would be repellent to most English speakers even if divisions by sex seem entirely natural to them. In a postscript he acknowledges that nonsexist language is

> like a foreign language that I am learning. I find that even after years of practice, I still have to translate sometimes from my native language, which is sexist English. I know of no human being who speaks Nonsexist as their native tongue. It will be very interesting to see if such people come to exist. (167)

Gender Marking and Related Usage

1. **In general, avoid feminine suffixes.**

2. **If objectionable feminine suffixes are necessary to refer accurately to another's usage, put them in quotation marks or find another way of showing your disapproval.**

3. **Avoid gender-marked clichés and stereotypes in your writing as you would avoid other kinds of clichés and stereotypes.**

4. **Use names and titles symmetrically.**

   a. Avoid asymmetrical usage: *Miss Austen* versus *Dickens*; *Ms. Jane Smith* versus *Doctor John Smith*, when both persons hold doctorates.

   b. Avoid diminutive or nonprofessional designations of authors: *Jane* (for Jane Austen); *Virginia* or *Mrs. Woolf* (for Virginia Woolf); *Dorothy* or *Dottie* (for Dorothy L. Sayers).

   c. Avoid referring to persons by names or titles that they would reject: *Miss Steinem* and *Mrs. Radway* (for the feminists Gloria Steinem and Janice Radway).

   d. Similarly, avoid Euro-American or feminist-centered usage when inappropriate: *Ms. Washington* for *Mrs. Booker T. Washington*.

   e. Use nonsexist titles with conviction; do not add a superfluous *Miss* or *Mrs.* parenthetically.

   f. Avoid the unthinking and exclusive use of male names as touchstones and symbols.

5. **Review language for gender stereotypes.** In the following example, Cordelia is compared to two figures, one female, the other male. The emphasis is appropriately on their roles, not on their sex:

   > That she dies as a sacrifice to her sense of filial love and duty puts her into the mythic role of Antigone or even Christ. (*PMLA* 1983)

6. **When using "female" metaphors, avoid stereotyped references to nurturance, passivity, and reproductive functions that are not directly relevant to the text.**

Special Concerns in Scholarly Writing and Other Professional Activities

False Universals

A central point of the previous sections, and an issue to which feminist theory repeatedly draws attention, is that discourse has a way of constructing false universals and making them seem natural. The feminist critical journey, in this respect, invokes the theories of Ferdinand de Saussure, Claude Lévi-Strauss, Sigmund Freud, and Jacques Lacan. And theories are often systems of rules that, as Teresa deLauretis writes,

> cannot but be obeyed if one is to communicate, speak, or participate in the social symbolic exchanges and precisely for this reason their theories have been considered pernicious or at least of little value to those eager to dismantle all systems (of power, oppression, or philosophy) and to theorize instead ideas of individual, class, race, gender, or group freedom. (*Alice* 3)

"Whoever defines the code or the context," Anthony Wilden observes, "has control . . . and all answers which accept that context abdicate the possibility of redefining it" (294). In many ways, the sexist language question is a challenge to both the context and the code: to both the ideology of gender and the code that naturalizes it. Such a challenge is embodied in Fetterley's call for women to become "resisting readers" and in Ruth Bleier's demonstration that in scientific research on gender "the voice of the natural" has always been a voice for the status quo (12). What Bleier calls man-the-hunter narratives celebrate evolutionary evidence repeatedly constructed through the language of the male generic. She argues that the use of the term *rape* to describe the male flower's act of pollinating a female flower enables the discourse of sociobiology to root male aggression in "the natural," for "plants that commit rape . . . are following evolutionary strategies that maximize their fitness" (32).

In pointing to such tendencies in masculinist traditions, feminist critics are themselves seeking to identify and resist temptations to universalize notions like *woman* and *the feminine subject* in their own writing. A woman who teaches and studies black women writers suggests that feminist literary critics should accurately specify the scope of their research on women:

> I read an analysis of nineteenth century French women's autobiographical writings that purported to offer a theory of women's literature—all women, all forms of literature. In my own work on nineteenth and twentieth century Black women writers, I would never make such a claim. Much feminist theory reproduces the same false notions of universality that we criticize in male theories.   (Qtd. in Treichler, "Teaching" 77)

Angela Y. Davis, tracing the African roots of the slave culture in the United States and the particular demands that slavery placed on black women, comments as follows: "Required by the masters' demands to be as 'masculine' in the performance of their work as men, Black women must have been profoundly affected by their experiences during slavery" (11). Answerable both to black men and to the white male owners, black women were from the outset beings who had "masculine" value as workers but who also had female value as breeders in the ongoing production of the labor force. Though not allowed to take their husbands' names, they must, in Davis's words, "have been aware nonetheless of their enormous power—the ability to produce and create" (11). The history of black women in the United States is thus dramatically different from that of the white middle-class women who became most vocal in the articulation of "women's experience" in the 1970s. Suggesting an alternative to this false universal, Cherríe Moraga and Gloria Anzaldúa argue that feminist theory should rest on the material realities and corporeal differences among women instead of trying to transcend those differences:

> A theory in the flesh means one where the physical realities of our lives—our skin color, the land or concrete we grew up on, our sexual longings—all fuse to create a politic born out of necessity.   (23)

Gloria I. Joseph argues, similarly, that feminism will ultimately need to encompass the powerful diversity of women's lives. This diversity is articulated more forcefully all the time. Anne Finger, for example, points out that if the feminist movement desires and claims to speak for all women, it will have to listen to the voices of women who have various disabilities. Feminism has focused on women's reproductive rights as a crucial goal, she observes, yet must do more to address the denial of those rights to women with disabilities, many of whom need the same information about birth control, abortion, pregnancy, and childbirth as able-bodied women do. Lesbians with disabilities are not credited with having chosen their sexuality but are often assumed (even by feminists) to have resigned themselves to "second best." Index entries under *disabled, retarded,* and the like in publications of the women's health movement refer almost exclusively to the fears and probabilities of having a "deformed" child and how to avoid this possibility. "The deeply-rooted fears that many women have of giving birth to a disabled child," writes Finger, "extend to our politics. They need to be worked through" (300–01).

Donna J. Haraway, who has helped deconstruct sociobiology's strategies for creating universal narratives, suggests that women may need to resist the apparent unity of their own female identities if they are to find a fundamental way of combating the universalizing and totalizing impulses of theory—including feminist theory. Feminism has brought about an acute consciousness of exclusion through naming, Haraway writes, and so "it has become difficult to name one's feminism by a single adjective—or even to insist in every circumstance upon the noun." She continues:

> Identities seem contradictory, partial, strategic. With the hard-won recognition of their social and historical constitution, gender, race, and class cannot provide the basis for belief in "essential" unity. There is nothing about being "female" that naturally binds women. There is not even such a state as "being" female, itself a highly complex category constructed in contested sexual scientific discourses and other social practices. ("Manifesto" 72)

Nor do other categories of women provide their members with natural identification:

> Women of color, a name contested at its origins by those whom it would incorporate, as well as a historical consciousness marking systematic breakdown of all the signs of Man in "Western" traditions,

constructs a kind of postmodernist identity out of otherness and difference. (73)

Haraway cites the work of Chela Sandoval, whose analysis of the new political voice called "women of color" denies any essential criterion for identifying members of this group: they represent not singularity but "a sea of differences" created by "a cascade of negative identities," such as nonwhite, nonblack, and nonmale. Women of color, Sandoval suggests, have themselves constructed a linguistic and political entity based on conscious coalition and political kinship rather than on natural identification.

Just as scrutiny and theoretical analysis fracture and destabilize unexamined concepts of such categories as *women, women of color*, and *feminism*, theoretical self-consciousness also seeks to extricate *race* from the discourse of the natural. Stephen Jay Gould, a scientist with highly developed linguistic sensitivities, recently suggested that unacknowledged racism may be at work in some scientists' preference for the hypothesis that the human species originated in Asia rather than—as solid evidence increasingly indicates—in Africa:

> [S]ubtle and largely unrecognized remnants of racist arguments viewed the tough climates of native Caucasians as prods to the evolution of higher things, and the languid tropics as a self-indulgent home for indolence and degeneration. . . . The racist traditions of our culture run so deep that vestiges remain, even among those who've struggled hard to overcome all prejudice. ("We" 53)

"Race," Writing, and Difference, a special issue of *Critical Inquiry* edited by Henry Louis Gates, Jr., explores the notion of race in considerable theoretical depth. Gates's introduction opens with the following question: "What importance does 'race' have as a meaningful category in the study of literature and the shaping of critical theory?" The quotation marks around *race* call attention to its status as a fictional construction: the term, Gates writes, "has both described and *inscribed* differences of language, belief system, artistic tradition, and gene pool, as well as all sorts of supposedly natural attributes such as rhythm, athletic ability, cerebration, usury, fidelity, and so forth." Indeed, it has become the trope of choice for "ultimate, irreducible difference"—in the total absence of evidence:

> The biological criteria used to determine "difference" in sex simply do not hold when applied to "race." Yet we carelessly use language in such a way as to *will* this sense of *natural* difference into our

formulations. To do so is to engage in a pernicious act of language, one which exacerbates the complex problem of cultural or ethnic difference, rather than to assuage or redress it.   (5)

This argument is designed not to deny that "race" operates in specific historical or cultural settings, including "everyday life," but to unmask its fraudulence as a scientific or objective designation. (As we have argued in this book, there are grounds for placing quotation marks around *sex* and *gender* as well, for they too are fictional constructions, despite the existence of actual women and men.) Thus the study of "race," writing, and difference requires scholars to examine how this fiction figures in their language, in the critical approaches they adopt—"recognizing especially that hermeneutic systems are not universal, color-blind, apolitical, or neutral" (15). Without such self-scrutiny, scholars can never begin to untangle the actual complexities signaled, inadequately, by the shorthand term *race*.

Responses to the "race" issue of *Critical Inquiry* displayed considerable preoccupation with both the quotation marks and the suggestion that notions of race may be embedded in critical theories. Replying to the widely divergent commentaries of the structuralist critic Tzvetan Todorov and the Afro-American critic Houston Baker, Gates takes issue with Todorov's view that analytical concepts are neutral and that their genesis—the traditions they come from—is irrelevant to the literary critic:

[F]or a critic of black literature to borrow European or American theories of literature regardless of *"where they come from"* is for that critic to be trapped in a relation of intellectual indenture or colonialism.   ("Talkin' " 207)

Gates concludes:

[My] call for vernacular theories of the Other was intended, as I state it to be, as an example of where [Houston Baker] and I found it necessary and fruitful to turn to escape the neocolonialism of the "egalitarian criticism" of Todorov and company, whose claims to "the universal" somehow always end up lopping off our arms, legs, and pug noses, muffling the peculiar timbres of our voices, and trying to straighten our always already kinky hair. . . .   (209)

Thus Gates completes his indictment of Euro-American theoretical dominance and its claims to "the universal"—what Baker in his piece calls the "whitemale hegemony" (188)—by usurping a favored and quintessentially lofty catch phrase from the critical theory lexicon to assert the inescapability of "race" as a factor in theory. Talking high theory at the same time that he's "talkin' that talk," Gates perfectly "signifies upon" Todorov's claims to an "egalitarian criticism," for he thus invokes the very specificities of identity that that criticism seeks to disclaim.

Textual Practices

This section deals first with difficulties that arise in discussing texts that, by today's standards, rest on discriminatory premises and use language now regarded as sexist. It goes on to point out biased practices in choosing examples and closes by addressing problems related to the established canon.

Gender, Genre, and Period

In scholarly writing, the voice of the interpreter is often difficult to extricate from the discourse under analysis. The scholar who focuses primarily on sex and gender issues has many opportunities to talk about the text's relevant assumptions and linguistic practices, but problems also arise in scholarship not directly concerned with these matters. Are all scholars now expected to index the beliefs about sex and gender they detect in the authors, discourses, or periods they are writing about? Or can they assume that readers will know what, say, *man* means in a given context?

In this passage from an article on Pope's *Essay on Man*, the scholar's use of *man* mirrors Pope's and provides the necessary referent for the *he* in the next clause and the *his* in the lines quoted from Pope:

> The relation of sameness and difference thus resembles that of self-love and reason in *An Essay on Man*. Without reason, man would blaze chaotically and destructively through the void; but without self-love—that is, governed by reason alone—he would be
>
> Fix'd like a plant on his peculiar spot,
> To draw nutrition, propagate, and rot. (*PMLA* 1982)

But if Pope is speaking of human beings, the generic *we* would be a workable alternative here, with the subsequent pronoun adjusted

Summary of Recommendations

False Universals

1. **Acknowledge alternative forms of representation.** "Mainstream" writers commonly generalize about, say, art or criticism as if their statements were universally applicable rather than applicable only to their own Euro-American tradition. They assume that this tradition is "tradition" and use modifiers to mark the productions of other groups. Modern poetry, for example, is their poetry as opposed to modern black poetry or Asian American poetry. Avoid this practice. Strive for a balanced treatment of groups and literary traditions, specifying those you include rather than treating the part as the whole.

2. **State your "speaking" position.** For example, in responding to Mary Daly's 1981 public lecture in Sydney, a member of the audience began, "I speak as a member of the third world women's group and also as a former Catholic." When Meaghan Morris quotes this statement in her analysis of Daly's poetry, she appends a note: "Since I am not a third world woman (nor a former Catholic), I would like to thank Laleen Jayamanne for her kind permission to appropriate her statement for my own purposes" ("A-mazing" 89). Donna J. Haraway declares her speaking position within the body of her text: "For me—and for many who share a similar historical location in white, professional middle class, female, radical, North American, mid-adult bodies—the sources of a crisis in political identity are legion" ("Manifesto" 73).

3. **Choose language that undermines the discourse of mastery.** Some feminists seek new ways of defining and doing scholarly work. One strategy is to conceptualize and portray feminist discourse as a collaborative effort, different from the male model in which individuals vie for sovereignty, for the "winning" theory. One feminist scholar, accordingly, describes feminist dialogues not as debates or competitions with other positions but as "conversations" among those who contribute the points of view appropriate to their own moments in history.

as appropriate to become a referent for Pope's "his":

> The relation of sameness and difference thus resembles that of self-love and reason in *An Essay on Man*. Without reason, we would blaze chaotically and destructively through the void; but without self-love—that is, governed by reason alone—each of us would be
>
> > Fix'd like a plant on his peculiar spot,
> > To draw nutrition, propagate, and rot.

Scholars may argue that a literary audience will not find Pope's use of *man* ambiguous and, further, that repeated quotation from the primary source may become cumbersome if an original referent like *man* cannot be used. On the first point, not all readers will necessarily know whether Pope intended *man* to include women. Part of the scholar's task is to show awareness that language and meaning change over time and to provide expert information about changes that are significant. Since the word *man* has functioned ambiguously for several hundred years, it is useful for scholars to indicate—though not elaborately—what this linguistic form meant to the authors they are discussing. Indeed, there may be scholars who have not themselves thought about this question; or there may be disagreement that is itself of intrinsic scholarly interest. The point here is to strive for accuracy, not to rewrite history to clear or convict Pope of what we would now call sexism. There is also the point that literature, linguistics, and the other humanities are at some level (no matter how technical or rarefied their scholarship) committed to a search for generalizable truths about human activity. Providing information about sex and gender can help teachers and other scholars formulate valid generalizations. Some comment about the status of women (or the conception of "Man") early in an essay may lessen the need to change the word *man* on every occasion in the course of a close reading.

Scholars can, moreover, make a point of shifting to genuinely generic language in their own texts. A bit further on in the essay on Pope, for example, the author shifts back to his own voice and to the scholarly community today:

> I suspect we too often read Pope's accounts of the relation of part to whole, in *An Essay on Man* and elsewhere, as though they were governed by a single spatial or perspectival model—as though, that is, the difference between man's view and God's view were that God stands farther back or has wide-angle vision.

Here we would suggest replacing *man's view* with *our view, the human view,* or *the individual's view.* Such a device potentially gives greater applicability to the scholar's conclusions and at the same time dissociates the scholar from the exclusion of women implied in the work under study.

A 1983 *PMLA* essay on Milton uses inclusive, nonsexist language in its opening section, with *human beings* replacing the *man* that would probably have appeared in years past:

> At the root of all these beneficial activities and therefore of civilization itself was Jove's initiative, which brought the golden age to an end and compelled human beings by the driving force of want to labor, to think, and to invent.

But as the author starts to analyze the texts and interpret the scholarly positions within his field, he reverts to traditional male generic forms:

> As the angel leads Adam and Eve from the garden at the conclusion of the epic, a last simile adumbrates man's condition in history.

Eve is present at the beginning of the sentence; where is she at the end? And:

> Milton evokes a timeless picture of georgic man but complicates the sorrow by introducing a return home from labor. For labor ends at death; and also, as the covenant of the flood reminds us, man's work will be accomplished at the end of time when he will return to paradise once more.

Such usage is problematic because it is ambiguous and leaves readers uncertain about the inclusion of woman in man's return to paradise. What did Milton intend? What does the critic intend? Is he reflecting the usage of the text he is commenting on? Or is the apparent ambiguity solely an inadvertent artifact of conventional male generic usage? Does *man* exclude women here? Will all readers know what Milton meant? Or is his intention to some extent not known or even knowable?

Again, we believe that scholarly awareness is what is called for, along with a willingness to disambiguate generic references. In the example just given, the critic needs to judge how much explanation is needed. An article intended for a broad general audience might appropriately include something about how Milton viewed women and where they fit into his cosmology; a highly specialized readership will need less background information. Here the scholar might have used a critical paraphrase to clarify Milton's intentions:

> As the angel leads Adam and Eve from the garden at the conclusion of the epic, a last simile adumbrates the human condition in history.

The adjective *human* would be sufficient to reinforce the gender-inclusive sense carried by *Adam and Eve*. If, however, the critic wished to convey "adult men" as the original meaning, the statement might read:

> As the angel leads Adam and Eve from the garden at the conclusion of the epic, a last simile adumbrates man's condition in history (though not woman's: Eve is to have a different fate).

Scholars commonly begin to echo the texts they are writing about; because their goal is in some sense to weave together the voices of the researcher and the researched, questions of language can be delicate and problematic. In the following sentence, for example, a critic who regularly uses *men and women* elsewhere in his writing presumably reflects here the male generic usage of the author he is discussing:

> [Althusser's work on ideology] defined ideologies as providing the frameworks of understanding through which men interpret, make sense of, experience, and "live" the material conditions in which they find themselves.   (Cultural studies anthology 1980)

Despite the closeness of commentator and text, critical distance enables the scholar to establish a voice separate from the text's and, in this voice, to offer information on sex and gender questions. Such clarification, which can be brief and uncondescending, not merely serves the interests of accuracy but helps the reader better understand how concepts of sex and gender function, making it possible to trace their construction in a multiplicity of contexts.

The description of Althusser's work in the last example does not indicate whom the term *man* encompasses. A key passage in an essay on Antonio Gramsci was similarly ambiguous. It was edited for publication, however, to clarify the term *man*—or at least to clarify the ways in which the critic finds the term problematic in Gramsci's work. Here is the passage, showing the editorial changes made on the original:

> But for the fuller, more developed meaning of this "arrival," this so-called "absolute historicized immanence," Gramsci directed our attention, once again, to the *Theses on Feuerbach*. ~~And~~ he comment~~s~~ed that, in the first Thesis, the unity of the theoretical and practical activity referred to by Marx is precisely the dialectical unity of matter and "man," where matter is understood to mean the material forces of production, the "economic elements," and ~~whereas~~ "man" ~~is understood~~ to mean "the complex social relations" or, "more exactly, the process of his actions." But as we have seen, since Gramsci acknowledged that for the philosophy of praxis there is no such thing as an objective truth free from error, no truth outside history, no thing-in-itself, this suggests that the meaning of both matter and "man" is constructed in and by reality and that, consequently, there neither exists a general or pure economic science nor a natural "man" or "man-in-general." In other words, the meaning of "what is man" is always subject to history; it is ~~one which is~~ historically created, and ~~one which~~ "changes with changes in the circumstances," and ~~one which~~ is the "synthesized" unitary moment of our ~~man's~~ theoretical and practical activity. It is a meaning that ~~which~~ Gramsci argued is always, ~~consequently,~~ in the process of becoming. This led him ~~leads Gramsci~~ to conclude, as well, that not only is the meaning of "what is man" an historical creation, but that meaning itself is an historical creation. Meaning is also, in other words, the synthesized unitary expression of our ~~man's~~ creation, our ~~man's~~ theoretical and practical activity. (Anthology on Marxism and culture 1987)

The quotation marks around one use of *man* in the original signal that the critic is self-conscious about Gramsci's term but not why: do they identify discriminatory language or some other problem? The edited version accomplishes several things: it preserves the terms of the original discourse, including the important *matter* and *man*; it indicates, however, that the quotation marks around *man* mark the word not merely as "sexist" but as incorrectly presumed to be "natural"; finally, having argued that "man" is a historically created construction, the passage makes this entity (even if constructed) universal and generic by replacing *man's* with *our*.

Often the critic is discussing a field, genre, or experience during a time when it *was* all male: are *man* and *he* then permitted? Before considering that question we want to stress the prior need of verifying the assumption of exclusive maleness. We repeat that language both reflects and constructs. A sentence like "The turn-of-the century US physician had begun to integrate scientific knowledge from Paris into his practice" reinforces a widespread but incorrect belief that during this period all physicians in this country were male. In fact, by 1900 many women physicians were teaching in medical schools or practicing medicine, more than at any other time until very recently. Women physicians have existed for thousands of years: tombstones with the feminine suffix on the word *medica* are part of the evidence, though scribes in later centuries often changed the endings in keeping with their own beliefs; the name of the famous Italian obstetrician Trotula was rendered in some later texts as Trottus, helping to perpetuate the myth that all physicians were male (Hurd-Mead v). A stylistic convention, then, takes on a life of its own in this context and helps to erase women from medical history. Indeed, the names of many black women physicians were literally erased from hospital registers (Aptheker 96; also see Hine). Similarly, lesbians are not named in the British statutes prohibiting homosexuality, not because there were no lesbians but because Queen Victoria claimed total ignorance of such persons and refused to sign the bill unless all references to female homosexual practices were removed (Bland 20; Crane 8–10).

If a scholar uses *he* to refer to an unspecified eighteenth-century ode writer, the pronoun may be making a claim about these writers or about the canon—or it may not. But it is important to repeat that the unthinking use of gender-neutral terms may also be misleading. One author objected to *scholars*, the nonsexist alternative to *men* proposed by an editor of her essay, arguing that this would alter and muddy her point: she meant *male* men—specifically the "university-trained gentlemen" (no women attended the university) who would have had access to a particular set of books:

> One didn't *have* to be a *scholar* to know these books; ordinary men at the university knew them (and only *men* attended the university —so I refer to them as university-trained gentlemen). It is not to say that women outside the university could not have known the books. But that's not part of my argument. I only want to establish the most likely place Milton might have come into contact with myth books. Therefore, retain gentlemen or at least men for clarity of argument.

This argument is valid, for *men*, as we have said, is unobjectionable as a sex-specific term. Scholarship seeks to communicate accurate information; neither the denial of women's participation in a given activity (like practicing medicine) nor the denial of their absence (e.g., in universities) serves this goal.

So what and how much background information does the reader need? We recommend that every use of *man* or *men* be briefly annotated if the context permits any ambiguity. The author just quoted was arguing, not that women could not have known about the myth books, just that the university was a likely place for Milton to have encountered them. We would suggest annotating the phrase "university-trained gentlemen" to offer precisely the explanation the author gave the editor.

Quotations: Preserving the Integrity of the Original

In scholarly writing, it is axiomatic that quotations must preserve the integrity of the original text. Accordingly, detailed conventions prescribe how to represent and document extracts from sources. Although there is considerable latitude here, certain rules are considered inviolate. Scholars may vary, for example, in what they consider fair ways of omitting portions of the original text, differing about how omissions should be indicated, how much text can be omitted without radically distorting meaning, how much information should be provided, how much subjective interpretation is permitted, and so on. But there is no disagreement about the need to indicate any omission from the original passage, even a single word. Likewise, though scholars may disagree about the fairness of making substitutions in the original, they agree that any changes must be identified. It is also routine to clarify any ambiguity about the accuracy of the reproduced text, through such remarks as "[italics mine]," "[*sic*]," or "[I have corrected only obvious typos]." Not all emendations are neutral, however: many take on a connotative life of their own. Here, for example, an author is discussing an argument made by two feminist linguists:

> They maintain that the borrowing of the word *husband* into late Old English from Old Norse is evidence that "the notion of males living with wimmin [sic] must have still been relatively recent." (Scholarly text on language and gender 1986)

As it happens, this author disagrees with the scholars he is quoting, and he may have quoted their alternative spelling of *women* deliberately to signal his skepticism about their argument. At times, then, *sic* is not a neutral assurance of accurate quotation but a warning to the reader to be on guard: "If they spell *women* in this crazy way, how can you believe a thing they tell you?" If this author had agreed with the argument, he might have paraphrased the original so that he could use the conventional spelling. In feminist writing, a *sic* following the quotation of a particularly outrageous instance of male chauvinism carries the connotation "Yes I know it's hard to believe, but the guy really said this."

Writers who adhere to gender-neutral usage face a problem when they quote a text that uses male "generic" pronouns. Often, as we have noted, they may have to do research to determine and clarify the original meaning. But they need not alter the text itself by, for example, supplying "understood" material or extrapolating what the meaning would be if the author were writing today. Sometimes a scholar who wants to present an author sympathetically tries to avoid exposing contemporary readers to material they will find offensive, such as unambiguously sexist or racist remarks. This classic problem in scholarship has occurred notoriously in the suppression of evidence linking an author to homosexuality or to "politically incorrect" views. We cannot address this issue here beyond saying that we do not recommend emending the original language. We would not advocate, say, changing Lacan's male pronoun to *elle* and translating it "she" as a linguistic form of feminist appropriation. Even adding *[or she]* after a *he* in Lacan would be highly questionable, because our taken-for-granted notions about sex and gender *are* precisely what he is often disputing.

The purpose of a scholarly undertaking will inevitably influence the way the critic copes with an author's discriminatory language.

In the following example, a present-day male critic adds bracketed expansions to a quotation from Gramsci:

> There do however exist certain general criteria which could be held to constitute the critical consciousness of every man [and woman] of science, whatever his [or her] specialization.   (Cultural studies anthology 1980)

A critic quoting this passage simply to report Gramsci's original argument might have reproduced it verbatim. But because this critic wanted to emphasize what he himself believes are crucial features of intellectual practice, it was important to adapt the original quotation to make it inclusive, to turn it into a broadly relevant statement that he, too, could endorse. But, again, purely mechanical solutions are rarely satisfactory. If the critic had decided to expand *all* instances of *he* and *man* in Gramsci to include female references, the next sentence in the quotation cited above would have read as follows:

> Thus one can say someone is not a scientist if he [or she] displays a lack of sureness in his [or her] particular criteria, if he [or she] does not have a full understanding of the concepts he [or she] is using, if he [or she] has scant information and understanding of the previous state of the problems he [or she] is dealing with, if he [or she] is not very cautious in his [or her] assertions, if he [or she] does not proceed in a necessary but an arbitrary or disconnected fashion, if he [or she] cannot take account of the gaps that exist in knowledge acquired, but covers over and contents himself [or herself] with purely verbal solutions and connections, instead of stating that one is dealing with provisional positions which may have to be gone over again and developed, etc.

The solution the critic chose—to annotate the first occurrence and then return to the original text—accurately preserves Gramsci's rhetorical style (at least in translation, a complicating factor discussed below), certainly makes the text more readable, and assumes that the reader can interpret the noun "scientist" generically, given the earlier inclusion of *women*. For some readers, however, the solution might be confusing or misleading. The critic might have chosen instead to retain the original wording throughout, explaining that the meaning should be understood to include women as well as men. Or the quotation could be paraphrased in the plural, with gender-neutral phrases from the original dropped in. The nature of the original text—what it most easily lends itself to—may influence which solution is least conspicuous.

Of course, one might also argue that this description of practices, such as displaying no "lack of sureness," is not generic but, rather, traditionally male. To some degree, Evelyn Fox Keller makes a distinction between "male science" and "female science" in *A Feeling for the Organism*, her biography of the scientist Barbara McClintock. But in the Gramsci quotation, as we noted, the critic seeks primarily to underscore the emphasis on intellectual practice as opposed simply to ideas. And it is this aspect of the text that he most carefully annotates and clarifies.

It is not feasible to annotate and explicate every term in a quotation, but it is helpful to disambiguate basic information about gender, providing explanations in the text, in endnotes, or in brackets within the quotation itself. Resurrecting an earlier example, we can more systematically illustrate how to clarify direct quotations:

> The depressed person often becomes aware of strong feelings of self-dislike; he feels worthless and guilty about his shortcomings. He believes that nothing he can do will alleviate his condition. . . . Food no longer tastes good, sex is not arousing, and people, even his wife and children, become wholly uninteresting.

We originally used this example to indicate ambiguity and an apparent shift from generic to sex-specific usage, and we suggested how rewriting might improve the text. But let us now suppose that this particular characterization of depression—written, say, by John Smith, PhD—has become famous and that we wish to explicate it in detail. Independent evidence, we further assume, indicates that the author intended his analysis to apply to both males and females and that he used the male pronoun strictly because it was conventional to do so. Indeed, depression exemplifies a disorder for which accurate information about sex is crucial, since studies of major depression in adults in industrialized countries estimate that depression is twice as common in women as in men (American Psychiatric Association 229). So the sex of the depressed person is relevant here, and there are several ways to convey it. One is to state the author's intention by way of introduction:

> In the following passage, Smith outlines his classic characterization of depression (though Smith speaks of "the depressed person" as male, scholars of his work generally agree that he intended the description to apply to women and men).

A second possibility is to quote the passage verbatim and to comment on it in an endnote:

> ¹Smith speaks here as though "the depressed person" is male, but scholars of his work generally agree that he intended the description to apply to both women and men. Indeed, correspondence in the Smith archive contains a lively dialogue on this very passage between Smith and Harry Bream, his editor at Watson and Woofson. "When I *mean* both men and women," Smith wrote prior to the first edition (1/15/43), "it seems less than straightforward—even clinically irresponsible—to use nouns and pronouns that disguise this fact and imply that only married males will meet this description." Bream responded as follows: "Our firm policy at W&W, as you know, is to use such standard English conventions as the one you cite; I do not think it will damage your argument to defer to us on this point. On the contrary, I think you will only lose credibility if you imply that a serious presentation of depression is identical in men and women"   (1/29/43).

(If we recovered Smith's original manuscript from the archive and found it to use gender-inclusive terms, then we might quote the published version and cite the original text in a note, or focus the analysis more centrally on the differences between the original and the published version, or argue for a new edition.)

Or we might clarify the meaning of the text internally, using brackets:

> The depressed person [male or female] often becomes aware of strong feelings of self dislike; he [or she] feels worthless and guilty about his [or her] shortcomings. He [or she] believes that nothing he [or she] can do will alleviate his [or her] condition. . . . Food no longer tastes good, sex is not arousing, and people, even his wife [or her husband] and children, become wholly uninteresting.

Here, as in the Gramsci quotation above, repeated internal emendations do not make for smooth reading. One alternative is to reproduce the original text and explain that *he* is used generically; another is to annotate the first usage only, as the Gramsci critic did:

> The depressed person [either male or female] often becomes aware of strong feelings of self-dislike; he feels worthless and guilty about his shortcomings.

Excerpts from a description of depression now in official use reveal other solutions:

> The essential feature of a Major Depressive Episode is either depressed mood . . . or loss of interest or pleasure in all, or almost all, activities, and associated symptoms, for a period of at least two weeks. . . . The associated symptoms include appetite disturbance, change in weight, psychomotor agitation or retardation, decreased energy, feelings of worthlessness or excessive or inappropriate guilt, difficulty in thinking or concentrating, and recurrent thoughts of death. . . .
>
> Loss of interest or pleasure is probably always present . . . to some degree, and is often described by the person as not being as interested in usual activities as previously, "not caring anymore," or, more rarely, a painful inability to experience pleasure.
>
> The sense of worthlessness varies from feelings of inadequacy to completely unrealistic negative evaluations of one's worth. The person may reproach himself or herself for minor failings that are exaggerated and search the environment for cues confirming the negative self-evaluation.   (American Psychiatric Association 218–19)

Notable here is a shift in emphasis from the person experiencing depression to the depression itself and its symptoms—a shift reflected in the syntactic structure:

> The feature of depression is depressed mood.
> The associated symptoms include appetite disturbance. . . .
> Loss of interest is always present to some degree.
> Loss of interest is described by the person as losing interest in activities,
>   not caring anymore, and lacking the ability to experience pleasure.

Although "the person" is still semantically involved—reporting symptoms, losing interest, becoming unable to experience pleasure—the syntax for the most part removes the person from the subject position and from most sentences entirely. Such agent deletion is accomplished through the use of passive and "there is" constructions, gerunds and participles, and abstract nominals.

While these structural features create their own set of problems (e.g., the much criticized tendency in modern medicine to treat diseases rather than patients), the description as a whole is steadfastly applicable to either gender as well as to people in diverse living arrangements; that is, unlike the previous example, it presumes no nuclear family.

Finally, some quoted passages containing discriminatory usage may call for more explicit comment. In the following examples, the author of an essay in *Profession 78* quotes verbatim from an essay published in a literature journal in 1967:

> The English Ph.D. does not often venture out into the cold, non-academic world. Faithful to his careful traditions, he enters the teaching profession at the rate of ninety-one to the hundred. The nine who stray in strange lands probably end up grading their husbands' themes.

The author of the 1978 essay then comments that this passage "reveals how much our consciousness has been raised in the past ten years by the women's movement."

Figures of Speech: Metaphors, Allusions, Idioms, Proverbs

Metaphors, writes Ronald Langacker, "have an enormous influence on how scholars deal with their subject matter, even when they regard their investigation as being fully objective" (387). Though some scholars would challenge this assertion, few would deny the pervasiveness of metaphors in the scholarly language of the humanities. Indeed, even investigators in the natural and physical sciences draw centrally on metaphors to represent theories and events. Gould shows how metaphors of evolution were deployed in the service of intelligence testing and eugenics (*Mismeasure*); Keller shows how a language of "masculinity" and "virility" was explicitly used as a foundation for modern science (*Reflections* 7). Elsewhere in this book we suggest that meaning is never pure but always partly dependent on how it is represented linguistically. The role of metaphor in representation is a vast topic, far beyond our present scope, and we can therefore give only a few examples.

It is not always a straightforward task to identify and address the problems of "sexist" metaphors and other figurative language. Some argue that all writing short of quoted primary material can be updated, changed, or rendered otherwise gender-neutral without consequence. And often one allusion, idiom, or proverb can indeed substitute for another. Many of the guidelines included in the bibliographical section list proverbs and suggested substitutes. For example, in some contexts the meaning of "he who hesitates is lost" could be captured by "a stitch in time saves nine." But language plays off history, and some contexts may require particular figures of speech. In the following example, an author discusses the deeply felt perceptions of John Dewey, Josiah Royce, and others that the posturbanization, postindustrialization world of twentieth-century America was out of joint. Progressive social thought struggled with the prospects for democracy in a society based on mass communication rather than on face-to-face communities:

> Is the vision of each "man" determining "his" own fate absolute in a society of such colossal scale, where things are in the saddle and ride mankind? Is political participation a chimera in a society of displaced city-dwellers and uprooted immigrants? (*Communication* 1988)

The author signals awareness of pseudogeneric terms like *man* in the so-called mass-culture debates and uses gender-neutral nouns in the last sentence (*city-dwellers, immigrants*). But in the first sentence the allusion to Emerson's "things are in the saddle and ride mankind" efficiently evokes and plays on an earlier assessment of American history. Although knowledgeable readers rarely need explicit signposts to identify allusions, the author could have disclaimed responsibility for the "sexist" *mankind* by inserting *in Emerson's words*, enclosed in commas, between *where* and *things*. In this instance, it seems to us that the quotation marks around *man* and *his* are all right. But in other contexts (perhaps even here for some readers) they might be ambiguous, seeming to function not to evoke the language of a given discourse but rather to question its terms: "men," that is, might seem to mean so-called men—persons who are actually less than that (say, cowards or beasts). One feature of some writing in critical theory is the profusion of quotation marks that aim to call terms into question, render them problematic. It is a stylistic device that may quickly become tiresome (see Morris's comments on the overuse of such "scare quotes" ["Pirate's" 24]). In this and similar examples, therefore, it might be better to use the first-person plural:

> Is the concept that we each determine our own fate absolute in a society of such colossal scale, where, in Emerson's words, things are in the saddle and ride mankind?

An anonymous male reader of a manuscript being considered by a university press argued that adding *[sic]* after a pseudogeneric use of *man* to citations from prefeminist texts is "incorrect." He suggests using [woman] next to *man* in the text or pointing out, in an introductory statement, the linguistic bias of earlier texts and urging the reader to read the material as gender-inclusive. He concludes by saying, "Since the feminist linguistic awakening, such offenses are no longer tolerable, but we cannot rewrite the whole of world literature." Certainly we agree that cluttering quotations from a primary text with *[sic]*s is not a desirable solution. Such interpolations interfere with reading, and when added to the words of a familiar author (Wordsworth, say), they often seem ludicrous as well as disruptive. If, of course, the point to be made involves the text's outrageous sexism, then the repetition of *[sic]* would underscore the magnitude of the problem (though it would also grow tiresome). But in general we agree that prefeminist texts should be left alone as much as possible, with a discussion offered external to the text. As we indicate elsewhere, the disclaimer needs to be accurate and to distinguish carefully between gender-inclusive and sex-specific (male) meanings.

Illustrative Material

Elsewhere in this book (in our introduction, and in Treichler's essay) we cite sexist sentences dictionary editors have constructed to illustrate word usages. Such illustrations and exemplary sentences can be found in all fields. An epidemiology and statistics text written in the 1960s uses the example of a sultan and his harem to illustrate the different ways of measuring the behavior of individuals within groups. In linguistics, the creation of clever, racy, or topical examples became popular in the 1960s:

> If he has a boring wife, a man should find a mistress.   (Reinhart 116)

Even more sober instances embody troubling representations of women. Opening at random the first volume of Keith Allan's linguistics text, which discusses many of these now standard examples, we find:

> *Discussion of singular and plural*
> The committee is/are composed of notable scholars.
> The committee consists/consist of both men and women.
> The committee contains/contain many men of distinction.   (128)

Discussion of literal vs. idiomatic meaning
The prime minister is an old woman.
If the prime minister is Gladstone, this means:
    The prime minister is a man who complains too much and is
    overconcerned with trivia.
If the prime minister is Golda Meir, this means:
    The prime minister is a woman of advancing years.   (67–68)

Discussion of meaning-changing transformations
a. John even kissed Kate!
b. Kate was even kissed by John!
c. Maísie didn't shoot her husband.
d. Maisie didn't shóot her husband.   (290–92)

Discussion of progressive tense marking
Will is hunting for deer.
Percy is holidaying in France.
He's telephoning her now.
She is crying.   (334)

Discussion of novel or untrue but grammatical sentences
John insisted that the smallest prime number is 2.
John diagonalized the differential manifold.
Almond Eyes ate her Kornies and listened to the radio.   (41–42)

Linguistics often assumes a male, heterosexual, and sex-stereo-
typical norm, a norm that influences the examples used for discussions of topics not directly concerned with gender. In fact, the
final examples cited, which serve to demonstrate an infinite capacity
to construct grammatical sentences unrelated to real-world conditions, also demonstrate an infinite capacity to reproduce sex stereotypes even in a world that does not exist.

Virginia L. Warren cites a number of classic and long-standing
discussions in philosophy that are founded on sexist illustrative
sentences. The most famous example is the complex question:

When did you stop beating your wife?   (473)

Warren notes that other classical texts draw on such statements as
the following:

As a citizen, for example, man abides by the law and works hard for
his wife and children.   (473)

The philosopher uses his reason to guide him.   (475)

For Aristotle, man is, above all, Political Man.

Consider what the ordinary man thinks about justice.

What would the rational man do in this situation?   (478)

Warren argues that one must take care in revising such sentences if they are not to misrepresent the issues they illustrate. For example, she notes that a standard gender-neutral revision might recast the last sentence either by changing *man* to *person* or by using the plural:

What would the rational person do in this situation?

What would rational persons (individuals) do in this situation?

Grammatically, the plural would be preferable because it facilitates pronoun use in the subsequent discussion. The philosopher, however, might prefer *the rational person* because the definite article here implies that all rational persons must come to the same conclusion. This consideration reveals the impulse in philosophical discourse to seek universals in place of diversity. Whether or not one agrees with such thinking, the point is that language is intrinsic to practices in the field, and revisions of the language need to take the discursive traditions and purposes of the particular discipline into account.

Questioning the Canon

Gender can complexly and diversely influence the ways contemporary scholars relate to the texts they study, and questions often arise about what constitutes linguistic sexism. In feminist scholarship and in much scholarship about women's writings, gender is a central and explicit topic. But familiar Euro-American literature was largely written by white educated males for a like audience. Feminist scholars have taken varied approaches to the question of gender in earlier periods. Some concern themselves with what Germaine Greer has called archaeology, unearthing "lost" women's writing, evaluating its contributions, and identifying how social and cultural biases may work to value and preserve some works but not others. The *Norton Anthology of Women's Literature* (ed. Gilbert and Gubar) demonstrates women's contributions to literature. Others seek to illuminate the "women's part" in the great works of literature—Shakespeare, Milton, and so on (see Lenz, Greene, and Neely). Similarly, as scholars encounter the works of the past with new eyes and new sensibilities, they often adopt what Annette Kolodny calls "maps for rereading," maps that enable them to identify what is now visible—knowing what they know—in what was written then. Kolodny demonstrates how a feminist rereading of nineteenth-century women's writing illuminates meanings that generally eluded contemporary readers. Other scholars seek to document exclusions and biases in the traditional male writing and scholarship that created "the canon" (Gilbert's essay "The Education of Henrietta Adams" is one example). Still others articulate and explore the notion of "writing as a woman," examining the gaps and silences of texts (e.g., Jardine, *Gynesis*). This "re-visioning" of texts also involves different approaches—for example, an examination of the heterosexist and ethnocentric assumptions of most scholarship. The vantage point of gay studies illuminates in new ways both biographical and interpretive aspects of criticism and, again, underlines the complexity of sexual identity in relation to texts.

Adrienne Rich wrote "Writing as Re-Vision" for a 1971 MLA forum on the woman writer in the twentieth century. Reprinting it in her 1979 collection, she added a prefatory note:

> The Modern Language Association is both marketplace and funeral parlor for the professional study of Western literature in North America. Like all gatherings of the professions, it has been and remains a "procession of the sons of educated men" (Virginia Woolf): a congeries of old-boys' networks, academicians rehearsing their numb canons in sessions dedicated to the literature of white males, junior scholars under the lash of "publish or perish" delivering papers in the bizarrely lit drawing-rooms of immense hotels: a ritual competition veering between cynicism and desperation.
>
> However, in the interstices of these gentlemanly rites (or, in Mary Daly's words, on the boundaries of this patriarchal space), some feminist scholars, teachers, and graduate students, joined by feminist writers, editors, and publishers, have for a decade been creating more subversive occasions, challenging the sacredness of the gentlemanly canon, sharing the rediscovery of buried works by women, asking women's questions, bringing literary history and criticism back to life in both senses.
>
> The challenge flung by feminists at the accepted literary canon,

at the methods of teaching it, and at the biased and astigmatic views of male "literary scholarship," has not diminished in the decade since the first Women's Forum; it has become broadened and intensified more recently by the challenges of black and lesbian feminists pointing out that feminist literary criticism itself has overlooked or held back from examining the work of black women and lesbians.

Much, much more is yet to be done; and university curricula have of course changed very little as a result of all this. What *is* changing is the availability of knowledge, of vital texts, the visible effects on women's lives of seeing, hearing our wordless or negated experience affirmed and pursued further in language.   (*On Lies* 33–34)

All around us are examples of challenges to existing canons and of the unease these challenges create:

It is hard to evaluate this work because it is not clear whether it should be evaluated against the standards set for literary criticism or women's studies.   (*Communication* 1983)

This book will undoubtedly become a classic, not only in cross-cultural psychology, but in social science in general. Its topic, sex stereotypes, is extremely timely but also very controversial. . . . [The authors] shows dispassionate objectivity and ideological restraint for which open-minded readers will be grateful.   (Publisher's flyer 1985)

While the proponents of other critical approaches—such as reader-response criticism, poststructuralism, Marxist criticism, and the sociology of literature—are also questioning canonicity, we specifically wished to expose the operations of a gender system in literary endeavors.   (Anthology on women and literary scholarship 1982)

Some consequences of the questioning appear in the work of male critics, often taking the form of hesitant language:

At the moment it seems clear that what follows here, both in its emerging clarities and remaining confusions, results from my somewhat surprised surrender to voices previously alien to me: the "Mikhail Bakhtin" who speaks to me, muffled by my ignorance of Russian, and the "feminist criticism" that in its vigor and diversity and challenge to canonic views has—belatedly, belatedly—forced me to begin listening.   (*Critical Inquiry* 1982)

The canonicity issue plays itself out in language in ways that require fairly subtle and informed analysis. In their introduction to *Shake-*

speare's Sisters, Sandra M. Gilbert and Susan Gubar discuss the devaluation of women poets:

> Whatever alternative tradition the woman poet attempts to substitute for "ancient rules" is subtly devalued. Ransom, for instance, asserts that Dickinson's meters, learned from "her father's hymnbook," are all based upon "Folk line, the popular form of verse and the oldest in our Language," adding that "the great classics of this meter are the English ballads and Mother Goose." Our instinctive sense that this is a backhanded compliment is confirmed when he remarks that "Folk line is disadvantageous . . . if it denies to the poet the use of English Pentameter," which is "the staple of what we may call the studied or 'university' poetry, and . . . is capable of containing and formalizing many kinds of substantive content which would be too complex for Folk Line. Emily Dickinson appears never to have tried it." If we read "pentameter" here as a substitute for "ancient rules," then we can see that once again "woman" and "poet" are being defined as contradictory terms.   (xxii)

A number of terms have been coined within feminist scholarship to mark new approaches to the canon. These include Moers's *heroinism*, noted above; Domna Stanton's *generic differences*, to describe the way women use and rewrite the rhetorical structures of memoirs, journals, letters, and autobiographies; Jardine's *gynesis*, an exploration of the female text and what it means to "write as a woman"; Showalter's *gynocritics*, the identification and exploration of themes and patterns in writing by women ("Women's Time"); and Marjorie Pryse and Hortense Spillers's *conjuring*, a term that disputes any rigid notion of literary tradition, whether male or female. Challenges to the canon, forcefully initiated by feminists and other underrepresented minorities, continue, though feminist proposals have achieved much less hegemony than is alleged by traditionalists (see Bate and "Reports from the Academy" for prime examples).

Summary of Recommendations

Textual Practices

1. **Clarify the meaning of sex and gender referents, inclusions, and exclusions.** The critic should alert the reader, briefly and without condescension, to the sex and gender assumptions reflected in the text under discussion. Such clarification not only serves the interests of accuracy but also helps those doing research

on gender, enabling them to assess the multiplicity of views about sexual similarities and differences. Thus a Milton scholar, for example, should give readers enough information about the author's views for them to know whether or where to interpret *men* in Milton's text as meaning "male adults."

2. **Clarify your use of sex-specific *man* or *men*, if any ambiguity is possible, by stating explicitly that you refer to male adults; further clarify what subset of men you refer to.** Thus use unambiguous terms like *men and women, human beings, university-trained gentlemen* and, if necessary, indicate (within parentheses, in an endnote, or within the text) why the sex-specific terms are accurate and appropriate.

3. **Do not substitute gender-neutral terms for sex-specific terms that would misrepresent the norms of the period.** The mechanical substitution of *men and women* for *gentlemen* in discussing eighteenth-century British university education, for example, misrepresents the social stratification by both sex and class that limited higher education to privileged male students. If in writing about the past you use terms like *scholars* and *the upper class*—which in today's usage are essentially generic—a brief note should explain to whom they referred at the time.

4. **Do not assume heterosexuality as a norm, whether for an author, a community, a culture, or a language.** It may be relevant to indicate a writer's sexual orientation, to the extent that it is known, even if the author was not sexually active. Linguistics scholarship often appears to assume that the human norm is male and heterosexual. In studies of both syntax and semantics, examples and even decisions about syntactic structure are often based on male heterosexist assumptions (e.g., that human nouns are masculine unless marked nonmale), as are etymologies, glosses for historical or reconstructed terms, and translations.

5. **If a text uses the same term in both generic and sex-specific senses, clarify the usage in individual contexts.** The following example shows how a scholar might annotate *Man's* in a sentence echoing or paraphrasing Milton's text:

Man's work (and here *Man's* certainly means "male human beings")

continued

[*or* (and here Milton is using *Man's* in its generic sense)] will be accomplished at the end of time when he will return to paradise once more.

6. Preserve the integrity of the original text. Direct quotations must preserve the original text. Commentary that clarifies or otherwise addresses sex and gender references may be provided before or after the quotation, in a note, or in brackets within the excerpt itself. Comments within the quoted passage should be minimal. Substitutions for the original are only rarely justified and should be clearly indicated.

Documentation and Associated Scholarly Tasks

A number of recent works suggest ways in which sexism may influence documentation practices. Susan Searing, for example, provides an overview of the scholarly process in women's studies from the perspective of a women's studies librarian (*Introduction*). Mary Ellen Capek headed the long-term project of preparing a women's studies thesaurus that would catalog terms, concepts, and coinages. Capek's *Women's Thesaurus* builds on efforts by J. K. Marshall and Sanford Berman to create models for nonsexist catalog and computer data bases. Joan Hartman and Ellen Messer-Davidow's two volumes remain enlightening assessments of sexist practices in bibliography, archival collections, publication, and so on.

Acknowledgments and Prefaces

In *A Feminist Dictionary*, Kramarae and Treichler define *acknowledgments* as follows:

> Before feminism, that portion of a book where authors acknowledged the ideas and intellectual contributions of males and the clerical and editorial assistance of females and where men thanked their wives for critically reading their manuscripts without asking for co-authorship. After feminism, the place where women authors often acknowledge the intellectual, emotional, editorial, and clerical contributions of women and sometimes of men. (28)

In a book we pulled randomly off the shelf, for example, an author thanks a sponsoring agency for encouragement and financial assistance and thanks his students "who generated ideas and provided feedback to various portions of this text." He continues:

> Also, I cite the determination of the typist Jane Smithers, who probably struggled as much as I in deciphering my handwritten manuscript. Lastly, my deepest appreciation to my wife, Alice, who sat alone for the many hours required for this project.   (Bioethics textbook 1979)

As women increasingly entered and completed doctoral training, some changes became apparent:

> I should also like to thank my husband . . . for aid and comfort above and beyond the vows of matrimony. His suggestions and comments have directly shaped this thesis; his [contribution to linguistic theory] is what makes such a work possible. He has lived for a year on hamburgers and TV dinners, suffering along with me the day-to-day crises of thesis writing. To him, a double portion of Peking Duck.   (1967 doctoral dissertation)

More recent feminist variations include the following:

> I am extremely grateful to . . . my father who helped with some of the typing and the bibliography.   (Feminist theory text 1983)

> My first thanks go to those women from and with whom I have learned what feminist practice is, what feminist theory should be, and, more rarely but far more delightfully, what the two can be together.   (Book on feminist film theory 1984)

> Most of all, I must thank my husband. . . . Perhaps the quality of his "sacrifice" might best be measured by totaling the hours he has spent of a Saturday afternoon in the sticky darkness of a movie theater with Walt Disney and two boisterous little boys—so that I might write.   (Book of feminist literary criticism 1977)

Notes and Citations

In most scholarship, men are overwhelmingly cited over women— and citation leads to further citation. Thus Otto Jespersen's 1922 book on language, with its sexist and racist assumptions, was initially cited by other language scholars because Jespersen was an established authority, because his argument was theoretically compatible with received wisdom, and, possibly, because he was male. Elsie Clews Parsons, writing on women and language in 1913, was, in contrast, virtually ignored (though she was later credited for her mainstream linguistic fieldwork). Recognition and thus accessibility geometrically increase with each citation. As a result, Jespersen's work continues to be cited frequently; Parsons—though she foreshadowed what many feminists are saying today—remains virtually unknown (see Kramarae, *Women*).

This domino effect of authority is what Donna Haraway calls "patrilineal naming" ("In the Beginning" 473), in part a fictive and rhetorical strategy for constructing a story in an official voice (470; see also Treichler's essay in this volume). As such, it has critical and theoretical consequences as well as implications for individual scholars. For example, male authors of past eras are much more likely than women writers of the same time to receive extended critical attention, and individual works by male authors are more likely to be prepared as scholarly critical editions. These advantages in turn increase the likelihood that the men's texts will be used as sources for other scholarship:

> The ongoing *Middle English Dictionary*, for instance, compiled its "m" words before Julian's 1393 *Revelations* was critically edited in 1978. The compilers used her shorter 1373 text. Consequently, under the lengthy entry, "mother," the *MED* does not record any figurative application of it to male divinity. Researchers who use the *MED* as a concordance to locate themes and ideas do not find any trace of an early feminization of religion, nor do those who rely upon such scholarly dictionaries in compiling more popular works such as thesauri, dictionaries of quotations, collections of proverbs, and the like.   (Schibanoff 483)

In the context of feminist writing, Elaine Showalter's essay "Critical Cross Dressing," on Dustin Hoffman in *Tootsie* as the "Woman of the Year," points accurately to a tendency among literary critics to confer respectability on feminist work only after it has been taken up and legitimized by a respected male scholar. Because Jonathan Culler has written about Luce Irigaray, Julia Kristeva, and other feminist theorists, other scholars who merely cite his work believe that they have made their bow to feminism without contaminating their own prose.

The expected outcome of these practices is confirmed in Eugene Garfield's report on the *Arts and Humanities Citation Index*, which demonstrates that, in 950 journals, a relatively small number of male names are repeatedly cited. (Conarroe's 1980 "Editor's Column" in *PMLA* and J. R. Kelly's letter to the editor also discuss the preponderance of a limited group of authors.) This pattern of patrilineal naming of texts reflects their authors' judgments about value and importance, in turn reproducing and reinforcing the hegemony of male authorship. To be cited is to have one's work recognized. Recognition can, of course, have practical consequences—for example, in tenure and promotion reviews, in appointments, and in other honors and awards.

We are not arguing that works should be listed simply because their authors are women or that gender is the only basis for unjust citation practices. Our point, rather—a point supported by considerable evidence—is that sociological factors other than the merit of the scholarship may influence bibliographic entries. Sexism, the long-standing area of "unfairness" we specifically challenge, is one such factor. Thus scholars should both recognize biased patterns of citation and seek conscientiously to make their own references inclusive and nondiscriminatory.

A related point is that scholars and administrators, especially those who are uninformed about feminist scholarship and potentially involved in hiring, promotion, and other forms of evaluation, should probably learn something about publishing policies in the field. A number of respected feminist journals, for example, are edited by feminist collectives (e.g., *Camera Obscura*, *Feminist Review*, *m/f*); the absence of a large editorial board composed of established scholars does not signal the absence of disinterested standards. It suggests, rather, interests and standards that are different, since a small but committed collective can be very rigorous.

The editorial collective of *Camera Obscura* directly addressed this question in response to an argument set forth in *Cinema Journal* (the journal of the Society for Cinema Studies) that "the objective procedures of refereed journals should serve as standards for editorial excellence in the field of film studies." In their editorial, the collective responds:

> In a field such as film studies, which has been particularly attentive to the ideological aspects of supposedly neutral or objective discourse, it is misguided to assume that the editorial policy of refereed journals can attain the ideal of objectivity lacking in non-refereed journals.
>
> The supposed objectivity of referee procedures (in the name of "professionalizing" the field of film studies) serves as a rhetorical strategy to reinforce or naturalize a scholarly bias against feminist, marxist, and minority discourses, and against theoretical work.
>
> Finally, it seems that rather than taking a normative position about

what constitutes scholarly writing on film and television, it would be
more productive for the Society for Cinema Studies and *Cinema
Journal* to support a diversity of journals and editorial policies.   (5)

Similarly, one might note that in linguistics some of the most significant and cited essays of the past 20 years have never existed as
other than mimeos; the dog-eared copies are all that are available
to scholars today.

A final point is that citation need not mean lining up those who
agree and those who disagree. Within feminist scholarship, gen-
erous citation practices have evolved. The author of a 1985 essay
on feminism and the philosophy of science, for example, takes a
firm and not entirely popular position, but the detailed endnotes
to the essay do not divide feminist sources into those that are "correct" and those that are "incorrect." Rather, they begin with such
phrases as the following:

Useful references include. . . .

Starting points for understanding the literature here include. . . .

For crucial guidance in thinking about the political/cultural implications of the history of women doing science in the United States,
see. . . .

Disclaimers, Apologia, and the Authorial Voice

Within the context of nonsexist guidelines, the term *disclaimer* designates a prefatory statement that denies any sexist intent, whatever
the actual language used. Disclaimers seem to us to be essentially
nonsensical or self-contradictory, for they ask the reader contin-
uously to disregard the written text. A typical disclaimer simply
says that whenever words like *men* and *he* occur, they are to be
interpreted as meaning "men and women" and "he or she." As
McConnell-Ginet asserts in her essay in this volume,

It does not suffice to put a footnote on the first page that announces
one's intentions to mean "he or she" since some readers will doubt
the sincerity of the announcement and others will forget it.

The sexist language controversy has generated some rather elaborate disclaimers:

My expository style relies heavily on the exemplary singular, and the construction "everybody . . . his" therefore comes up frequently. This "his" is generic, not gendered. "His or her" becomes clumsy with repetition and suggests that "his" alone elsewhere is masculine, which it isn't.

"Her" alone draws attention to itself and distracts from the topic at hand. "Their" solves the problem neatly but substitutes another. "Ter" is bolder than I am ready for. "One's" defeats the purpose of the construction, which is meant to be vivid and particular. "Its" is too harsh a joke. Rather than play hob with the language, we feminists might adopt the position of pitying men for being forced to share their pronouns around.   (English handbook 1978)

Sharon Veach, editor of *Women and Language News* for several years, regularly ran what she termed *Male Apologia*—disclaimers coupled with a certain degree of male self-consciousness:

Given the title and the text, the *reader* is encouraged to make a poem. He is not forced to do so, but there is not much else he can do with this material, and certainly nothing else so rewarding. (I will use the masculine pronoun here to refer to the reader, not because all readers are male but because I am, and my hypothetical reader is not a pure construct but an idealized version of myself.)   (Book of literary criticism 1982)

Earlier we quoted a woman author who on similar grounds had used the generic *she* to refer to *the reader*. When women use generic *she*, however, they may intend to protest and disrupt a long-established code as much as to delineate the gender of a particular reader. It is questionable whether this rationale from a male serves the same function: the contention that *the reader* now refers only to the authorial "I" seems ineffective as a blanket disclaimer. Once the statement has been made, both author and reader can forget it and proceed according to long-standing convention. The following passage reflects a different view about what disrupts the reading process; at the same time it shows an apparent indifference to the reading experience many women report:

What is offending and interruptive in the reading act is the doubling of the pronouns or adjectives—he or she, his or her, etc. As editor of a literary journal I am highly supportive of our policy to edit out such expensive space wasters when a simple generic form is all that is needed.   (Letter to the editors of this book 1983)

The feminist attack on sexist language has had partial success but, perhaps for that reason, has also created "disclaimer backlash," a refusal even to attempt inclusiveness:

> For the sake of simplicity in exposition, it is generally assumed that both [the speaker and the hearer] are male. My apologies to any readers who might be offended by this.   (Linguistics text 1986)

> In an attempt to enhance the readability of my own page, I have renounced all claims of conscience and elected to use the masculine form for all references to the hypothetical reader or critic.   (Book of literary criticism 1984)

Recently, disclaimers have entered a new field of discourse. The following example is from the first page of a 1984 brochure called "Your Dog's New Home," published by KalKan Foods:

> All cats and dogs are created equal . . . but in talking about them in our Pet Care Series, we'll use "he" and "his" in reference to all pets, regardless of their sex, for the sake of consistency and simplicity. The only exception would be in the case of a pregnant or lactating dog or cat.

The language of animal-care books needs a general overhaul. One objectionable practice is the stereotypical use of the pronoun (*he* for dogs and *she* for cats). The KalKan publication at least suggests that someone is thinking about the problem. And in mentioning human beings, the brochure uses nonsexist language:

> Be sure, too, to consult your veterinarian, since he or she knows your dog and can provide a recommendation based on personal observation.

Not all disclaimers concern sexist language, of course, and some of them can be useful. The following example gives specificity to a research project, as these guidelines recommend; by noting the universe in which the research takes place, the author qualifies the conclusions and signals the necessity for further research:

> I should add as well that because the generic assumptions I am mainly concerned with questioning derive in the greater part from Anglo-American attitudes, my examples are drawn almost exclusively from British, American, and Canadian fiction. How much my argument

could profit from or will require qualification in the light of the theory and practice of other nationalities and cultures is something that, for the moment, I must leave in abeyance. (*PMLA* 1976)

Feminist disclaimers typically serve to undermine the voice of authority that is traditionally expected of the scholarly text. Not infrequently the feminist scholar will add a note renouncing any claim to universality or omniscience, emphasizing the provisional nature of the research, noting the collective development of the ideas to follow, or otherwise destabilizing the authorial voice:

> Let this be a warning about what follows: this text probably involves certain "naiveties," that is to say unconscious adherence to ideological structures which have not yet been completely deconstructed. (*Radical Philosophy* 1977)

As male critics begin to take an increasing interest in feminist criticism and feminist theory, their writing sometimes reflects an attempt to mediate between a voice of male critical authority and the various tenets of feminist criticism that challenge that authority. The following two examples embody such a self-conscious and careful linguistic negotiation, a contest between the writers' authority and their uneasiness about being involved in feminist projects:

> Where to begin is always a problem when writing a book, but particularly a book about feminist criticism, especially if you happen to be a man. The reason for this is that feminist theory has politicised all the usual maneuvers engaged in by men who write books about books, so that whatever they do is likely to be considered symptomatic of the problem of male domination to which feminists address themselves. If you are a man and you decide (as I have done) to take a look at feminist criticism, you may find yourself at risk from a feminist mode of cinematic discourse which categorizes "looking" as a morbid activity engaged in by men to the detriment of women, who are reduced consequently to mere objects of voyeuristic attention. To want to "look" at feminist criticism, therefore, is only what you would expect of a man in a male-dominated society, for in doing so he simply complies with the rules of a symbolic order of representation which displays women's ideas in the same way that films and girlie magazines display their bodies, and for the same purposes: vulgar curiosity and the arousal of desire. (Book on feminist criticism 1984)

How does a man begin to write about feminist criticism? Several personae are readily available—the benign paterfamilias, the cornered rat, the condescending authority, the defender of the sacred, the guilty supplicant. None of these is very appealing, especially since whatever anxiety and defensiveness I feel in beginning to write about the subject is countered by my conviction that feminist criticism has been one of the most successful and revolutionary enterprises of the past decade. Nevertheless, each of these personae no doubt makes at least a fleeting appearance here. For men to acknowledge the difficulties we have in writing about feminist criticism does not do away with those difficulties. What follows is the result not only of an awareness of the problematics of my voice (and some uneasiness about it) but also of an effort to think through both the internal potential of feminist theoretical writing and its challenge to other bodies of theory.   (Book on feminist theory 1985)

Jane Gallop describes a reader's report that criticized her for not being "in control of the text" in her book on Lacan. Because control was an authorial position she had avoided deliberately and disclaimed at length, she wrote to the press disputing the reader's evaluation, with the result that the book was accepted for publication. "I am well aware of the irony," she writes, "of the fact that my non-authoritative position was accepted by the press only because I could argue it with sufficient authority" ("Castration").

Indexes

Sexism in indexing can take a variety of forms. For example, it can reflect discriminatory assumptions, as in this 1955 index of folk literature:

> *Man*, see also *Person*
> *Person*, see also *Human Being, Man*
> *Persons*, see also *Men, People*
> *Wife*, see also *Adultress, Marriage, Woman*
> *Woman*, see also *Wife*

Scholars should be sensitive to the interests of researchers whose studies focus on women and prepare indexes accordingly. In addition to discriminatory conceptualizations like those in the example above, other objectionable practices to guard against include entering the names of women solely under the names of their fathers or husbands; omitting significant women figures; trivializing or stereotyping women's contributions to, say, a particular historical period (e.g., by listing women's social service contributions but not their intellectual ones); and categorizing women exclusively under male-conceived and male-oriented entries, as described in this comment:

> Asian American women have . . . been victimized in historical accounts and current literature. . . . A search of historical literature on Hawaii reveals that Asian and Pacific women are not mentioned except in stereotypical categories, such as "picture brides," "mothers," "prostitutes," "war brides," "entertainers," and "queens." (*Women's Studies International Forum* 1985)

Some feminists believe that explicitly labeling index entries for women's concepts, activities, products, and accomplishments (*Women and education, Women's views on segregation*) will set women apart from the rest of the world; such separatism, they argue, is ultimately retrogressive. Some years ago one feminist librarian advocated a different strategy for indexes and card catalogs: librarians should delete *women's* wherever it appears in article and book titles and at the same time add *men's* wherever this would be more accurate—thus *Modern European History* would become *Modern [Male] European History*. Dale Spender used this strategy in titling her book on women's studies *Men's Studies Modified*. Our view is that the growing scholarly interest in women mandates more detailed indexing. Further, this practice leaves women's mark on texts and makes erasure more difficult.

Some authors work hard to overcome indexing conventions they see as masculine. Dale Spender notes that her index for *Women of Ideas* includes entries created to be meaningful to women; she cites *completion complex*—the conviction that a woman is not complete without a man—as a term she coined to capture women's experience. Another unconventional entry appears in the index of Moers's *Literary Women*:

Advice, masculine
    bad, 271, 415, 443
    good, 450

Women's names pose special problems for indexes and bibliographies. Though men also write under pseudonyms and sometimes change their names (Leroi Jones, for example, became Amiri Baraka), women are likely to change their names a number of times in the course of their professional lives—not only when they marry, divorce, or remarry but also when they wish to commemorate other significant life changes or to demonstrate ideological commitments. As we noted above, some women scholars may therefore publish under several names, successively or simultaneously. Women who choose to maintain one name for professional purposes present little problem. Those who use different names at different times, however, may create some confusion, though their wishes also deserve respect.

But even if one is willing to honor their preferences, it is not always simple to produce accurate and appropriate citations and cross-references. As we examined style handbooks, we identified a number of approaches, including bracketing the alternative names, citing them in parentheses, and providing *See* and *See also* directions. But these suggestions were not easy to locate. In one handbook, we searched through the entire section on cross-referencing to find, among the examples of cross-references in indexes, an unlabeled entry describing married women's names. The entry was not indexed under *Personal Names* or *Author's Names*. Like other handbooks, however, this one did have the entries *Married Women's Names* and *Pseudonyms*.

In handbooks generally, a guiding principle is to treat as the main entry the name the woman prefers, or is "known by" according to accumulated tradition; parenthetical data or cross-references to and from secondary entries guide the reader to the woman's other names, roles, or identities:

Baker, Norma Jean. *See* Monroe, Marilyn
Barrett, Elizabeth (later Elizabeth Barrett Browning)
Bell, Currer. *See* Brontë, Charlotte
Dunbar-Nelson, Alice (born Alice Ruth Moore)
King, Coretta Scott (Mrs. Martin Luther King, Jr.)
Monroe, Marilyn (Norma Jean Baker)

A second guiding principle is to consider the overall context and purpose of the scholarly work in determining the relationship of one name to another. *See also* references guide the reader to all the names that are equally "primary":

Barrett, Elizabeth. *See also* Browning, Elizabeth Barrett.
Browning, Elizabeth Barrett. *See also* Barrett, Elizabeth.

We found no special directions for citing variations in the names of single or divorced women. Certainly it is not accurate to call these variations pseudonyms. We propose the entry *Multiple Names* for this purpose and suggest that it be routinely included in style manuals. This listing will not guarantee accurate information on the chronology or context of the various names or the primacy of one name over another, but it will cause people to attend more carefully to these problems. The following example is from Rosalie L. Colie's *Shakespeare's Living Art*:

> He serves, as Anne Barton has rightly observed,[9] as a chorus commentary upon the behavior and occupations of the people he sees before him.   (37)

A footnote includes information about Barton's names:

> [9]Anne Barton (also writing under the names Bobbyann Roesen and Anne Righter), "Love's Labour Lost," *SQ*, IV (1963), 411–26.

The information is particularly valuable here because the *Shakespeare Quarterly* article is published under the name Bobbyann Roesen. Colie's text suggests that the scholar currently known by the name Anne Barton has also written under the names Bobbyann Roesen and Anne Righter. But the index includes no entry for Roesen, thus suggesting that Barton has abandoned the name Bobbyann Roesen altogether:

> Barton, Anne, 37, 48n. *See also* Righter, Anne (363)
> Righter, Anne, 37n, 212n, etc. *See also* Barton, Anne (368)

Thus anyone who knew only the name Roesen would not find the listings for Barton and Righter. This problem would be solved by an entry for Bobbyann Roesen referring the reader to Barton (the author's most recent writing name) and hence the main entry, which would lead back to both Righter and Roesen):

> Roesen, Bobbyann. *See* Barton, Anne

Translations, Critical Editions, Interpretations

We have noted throughout this volume a pervasive view of women as transmitters rather than originators of scholarship (see Kramarae and Treichler, *Feminist*, and Treichler's essay in this volume). Because this view is widely accepted, it may enter into scholarly activities that involve decisions about the texts of writers other than oneself. For example, Margaret A. Simons claims that the changes introduced into Simone de Beauvoir's *Second Sex* by the translator and editor, H. M. Parshley, turned the English version into a book about women rather than a book about philosophy (559).

Susan Schibanoff traces what she calls covert "paternalistic rewriting" by textual critics and translators of "Four Sorrows or the Unfortunate Man," by Marie of France, and other works by early women writers; she uses the term *in-scribing* to signify a feminist reading of the fine print of primary works known to us only through layers of androcentric practices (she argues that women's texts are botched in ways quite different from men's texts, chiefly because female writers are made to conform to conventional feminine stereotypes). "Unlike critical editions," she writes, "translations rarely pretend to objectivity or exactness" (483–84). In their introductions, translators often indicate the necessity for certain kinds of changes, usually to preserve the flavor of the original text. Schibanoff examines successive translations of *Beowulf* in which the strength of Grendel's mother is downplayed in a variety of ways, none preserving the meaning of the original language (484). Because few scholars have either the time or the money (or, often, the expertise) to inspect the original texts in rare-book rooms, they must rely on primary professional readers and translators for access to these texts. Thus not only translations but the related guides and critical volumes potentially reflect established, androcentric views.

The French philosopher Michèle Le Doeuff describes how this exclusion of the feminine mind from originality and authority severely limits what women as intellectuals and scholars are allowed to do. They are not permitted, for instance, to provide their own interpretations of texts. Only men, she writes, can "manhandle" a text. Women are its vestals, keepers of the sacred:

> Who better than a woman to show fidelity, respect, and remembrance? A woman can be trusted to perpetuate the words of the Great Discourse: she will add none of her own. . . . The vestal of a discourse which time threatens to eclipse, the nurse of dismembered texts, the healer of works battered by false editions, the housewife whom one hopes will dust off the grey film that successive readings

have left on the fine object, she takes on the upkeep of the monuments, the forms which the mind has deserted. (10–11)

These feminine qualities have enabled women to find a place for themselves in philosophical work: "A minor one, however: as in cooking, so in commentary—the high class works are always reserved for a Hyppolite or a Bocuse" (11).

This point is echoed by Barbara Godard in writing about translation, a field currently under reevaluation:

> For a long time in the Anglo-Saxon world translation has been seen as a derivative and subsidiary activity in which a "servant-translator" somewhat mechanically . . . renders a source language text into a target language. . . . [but] contemporary tendencies defining translation as an *art*, not a craft, stress the preeminence of the translator's creative freedom. More than just a transference of "meaning" contained in one set of language signs into another set of language signs, translation involves the interpretation of a whole set of extra-linguistic criteria. An entire culture and system of aesthetic features must be interpreted for a new audience. (13)

Arguing that translation is political as well as social, Godard cites a 1983 study by Evelyne Voldeng that systematically examines and compares the translations of French feminist texts into (Canadian) English by men and by women. Voldeng concludes that men generally are less aware of the political and discursive resonances that certain notions and words have come to have for feminists; at the same time, women translators tend toward "a more systematic exploration of concrete terms especially as concerns biophysiology" (qtd. in Godard 14). For example, she cites this line from Nicole Brossard's "L'écrivain": "ce soir j'entre dans l'histoire sans relever ma jupe." Linda Gaboriau translates this as "Tonight I enter into history without opening my legs," while David Ellis translates the same passage more literally as "Tonight I enter into history without pulling up my skirt." "Gaboriau's version," writes Godard,

> has a greater shock effect, but makes explicit a major feminist topos, namely the repossession of the words, the naming and writing of the life of the body, the exploration of its images, as experienced by women. The male translator frequently fails to comprehend the full range of this experience, as is evident in David Ellis's translation of Brossard's "les mots affluent autour de clitoris" by "the words flow

by the clitoris," while Gaboriau chooses the translation "the words gather around the clitoris." Again in a translation of a Brossard text, "Simulation," Larry Shouldice translates "la perte blanche" literally as "white loss," failing to note an alternate meaning of "discharge" which is suggested by the textual allusions to bodily secretions. Such shifts in meaning away from the concrete realities of female sexuality are not unique in English Canada. Voldeng notes similar cases in other translations, including those of Sylvia Plath into French where the male translator was also not precise in his knowledge of female biology.   (14)

As for critical editions and interpretations, we want only to emphasize the importance of incorporating feminist scholarly insights into such works and of disambiguating the usage of male nouns and pronouns. The subtlety of this process—along with the importance of retaining the meaning of the original—is articulated as follows by an author responding to editorial changes suggested by her publisher:

> Some of the efforts to un-sex my text result in mistranslations of Greek, Latin, or Italian. When Pindar says ἀνήρ, he means man, not person. The word is NEVER generic in Greek; it is always used to refer to a male person. The sexism is Pindar's not mine. . . . Similarly, the Renaissance mythographers use *homines* to refer to men, not people. When they say the Muses lead learned men to heaven, I cannot be sure whether they mean men as males (who are learned) or men as people. I prefer to translate what I find and let the reader interpret whether "men" is generic. . . . The Renaissance was a sexist society—I prefer to represent it accurately.

As we indicated earlier, we have no argument with an author's desire to preserve the integrity of the original text, but if doing so involves what appears to be discriminatory usage, the author should, we believe, include an introductory statement or a note of the sort offered here.

Issues in Other Professional Activities

This book focuses primarily on the problem of sexist language in scholarly and professional writing. But even scholars who take care in preparing texts may be guilty of discriminatory usage in other

Summary of Recommendations

Documentation and Associated Scholarly Tasks

1. **Cite men and women in parallel ways.**

2. **If a study by a woman is relevant but has also been cited by a male author, cite the original female author's work as well as the male author's.**

3. **Preserve the language and meaning of original texts, even if they contain sexist usage.** Do not use facile disclaimers to offset, justify, or disguise the sexist language of the original. Use your own words to signal your commitment to inclusive language.

4. **In general, do not clutter the text with internal bracketed annotations after each pseudogeneric usage, a practice that in familiar texts sounds especially silly:**

   God created man [sic] in His [sic] own image.
   Man [and Woman] created God in his [and her] own image.

5. **Think about how potentially ambiguous language is used and provide intelligent guidance, so that the reader can interpret what the author meant.** If the meaning is disputed, acknowledge the controversy and offer your interpretation. If you believe the sexist language of the original was in fact intended to be inclusive, you can make this point by alternating verbatim quotations with paraphrases.

6. **Prepare indexes so that information about women is easy to locate and need not be sought only under broad generic categories like *Family*.**

7. **If a woman is known by multiple names, include them in the index or bibliography with the necessary cross-references.**

8. **Try to cite women by the names they prefer.**

9. **Do not cite a married woman by her husband's first name unless this form is dictated by her own preference, established practice, or lack of information.** Use the woman's given name instead, along with information about her married identity (when this is relevant):

   Roosevelt, Eleanor (married to Franklin Delano Roosevelt) or (wife of Franklin Delano Roosevelt)
   Roosevelt, Mrs. Franklin Delano. *See* Roosevelt, Eleanor

circumstances, either through a lack of awareness or a lapse in attentiveness. Thus, members of an English department search committee in the mid-1980s were astonished to read recommendations for women applicants that included comments like "You will know her by her flaming red hair" and "She reminds one of the young Greer Garson." Though feminist efforts over the past 15 years have raised consciousness to the point where many readers can now interpret such remarks critically, without prejudice to the applicant, situations commonly arise that continue to leave much room for improvement.

Research and reports by many professional organizations confirm that job searches, interviews, letters of reference, and other aspects of routine professional conduct are potential sources of discrimination against women and minorities. In such critical areas, individual faculty members can have considerable influence on the lives of individuals and on the climate of the institution as a whole. For this reason it is important that evaluations and recommendations for women students and colleagues become a site of ongoing consciousness-raising. Many views that scholars hold about gender are almost wholly internalized and often available to them only through such self-conscious processes as scrutinizing the language of their own letters of recommendation. We encourage attention of this kind and believe that it is a powerful step toward conceptual and behavioral change. We therefore conclude these guidelines with some brief comments on sexist practices in professional activities other than scholarly writing.

Professional interaction with students and colleagues constitutes one such activity. A current myth about coeducation is that the problems women once faced on campuses no longer exist. Assessments made in 1987 indicate that, despite the progress of recent decades, college and university women faculty members continue to lag behind men in salaries, to hold fewer tenured or tenure-track appointments, and to be underrepresented in traditionally male disciplines and in important leadership positions (Shavlik, Touchton, and Pearson; Rohter). Of the more than 400,000 full-time faculty members on college and university campuses in 1987, women accounted for 27.3%. Though this figure is up from 22.3% in 1972, it does not approach the percentage of over a century ago—36.4% in 1879 (Shavlik and Touchton 240). The classroom behavior of female instructors is judged and interpreted differently from the behavior of male instructors (Treichler and Kramarae

121). In addition, considerable evidence suggests that instructors tend to treat female and male students differently. The Association of American Colleges' Project on the Status and Education of Women identified over 30 distinctive types of conduct: for example, instructors interrupt women more often than they do men, establish more frequent eye contact with men, call on women less, and less often engage in dialogue with women who do speak. Both male and female instructors vary in their conduct toward male and female students; yet for the most part neither instructor nor student is aware of this discrimination (R. M. Hall).

Professional behavior at public events such as meetings and conferences may also be marred by sexist practices. For a woman to be introduced formally to a roomful of new colleagues as a "sweet young thing" (as one of us was a few years ago) is neither a compliment nor a good joke, but such incidents still occur. One woman faculty member in this situation was presented as "our affirmative-action candidate"; another, at a different university, as "our new colleague, Doctress Smythe." Ignorance about women as professional colleagues has now given way to acceptance and collegiality from some men and to a determined self-consciousness from others; but there are still no good jokes, and inappropriateness remains common. Women are more likely to be called by their first names (by other women as well as by men) and otherwise treated less professionally. At a university lecture series, for example, when two male faculty members gave formal responses to a paper delivered by a female colleague, one of the two compared the order of the speakers—two men following one woman—to a "gang bang." Presumably he simply meant to acknowledge the gender imbalance; yet the simile, intended ironically, was uncalled for and offensive. On another occasion and in a somewhat different vein, a male faculty member caused distress when he lectured to students on the "rape" of the text, deliberately echoing a metaphor used by Barthes, Derrida, and others precisely to challenge widely accepted critical assumptions about the critic's control over the text; here, an explanation to the class would have clarified his own use of the term. This tendency toward sexualized discourse was also manifested by a male researcher at a medical conference in the late 1970s. He reported finding that men who are denied admission to medical school interpret the rejection as unfair ("I know I could be a good doctor") whereas women who are turned down blame themselves ("there must be something wrong with me"). The researcher then commented, "What this research means—according to streetwalker psychology—I mean streetcorner psychology—is that men see the problem as external, women as internal."

Another male scholar showed a similar lack of tact in discussing historical periodization. Citing Joan Kelly's insight that traditional male-oriented periodization does not adequately capture women's historical development or experiences, he added, "Women, forgive me, have periods of their own." He was trying to be a "good feminist," but it was perhaps another instance of the gang-bang syndrome: out of hundreds of possible expressions, the one he selected—even for a bad pun—characterized women unequivocally in terms of their reproductive and sexual identity. And he could be faulted as well for presuming too much intimacy in speaking to women he did not know well. "Thank you all for coming out tonight," lesbian comic Kate Clinton typically tells her mostly lesbian audience when she opens her live performances; but her own identity is part of what authorizes her to take this liberty with her listeners.

One more issue is worth noting here. Although studies of language and gender show few individual linguistic features characteristic of women or men, research does suggest differences in interaction patterns. Treichler and Kramarae summarize findings from these studies (based chiefly on the behavior of men, both white and black) as follows:

> Men interpret questions as requests for information; they interrupt women and each other more than women do; they engage in open argumentation and conflict; they typically ignore comments of previous speakers; they use more mechanisms to control conversational topics; they more frequently make declarations of fact and opinion; and they talk more frequently, and for longer periods.   (120)

Anthropologists Daniel Maltz and Ruth Borker, noting the different "cultural rules" for male and female interaction—rules that children and teenagers evolve out of years of same-sex interaction—suggest specific areas where these rules may conflict in cross-sex interaction: (1) women see questions as part of conversational maintenance, while men see them as requests for information; (2) women explicitly acknowledge previous utterances and try to connect with them, while men have no such rule and often ignore preceding comments; (3) women interpret verbal aggression as personal, negative, and disruptive, while men view it as a conventional organizing feature of conversation; (4) men shift topics quickly, while women tend to develop them progressively and to shift gradually; (5) women share experiences and talk over problems as a form of mutual support, while men hear problems as requests for solutions and respond by giving advice, acting as experts, or lecturing their audience (Maltz and Borker 213; see also Fishman, "What"; Tannen). It is perhaps for these reasons that many women prefer and seem to excel at speaking in more collaborative structures and settings: meetings with a rotating chair, participatory conference sessions, and decision making by consensus rather than by strict parliamentary procedure. (These issues are discussed and interpreted in Boxer; McConnell-Ginet, "Language," "Review"; Treichler and Kramarae.)

For women feminists, the connection between the personal and the professional has always been a central commitment. It is therefore important to evaluate male participation in feminist scholarship not just by what men write but by how they act within the field. In this spirit, Alice Jardine, at a 1984 MLA session on men in feminism, suggested that male feminist scholars educate themselves about women writers and feminist scholarship; acknowledge in writing debts to feminism (not merely to male critics who have read feminist writing); sponsor women students and encourage the reviewing of women's books; evaluate their male colleagues on feminist issues; and, above all, become *active* rather than *reactive* feminists ("Men" 60–61).

This is not the place for an extended discussion of gender in relation to computers and technology, but a couple of points can be noted. The computer industry is at this time relatively unregulated, with few accepted standards for such practices as advertising, marketing, communicating through networks, and developing software. It is a dominantly male industry as well. There is sexism in virtually all areas, from programs for "ladies" packaged like pantyhose, to job discrimination, to obscene-talk networks, to pornographic software. Though there are feminist computer networks and even computer programs for detecting and removing sexist language (*MacProof* is the best known), the field needs closer and more systematic monitoring. Instances of blatant sexism should be brought to the attention of the National Organization for Women, *Ms.* (which runs a regular column on computers for women), or the Modern Language Association (which has invited members to share computer-related information and experiences).

Some feminists have expressed concern about the implications of the "computer revolution" for women (see Leveen; J. Zimmerman, *Once, Technological*; and Turkle). They cite studies that show continuing differences between men and women in relation to computers; compared with men, women experience greater anxiety and technophobia and use computers less frequently and for fewer kinds of operations. For feminist writers and scholars, Schibanoff points out, the computerization of texts and data bases promises to reproduce the same kind of "triage" that male scholars, archivists, and other gatekeepers have performed on women's works in the past (488). As bibliographies, indexes, and texts are computerized, she argues, feminist texts—unlikely to be given a high priority by those making the decisions—will be especially vulnerable to loss, suppression, and distortion. For this reason feminist scholars need to be particularly vigilant in attending to the computerization of their field. They should also recognize that it is frequently the first few words of titles that are entered into computerized bibliographies, indexes, and other data bases; feminists who wish their works to be accessible through these channels might want to take that practice into account in deciding what to call their books and articles.

The discriminatory practices we have been discussing, some more subtle than others, are not unrelated to the more blatant issue of sexual harassment. Studies consistently show that between 20 and 30% of all female students report some form of sexual harassment during their college years, primarily from male faculty members. While policies at many academic institutions explicitly or implicitly prohibit sexual and gender harassment (see Franklin, Moglen, Zatlin-Boring, and Angress for an excellent outline of these issues), the Supreme Court's 1986 decision in the case of *Meritor Savings Bank, FSB v. Vinson* seems certain to make administrative enforcement more common and more aggressive. The Court held that the prohibition of employment discrimination on the basis of sex under Title VII of the Civil Rights Act of 1964 does encompass discrimination through sexual harassment; more significantly, perhaps, the Court determined unanimously that sexual harassment complaints can be made not only by those who have been harassed but by those subjected to an offensive, discriminatory work environment—a "hostile environment," one in which sexual harassment takes place. Further, under some circumstances, the employer can be held responsible for a hostile environment (for a discussion of this point see Bennett-Alexander). While we cannot entirely foresee the impact of the *Meritor* decision on various employment settings, leading attorneys as well as a body of related cases and court decisions suggest that academic institutions have begun to take this issue very seriously. It is important that faculty members do so as well.

As Phyllis Franklin, Helene Moglen, Phyllis Zatlin-Boring, and Ruth Angress point out, sexist language may in some instances be considered sexual harassment. Sexual harassment does not usually occur in isolation—that is, it rarely involves simply the aberrant behavior of a single individual. Rather it exists as part of a larger institutional climate in which related forms of linguistic discrimination are liable to occur as well: women graduate and professional students, for example, are more apt than men to feel alienated and reluctant to speak in institutional settings such as classrooms; they are less likely than men students to receive informal advising and guidance; and sexist remarks in classrooms are more often at the expense of women than of men. We have argued that nonsexist language promotes fairness and justice. In addition, however, when sexist language takes the form of sexual harassment, it is prohibited and illegal. This point should be clearly understood because sexual harassment can have grave legal and professional consequences. (For more information see Boxer; DeSole and Hoffman; El-Khawas; Farley; R. M. Hall; Jenkins; Kramarae and Treichler, "Power"; Sandler, "Women" and "Classroom"; and Treichler and Kramarae. Also of relevance are McMillen and Rix.)

This point leads, finally, to the question of academic freedom. One of the standard arguments against guidelines that call for nonsexist language is that their mandates threaten academic freedom. Most guidelines, of course, do not and cannot "mandate" anything. Even so, we decided in this book to be less prescriptive than other guidelines and to provide alternatives rather than imperatives. We want to open up discourse on this topic, not close it off.

We believe academic freedom is important. We do not believe it is threatened by the use of nonsexist language or by guidelines recommending such language. Indeed, after reviewing the concept of academic freedom in American universities, we argue (1) that if "nonsexist language" is given its broadest possible social interpretation, it exemplifies rather than threatens academic freedom and (2) that a set of guidelines encouraging the academic community to modify specific professional practices involves not a question of academic freedom but the more mundane question of professional propriety.

The broad concept of academic freedom—liberty of thought without external or internal restraint—has a long tradition in Anglo-American intellectual life. Francis Bacon's 1605 *Advancement of Learning* provided philosophical underpinnings for the right to carry out experimental inquiry. The rise of commerce established the value of economic competition; in parallel fashion, the rise of the liberal state encouraged the notion that ideas should stand up under competition: the competition of the marketplace was a model for the competition of ideas ("the academic marketplace"). Their worth would be determined by testing, not established by the power of those who hold them. Out of this background, the term *academic freedom* has come into common use in two senses: in Britain, it means the freedom of the institution from outside influences; in the United States it means the freedom of the individual professor from outside influences:

> Academic freedom is usually described as the right of each individual member of the faculty of an institution to enjoy the freedom to study, to inquire, to speak his mind, to communicate his ideas, and to assert the truth as he sees it. In the United States, the professor's academic freedom is often defined in terms of full freedom in research and in the publication of results, in classroom discussion of his subject, and in the exercise extra-murally of his basic rights as a citizen. (Fellman 10)

Despite the pronouns in this passage, academic freedom as a concept has protected women as well as men. It was especially important for women faculty members, Helen Horowitz argues, at the point that they began to move off campus and establish private lives—singly, in pairs, and collectively. As their sense of autonomy and collective strength grew, they came into political conflict for the first time with the college administration—often over such issues as women's suffrage. Academic freedom came to have real meaning then; though many women were nevertheless fired for their beliefs, academic freedom continues to serve as a central principle in the life of American colleges and universities.

In 1940 the American Association of University Professors (AAUP), founded in 1915, published its *Statement of Principles on Academic Freedom and Tenure*, delineating a role for faculty members in keeping with the notion of freedom from external supervision: professors are appointed by the trustees of an institution but are not, strictly speaking, their "employees." The AAUP's Committee A on Academic Freedom and Tenure continues to articulate and develop the concept of academic freedom, a concept further supported by a series of Supreme Court decisions. In addition to protecting the rights of individual professors, the principle of academic freedom fosters the unhampered search for truth and thus benefits society as a whole. Truth will emerge only as ideas clash in an unrestricted marketplace. In more recent times, particularly over the last two turbulent decades, the concept of academic freedom (in the United States and elsewhere) has been broadened to include students as well as teachers. As one commentator puts it, "the freedom of the professor to teach is merely one side of the coin of academic freedom, the other side being the freedom of the student to learn" (Fellman 10). Thus the important "Joint Statement on Rights and Freedom of Students," drawn up collaboratively in 1967 by the AAUP and four other educational associations, asserts that "freedom to teach and freedom to learn are inseparable facets of academic freedom." For only a free educational system is free to change with the times—an essential quality if it is to produce leaders, because "leaders in a rapidly changing world should not be slaves to routine." And, finally, in a free university—one not bound by orthodoxy—truth must emerge "out of a multitude of tongues" (Fellman 12).

Interpreted broadly, academic freedom seems to us to encourage "a multitude of tongues," unbound by orthodoxy. In our view a shift in perspective to encompass women within this multitude is consistent with that concept. Yet in the context of this broad history, we need to emphasize that academic freedom is a principle: it is not a carte blanche that authorizes any and all behaviors or professional activities. All members of the academic community are supposed to display standards of professional propriety and behavior appropriate to an academic setting. This obligation certainly extends to their language. In closing, we draw on a statement made by John H. Fisher in his 1974 MLA presidential address. Though his words were spoken in a different context, they suit our present purposes:

> As teachers of language and literature we live, move, have our being in the world of symbols. We cannot expect to be absolved from the practical effects these symbols have in the real world. In our responsibility or irresponsibility we *become* these symbols. . . . (365)

Fisher concluded by asking, on behalf of the association, "that our individual and collective symbolic behavior be responsible" (365).

We conclude by repeating the argument of this book: that symbolic behavior has significant practical and theoretical consequences in the real world and that these are often negative for women. The use of nonsexist language is, therefore, at this point in history, the only linguistic choice that enables us, individually and collectively, to be responsible members of our profession.

Part Three

Bibliography

Works Cited

Abel, Elizabeth, ed. *Writing and Sexual Difference*. Spec. issue of *Critical Inquiry* 8 (1981): 173–403.

Ahmed, Leila. "Western Ethnocentrism and Perceptions of the Harem." *Feminist Studies* 8 (1982): 521–34.

Allan, Keith. *Linguistic Meaning*. 2 vols. New York: Methuen, 1986.

Allen, Paula Gunn, ed. *Studies in American Indian Literature: Critical Essays and Course Designs*. New York: MLA, 1983.

Alter, Lance. "Do the NCTE Guidelines on Nonsexist Use of Language Serve a Positive Purpose?" *English Journal* 65.9 (1976): 10–13.

American Association of University Professors et al. "Joint Statement on Rights and Freedoms of Students." 1967. *AAUP Policy Documents and Reports*. Washington: AAUP, 1977. 73–76.

———. "Statement of Principles on Academic Freedom and Tenure." 1940. *AAUP Policy Documents and Reports*. Washington: AAUP, 1977. 1–4.

American Psychiatric Association. *Diagnostic and Statistical Manual of Mental Disorders*. 3rd rev. ed. [*DSM-3-r*]. Washington: APA, 1987.

American Psychological Association. "Guidelines for Nonsexist Language in APA Journals." *American Psychologist* 32 (1977): 487–94.

———. Task Force on Issues of Sexual Bias in Graduate Education. "Guidelines for Nonsexist Use of Language." *American Psychologist* 30 (1975): 682–84.

Aptheker, Bettina. "Quest for Dignity: Black Women in the Professions, 1865–1900." *Woman's Legacy: Essays on Race, Sex, and Class in American History*. Amherst: U of Massachusetts P, 1982. 89–110.

Ardener, Edwin. "The 'Problem' Revisited." S. Ardener, *Perceiving* 19–27.

———. "Some Outstanding Problems in the Analysis of Events." Assn. of Social Anthropologists of the Commonwealth Decennial Conference, 1973.

Ardener, Shirley, ed. *Defining Females: The Nature of Women in Society.* New York: Wiley, 1978.

———. *Perceiving Women.* London: Malaby, 1975.

Atwood, Margaret. *The Handmaid's Tale.* Boston: Houghton, 1986.

Bach, K., and R. M. Harnish. *Linguistic Communication and Speech Acts.* Cambridge: MIT P, 1979.

Baker, Houston A., Jr. "Caliban's Triple Play." *Critical Inquiry* 13 (1986): 182–96.

Bakhtin, Mikhail. *The Dialogic Imagination: Four Essays.* Ed. M. Holquist. Austin: U of Texas P, 1981.

Balsamo, Anne. "Un-wrapping the Postmodern: A Feminist Glance." *Journal of Communication Inquiry* 11.1 (1987): 64–71.

Barnhart, Clarence L. *Second Barnhart Dictionary of New English.* New York: Harper, 1980.

Baron, Dennis E. "The Epicene Pronoun: The Word That Failed." *American Speech* 56 (1981): 83–97.

———. *Grammar and Gender.* New Haven: Yale UP, 1986.

———. *Grammar and Good Taste: Reforming the American Language.* New Haven: Yale UP, 1982.

———. "Is it [mIs] or [mIz]?" *Verbatim* 11.2 (1984): 10.

Bart, Pauline. "Being a Feminist Academic: What a Nice Feminist like Me Is Doing in a Place like This." Treichler, Kramarae, and Stafford 402–18.

Bate, Walter Jackson. "The Crisis in English Studies." *Harvard Magazine* Sept.–Oct. 1982: 46–53.

Bates, Elizabeth, and Laura Benigni. "Rules of Address in Italy: A Sociological Survey." *Language in Society* 4 (1975): 271–88.

Bauer, Laurie. *English Word Formation.* Cambridge: Cambridge UP, 1983.

Baym, Nina. *Woman's Fiction: A Guide to Novels by and about Women in America 1820–1870.* Ithaca: Cornell UP, 1978.

Beanland, J. "The Sex War in Language." *The Vote* 18 Feb. 1911: 207–08. Excerpts rpt. in *Women and Language News* 7.2–3 (1984): 24–25.

Beard, Mary R. *Woman as Force in History.* New York: Macmillan, 1946.

Beattie, James. *The Theory of Language.* London, 1788.

Beck, Evelyn Torton. " 'No More Masks': Anti-Semitism as Jew Hating." *Women's Studies Quarterly* 11.3 (1983): 11–14.

Bell, Roger T. *Sociolinguistics: Goals, Methods and Problems.* New York: St. Martin's, 1976.

Belsey, Catherine. *Critical Practice.* New York: Methuen, 1980.

Bem, Sandra Lipsitz. "The Developmental Implications of Gender Schema Theory: Raising Gender-Aschematic Children in a Gender-Schematic

Society." *Signs: Journal of Women in Culture and Society* 8 (1983): 598–616.

Bem, Sandra Lipsitz, and Daryl J. Bem. "Does Sex-Biased Job Advertising 'Aid and Abet' Sex Discrimination?" *Journal of Applied Social Psychology* 3 (1973): 6–18.

Bennett-Alexander, Dawn D. "The Supreme Court Finally Speaks on the Issue of Sexual Harassment—What Did It Say?" *Women's Rights Law Reporter* 10 (1987): 65–78.

Benstock, Shari, ed. *Feminist Issues in Literary Scholarship.* Bloomington: Indiana UP, 1987.

Benveniste, Emile. *Indo-European Language and Society.* Coral Gables: U of Miami P, 1973.

Berman, Sanford, ed. *Subject Cataloging: Critiques and Innovations.* Spec. issue of *Technical Services Quarterly* 2.1–2 (1984): 1–252.

Berryman, Cynthia, and Virginia A. Eman, eds. *Communication, Language, and Sex: Proceedings of the First Annual Conference.* Rowley: Newbury, 1980.

Bethel, Lorraine. "What Chou Mean *We*, White Girl?" *Conditions* 5 (1979): 86–92.

Bickerton, Derek. *The Roots of Language.* Ann Arbor: Karoma, 1981.

Bierce, Ambrose. *The Devil's Dictionary.* 1911. New York: Dover, 1958.

Black, Maria, and Rosalind Coward. "Linguistic, Social and Sexual Relations: A Review of Dale Spender's *Man Made Language.*" *Screen Education* 39 (1981): 69–85.

Bland, Lucy. "Purity, Motherhood, Pleasure, or Threat? Definitions of Female Sexuality 1900–1970s." *Sex and Love: New Thoughts on Old Contradictions.* Ed. Sue Cartledge and Joanna Ryan. London: Women's, 1983. 8–29.

Blaubergs, Maija S. "An Analysis of Classic Arguments against Changing Sexist Language." Kramarae, *Voices* 135–47.

———. "Changing the Sexist Language: The Theory behind the Practice." *Psychology of Women Quarterly* 2 (1978): 244–61.

Bleier, Ruth. *Science and Gender: A Critique of Biology and Its Theories on Women.* New York: Pergamon, 1984.

Bloomfield, Leonard. *Language.* New York: Holt, 1933.

Bodine, Ann. "Androcentrism in Prescriptive Grammar: Singular 'They,' Sex-Indefinite 'He' and 'He or She.'" *Language in Society* 4 (1975): 129–46.

Bolinger, Dwight. "Truth Is a Linguistic Question." *Language* 49 (1973): 539–50.

Boxer, Marilyn J. "For and about Women: The Theory and Practice of Women's Studies in the United States." *Signs: Journal of Women in Culture and Society* 7 (1982): 661–95.

Breines, Wini, and Linda Gordon. "The New Scholarship on Family Violence." *Signs: Journal of Women in Culture and Society* 8 (1983): 490–531.

Brooke. "The Chador of Women's Liberation: Cultural Feminism and the Movement Press." *Heresies* 3.9 (1980): 70–74.

Brophy, Brigid. Rev. of *The Handbook of Non-Sexist Writing*, by Casey Miller and Kate Swift. *London Review of Books* 14–18 Feb. 1982: 17.

Brown, Goold. *Grammar of English Grammars*. New York, 1851.

Brown, Penelope. "How and Why Are Women More Polite: Some Evidence from a Mayan Community." McConnell-Ginet, Borker, and Furman 111–36.

Brown, Roger W., and Albert Gilman. "The Pronouns of Power and Solidarity." *Style in Language*. Ed. T. A. Sebeok. Cambridge: MIT P, 1960. 253–76. Rpt. in *Readings in the Sociology of Language*. Ed. J. A. Fishman. The Hague: Mouton, 1968; and in *Language and Social Context: Selected Readings*. Ed. P. P. Giglioli. Harmondsworth, Eng.: Penguin, 1972.

Browne, Susan E., Debra Connors, and Nanci Stern, eds. *With the Power of Each Breath: A Disabled Women's Anthology*. Pittsburgh: Cleis, 1985.

Burchfield, Robert W., ed. *Supplement to the* Oxford English Dictionary. Oxford: Oxford UP, 1972–86.

Burgess, Anthony. "Penile Servitude." *London Observer* 27 Oct. 1985: 26.

Butler, Matilda, and William Paisley. *Women and the Mass Media: Sourcebook for Research and Action*. New York: Human Sciences, 1980.

Butturff, Douglas, and Edmund L. Epstein, eds. *Women's Language and Style*. Akron: L&S with U of Akron, 1978.

Camera Obscura Collective. Editorial. *Camera Obscura: A Journal of Feminism and Film Theory* 15 (1986): 4–5.

Cameron, Deborah. *Feminism and Linguistic Theory*. New York: St. Martin's, 1984.

Cannon, Garland, and Susan Robertson. "Sexism in Present-Day English: Is It Diminishing?" *Word* 36 (1985): 23–35.

Capek, Mary Ellen. *A Women's Thesaurus: An Index of Language Used to Describe and Locate Information by and about Women*. New York: Harper, 1987.

Carby, Hazel V. *Reconstructing Womanhood: The Emergence of the Afro-American Woman Novelist*. New York: Oxford UP, 1987.

Caroll, Berenice A. *Liberating Women's History*. Urbana: U of Illinois P, 1978.

———. "The Politics of Originality: Women and the Class System of the Intellect." Unit for Criticism and Interpretive Theory Colloquium, U of Illinois, Urbana. Apr. 1984.

Cassidy, Frederick G., ed. *The Dictionary of American Regional English*. Vol. 1. Cambridge: Belknap-Harvard UP, 1985.

Chafe, William H. *The American Woman: Her Changing Social, Economic, and Political Roles, 1920–1970.* Oxford: Oxford UP, 1974.

Christian, Barbara. *Black Feminist Criticism: Perspectives on Black Women Writers.* New York: Pergamon, 1985.

———. "Shadows Uplifted." *Feminist Criticism and Social Change: Sex, Class, and Race in Literature and Culture.* Ed. Judith Newton and Deborah Rosenfelt. New York: Methuen, 1985. 181–215.

Clarke, Cheryl, Jewelle Gomez, Evelynn Hammonds, Bonnie Johnson, and Linda Powell. "Black Women on Black Women Writers: Conversations and Questions." *Conditions* 9 (1983): 88–137.

Clines, Francis X. "OED's Gigabyte Task: Transferring to Disks." *New York Times* 17 Oct. 1987: 13.

Coleman, Linda, and Paul Kay. "Prototype Semantics: The English Verb *lie.*" *Language* 57 (1981): 26–44.

Colie, Rosalie L. *Shakespeare's Living Art.* Princeton: Princeton UP, 1974.

Conarroe, Joel. "Comments from the Editor." *MLA Newsletter* 12.1 (1980): 1–2.

———. "Editor's Column." *PMLA* 95 (1980): 3–4.

Connors, Debra. "Disability, Sexism and the Social Order." Browne, Connors, and Stern 92–107.

Cook, Claire Kehrwald. *Line by Line: How to Improve Your Own Writing.* Boston: Houghton, 1985.

Cook, Stanley J., and Richard W. Suter. *The Scope of Grammar: A Study of Modern English.* New York: McGraw, 1980.

Cooper, Robert L. "The Avoidance of Androcentric Generics." *International Journal of the Sociology of Language* 50 (1984): 5–20.

Copleman, Martha. "Sexism in the Courtroom: Report from a 'Little Girl Lawyer.' " *Women's Rights Law Reporter* 9 (1986): 107–08.

Corea, Gena. *The Hidden Malpractice: How American Medicine Treats Women as Patients and Professionals.* New York: Morrow, 1977.

Costello, Bonnie. "The 'Feminine' Language of Marianne Moore." McConnell-Ginet, Borker, and Furman 222–38.

Crane, Paul. *Gays and the Law.* London: Pluto, 1983.

Cuddon, J. A. *A Dictionary of Literary Terms.* Garden City: Doubleday, 1977.

Culler, Jonathan. "Reading as a Woman." *On Deconstruction: Theory and Criticism after Structuralism.* Ithaca: Cornell UP, 1982. 43–64.

Culley, Margo, and Catherine Portuges, eds. *Gendered Subjects: The Dynamics of Feminist Teaching.* London: Routledge, 1985.

Dahl, Östen. "On Generics." *Cambridge Colloquium on Formal Semantics of Natural Language.* Ed. Edward L. Keenan. London: Cambridge UP, 1975. 99–111.

Daly, Mary. *Beyond God the Father: Towards a Philosophy of Women's Liberation.* Boston: Beacon, 1973.

———. *Gyn/Ecology: The Metaethics of Radical Feminism.* Boston: Beacon, 1978.

Daly, Mary, with Jane Caputi. *Websters' First New Intergalactic Wickedary of the English Language.* Boston: Beacon, 1987.

Davis, Angela Y. *Women, Race, and Class.* New York: Random, 1981.

deLauretis, Teresa. *Alice Doesn't: Feminism, Semiotics, Cinema.* Bloomington: Indiana UP, 1984.

———. "The Violence of Rhetoric: Considerations on Representation of Gender." *Semiotica* 54 (1985): 11–31.

Delbridge, Arthur, ed. *Macquarie Dictionary.* Sidney: Macquarie, 1981.

DeLee, Joseph B. "The Prophylactic Forceps Operation." *American Journal of Obstetrics and Gynecology* 1 (1920): 34–44.

Delphy, Christine. "The Main Enemy." *Close to Home: A Materialist Analysis of Women's Oppression.* Trans. and ed. Diana Leonard. Amherst: U of Massachusetts P, 1984.

Densmore, Dana. "Speech Is the Form of Thought." *The Female State: A Journal of Female Liberation* 4 (1970): 9–15. Rpt. Pittsburgh: KNOW, 1970.

DeShazer, Mary K. "Reply [to A. M. Tibbetts and Charlene Tibbetts]." *College Composition and Communication* 34 (1983): 490–91.

———. "Sexist Language in Composition Textbooks: Still a Major Issue?" *College Composition and Communication* 32 (1981): 57–64.

DeSole, Gloria, and Leonore Hoffman, eds. *Rocking the Boat: Academic Women and Academic Processes.* New York: MLA, 1981.

DeStefano, Johanna S., Mary W. Kuhner, and Harold B. Pepinsky. "An Investigation of Referents of Selected Sex-Indefinite Terms in English." Ninth World Congress of Sociology. Uppsala, Swed., Aug. 1978.

Diamond, Irene, and Lee Quinby, eds. *Feminism and Foucault: Reflections on Resistance.* Boston: Northeastern UP, 1988.

Dictionaries of the World. New York: Pergamon, 1982.

Douglas, Mary. *How Institutions Think.* Syracuse: Syracuse UP, 1986.

Dubois, Betty Lou. "Nontechnical Arguments in Biomedical Speeches." *Perspectives in Biology and Medicine* 24 (1981): 399–410.

Dubois, Betty Lou, and Isabel Crouch. "Linguistic Disruption: He/She, S/He, He or She, He-She." Penfield 28–35.

———, eds. *Proceedings of the Conference on the Sociology of the Languages of American Women.* Papers in Southwest English. San Antonio: Trinity U, 1976.

DuBois, Ellen Carol, Gail Paradise Kelly, Elizabeth Lapovsky Kennedy, Carolyn W. Korsmeyer, and Lillian S. Robinson. *Feminist Scholarship: Kindling in the Groves of Academe.* Urbana: U of Illinois P, 1987.

Dworkin, Andrea. *Woman Hating.* New York: Dutton, 1974.

Dykeman, Wilma. "Honoring a Cherokee." *New York Times* 2 Aug. 1987, sec. 10: 21 +.

Eakins, Barbara Westbrook, and R. Gene Eakins. *Sex Differences in Human Communication.* Boston: Houghton, 1978.

———. "Verbal Turn-Taking and Exchanges in Faculty Dialogue." Dubois and Crouch, *Proceedings* 53–62.

Edelsky, Carole. "Observation of a Second-Grade Classroom." *Women and Language News* 7.2–3 (1984): 29.

———. "When She's/He's Got the Floor, We've/He's Got It." Tenth World Congress of Sociology. Mexico City, Aug. 1982.

———. "Who's Got the Floor?" *Language in Society* 10 (1981): 383–421.

Eisenstein, Hester, and Alice Jardine, eds. *The Future of Difference.* Boston: Hall, 1980.

Elgin, Suzette Haden. *Native Tongue.* New York: DAW, 1984.

———. "Some Proposed Additions to the Glossary of Needed Lexical Items for the Expression of Women's Perceptions." *Lonesome Node* 1 (1981): 2–3.

———. "Why a Woman Is Not like a Physicist." *Aurora: Speculative Feminism* 8.1 (1982): 30–34.

Eliminating Stereotypes. Boston: Houghton, 1981.

El-Khawas, Elaine H. *Differences in Academic Development during College. Men and Women Learning Together: A Study of College Students in the Late 1970s.* Providence: Brown U, 1980.

Elstob, Elizabeth. *The Rudiments of Grammar for the English-Saxon Tongue, First Given in English: With an Apology for the Study of Northern Antiquities.* London, 1715.

Falco, Kristine L. "Word Consciousness: A Look at Sexist Language and Attitudes." *Women on the Move: A Feminist Perspective.* Ed. J. R. Leppaluoto et al. Pittsburgh: KNOW, 1973. 289–95.

Farley, Jennie. *Academic Women and Employment Discrimination: A Critical Annotated Bibliography.* Ithaca: ILR, 1982.

Faust, Jean. "Words That Oppress." *Women Speaking.* Pittsburgh: KNOW, 1970.

Federbush, Marsha. "The Sex Problems of School Math Books." Stacey, Béreaud, and Daniels 178–84.

Fell, John. *An Essay towards an English Grammar.* London, 1784.

Fellman, David. "Academic Freedom." *Dictionary of the History of Ideas.* Ed. Philip P. Wiener. Vol. 1. New York: Scribner's, 1973. 9–17.

Fern, Fanny. "Aunt Hetty on Matrimony." *Fern Leaves from Fanny's Port Folio.* 1853. New York: Arundel, 1881.

Fetterley, Judith. *The Resisting Reader: A Feminist Approach to American Fiction.* Bloomington: Indiana UP, 1978.

Finger, Anne. "Reproductive Rights and Disability." Browne, Connors, and Stern 292–307.

Fishbein, Martin. "Attitudes and the Prediction of Behavior." *Readings in Attitude Theory and Measurement.* Ed. Fishbein. New York: Wiley, 1967. 477–92.

Fishel, Andrew, and Janice Pottker. *National Politics and Sex Discrimination in Education.* Lexington: Heath, 1977.

Fisher, Dexter, ed. *The Third Woman: Minority Women Writers of the United States.* Boston: Houghton, 1980.

Fisher, John H. "The Dancer and the Dance." *PMLA* 90 (1975): 361–65.

Fisher, Sue. *In the Patient's Best Interest: Women and the Politics of Medical Decisions.* New Brunswick: Rutgers UP, 1986.

Fisher, Sue, and Alexandra Dundas Todd, eds. *Discourse and Institutional Authority: Medicine, Education, and Law.* Norwood: Ablex, 1986.

———, eds. *The Social Organization of Doctor-Patient Communication.* Washington: Center for Applied Linguistics, 1983.

Fishman, Pamela. "Interaction: The Work Women Do." Thorne, Kramarae, and Henley 89–101.

———. "What Do Couples Talk about When They're Alone?" Butturff and Epstein 11–22.

Fiske, Edmund B. "The Push for Smarter Schoolbooks." *New York Times* 2 Aug. 1987, sec. 12: 20–23.

Flaubert, Gustave. *Dictionnaire des idées reçues.* 1881. *Dictionary of Accepted Ideas.* Trans. Jacques Barzun. New York: New Directions, 1967.

Fleck, Ludwik. *Genesis and Development of a Scientific Fact.* Trans. Fred Bradley and Thaddeus J. Trenn. Ed. Thaddeus J. Trenn and Robert K. Merton. Chicago: U of Chicago P, 1979.

Follett, Wilson. *Modern American Usage: A Guide.* Ed. Jacques Barzun. New York: Hill, 1966.

Foucault, Michel. *The Archeology of Knowledge.* Trans. A. M. Sheridan Smith. London: Tavistock, 1972.

———. "Politics and the Study of Discourse." *Ideology and Consciousness* 3 (1978): 7–26.

Frank, Francine W. "Guidelines for Non-sexist Writing: Sources and Consequences." Tenth World Congress of Sociology. Mexico City, Aug. 1982.

———. "Sexism, Grammatical Gender, and Social Change." Ninth World Congress of Sociology. Uppsala, Swed., Aug. 1978. ERIC, 1979. ED 168 368.

———. "Women's Language in America: Myth and Reality." Butturff and Epstein 47–61.

Franklin, Phyllis, Helene Moglen, Phyllis Zatlin-Boring, and Ruth Angress. *Sexual and Gender Harassment in the Academy.* New York: MLA, 1981.

Friedan, Betty. *The Feminine Mystique*. New York: Norton, 1963.

Friendly, Alfred. "Language and the Wopersons' Movement." *Washington Post* 2 May 1978: A19.

Fromkin, Victoria, and Robert Rodman. *An Introduction to Language*. 3rd ed. New York: Holt, 1983.

Frye, Marilyn. "Male Chauvinism—A Conceptual Analysis." Vetterling-Braggin 7–51. Rpt. in Frye, *Politics* 5–79.

———. *The Politics of Reality: Essays in Feminist Theory*. Trumansburg: Crossing, 1983.

Furman, Nelly. "The Politics of Language: Beyond the Gender Principle?" Greene and Kahn 59–79.

Gallop, Jane. "Castration, Authority, and the Politics of Writing." MLA Convention. Los Angeles, 29 Dec. 1982.

———. "Writing and Sexual Difference: The Difference Within." *Critical Inquiry* 8 (1982): 797–804.

Garfield, Eugene. "Is Information Retrieval in the Arts and Humanities Inherently Different from That in Science? The Effect That ISI®'s Citation Index for the Arts and Humanities Is Expected to Have on Future Scholarship." *Library Quarterly* 50 (1980): 40–57.

Garner, Shirley Nelson, Claire Kahane, and Madelon Sprengnether, eds. *The (M)Other Tongue: Essays in Feminist Psychoanalytic Interpretation*. Ithaca: Cornell UP, 1985.

Gates, Henry Louis, Jr. "The Blackness of Blackness: A Critique of the Sign and the Signifying Monkey." *Black Literature and Literary Theory*. Ed. Gates. New York: Methuen, 1984. 285–321.

———. Introduction. Gates, *"Race"* 1–20.

———, ed. *"Race," Writing, and Difference*. Spec. issue of *Critical Inquiry* 12 (1985): 1–300. Chicago: U of Chicago P, 1986.

———. "Talkin' That Talk." *Critical Inquiry* 13 (1986): 203–10.

Gershuny, H. Lee. "Public Doublespeak: The Dictionary." *College English* 36 (1975): 938–42.

———. "Sexism in Dictionaries and Texts: Omissions and Commissions." Nilsen et al. 143–59.

———. "Sexist Semantics in the Dictionary." *ETC.: Review of General Semantics* 31.2 (1974): 159–69.

Gibaldi, Joseph, ed. *Introduction to Scholarship in Modern Languages and Literatures*. New York: MLA, 1981.

Gilbert, Sandra M. "The Education of Henrietta Adams." *Profession 84*. New York: MLA, 1984. 5–9.

Gilbert, Sandra M., and Susan Gubar. "Ceremonies of the Alphabet: Female Grandmatologies and the Female Autograph." D. Stanton 23–52.

———, eds. *The Norton Anthology of Women's Literature.* New York: Norton, 1985.

———. "Sexual Linguistics: Gender, Language, Sexuality." *New Literary History* 16 (1985): 515–43.

———, eds. *Shakespeare's Sisters: Feminist Essays on Women Poets.* Bloomington: Indiana UP, 1979.

Godard, Barbara. "Translating and Sexual Difference." *Resources for Feminist Research* 13.3 (1984): 13–16.

Goldfield, Bina. *The Efemcipated Handbook.* New York: Westover, 1983.

Goodwin, Marjorie Harness. "Directive-Response Speech Sequences in Girls' and Boys' Task Activities." McConnell-Ginet, Borker, and Furman 157–73.

Goodwin, Marjorie Harness, and Charles Goodwin. "Children's Arguing." Philips, Steele, and Tanz 200–48.

Gornick, Vivian, and Barbara K. Moran, eds. *Woman in Sexist Society.* New York: Basic, 1971. New York: Signet-NAL, 1972.

Gould, Stephen Jay. *The Mismeasure of Man.* New York: Norton, 1981.

———. "We First Stood on Our Own Two Feet in Africa, Not Asia." *Discover* May 1986: 52–55.

Gove, Philip Babcock, ed. *Webster's Third New International Dictionary of the English Language.* Springfield: Merriam, 1971.

Graham, Alma. Letter to the Editor. *Columbia Forum* 3.4 (1974): n. pag.

———. "The Making of a Nonsexist Dictionary." *Ms.* Dec. 1973: 12–16. Rpt. in Thorne and Henley 57–63.

Grahn, Judy. *Another Mother Tongue: Gay Words, Gay Worlds.* Boston: Beacon, 1984.

Greene, Gayle, and Coppélia Kahn. *Making a Difference: Feminist Literary Criticism.* New York: Methuen, 1985.

Greer, Germaine. "The Tulsa Center for the Study of Women's Literature: What We Are Doing and Why We Are Doing It." *Tulsa Studies in Women's Literature* 1 (1982): 5–26.

Gregersen, Edgar A. "Sexual Linguistics." Orasanu, Slater, and Adler 3–19.

Grice, H. P. "Meaning." *Philosophical Review* 66 (1957): 377–88.

———. "Utterer's Meaning, Sentence-Meaning and Word-Meaning." *Foundations of Language* 4 (1968): 225–42.

———. "Utterer's Meanings and Intentions." *Philosophical Review* 78 (1969): 147–77.

———. William James Lectures. Harvard University. Cambridge, 1967.

Hall, Deanna, and Kristin Langellier. "Mother-Daughter Storytelling." International Communication Assn. Montreal, May 1987.

Hall, Robert A., Jr. *Leave Your Language Alone.* Ithaca: Linguistica, 1950.

Hall, Roberta M., with the assistance of Bernice Sandler. *The Classroom Climate: A Chilly One for Women.* Washington: AAC Project on the Status and Education of Women, 1982.

Haraway, Donna J. "In the Beginning Was the Word: The Genesis of Biological Theory." *Signs: Journal of Women in Culture and Society* 6 (1981): 469–81.

———. "A Manifesto for Cyborgs: Science, Technology, and Socialist Feminism in the 1980s." *Socialist Review* 80 (1985): 65–108.

Harding, Susan. "Women and Words in a Spanish Village." *Toward an Anthropology of Women.* Ed. Rayna Reiter. New York: Monthly Review, 1975. 283–308.

Harrison, Linda. "Cro-Magnon Woman—in Eclipse." *Science Teacher* 42.4 (1975): 8–11.

Harrison, Linda, and Richard N. Passero. "Sexism in the Language of Elementary School Textbooks." *Science and Children* 12.4 (1975): 22–25.

Harrison, Ralph. *Institutes of English Grammar.* Manchester, 1777.

Hartman, Joan, and Ellen Messer-Davidow, eds. *Women in Print I: Opportunities for Women's Studies Research in Language and Literature.* New York: MLA, 1982.

———. *Women in Print II: Opportunities for Women's Studies Publication in Language and Literature.* New York: MLA, 1982.

Hearn, Kirsten. Letter. *Spare Rib* 136 (Nov. 1983): 5.

Heath, Shirley Brice. "The Context of Professional Languages: An Historical Overview." *Language and Public Life.* Ed. J. Alatis and R. Tucker. Washington: Georgetown UP, 1979. 102–18.

Heilbrun, Carolyn G. "Presidential Address 1984." *PMLA* 100 (1985): 281–85.

Hellinger, Marlis. "Effecting Social Change through Group Action." *Language and Power.* Ed. Cheris Kramarae, Muriel Schulz, and William M. O'Barr. Beverly Hills: Sage, 1984. 136–53.

———, ed. *Sprachwandel und Feministische Sprachpolitik: Internationale Perspektiven.* Wiesbaden: Westdeutscher, 1985.

Heschel, Susannah, ed. *On Being a Jewish Feminist: A Reader.* New York: Schocken, 1983.

Hine, Darlene Clark. "Opportunity and Fulfillment: Sex, Race, and Class in Health Care Education." *Sage* 2 (Fall 1985): 14–19.

Hofstadter, Douglas. "A Person Paper on Purity in Language." *Metamagical Themas: Questing for the Essence of Mind and Pattern.* New York: Basic, 1985. 159–67.

Hole, Judith, and Ellen Levine. "The First Feminists." Koedt, Levine, and Rapone 3–16.

Horowitz, Helen Lefkowitz. *Alma Mater: Design and Experience in the Women's*

Colleges from Their Nineteenth-Century Beginnings to the 1930s. Boston: Beacon, 1984.

Howard, Maureen. Rev. of *Literary Women,* by Ellen Moers. *New York Times Book Review* 7 March 1976: 6.

Hull, Gloria, Patricia Bell Scott, and Barbara Smith, eds. *All the Women Are White, All the Blacks Are Men, but Some of Us Are Brave: Black Women's Studies.* Old Westbury: Feminist, 1982.

Hurd-Mead, Kate Campbell. *A History of Women in Medicine.* Haddam: Haddam, 1938.

Jacobs, Roderick A., and Peter S. Rosenbaum. *Transformations, Style, and Meaning.* Waltham: Xerox Coll., 1971.

Jacobus, Mary. *Reading Woman: Essays in Feminist Criticism.* New York: Columbia UP, 1986.

Jardine, Alice. *Gynesis: Configurations of Women and Modernity.* Ithaca: Cornell UP, 1985.

———. "Men in Feminism: Odor di Uomo or Compagnons de Route?" Jardine and Smith 54–61.

Jardine, Alice, and Paul Smith, eds. *Men in Feminism.* New York: Methuen, 1987.

Jenkins, Mercilee M. "Guidelines for Student-Faculty Communication." *Sex and Gender in the Social Sciences: Reassessing the Introductory Course.* Ed. Judith M. Gappa and Janice Pearce. Washington: Women's Educational Equity Act Program, 1982. Rpt. as *Removing Bias: Guidelines for Student-Faculty Communication.* Annandale: Speech Communication Assn., 1983.

Jespersen, Otto. *Essentials of English Grammar.* 1933. University: U of Alabama P, 1964.

———. *Language: Its Nature, Development, and Origin.* London: Allen, 1922.

———. *The Philosophy of Grammar.* 1924. New York: Norton, 1965.

Johnson, Barbara. "Thresholds of Difference: Structures of Address in Zora Neale Hurston." Gates, *"Race"* 278–89.

Johnson, Samuel. *A Dictionary of the English Language: In Which the Words Are Deduced from Their Originals and Illustrated in Their Different Significations by Examples from the Best Writers.* 1755. New York: Adler, 1968.

Jones, Charles. *An Introduction to Middle English.* New York: Holt, 1972.

Jones, Deborah. "Gossip: Notes on Women's Oral Culture." Kramarae, *Voices* 193–98.

Joseph, Gloria I. Rev. of *Women, Race, and Class,* by Angela Y. Davis. *Signs: A Journal of Women in Culture and Society* 9 (1983): 134–36.

Justus, Carol F. "Indo-Europeanization of Myth and Syntax in Anatolian Hittite: Dating of Texts as an Index." *Journal of Indo-European Studies* 11 (1983): 59–103.

Kalčik, Susan. " '. . . Like Ann's Gynecologist or the Time I Was Almost Raped': Personal Narratives in Women's Rap Groups." *Journal of American Folklore* 88 (1975): 3–11.

Kamuf, Peggy. "Writing like a Woman." McConnell-Ginet, Borker, and Furman 284–99.

Kantrowitz, Joanne Spencer. "Paying Your Dues, Part-Time." DeSole and Hoffmann 15–36.

Kaplan, Cora. "Pandora's Box: Subjectivity, Class and Sexuality in Socialist Feminist Criticism." Greene and Kahn 146–76.

Keesing, Nancy. *Lily on the Dustbin: Slang of Australian Women and Their Families*. Ringwood, Vic., Austral.: Penguin, 1982.

Keller, Evelyn Fox. *A Feeling for the Organism: The Life and Work of Barbara McClintock*. San Francisco: Freeman, 1983.

———. *Reflections on Gender and Science*. New Haven: Yale UP, 1985.

Kelly, James R. Letter. *PMLA* 95 (1980): 873.

Kelly, Mary. *Post-partum Document*. London: Pandora, 1984.

Kessler, Suzanne, and Wendy McKenna. *Gender: An Ethnomethodological Approach*. New York: Wiley, 1978.

Ketchum, Sara Ann. "Reflections on Meaning and Power." Eastern Div., Fall Meeting, Soc. for Women in Philosophy. Ithaca, Nov. 1979.

Kett, Merriellyn, and Virginia Underwood. *How to Avoid Sexism: A Guide for Writers, Editors and Publishers*. Chicago: Ragan, 1978.

Kidd, Virginia. "A Study of the Images Produced through the Use of the Male Pronoun as the Generic." *Moments in Contemporary Rhetoric and Communication* 1.2 (1971): 25–30.

Kloss, Heinz. "Notes concerning a Language-Nation Typology." *Language Problems of Developing Nations*. Ed. J. A. Fishman, C. A. Ferguson, and J. Das Gupta. New York: Wiley, 1968. 69–85.

Knorr-Cetina, Karin D. *The Manufacture of Knowledge: An Essay on the Constructivist and Contextual Nature of Science*. Oxford: Pergamon, 1981.

Koedt, Anne. "The Myth of the Vaginal Orgasm." Koedt, Levine, and Rapone 198–207.

Koedt, Anne, Ellen Levine, and Anita Rapone, eds. *Radical Feminism*. New York: Quadrangle-New York Times, 1973.

Kolodny, Annette. "A Map for Rereading: Or, Gender and the Interpretation of Literary Texts." *New Literary History* 11 (1980): 451–67.

Kramarae, Cheris (see also Kramer, Cheris). "Gender: How She Speaks." *Attitudes toward Language Variation: Social and Applied Contexts*. Ed. Ellen Bouchard Ryan and Howard Giles. London: Arnold, 1982. 84–98.

———. "Proprietors of Language." McConnell-Ginet, Borker, and Furman 58–68.

———, ed. *The Voices and Words of Women and Men*. Oxford: Pergamon, 1980.

——. *Women and Men Speaking: Frameworks for Analysis.* Rowley: Newbury, 1981.

Kramarae, Cheris, and Paula A. Treichler. "Power Relationships in the Classroom." *Gender Studies: Reading, Writing, and Teaching.* Ed. Susan Gabriel and Isaiah Smithson. Urbana: U of Illinois P (in press).

Kramarae, Cheris, and Paula A. Treichler, with the assistance of Ann Russo. *A Feminist Dictionary.* London: Pandora-Routledge, 1985. New York: Methuen, 1986.

Kramer, Cheris (see also Kramarae, Cheris). "Stereotypes of Women's Speech: The Word from Cartoons." *Journal of Popular Culture* 8 (1974): 624–30.

Kramer, Cheris, Barrie Thorne, and Nancy Henley. "Review Essay: Perspectives on Language and Communication." *Signs: Journal of Women in Culture and Society* 3 (1978): 638–51.

Küpper, Heinz, ed. *Illustriertes Lexikon der deutschen Umgangssprache [Illustrated Dictionary of German Colloquial Language].* Stuttgart: Klett, 1984.

Labov, William, ed. *Locating Language in Time and Space.* New York: Academic, 1980.

——. *Sociolinguistic Patterns.* Philadelphia: U of Pennsylvania P, 1972.

Labov, William, and David Fanshel. *Therapeutic Discourse: Psychotherapy as Conversation.* New York: Academic, 1977.

Lakoff, George, and Mark Johnson. *Metaphors We Live By.* Chicago: U of Chicago P, 1980.

Lakoff, Robin. *Language and Woman's Place.* New York: Harper, 1975.

Langacker, Ronald W. Rev. of *Women, Fire, and Dangerous Things,* by George L. Lakoff. *Language* 64 (1988): 384–95.

Latour, Bruno, and Steve Woolgar. *Laboratory Life: The Construction of Scientific Facts.* Cambridge: Cambridge UP, 1985.

Le Doeuff, Michèle. "Women and Philosophy." Trans. Debbie Pope. *Radical Philosophy* 17 (1977): 2–11.

Leffler, Ann, Dair L. Gillespie, and Elinor Lerner. *Academic Feminists and the Women's Movement.* Iowa City: Iowa City Women's, 1973.

Lennert, Midge, and Norma Willson, eds. *A Woman's New World Dictionary.* Lomita: 51%, 1973.

Lenz, Carolyn Ruth Swift, Gayle Greene, and Carol Thomas Neely, eds. *The Woman's Part: Feminist Criticism of Shakespeare.* Urbana: U of Illinois P, 1980.

Leveen, Steven. "Technosexism." *New York Times* 12 Nov. 1983, sec. 1: 23.

Levelt, W. J. M. "What Became of LAD?" Lisse, Neth.: de Ridder, 1975.

Lewis, D. *Convention.* Cambridge: Harvard UP, 1969.

Lindsey, Karen. "The Pitfalls of Politically Correct Language." *Sojourner* Oct. 1985: 16–17.

"Linguistic Sexism." Editorial. *Journal of Ecumenical Studies* 11 (1974): n. pag.

Lockwood, W. B. *Indo-European Philology.* London: Hutchinson, 1969.

Loftus, Marilyn. "The First Year Report of the New Jersey Supreme Court Task Force on Women in the Courts—June 1984." *Women's Rights Law Reporter* 9 (1986): 129–77.

Lorde, Audre. "The Master's Tools Will Never Dismantle the Master's House." Moraga and Anzaldúa 98–101.

Lowe, Marian, and Ruth Hubbard, eds. *Woman's Nature.* New York: Pergamon, 1983.

Lyons, John. *Semantics.* 2 vols. Cambridge: Cambridge UP, 1977.

MacKay, Donald G. "On the Goals, Principles, and Procedures for Prescriptive Grammar: Singular *they.*" *Language in Society* 9 (1980): 349–67.

MacKay, Donald G., and David C. Fulkerson. "On the Comprehension and Production of Pronouns." *Journal of Verbal Learning and Verbal Behavior* 18 (1979): 661–73.

Mager, Donald N. "Discourse of Homophobia: Female and Male Contexts." MLA Convention. New York, 30 Dec. 1986.

Maittaire, Michael. *The English Grammar.* London, 1712.

Makward, Christiane. "To Be or Not to Be . . . a Feminist Speaker." Eisenstein and Jardine 95–105.

Maltz, Daniel N., and Ruth A. Borker. "A Cultural Approach to Male-Female Miscommunication." *Language and Social Identity.* Ed. John J. Gumperz. Cambridge: Cambridge UP, 1982. 195–216.

Marcus, Jane. "Still Practice, A/Wrested Alphabet: Toward a Feminist Aesthetic." Benstock 79–97.

———. "Storming the Toolshed." *Signs: Journal of Women in Culture and Society* 7 (1982): 622–40.

Marshall, J. K. *On Equal Terms: A Thesaurus for Nonsexist Indexing and Cataloging.* New York: Neal, 1977.

Marshall, Thurgood. Address to the annual seminar of the San Francisco Patent and Trademark Law Association. Maui, 6 May 1987. Reported in the *New York Times* by Stuart Taylor, 7 May 1987, sec. 1:1.

Martin, Emily. *The Woman in the Body: A Cultural Analysis of Reproduction.* Boston: Beacon, 1987.

Martyna, Wendy. "Beyond the He/Man Approach: The Case for Nonsexist Language." *Signs: Journal of Women in Culture and Society* 5 (1980): 482–93. Rev. and rpt. in Thorne, Kramarae, and Henley 25–37.

———. "The Psychology of the Generic Masculine." McConnell-Ginet, Borker, and Furman 69–78.

———. "Using and Understanding the Generic Masculine: A Social Psychological Approach to Language and the Sexes." Diss. Stanford U, 1978.

———. "What Does 'He' Mean? Use of the Generic Masculine." *Journal of Communication* 28.1 (1978): 131–38.

McArthur, Leslie Z., and Susan V. Eisen. "Achievements of Male and Female Storybook Characters as Determinants of Achievement Behavior by Boys and Girls." *Journal of Personality and Social Psychology* 33 (1976): 467–73.

McConnell-Ginet, Sally. "Address Forms in Sexual Politics." Butturff and Epstein 23–35.

———. "Feminism in Linguistics." Treichler, Kramarae, and Stafford 159–76.

———. "Intonation in a Man's World." *Signs: Journal of Women in Culture and Society* 3 (1978): 541–59. Rpt. in Thorne, Kramarae, and Henley 69–88.

———. "Language and Gender." *Cambridge Survey of Linguistics.* Ed. Frederick J. Newmeyer. Vol. 4. Cambridge: Cambridge UP, 1987. 75–99.

———. "Linguistics and the Feminist Challenge." McConnell-Ginet, Borker, and Furman 3–25.

———. "The Origins of Sexist Language in Discourse." *Discourses in Reading and Linguistics.* Ed. Sheila J. White and Virginia Teller. *Annals of the New York Academy of Sciences* 433 (1984): 123–35.

———. "Our Father Tongue." *Diacritics* 5 (1975): 44–50.

———. "Review Article [on Language, Sex, and Gender]." *Language* 59 (1983): 373–91.

McConnell-Ginet, Sally, Ruth Borker, and Nelly Furman, eds. *Women and Language in Literature and Society.* New York: Praeger, 1980. Westport: Greenwood, 1986.

McDermott, Ray P., and Henry Tylbor. "On the Necessity of Collusion in Conversation." Fisher and Todd, *Discourse* 123–39.

McDowell, Deborah. "New Directions for Black Feminist Criticism." Showalter, *New* 186–99.

McHoul, A. W. "Writing, Sexism, and Schooling: A Discourse-Analytic Investigation of Some Recent Documents on Sexism and Education in Queensland." Fisher and Todd, *Discourse* 186–202.

McKluskie, Kate. "Women's Language and Literature: A Problem in Women's Studies." *Feminist Review* 14 (1983): 51–61.

McMillen, Liz. "Job-Related Tension and Anxiety Taking a Toll among Employees in Academe's 'Stress Factories.'" *Chronicle of Higher Education* 4 Feb. 1987, sec. 1: 10–12.

Medin, Douglas L., and Edward E. Smith. "Concepts and Concept Formation." *Annual Review of Psychology* 35 (1984): 113–38.

Meese, Elizabeth A. *Crossing the Double-Cross: The Practice of Feminist Criticism.* Chapel Hill: U of North Carolina P, 1986.

Meillet, Antoine. "L'État actuel des études de linguistique générale." Opening lecture of the cours de grammaire comparée, Coll. de France, 13 Feb. 1906. *Linguistique historique et linguistique générale*. Paris: Champion, 1958. 1–18.

Merchant, Carolyn. *The Death of Nature: Women, Ecology, and the Scientific Revolution*. New York: Harper, 1980.

Meyers, Walter E. *Handbook of Contemporary English*. New York: Harcourt, 1974.

Michard-Marchal, Claire, and Claudine Ribéry. "Enunciation and Ideological Effects: 'Women' and 'Men' as Subjects of Discourse in Ethnology." *Feminist Issues* 6.2 (1986): 53–74.

Miller, Casey, and Kate Swift. *The Handbook of Nonsexist Writing*. 1980. 2nd rev. ed. New York: Harper, 1988.

———. *Words and Women: New Language in New Times*. Garden City: Anchor-Doubleday, 1976.

Millet, Kate. *Sexual Politics*. New York: Avon, 1971.

Milroy, James, and Lesley Milroy. *Authority in Language: Investigating Language Prescription and Standardisation*. London: Routledge, 1985.

Mitchell, Juliet. Introduction 1. Mitchell and Rose 1–26.

Mitchell, Juliet, and Jacqueline Rose, eds. *Feminine Sexuality: Jacques Lacan and the école freudienne*. Trans. Rose. New York: Norton, 1982.

Mitchell-Kernan, Claudia. "Signifying, Loud-Talking, and Marking." *Rappin' and Stylin' Out: Communication in Urban Black America*. Ed. Thomas Kochman. Urbana: U of Illinois P, 1972. 315–35.

MLA Commission on the Status of Women in the Profession. "Sexism in the Profession: One More Time." *MLA Newsletter* 9.2 (1977): 4–5.

MLA Delegate Assembly. Minutes of the 1979 Meeting. *PMLA* 95 (1980): 430+.

Moers, Ellen. *Literary Women*. Garden City: Doubleday, 1976. New York: Oxford UP, 1985.

Mohanty, Chandra Talpade. "Under Western Eyes: Feminist Discourse of Appropriation." MLA Convention. New York, Dec. 1984.

Mohr, Richard D. *Gays/Justice: A Study of Ethics, Society, and the Law*. New York: Columbia UP, 1988.

Moi, Toril. *Sexual/Textual Politics: Feminist Literary Theory*. New York: Methuen, 1985.

Money, John. "The Conceptual Neutering of Gender and the Criminalization of Sex." *Archives of Sexual Behavior* 14 (1985): 279–90.

———. "Gender: History, Theory and Usage of the Term in Sexology and Its Relationship to Nature/Nurture." *Journal of Sex and Marital Therapy* 11.2 (1985): 71–79.

Moraga, Cherríe, and Gloria Anzaldúa, eds. *This Bridge Called My Back: Writings by Radical Women of Color*. Boston: Persephone, 1981.

Morris, Meaghan. "A-mazing Grace: Notes on Mary Daly's Poetics." *Intervention* 16 (1982): 70–92.

————. "The Pirate's Fiancée: Feminists and Philosophers, or Maybe Tonight It'll Happen." Diamond and Quinby 21–42.

Morton, Nelle. "The Rising Woman's Consciousness in a Male Language Structure." *Andover Newton Quarterly* 12 (1972): 177–90.

Mossé, Fernand. *A Handbook of Middle English.* Baltimore: Johns Hopkins P, 1952.

Moulton, Janice. "The Myth of the Neutral 'Man.' " Vetterling-Braggin 100–15.

Muller, Marcia. *The Cheshire Cat's Eye.* New York: St. Martin's, 1983.

Müller, Max. *Biographies of Words and the Home of the Aryas.* London, 1888.

Murphy, Gregory L., and Douglas L. Medin. "The Role of Theories in Conceptual Coherence." *Psychological Review* 92 (1985): 289–316.

Murray, James A. *The Evolution of English Lexicography.* Romanes Lecture, 1900. Oxford: Clarendon, 1900. College Park: McGrath, 1970.

Murray, James A., ed. *Oxford English Dictionary.* 1874–1928. Compact ed. Oxford: Oxford UP, 1971.

Murray, K. M. Elisabeth. *Caught in the Web of Words: James Murray and the Oxford English Dictionary.* Oxford: Oxford UP, 1977.

Murray, Lindley. *Murray's English Grammar.* York, 1795. Rpt. Delmar: Scholars Facsimiles and Reprints, 1981.

Nelson, Cary. "Envoys of Otherness: Difference and Continuity in Feminist Criticism." Treichler, Kramarae, and Stafford 91–118.

————. Letter to the authors. 18 Apr. 1985.

Nelson, Cary, and Lawrence Grossberg, eds. *Marxism and the Interpretation of Culture.* Urbana: U of Illinois P, 1988.

Newmeyer, Frederick J. *The Politics of Linguistics.* Chicago: U of Chicago P, 1986.

Newton, Esther. *Mother Camp: Female Impersonators in America.* Chicago: U of Chicago P, 1972.

Nichols, Patricia C. "Black Women in the Rural South." DuBois and Crouch 103–114. Rpt. in *International Journal of the Sociology of Language* 17 (1978): 45–54.

————. "Women in Their Speech Communities." McConnell-Ginet, Borker, and Furman 140–49.

Nilsen, Alleen Pace. "Guidelines against Sexist Language: A Case History." Penfield 37–64.

————. "Sexism in English: A Feminist View." *Female Studies* 6 (1972): 102–09.

Nilsen, Alleen Pace, Haig Bosmajian, H. Lee Gershuny, and Julia P. Stanley, eds. *Sexism and Language.* Urbana: NCTE, 1977.

"No Comment." *Ms.* Dec. 1978: 102.

Oakley, Ann. *Sex, Gender, and Society.* New York: Harper, 1972.

O'Barr, William M., and Bowman K. Atkins. " 'Women's Language' or 'Powerless Language'?" McConnell-Ginet, Borker, and Furman 93–110.

Orasanu, Judith, Mariam K. Slater, and Leonore Loeb Adler, eds. *Language, Sex and Gender: Does "la différence" Make a Difference? Annals of the New York Academy of Sciences* 327 (1979): 1–121.

Orr, Chris. "Moms and Whoopi: Pioneers of Black Theater." *Plexus* Nov. 1983: 15.

Parker, Frank. "Typology as an Inadequate Explanation for Language Change." Div. on Language Change, MLA Convention. Chicago, Dec. 1977.

Parker, Robert B. *A Catskill Eagle.* New York: Delacorte, 1985.

Parsons, Elsie Clews. *The Old-Fashioned Woman: Primitive Fancies about the Sex.* New York: Putnam's, 1913.

Penelope, Julia (see also Stanley, Julia Penelope). "Lexicon of Liberation." *Women's Review of Books* 3.2 (1986): 9.

Penfield, Joyce, ed. *Women and Language in Transition.* Albany: State U of New York P, 1987.

Penley, Constance. *The Future of an Illusion: Film, Feminism, and Psychoanalysis.* Minneapolis: U of Minnesota P, 1989.

Philips, Susan U. "Sex Differences and Language." *Annual Review of Anthropology* 9 (1980): 523–44.

Philips, Susan U., Susan Steele, and Christine Tanz. *Language, Gender, and Sex in Comparative Perspective.* Cambridge: Cambridge UP, 1987.

Piercy, Marge. *Woman on the Edge of Time.* New York: Knopf, 1976.

Poovey, Mary. "My Hideous Progeny: Mary Shelley and the Feminization of Romanticism," *PMLA* 95 (1980): 332–47.

———. " 'Scenes of an Indelicate Character': The Medical 'Treatment' of Victorian Women." *The Making of the Modern Body.* Ed. Catherine Gallagher and Thomas Laqueur. Berkeley: U of California P, 1987. 137–68.

———. "Speaking of the Body: A Discursive Division of Labor in Mid-Victorian Britain." Colloquium on Women, Science, and the Body: Discourses and Representations. Soc. for the Humanities, Cornell U, Ithaca. May 1987.

Posner, Herbert S. "Unambiguous Reporting of the Sex of Human Beings." *Lancet* 22 Jan. 1983: 175–76.

Pratt, Mary Louise. "The Ideology of Speech-Act Theory." *Centrum* ns 1.1 (1981): 5–18.

Prince, Virginia. "Sex, Gender, and Semantics." *Journal of Sex Research* 21 (1985): 92–96.

Pritchard, Jack A., and Paul C. MacDonald, eds. *Williams' Obstetrics.* 15th ed. New York: Appleton, 1976.

Pryse, Marjorie, and Hortense J. Spillers, eds. *Conjuring: Black Women, Fiction, and Literary Tradition.* Bloomington: Indiana UP, 1985.

Putnam, Hilary. *Philosophical Papers.* Vol. 2. Cambridge: Cambridge UP, 1975.

Pyles, Thomas. *The Origins and Development of the English Language.* New York: Harcourt, 1971.

Radway, Janice A. "Identifying Ideological Seams: Mass Culture, Analytic Method, and Political Practice." *Feminist Critiques of Popular Culture.* Ed. Ellen Wartella and Paula A. Treichler. Spec. issue of *Communication* 9.1 (1985): 93–123.

———. *Reading the Romance: Women, Patriarchy, and Popular Literature.* Chapel Hill: U of North Carolina P, 1984.

Rebolledo, Tey Diana. "The Maturing of Chicana Poetry: The Quiet Revolution of the 1980s." Treichler, Kramarae, and Stafford 143–58.

Reinhart, Tanya. *Anaphora and Semantic Interpretation.* Chicago: U of Chicago P, 1983.

"Reports from the Academy: The Uses and Abuses of Literature at the Modern Language Association Conference." *Academic Questions* 1.1 (1987–88): 36–47.

Rice, Nancy Hall. "From *Hose* to *Hoser* to *Hosebag*: Folk Humor and Misogyny in the Cornfields." *Women and Language* 7.1–2 (1984): 44–46.

Rich, Adrienne. *On Lies, Secrets, and Silence: Selected Prose 1966–1978.* New York: Norton, 1979.

———. "When We Dead Awaken: Writing as Re-vision." Rich, *On Lies* 33–49.

———. *The Will to Change: Poems 1968–1970.* New York: Norton, 1971.

Richards, Janet Radcliffe. *The Skeptical Feminist.* London: Routledge, 1982.

Rix, Sara E., ed. *The American Woman 1987–88: A Report in Depth.* New York: Norton, 1987.

Roberts, Paul. *Modern Grammar.* New York: Harcourt, 1968.

Rohter, Larry. "Women Gain Degrees, but Not Tenure." *New York Times* 4 Jan. 1987, sec. 4: 9.

Rose, Hilary. "Hand, Brain, and Heart: A Feminist Epistemology for the Natural Sciences." *Signs: Journal of Women in Culture and Society* 9 (1984): 73–90.

Rose, Jacqueline. Introduction 2. Mitchell and Rose 27–57.

Rosenberg, Rosalind. "From the Witness Stand: Previously Unpublished Testimony in the Sex Discrimination Case against Sears." *Academic Questions* 1.1 (1987–88): 15–35.

Ross, Alan S. C. "U and Non-U." *Noblesse Oblige.* Ed. Nancy Mitford. New York: Harper, 1956. 55–89.

Rosser, Sue. *Teaching Science and Health from a Feminist Perspective.* New York: Pergamon, 1986.

Rothstein, Robert A. "Sex, Gender, and the October Revolution." *Festschrift for Morris Halle.* Ed. S. R. Anderson and Paul Kiparsky. New York: Holt, 1973. 460–66.

Rousmaniere, John. "Little Words That Exclude." Letter. *New York Times* 26 May 1985: E14.

Rubin, Gayle. "The Traffic in Women: Notes on the 'Political Economy' of Sex." *Toward an Anthropology of Women.* Ed. Rayna R. Reiter. New York: Monthly Review, 1975. 157–210.

Ruether, Rosemary Radford, ed. *Religion and Sexism.* New York: Simon, 1974.

——. *Sexism and God-Talk: Toward a Feminist Theology.* Boston: Beacon, 1983.

Russell, Letty M. "Changing Language and the Church." *The Liberating Word: A Guide to Nonsexist Interpretation of the Bible.* Ed. Letty M. Russell. Philadelphia: Westminster, 1976.

Ruthven, K. K. *Feminist Literary Studies: An Introduction.* Cambridge: Cambridge UP, 1984.

Safire, William. "On Language: Dust Heaps of History." *New York Times Magazine* 16 Oct. 1983: 14–16.

——. "On Language: Hypersexism and the Feds." *New York Times Magazine* 26 May 1985: 10–11.

Sage, Lorna. "Seminal Semantics." Rev. of *Dissemination,* by Jacques Derrida. *Observer* 10 Jan. 1982: 45.

Sandler, Bernice R. "The Classroom Climate for Women." Rix 243–47.

——, ed. "Women on Campus: A Ten-Year Retrospect." *On Campus with Women* 26 (1980): 2–3.

Sandoval, Chela. "Dis-illusionment and the Poetry of the Future: The Making of Oppositional Consciousness." Unpublished essay, 1984.

Sapir, Edward. Abstract of "Conceptual Categories in Primitive Languages" (paper presented to the National Academy of Sciences). *Science* 74 (1931): 578.

——. "The Status of Linguistics as a Science." *Language* 5 (1929): 207–14. Rpt. in *Culture, Language, and Personality.* Ed. David Mandelbaum. Berkeley: U of California P, 1966. 65–77.

Schaefer, William D. "Editor's Column." *PMLA* 91 (1976): 795–96.

Scheman, Naomi. "Anger and the Politics of Naming." McConnell-Ginet, Borker, and Furman 174–87.

Schibanoff, Susan. "Early Women Writers: In-scribing: Or, Reading the Fine Print." *Women's Studies International Forum* 6 (1983): 475–89.

Schiffer, S. *Meaning.* London: Oxford UP, 1972.

Schneider, Joseph, and Sally Hacker. "Sex Role Imagery and the Use of

Generic 'Man' in Introductory Texts." *American Sociologist* 8 (1973): 12–18.

Schneider, Michael J., and Karen A. Foss. "Thought, Sex, and Language: The Sapir-Whorf Hypothesis in the American Women's Movement." *Bulletin: Women's Studies in Communication* 1.2 (1977): 1–7.

Schulz, Muriel R. "The Semantic Derogation of Women." Thorne and Henley 64–75.

Scott, Joan W. "Gender: A Useful Category of Historical Analysis." *American Historical Review* 91 (1986): 1053–75.

Scott, Patricia Bell. "Debunking Sapphire: Toward a Non-racist and Non-sexist Social Science." Hull, Scott, and Smith 85–92.

Scruton, Roger. "Doing without Gender." Rev. of *Sexist Language*, ed. Mary Vetterling-Braggin. *Times Literary Supplement* 1 Jan. 1982: 6.

Scully, Diana, and Pauline Bart. "A Funny Thing Happened on the Way to the Orifice: Women in Gynecology Textbooks." *American Journal of Sociology* 78 (1973): 1045–50.

Searing, Susan E. "Empowerment and Library Instruction." *Feminist Teacher* 1.1 (1984): 8–9.

———. *Introduction to Library Research in Women's Studies*. Boulder: Westview, 1985.

Shavlik, Donna L., and Judith G. Touchton. "Women in Higher Education." Rix 239–42.

Shavlik, Donna L., Judith G. Touchton, and Carol S. Pearson. *The New Agenda of Women for Higher Education: A Report of the ACE Commission on Women in Higher Education*. Washington: ACE, 1988.

Shear, Marie. "Solving the Great Pronoun Problem: Twelve Ways to Avoid the Sexist Singular." *Perspectives* 13.1 (1981): 17–24.

Shenker, Israel. *Harmless Drudges: Wizards of Language—Ancient, Medieval, and Modern*. New York: Barnhart, 1979.

Shepard, Richard F. " 'Yuppie,' 'Sputnik' and 'Wimmin' Officially Join the Queen's English." *Chicago Tribune* 22 May 1986, sec. 1A: 38.

Shepelak, Norma J. "Does 'He' Mean 'She' Too? The Case of the Generic Anomaly." Fourth National Conference, Assn. for Women in Psychology. St. Louis, 1977.

Shepelak, Norma J., D. Ogden, and D. Tobin-Bennett. "Students' Perceptions of Careers as a Function of Gender Cues." Unpublished essay, 1976.

Shimanoff, Susan B. "Man = Human: Empirical Support for the Whorfian Hypothesis." *Bulletin: Women's Studies in Communication* 1.2 (1977): 21–27.

Showalter, Elaine. "Critical Cross Dressing: Male Feminists and the Woman of the Year." *Raritan* 3.2 (1983): 130–49.

———, ed. *The New Feminist Criticism: Essays on Women, Literature, and Theory.* New York: Pantheon, 1985.

———. "Toward a Feminist Poetics." Showalter, *New* 125–43.

———. "Women's Time, Women's Space: Writing the History of Feminist Criticism." *Tulsa Studies in Women's Literature* 3 (1984): 29–43. Rpt. in Benstock 30–44.

Sicherman, Barbara. "The Uses of Diagnosis: Doctors, Patients, and Neurasthenia." *Journal of the History of Medicine and Allied Sciences* 32 (1977): 33–54.

Simon, John. "A Handbook for Maidens." Rev. of *The Handbook of Nonsexist Writing*, by Casey Miller and Kate Swift. *American Spectator* 13.11 (1980): 29–31.

Simons, Margaret A. "The Silencing of Simone de Beauvoir: Guess What's Missing from *The Second Sex.*" *Women's Studies International Forum* 6 (1983): 559–64.

Sklar, Elizabeth S. "Sexist Grammar Revisited." *College English* 45 (1983): 348–58.

Sledd, James. "Dollars and Dictionaries: The Limits of Commercial Lexicography." *New Aspects of Lexicography: Literary Criticism, Intellectual History, and Social Change.* Ed. Howard D. Weinbrot. Carbondale: Southern Illinois UP, 1972. 119–37.

Sledd, James, and Wilma R. Ebbitt. *Dictionaries and That Dictionary: A Case Book on the Aims of Lexicographers and the Targets of Reviewers.* Chicago: Scott, 1962.

Smith, Barbara. "Word Play." Rev. of *A Feminist Dictionary*, by Cheris Kramarae and Paula A. Treichler. *New Statesman* 3 Jan. 1986: 23.

Smith, David. "Language, Speech, and Ideology." *Language Attitudes: Current Trends and Prospects.* Ed. Roger Shuy and R. W. Fasold. Washington: Georgetown UP, 1973. 97–112.

Smith, N., ed. *Mutual Knowledge.* New York: Academic, 1981.

Smith, Patricia Clark. "Ain't Seen You Since: Dissent among Female Relations in American Indian Women's Poetry." Allen 108–26.

Smith, Philip M. *Language, the Sexes and Society.* Oxford: Blackwell, 1985.

Smitherman, Geneva. *Talkin' and Testifyin': The Language of Black America.* Boston: Houghton, 1977.

Sniezek, Janet A., and Christine H. Jazwinski. "Gender Bias in English: In Search of Fair Language." *Journal of Applied Social Psychology* 16 (1986): 642–62.

Sorrels, Bobbye D. *The Nonsexist Communicator: Solving the Problems of Gender and Awkwardness in Modern English.* Englewood Cliffs: Prentice, 1983.

Spender, Dale. *Man Made Language.* London: Routledge, 1980.

———. *Men's Studies Modified.* Oxford: Pergamon, 1981.

————. *Women of Ideas (and What Men Have Done to Them)*. London: Routledge, 1982.

Spender, Lynne. "The Politics of Publishing: Selection and Rejection of Women's Words in Print." *Women's Studies International Forum* 6 (1983): 469–73.

Spillers, Hortense. "A Hateful Passion, A Lost Love." Benstock 181–207.

————. "Interstices: A Small Drama of Words." *Pleasure and Danger*. Ed. Carole S. Vance. New York: Routledge, 1984. 73–100.

Spivak, Gayatri Chakravorty. "Can the Subaltern Speak?" Nelson and Grossberg 271–313.

Stacey, Judith, Susan Béreaud, and Joan Daniels, eds. *And Jill Came Tumbling After: Sexism in American Education*. New York: Dell, 1974.

Stanback, Marsha Houston. "Language and Black Woman's Place: Some Evidence from the Black Middle Class." Treichler, Kramarae, and Stafford 177–93.

Stanley, Julia Penelope (see also Penelope, Julia). "Gender-Marking in American English." Nilsen et al. 43–74.

————. "Sexist Grammar." *College English* 39 (1978): 800–12.

————. "Generics, Gender, and Common Nouns in English: Usage and Reference." Unpublished essay, 1976.

————. "Paradigmatic Woman: The Prostitute." *Papers in Language Variation*. Ed. D. L. Shores. Birmingham: U of Alabama P, 1977.

Stanley, Julia P., and Susan W. Robbins (see also Wolfe, Susan J.). "Going through the Changes: The Pronoun 'She' in Middle English." *Papers in Linguistics* 11 (1978): 71–88.

————. "Truncated Passives: Some of Our Agents Are Missing." *Linguistic Theory and the Real World* 1.2 (1976): 33–37.

Stannard, Una. *Mrs. Man*. San Francisco: Germainbooks, 1977.

Stanton, Domna, ed. *The Female Autograph*. New York: New Literary Forum, 1984.

Stanton, Elizabeth Cady. *The Woman's Bible*. New York, 1895. Rpt. as *The Original Feminist Attack on the Bible*. New York: Arno, 1974.

"A Statement of Editorial Policy." *PMLA* 96 (1981): 7.

Stedman's Medical Dictionary. 23rd ed. Baltimore: Williams, 1979.

Stein, Jess, ed. *Random House Dictionary of the English Language*. New York: Random, 1967.

Steinem, Gloria. *Outrageous Acts and Everyday Rebellions*. New York: Holt, 1983.

Steinmetz, Sol. "On Language: The Desexing of English." *New York Times Magazine* 1 Aug. 1982: 7–8.

Stopes, Charlotte Carmichael. *The Sphere of "Man": In Relation to That of "Woman" in the Constitution*. London: Unwin, 1908.

Strainchamps, Ethel. "Our Sexist Language." Gornick and Moran 347–61.

Strang, Barbara. *A History of English.* London: Methuen, 1970.

Swacker, Marjorie. "Women's Verbal Behavior at Learned and Professional Conferences." Dubois and Crouch 155–60.

Szemerényi, Otto. "Studies in the Kinship Terminology of the Indo-European Languages, with Special Reference to Indian, Iranian, Greek and Latin." *Acta Iranica Encyclopédie Permanente des Études Iraniennes.* 3rd ser. Vol. 7. Téhran: Pahlavi, 1977.

Tannen, Deborah. *That's Not What I Meant! How Conversational Style Makes or Breaks Your Relations with Others.* New York: Morrow, 1986.

Tate, Claudia. "Review Essay: Reshuffling the Deck: Or, (Re)Reading Race and Gender in Black Women's Writing." *Tulsa Studies in Women's Literature* 7 (1988): 119–32.

Taylor, Janet. *The Mariner's Friend: Or, Polyglot Indispensable and Technical Dictionary containing Upwards of Five Thousand Modern Nautical, Steam, and Shipbuilding Terms, Commercial and Scientific Expressions, Denominations of Art and an Explanatory Preface of Requirements in Ten Different Languages.* London, 1865.

Thomas, K. E. "The Influence of Feminism on Language: A Decade of Letters to *The Times.*" *Quaderni di Filologia Germanica della Facoltà di Lettere e Filosofia dell'Università di Bologna* 1 (1980): 247–59.

Thorne, Barrie, and Nancy Henley, eds. *Language and Sex: Difference and Dominance.* Rowley: Newbury, 1975.

Thorne, Barrie, Cheris Kramarae, and Nancy Henley, eds. *Language, Gender and Society.* Rowley: Newbury, 1983.

Tibbetts, A. M., and Charlene Tibbetts. "Response to Mary K. DeShazer." *College Composition and Communication* 34 (1983): 485–90.

Todasco, Ruth, ed. *The Feminist English Dictionary: An Intelligent Woman's Guide to Dirty Words.* Chicago: Loop Center YWCA, 1973.

Todd, Roy. "Social Policies towards Gypsies." *The Year Book of Social Policy in Britain 1977.* Ed. Muriel Brown and Sally Baldwin. London: Routledge, 1978. 180–200.

Traugott, Elizabeth Closs. *A History of English Syntax.* New York: Holt, 1972.

Treichler, Paula A. "AIDS, Homophobia, and Biomedical Discourse: An Epidemic of Signification." *Cultural Studies* 1 (1987): 263–305. Rpt. in *AIDS: Cultural Analysis/Cultural Activism.* Ed. Douglas Crimp. Cambridge: MIT P, 1988. 31–70.

———. "The Construction of Ambiguity in *The Awakening*: A Linguistic Analysis." McConnell-Ginet, Borker, and Furman 239–57.

———. "Escaping the Sentence: Diagnosis and Discourse in 'The Yellow Wallpaper.'" Benstock 62–78.

————. "Language, Feminism, Theory: Entering Decade Three." *Women and Language* 10.1 (1986): 5–36.

————. "Teaching Feminist Theory." *Theory in the Classroom.* Ed. Cary Nelson. Urbana: U of Illinois P, 1986. 57–128.

————. "The Wall behind the Yellow Wallpaper." *Tulsa Studies in Women's Literature* 4 (1985): 323–30.

Treichler, Paula A., and Cheris Kramarae. "Women's Talk in the Ivory Tower." *Communication Quarterly* 31 (1983): 118–32.

Treichler, Paula A., Cheris Kramarae, and Beth Stafford, eds. *For Alma Mater: Theory and Practice in Feminist Scholarship.* Urbana: U of Illinois P, 1985.

Treichler, Paula A., et al. "*The Dictionary of German Colloquial Language*: A Collective Critique." *Women and Language* 9.3 (1986): 18–21.

Trible, Phyllis. *God and the Rhetoric of Sexuality.* Philadelphia: Fortress, 1978.

Tschudi, Finn. "Gender Stereotypes Reflected in Asymmetric Similarities in Language." Annual Meeting of the American Psychological Assn. New York, Sept. 1979.

Turkle, Sherry. *The Second Self: Computers and the Human Spirit.* New York: Simon, 1985.

United Presbyterian Church in the U.S.A. Advisory Council on Discipleship and Worship. *The Power of Language among the People of God and the Language about God "Opening the Door": A Resource Document.* New York: United Presbyterian Church, 1979.

U'Ren, Marjorie B. "The Image of Woman in Textbooks." Gornick and Moran 318–28.

Varda One. "Manglish." Weekly column in *Everywoman* 8 May 1970–June 1972. Excerpts rpt. Pittsburgh: KNOW, 1971.

Vetterling-Braggin, Mary, ed. *Sexist Language: A Modern Philosophical Analysis.* Totowa: Littlefield, 1981.

Walker, Alice. Letter. *New York Times Magazine* 12 Feb. 1984: 94.

————. "One Child of One's Own: A Meaningful Digression within the Work(s)—An Excerpt." Hull, Scott, and Smith 37–44.

Walkowitz, Judith R. "Male Vice and Female Virtue: Feminism and the Politics of Prostitution in Nineteenth-Century Britain." *Powers of Desire.* Ed. Ann Snitow, Christine Stansell, and Sharon Thompson. New York: Monthly Review, 1983. 419–38.

Walsh, Mary Roth. *"Doctors Wanted: No Women Need Apply": Sexual Barriers in the Medical Profession, 1835–1975.* New Haven: Yale UP, 1977.

Warren, Mary Anne. *The Nature of Woman: An Encyclopedia and Guide to the Literature.* Inverness: Edgepress, 1980.

Warren, Virginia L. "Issues in the Profession: Guidelines for the Nonsexist Use of Language." *American Philosophical Association Proceedings* 59 (1986): 471–84.

Waugh, Evelyn. *The Loved One.* Boston: Little, 1948.

Weinreich, Uriel, William Labov, and Marvin I. Herzog. "Empirical Foundations for a Theory of Language Change." *Directions for Historical Linguistics: A Symposium.* Ed. W. P. Lehmann and Yakov Malkiel. Austin: U of Texas P, 1968. 95–188.

Wellman, David. "The New Political Linguistics of Race." *Socialist Review* 87–88 (1986): 43–62.

Welter, Barbara. Introduction. E. C. Stanton v–xxxiv.

West, Candace. *Routine Complications: Troubles with Talk between Doctors and Patients.* Bloomington: Indiana UP, 1984.

West, Candace, and Don H. Zimmerman. "Small Insults: A Study of Interruptions in Cross-Sex Conversations between Unacquainted Persons." Thorne, Kramarae, and Henley 103–17.

Whitehall, Harold. "The English Language." *Webster's New World Dictionary of the American Language, College Edition.* Ed. Joseph H. Friend and David Guralnik. Cleveland: World, 1959. xv–xxxiv.

Whitehead, Tony Larry, and Mary Ellen Conaway, eds. *Self, Sex, and Gender in Cross-Cultural Field Work.* Urbana: U of Illinois P, 1986.

Whorf, Benjamin Lee. *Language, Thought, and Reality: Selected Writings of Benjamin Lee Whorf.* Ed. J. B. Carroll. Cambridge: MIT P, 1956.

Wilden, Anthony. *System and Structure: Essays in Communication and Exchange.* London: Tavistock, 1972.

Wiley Guidelines on Sexism in Language. New York: Wiley, 1977.

Wilkins, Roger, Richard P. Young, and David Wellman. "The New Political Linguistics of Race: A Debate." *Socialist Review* 87–88 (1986): 63–79.

Williams, Raymond. *Keywords: A Vocabulary of Culture and Society.* New York: Oxford UP, 1976.

Wittig, Monique. *The Lesbian Body.* Trans. David Le Vay. New York: Morrow, 1975.

———. "The Mark of Gender." *Feminist Issues* 5.2 (1985): 3–12.

———. "One Is Not Born a Woman." *Feminist Issues* 1.2 (1981): 47–54.

Wittig, Monique, and Sande Zeig. *Lesbian Peoples: Material for a Dictionary.* 1976. New York: Avon, 1979.

Wolfe, Susan J. "The Codification of Sexist Language Use." Linguistic Society of America Annual Meeting. Baltimore, Dec. 1984.

———. "Constructing and Reconstructing Patriarchy: Sexism and Diachronic Semantics." *Papers in Linguistics* 13 (1980): 321–44.

———. "Gender and Agency in Indo-European Languages." *Papers in Linguistics* 13 (1980): 773–94.

———. "On Terms of Consanguineal Kinship in Proto-Indo-European." *Papers in Linguistics* 19 (1986): 425–47.

———. " 'Sister,' 'Sister's Son' and 'Mother's Brother': Linguistic Evidence for Matrilineal Kinship." *1982 Mid-America Linguistics Conference Papers*. Ed. Frances Ingemann. Lawrence: U of Kansas Dept. of Linguistics, 1983. 254–68.

Wolfe, Susan J., and Julia Penelope Stanley. "Linguistic Problems with Patriarchal Reconstructions of Indo-European Culture: A Little More than Kin, a Little Less than Kind." Kramarae, *Voices* 227–37.

"Woman May Be Rapist, Maine High Court Holds." *New York Times* 24 June 1986: 16.

Women on Words and Images. *Dick and Jane as Victims: Sex-Role Stereotyping in Children's Readers*. Princeton: Women on Words and Images, 1970.

———. "Look Jane Look. See Sex Stereotypes." Stacey, Béreaud, and Daniels 159–77.

Wood, Michael. "Heroine Addiction." *New York Review of Books* 2 Apr. 1978: 12–13.

Worby, Diana Zacharia. "In Search of a Common Language: Women and Educational Texts." *College English* 41 (1979): 101–05.

Yelin, Shulamis. Personal communication, Sept. 1987.

Zgusta, Ladislav, ed. *Theory and Method in Lexicography: Western and Non-Western Perspectives*. Columbia: Hornbeam, 1980.

Zimmerman, Bonnie. "What Has Never Been: An Overview of Lesbian Feminist Criticism." Greene and Kahn 177–210.

Zimmerman, Jan. *Once upon the Future: A Woman's Guide to Tomorrow's Technology*. New York: Pandora, 1986.

———, ed. *The Technological Woman: Interfacing with Tomorrow*. New York: Praeger, 1983.

Bibliography of English Handbooks

Coulthard, A. R. *The Writer's Craft: A Concise Rhetoric and Handbook.* Belmont: Wadsworth, 1980.

Crews, Frederick. *The Random House Handbook.* 3rd ed. New York: Random, 1980. 4th ed., 1984.

Fear, David E., and Gerald J. Schiffhorst. *Short English Handbook.* 2nd ed. Oakland: Scott, 1982.

Flachmann, Kim. *Focus: A College Handbook.* Boston: Houghton, 1981.

Fowler, H. Ramsey. *The Little, Brown Handbook.* 2nd ed. Boston: Little, 1983.

Guth, Hans P. *New English Handbook.* Belmont: Wadsworth, 1982. 2nd ed., 1985.

Heffernan, James A. W., and John E. Lincoln. *Writing: A College Handbook.* New York: Norton, 1982.

Herman, William. *The Portable English Handbook.* 2nd ed. New York: Holt, 1982.

Hodges, John C., and Mary E. Whitten. *Harbrace College Handbook.* 9th ed. New York: Harcourt, 1982.

McMahan, Elizabeth, and Susan Day. *The Writer's Handbook.* New York: McGraw, 1980. 2nd ed., 1986.

Millward, Celia. *Handbook for Writers.* 2nd ed. New York: Holt, 1983.

Strunk, William, Jr., and E. B. White. *The Elements of Style.* 3rd ed. New York: Macmillan, 1979.

Watkins, Floyd C., and William B. Dillingham. *Practical English Handbook.* 6th ed. Boston: Houghton, 1982.

Bibliography of and about Guidelines

From Book Publishers

Ginn and Co. *Treatment of Women and Minority Groups.* Lexington, MA, 1975. 2 pp.

———. *Editorial and Graphic Criteria for Art and Design.* Lexington, MA, 1975. 5 pp.

Harper and Row Publishers, Inc. College Dept. *Harper and Row Guidelines on Equal Treatment of the Sexes in Textbooks.* New York, 1976. 5 pp.

Holt, Rinehart, and Winston, Inc. *Guidelines for the Development of Elementary and Secondary Instructional Materials.* New York, 1975. 25 pp.

———. College Dept. *The Treatment of Sex Roles and Minorities.* New York, 1976. 8 pp.

Houghton Mifflin Co. School Div. *Avoiding Stereotypes: Principles and Applications.* 1975. Rev. and rpt. as *Eliminating Stereotypes.* Boston, 1981. 42 pp.

Richard D. Irwin, Inc. *Richard D. Irwin Handbook for Authors and Copy Editors.* Homewood, IL, 1980. 5 pp. Appendix concerns equal treatment of men and women.

Macmillan Publishing Co. School Div. *Guidelines for Creating Positive Sexual and Racial Images in Educational Materials.* New York, 1975. 96 pp.

McGraw-Hill Book Co. *Guidelines for Bias-Free Publishing.* New York, 1983. 38 pp.

———. *Guidelines for Equal Treatment of the Sexes in McGraw-Hill Book Company Publications.* New York, 1974. ERIC ED 098 574. Rpt. in *Elementary English* 52 (1975): 725–33.

Prentice-Hall, Inc. *Prentice-Hall Author's Guide.* 5th ed. Englewood Cliffs, NJ, 1975. 127 pp.

Random House, Inc. *Guidelines for Multiethnic/Nonsexist Survey.* New York, 1976. 28 pp.

Scott, Foresman, and Co. *Guidelines for Improving the Image of Women in Textbooks.* Glenview, IL, 1972. 11 pp.

South-Western Publishing Co. *Fair and Balanced Treatment of Minorities and Women.* Cincinnati, 1976. 27 pp.

John Wiley and Sons, Inc. College Editing Dept. *Wiley Guidelines on Sexism in Language.* New York, 1977. 20 pp.

From Organizations and Professional Associations

Academy of Management Review. "Addendum to Style Guide for Authors." *Academy of Management Review* 1.3 (1976): 150–52.

American Psychological Assn. "Guidelines for Nonsexist Language in APA Journals." Publication Manual Change Sheet 2. *American Psychologist* 32 (1977): 487–94. Rpt. in *Educational Researcher* 7.3 (1978): 15–17.

———. Task Force on Issues of Sexual Bias in Graduate Education. "Guidelines for Nonsexist Use of Language." *American Psychologist* 30 (1975): 682–84.

American Soc. for Public Administration. National Comm. on Women in Public Administration. *The Right Word: Guidelines for Avoiding Sex-Biased Language.* Ed. E. Siedman. Washington, 1979. 8 pp.

American Sociological Assn. Comm. on the Status of Women in Sociology. "Sexist Biases in Sociological Research: Problems and Issues." *Footnotes* 8.1 (1980): 8–9. Rpt. Washington: Project on the Status and Education of Women, AAC, 1981. 2 pp.

American Speech-Language-Hearing Assn. "Guidelines for Nonsexist Language in Journals of ASHA." *ASHA* 21 (1979): 973–77.

Assn. for Women in Psychology. Ad Hoc Comm. on Sexist Language. "Help Stamp Out Sexism! Change the Language!" *APA Monitor* 6.11 (1975): 16.

International Assn. of Business Communicators. *Without Bias: A Guidebook for Nondiscriminatory Communication.* Ed. J. E. Pickens, P. W. Rao, and L. C. Roberts. San Francisco, 1977. 77 pp. 2nd rev. ed. 1982. 200 pp.

National Council of Teachers of English. *Guidelines for Nonsexist Use of Language in NCTE Publications.* Urbana, IL. 1975. 8 pp. Rpt. in *Sexism and Language.* Ed. A. P. Nilsen et al. Urbana: NCTE, 1977. 181–91. Rev. ed. 1985.

Soc. of Automotive Engineers, Inc. *Communication Alternatives: Guidelines for the Use of Non-sexist Language.* Warrendale, PA, 1984. 12 pp.

Teachers of English to Speakers of Other Languages. "TESOL Quarterly Style Sheet." *TESOL Quarterly* 13 (1979): 606–11. Rpt. in *TESOL Quarterly* 14 (1980): 543–48.

Texas Education Agency. *Establishing Equity in Language and Illustrations.* Austin, 1985. 24 pp.

Warren, Virginia L. "Guidelines for the Nonsexist Use of Language." *American Philosophical Association Proceedings* 59 (1986): 471–84.

From General Sources

American Insts. for Research. Document Design Center. "Eliminating Gender Bias in Language." *Simply Stated* 28 (Aug. 1982): 1–2.

Associated Press. *Stylebook and Libel Manual*. New York, 1977. 330 pp.

Bank of America Communications Dept. *Guidelines for the Equal Treatment of All Employees in Bank of America Internal Communications*. San Francisco, 1975. 18 pp.

Blaubergs, Maija, and M. Rieger. "Guidelines for Non-sexist Language: A Bibliography." Mimeo. ms. Athens: U of Georgia Inst. for Behavioral Research, 1979.

Burr, E., S. Dunn, and N. Farquhar. *Guidelines for Equal Treatment of the Sexes in Social Studies Textbooks*. Los Angeles: Westside Women's Comm., 1973.

Chicago Women in Publishing. *Equality in Print: A Guide for Editors and Publishers*. Chicago, n.d. 23 pp.

Eichler, Margrit, and Jeanne Lapointe. *On the Treatment of the Sexes in Research*. Ottawa: Social Sciences and Humanities Research Council of Canada. 1985. 60 pp. Bilingual.

Employment and Immigration Canada. *Eliminating Sex-Role Stereotyping: Editorial Guidelines for Employment and Immigration Canada Communications*. Ottawa: Minister of Supply and Services, 1983. 44 pp. Bilingual.

Franklin and Marshall College Writing Center. "(S)He: A Guide to Non-sexist Language." 2nd ed. Lancaster, 1986. 9 pp.

Graham, Alma. *Non-sexist Language Guidelines*. New York: Graham, n.d.

Hogan, Pat. "Sexism in the Corporate Press." *Journal of Organizational Communications* 2.2 (1973): 1–6.

Jenkins, Mercilee M. "Guidelines for Student-Faculty Communication." *Sex and Gender in the Social Sciences: Reassessing the Introductory Course*. Ed. Judith M. Gappa and Janice Pearce. Washington: Women's Educational Equity Act Program, 1982. Rpt. as *Removing Bias: Guidelines for Student-Faculty Communication*. Annandale: Speech Communication Assn., 1983.

Kett, Merriellyn, and Virginia Underwood. *How to Avoid Sexism: A Guide for Writers, Editors and Publishers*. Chicago: Ragan, 1978. 115 pp.

"Kissing 'the Girls' Goodbye: A Discussion of Guidelines for Journalists." *Columbia Journalism Review* 14.1 (1975): 28–33.

"Linguistic Sexism." *Journal of Ecumenical Studies* 11.2 (1974): n. pag.

Lutheran Church in America. Office of Communications. *Guidelines for Screening Bias for Writers and Editors*. New York, 1974. 14 pp.

Miller, Casey, and Kate Swift. *The Handbook of Nonsexist Writing*. New York: Lippincott, 1980. 2nd rev. ed. New York: Harper, 1988. 134 pp.

Newsday. Editorial Guidelines. Garden City, NY, 1976. 20 pp.

Ontario Press Council. *Sexism and the Newspapers.* Ottawa, 1978. 26 pp.

Orovan, Mary. *Humanizing English.* New York: Orovan, 1972.

Persing, Bobbye Sorrels (see also Sorrels, Bobbye D.). "Sticks and Stones and Words: Women in the Language." *Journal of Business Communication* 14.2 (1977): 11–19.

Posner, Herbert S. "Unambiguous Reporting of the Sex of Human Beings." *Lancet* 22 Jan. 1983: 175–76.

Project on the Status and Education of Women. *Guide to Nonsexist Language.* Washington: AAC, 1986. 4 pp.

"Publishers' Guidelines." *Women in Media: A Documentary Source Book.* Ed. Maureen Beasley and Sheila Gibbons. Washington: Women's Inst. for Freedom of the Press, 1977. 170–75.

Randall, Phyllis. "Sexist Language and Speech Communication Texts: Another Case of Benign Neglect." Annual Communication, Language and Gender Conference. Oxford, OH, Oct. 1984.

Schulz, Muriel R. "How Serious Is Sex Bias in Language?" *College Composition and Communication* 26 (1975): 163–67.

Scott, K. P., and C. G. Schau. "Sex Equity and Sex Bias in Instructional Materials." *Handbook for Achieving Sex Equity through Education.* Ed. Susan S. Klein. Baltimore: Johns Hopkins UP, 1985. 218–32.

Shear, Marie. "Equal Writes." *Women's Review of Books* 1.11 (1984): 12–13.

———. "Overcoming Language Barriers to Equality." *Perspectives: The Civil Rights Quarterly* 13.1 (1981): 17–24. Includes a section called "Solving the Great Pronoun Problem: Twelve Ways to Avoid the Sexist Singular."

Sorrels, Bobbye D. *The Nonsexist Communicator: Solving the Problems of Gender and Awkwardness in Modern English.* Englewood Cliffs: Prentice, 1983.

Stephenson, Harriet B. "De-stereotyping Personnel Language." *Personnel Journal* 54 (1975): 334–55.

United Presbyterian Church in the U.S.A. Advisory Council on Discipleship and Worship. *The Power of Language among the People of God and the Language about God "Opening the Door": A Resource Document.* New York, 1979. 48 pp.

US Commission on Civil Rights. *Fair Textbooks: A Resource Guide.* Alexandria, 1986. 430 pp.

U.S. Dept. of Labor. Manpower Administration. *Job Title Revisions to Eliminate Sex- and Age-Referent Language from the Dictionary of Occupational Titles, Third Edition.* Washington: GPO, 1975. 363 pp.

Wendlinger, Robert M., and Lucille Matthews. "How to Eliminate Sexist Language from Your Organization's Writing: Some Guidelines for the Manager and Supervisor." *Affirmative Action for Women: A Practical Guide.* Ed. D. Jongeward et al. Reading, MA: Addison, 1973. 309–20.

Wisconsin Dept. of Public Instruction. Sex Equity Project. *Guidelines for the Creative Use of Biased Materials in a Non-biased Way.* Madison, 1980. 8 pp.

Women on Words and Images, Inc. *Sex Fairness in Education Division Communications, Products and Dissemination Strategies.* Washington: National Advisory Council on Women's Educational Programs, 1977.

Suggestions for Further Reading

This bibliography annotates a selective sampling of recommended publications; it is not intended to be a comprehensive list. See also Works Cited, the first bibliography in part 3.

Baron, Dennis. *Grammar and Gender*. New Haven: Yale UP, 1986. Examines how linguists, language scholars, and usage commentators have described, etymologized, interpreted, and misinterpreted many gender-related linguistic forms. Includes a comprehensive chronological catalog of proposals for an epicene pronoun.

Benstock, Shari, ed. *Feminist Issues in Literary Scholarship*. Bloomington: Indiana UP, 1987. An expanded version of *Tulsa Studies in Women's Literature* 3.1–2 (1984), a special issue. Several essays, including those by Benstock, Nina Baym, Jane Marcus, Hortense Spillers, and Paula A. Treichler, examine linguistic aspects of feminist literary scholarship.

Berryman, Cynthia L., and Virginia A. Eman, eds. *Communication, Language and Sex: Proceedings of the First Annual Conference*. Rowley: Newbury, 1980. A collection of 16 papers from the 1978 Conference on Communication, Language and Sex held at Bowling Green State University, 2 sample syllabi for courses in communication and the sexes, and a summary of the discussion among conference participants about pedagogy and research. Contributions focus on stereotypes, research on sex differences in communication, and pedagogical approaches to these topics. Includes an introductory essay by Cheris Kramarae.

Butler, Matilda, and William Paisley. *Women and the Mass Media: Sourcebook for Research and Action*. New York: Human Science, 1980. Summarizes the major quantitative content studies of media images, effects on audiences, and sexism in employment and other practices in the communication industry.

Cameron, Deborah. *Feminism and Linguistic Theory*. New York: St. Martin's, 1984. Suggests that traditional linguistic theory may not provide the appropriate theoretical framework for investigating the kinds of questions that interest feminists.

Capek, Mary Ellen. *A Women's Thesaurus: An Index of Language Used to Describe and Locate Information by and about Women.* New York: Harper, 1987. Lists 5,000 terms that describe the broad range of concerns shaping women's lives—including self-image, work, personal relationships, families, and larger spheres of cultural, social, political, and economic concerns. Includes main entries on language (including nonsexist language), religion and philosophy, and education. The Use/Do Not Use section is interesting.

deLauretis, Teresa. *Alice Doesn't: Feminism, Semiotics, Cinema.* Bloomington: Indiana UP, 1984. The essays in this book explore representations of "woman" in cinema, language, narrative, imaging.

———, ed. *Feminist Studies/Critical Studies.* Bloomington: Indiana UP, 1986. Thirteen essays based on a 1985 conference at the Center for Twentieth-Century Studies (U of Wisconsin, Milwaukee) explore the relation of feminist work to critical studies in history, science, literature, and critical theory. A number of essays examine "the notion of a feminist discourse, a configuration of rhetorical and interpretive strategies," and the implications for a definition of feminism and its relation to "femaleness."

Eakins, Barbara Westbrook, and R. Gene Eakins. *Sex Differences in Human Communication.* Boston: Houghton, 1978. A textbook for communication courses. Discusses sex differences in verbal and nonverbal communication and sex-biased language usage. Includes suggested activities for students.

Elgin, Suzette Haden. *Native Tongue.* New York: DAW, 1984. A science fiction novel about female linguists whose central project involves the creation of a language sensitive to female perceptions and experience—and hence about the envisioning of an altogether new reality rather than one that extrapolates from what already exists.

Ellmann, Mary. *Thinking About Women.* New York: Harcourt, 1968. A literary and feminist meditation on women's writing and "phallic criticism" that predates current feminist literary criticism. Hilarious, intelligent, and, as Toril Moi writes, "Still hard to beat" (182).

Flynn, Elizabeth A., and Patrocinio P. Schweickart, eds. *Gender and Reading.* Baltimore: Johns Hopkins UP, 1986. Thirteen essays and an annotated bibliography extend reader-response criticism to explore issues of gender in the reading of criticism and theory, including interdisciplinary perspectives, feminist and lesbian readings, the appeal of best-sellers, and the ambiguity of "reading as a woman."

Frank, Francine, and Frank Anshen. *Language and the Sexes.* Albany: State U of New York P, 1984. Focusing on contemporary issues, this book synthesizes a wide range of research related to English and several other languages. Topics include naming, stereotypes of language behavior, the politics of conversation, sexist language usage, and possibilities of reform. Contains suggested projects and nonsexist language guidelines.

Gilbert, Sandra M., and Susan Gubar. "Ceremonies of the Alphabet: Female Grandmatologies and the Female Autograph." *The Female Autograph.* Ed. Domna Stanton. New York: New York Literary Forum, 1984. 23–52. Argues that the women modernists and other women writers have used the alphabet as a figure for language—in the face of silencing attempts by their fellow male writers.

————. "Sexual Linguistics: Gender, Language, Sexuality." *New Literary History* 16 (1985): 515–43. Companion to "Ceremonies of the Alphabet." Reviews writing on women, language, and language acquisition and posits the long-standing existence of a potentially uncorrupted mother tongue.

Grahn, Judy. *Another Mother Tongue.* Boston: Beacon, 1984. A search for the language and linguistic history of lesbian and gay culture. Includes scholarship, reports from the field, interviews, poetry, and other material. Grahn, a San Francisco Bay Area lesbian poet and activist, is the author of *The Psychoanalysis of Edward the Dyke, The Work of a Common Woman,* and *The Queen of Wands. Another Mother Tongue* is the result of ten years of writing and research.

Greene, Gayle, and Coppélia Kahn, eds. *Making a Difference: Feminist Literary Criticism.* New York: Methuen, 1985. While explicitly focused on issues in literary theory and canon formation, this diverse and challenging collection of essays is in fact multidimensional and interdisciplinary. Informed by anthropology, psychoanalysis, and history, as well as literary theory, it aims to interpret and define relations between ideology and cultural practices.

Hall, Roberta M., with the assistance of Bernice Sandler. *The Classroom Climate: A Chilly One for Women.* Washington: AAC Project on the Status and Education of Women, 1982. Reviews reports, research, surveys, anecdotes, and other sources to document numerous ways that current college and university classrooms appear to discriminate against and alienate women students and faculty.

Hartman, Joan E., and Ellen Messer-Davidow, eds. *Women in Print I* and *Women in Print II.* New York: MLA, 1982. Volume 1 documents sexist practices in several areas of writing and publication, as well as feminist research and other efforts aimed at reversing these practices. Includes chapters on bibliography; archives; language research; lesbian literature; black women's writing and scholarship; working-class women's literature; women in German, Russian, Hispanic, and French literature; women in eighteenth-century literature. Volume 2 provides information about opportunities for feminist publishing.

Hull, Gloria T., Patricia Bell Scott, and Barbara Smith. *All the Women Are White, All the Blacks Are Men, but Some of Us Are Brave: Black Women's Studies.* Old Westbury: Feminist, 1982. Essays, reviews, bibliographies, and other writings designed to fill the gap in women's studies and black studies that the title implies.

Jenkins, Mercilee M. "Guidelines for Student-Faculty Communication." *Sex and Gender in the Social Sciences: Reassessing the Introductory Course.* Ed. Judith M. Gappa and Janice Pearce. Washington: Women's Educational Equity Act Program, 1982. Rpt. as *Removing Bias: Guidelines for Student-Faculty Communication*. Annandale: Speech communication Assn., 1983. Comprehensive guidelines and suggestions for facilitating sex equity in and outside the classroom.

Knight, Diana, ed. *Feminism*. Spec. issue of *Paragraph: The Journal of the Modern Critical Theory Group* 8 (1986): 1–120. An "unashamedly separatist" collection of essays by 12 female contributors designed to counter not only the "thoroughly male" composition and outlook of recent issues of *Paragraph* but also the broader "macho-cum-*Scouting for Boys* ethos of . . . critical theorizing" (1).

Kramarae, Cheris. *Women and Men Speaking: Frameworks for Analysis*. Rowley: Newbury, 1981. Presents an analysis of theory and empirical research about language, speech, and the ethnography of speaking.

Kramarae, Cheris, Muriel R. Schulz, and William M. O'Barr, eds. *Language and Power*. Beverly Hills: Sage, 1984. Essays on the existence and role of power in linguistic interactions by Susan Ervin-Tripp, Marlis Hellinger, Noëlle Bisseret Moreau, Dale Spender, Jean F. O'Barr, Patricia C. Nichols, Muriel Schulz, and others.

Kramarae, Cheris, and Paula A. Treichler, with the assistance of Ann Russo. *A Feminist Dictionary*. London: Pandora-Routledge, 1985. New York: Methuen, 1986. Documents words, definitions, and linguistic theories of the English-speaking feminist movements. Starts by placing women at the center of the lexicographic project and contrasts traditional with feminist assumptions about dictionary making. The 586-page work includes an extensive bibliography.

Lakoff, Robin. *Language and Woman's Place*. New York: Harper, 1975. An early examination of women and language. Though criticized by some for its linguistic methodology ("data gathered mostly by introspection") and for its devaluing of women's language, it remains a germinal linguistic analysis.

Maggio, Rosalie. *The Nonsexist Word Finder: A Dictionary of Gender-Free Usage*. Phoenix: Oryx, 1987. An alphabetical list of sexist words and phrases along with their nonsexist alternatives. This reference tool helps users quickly find substitutes for exclusive language, and appendixes contain writing guidelines, readings, and a bibliography.

McConnell-Ginet, Sally. "Language and Gender." *Cambridge Survey of Linguistics*. Ed. Frederick J. Newmeyer. Vol. 4. Cambridge: Cambridge UP, 1987. 75–99. Explores why sex and gender questions have been more central to literary studies and anthropology than to linguistics. Reviews recent research on gender in relation to linguistic production (by speakers and writers) and to meaning. Includes a useful discussion of language systems versus language use.

———. "Review Article [on Language, Sex, and Gender]." *Language* 59 (1983): 373–91. Provides an overview of current American theory and research on language and sex, including issues of context, meaning, and sexist and nonsexist usage.

McConnell-Ginet, Sally, Ruth Borker, and Nelly Furman, eds. *Women and*

Language in Literature and Society. New York: Praeger, 1980. Westport: Greenwood, 1986. A still unrivaled collection of essays, edited by a linguist, an anthropologist, and a literary critic, that includes both sociolinguistic and anthropological research on language and gender and feminist analyses of literary texts.

Moi, Toril. *Sexual/Textual Politics: Feminist Literary Theory.* New York: Methuen, 1985. Through a detailed exposition of the major works and authors in the field, Moi critically examines the strengths and limitations of the two main strands of feminist criticism, the Anglo-American and the French.

Moraga, Cherríe, and Gloria Anzaldúa, eds. *This Bridge Called My Back: Writings by Radical Women of Color.* Boston: Persephone, 1981. A unique collection of powerful writing by women who explore their identities as feminists, lesbians, and women of color. Many of the essays, poems, and letters address linguistic questions.

Nelson, Cary, and Lawrence Grossberg, eds. *Marxism and the Interpretation of Culture.* Urbana: U of Illinois P, 1987. An interdisciplinary and international collection representing the state of Marxist cultural theory in the 1980s. Includes feminist essays that address language issues by Catherine A. MacKinnon, Christine Delphy, Gayatri Chakravorty Spivak, Julia Lesage, Michèle Mattelart, and Jean Franco.

Newton, Judith, and Deborah Rosenfelt, eds. *Feminist Criticism and Social Change: Sex, Class and Race in Literature and Culture.* New York: Methuen, 1985. Essays that explore the possibilities for a materialist-feminist criticism of literature and culture. Language is a central feature for many of these authors.

Nilsen, Alleen Pace. *Changing Words in a Changing World: Pop! Goes the Language.* Tempe: Arizona State U, 1979. Teaching guide designed to provide young adults with an understanding of language as a social phenomenon. Includes material, classroom exercises, and fieldwork assignments on nonsexist, inclusive language usage.

Ostriker, Alicia Suskin. *Stealing the Language: The Emergence of Women's Poetry in America.* Boston: Beacon, 1986. Surveys women's poetry from the seventeenth century to the present—the forms, styles, and criticism. Considering whether there exists an especially female language, a "mother tongue," Ostriker argues that what distinguishes this poetry is not a specific, shared, exclusive female language but "a vigorous and varied invasion of the sanctuaries of existing language." She suggests that revisionist mythmaking in women's poetry is a way to redefine both women and culture.

Penfield, Joyce, ed. *Women and Language in Transition.* Albany: State U of New York P, 1987. A collection of 10 essays on women and language with sections on "liberating language," "identity creation," and on the linguistic experiences of women of color.

Perspectives: On Overcoming Language Barriers to Equality. Spec. issue of *Civil Rights Quarterly* 3 (1981). Includes a discussion of linguistic discrimination against women and against black and Hispanic people.

Pryse, Marjorie, and Hortense Spillers, eds. *Conjuring: Black Women, Fiction, and Literary Tradition.* Bloomington: Indiana UP, 1985. An important collection that identifies and describes the diversity of writing by black women and challenges conventional notions about literary "tradition."

Rich, Adrienne. *On Lies, Secrets, and Silence: Selected Prose 1966–1978.* New York: Norton, 1979. Rich moves from concerns with writing and literature into social and political topics, always asserting links connecting history, writing, politics, and radical feminism. Essays on the poets Anne Bradstreet and Emily Dickinson intersect with writings on motherhood, lesbianism, and racism. Throughout, Rich is interested in describing women's culture: "to name and found a culture of our own means a real break from the passivity of the twentieth-century Western mind" (13).

Roberts, J. R. *Black Lesbian: An Annotated Bibliography.* Tallahassee: Naiad, 1981. Includes material on erasure, silencing, and oppression in black women's lives.

Ruether, Rosemary. *Sexism and God-Talk: Toward a Feminist Theology.* Boston: Beacon, 1983. A systematic feminist critique of Christian theology with strong emphasis on sexism in language. Ruether's work has been influential in the widespread movement among American religious groups (national and local) to modify sexist aspects of texts, services, rituals, and rules.

Ruthven, K. K. *Feminist Literary Studies: An Introduction.* Cambridge: Cambridge UP, 1984. Though this Australian critic writes with little apparent understanding of the political commitments of feminist literary scholarship, his study is a competent survey of approaches to language and critical practices that characterize the major theories of feminist criticism. He argues that gender is a crucial factor in the production, circulation, and interpretation of literary texts.

Shibamota, Janet S. *Japanese Women's Language.* London: Academic, 1985. Sociolinguistic study; in an introduction, the author reviews research on women's speech in Japan and reports original fieldwork; elsewhere she describes grammatical rules and summarizes her conclusions.

Showalter, Elaine, ed. *The New Feminist Criticism.* New York: Pantheon, 1985. A number of threads make up the fabric of feminist criticism today, including gynesis and gynocritics. Though Showalter does not find the two to be in competition, she places gynocritics—the study of women writers—at the heart of the enterprise.

Smith, Philip M. *Language, the Sexes and Society.* Oxford: Blackwell, 1985. Reviews research on language and sex roles in both Britain and the United States.

Sorrels, Bobbye D. *The Nonsexist Communicator: Solving the Problems of Gender and Awkwardness in Modern English.* Englewood Cliffs: Prentice, 1983. Practical guidelines for overcoming sexism in written, oral, and nonverbal communication. Includes examples, solutions, self-tests, and a glossary.

Spender, Dale. *Man Made Language.* London: Routledge, 1980. Argues that language is inherently male-biased. Despite its problems (see essays by Black and Coward and by McKluskie in Works Cited), Spender's book remains a major influence on girls and women who are beginning to think about inequalities in language and speech.

Stannard, Una. *Mrs. Man.* San Francisco: Germainbooks, 1977. A rich and unique study of the customs and laws regarding married women's names.

Tannen, Deborah. *That's Not What I Meant! How Conversational Style Makes or Breaks Your Relations with Others.* New York: Morrow, 1986. A linguist and discourse analyst's discussion for a general audience of the workings of conversation in everyday life. Discusses male-female differences in conversation as "cross-cultural differences" in a chapter on "talk in the intimate relationship" (133–51).

Thorne, Barrie, and Nancy Henley, eds. *Language and Sex: Difference and Dominance.* Rowley: Newbury, 1975. Important essays with a comprehensive annotated bibliography.

Thorne, Barrie, Cheris Kramarae, and Nancy Henley, eds. *Language, Gender and Society.* Rowley: Newbury, 1983. New essays with an updated and splendidly comprehensive annotated bibliography.

Treichler, Paula A. "Language, Feminism, Theory: An Annotated Bibliography." *Women and Language* 10.1 (1986): 5–36. A partial bibliography of recent feminist scholarship on language that takes a more or less explicitly theoretical perspective.

Treichler, Paula A., and Cheris Kramarae. "Women's Talk in the Ivory Tower." *Communication Quarterly* 31 (1983): 118–32. Reviews research on women and language in academia and suggests both an analytic framework and an alternative approach to academic structures that can enable women to participate more fully in the life of the academic community.

Treichler, Paula A., Cheris Kramarae, and Beth Stafford, eds. *For Alma Mater: Theory and Practice in Feminist Scholarship.* Urbana: U of Illinois P, 1985. One section of this collection, "On Language," includes essays on linguistic and literary topics by Carol Thomas Neely, Cary Nelson, Gayatri Chakravorty Spivak, Tey Diana Rebolledo, Sally McConnell-Ginet, and Marsha Houston Stanback.

Vetterling-Braggin, Mary, ed. *Sexist Language: A Modern Philosophical Analysis.* Totowa: Littlefield, 1981. This useful collection of 23 essays and a general introduction seeks to "elucidate current philosophical positions" for and against the claim that ordinary language is sexist. Among the topics covered are defining sexist language, the moral significance of using it, examples (including "generics" like *he* and *man*, gender-neutral terms, terms for sexual activity, and courtesy titles), and sexist versus racist language. Marilyn Frye's "Male Chauvinism: A Conceptual Analysis" and Janice Moulton's "Sex and Reference" are especially interesting and solid; many essays comment on one another, contributing to a stimulating dialogue. (See McConnell-Ginet's "Review Article" in *Language* for a detailed review.)

Wandor, Michelene, ed. *On Gender and Writing*. London: Pandora, 1983. Essays by writers, mostly women, in many genres (including fiction, dramatic literature, and scholarly writing) explore the relationship between a writer's gender and his or her choices about topic, style, ideas, and approach.

Wittig, Monique, and Sande Zeig. *Lesbian Peoples: Notes for a Dictionary*. New York: Avon, 1979. A witty utopian science fiction "dictionary" that explores what might have been, never was, and might yet be.

Women and Language. An interdisciplinary research periodical published at Stanford University from 1976 to 1981, at the University of Illinois, Urbana, from 1981 to 1989, and since 1989 at George Mason University.

Women and Language/Femmes et langage. Spec. issue of *RFR/DRF* [*Resources for Feminist Research/Documentation sur la recherche feministe*] 13.3 (1984). This special issue of *RFR/DRF*, an English-French feminist journal published in Toronto, includes editorials, articles, abstracts, research reviews, and bibliographies on women and language. Especially welcome are a number of pieces on translation.

Women's Studies in Communication. The Organization for Research on Women and Communication of the Western Speech Communication Division has published this journal since 1977 at Humboldt State University and the University of Oregon. It emphasizes interpersonal, rhetorical, and organizational studies in communication.

Notes on Contributors

Francine Wattman Frank is Dean of the College of Humanities and Fine Arts at the State University of New York, Albany, where she also teaches linguistics, Spanish, and women's studies. She has published widely on sexism and language, and she is the coauthor, with Frank Anshen, of *Language and the Sexes*. From 1981 to 1984 she was a member of the MLA Commission on the Status of Women in the Profession.

H. Lee Gershuny is Professor of English at Borough of Manhattan Community College and the author of many publications and conference papers on sexism in English writing and teaching, among them a series of essays on the dictionary as the cultural codifier of sexist meanings.

Sally McConnell-Ginet chairs the Department of Modern Languages and Linguistics at Cornell University, where she has been actively involved in the Women's Studies Program since 1973. She has published widely in the general area of language and gender, and she coedited *Women and Language in Literature and Society* with Ruth Borker and Nelly Furman. She is currently coauthoring a textbook on semantics and completing a study on the "looseness" of language meaning.

Paula A. Treichler is Associate Professor at the University of Illinois College of Medicine and Institute of Communications Research, Urbana. A linguist, she is a coauthor of *A Feminist Dictionary* and a coeditor of *For Alma Mater: Theory and Practice in Feminist Scholarship* and the interdisciplinary research periodical *Women and Language*. Her research is in cultural studies, medicine, and feminist theory. From 1982 to 1985, she was a member of the MLA Commission on the Status of Women in the Profession.

Susan J. Wolfe is Professor of English at the University of South Dakota. She is the author of several key articles on language and gender, especially in the history of English and in English grammar and syntax. Her other research interests include language acquisition and humor.

Author and Name Index

Subject Index

This index includes dictionaries and English handbooks cited in the text. A publication (such as *Camera Obscura* or the *New York Times*) is listed only if its editorial policy is discussed within the text. To locate other works cited, look up the author in the name index. Italicized entries other than titles designate words and phrases discussed as terms.